Beyond
The Palace

By Gary Wien
Photos by Debra L. Rothenberg

Front cover and back cover art photos:
© Debra L. Rothenberg/rothenbergphoto.com

Printed in Victoria, Canada

National Library of Canada Cataloguing in Publication Data

Wien, Gary, 1970-
    Beyond the palace / Gary Wien, Debra L. Rothenberg.
ISBN 1-4120-0314-8
    1. Music—New Jersey—Asbury Park—History and criticism. 2. Rock music—New Jersey—Asbury Park—History and criticism.
I. Rothenberg, Debra L. II. Title.
ML200.8.A799W64 2003   780'.9749'46   C2003-902511-X

TRAFFORD

This book was published *on-demand* in cooperation with Trafford Publishing. On-demand publishing is a unique process and service of making a book available for retail sale to the public taking advantage of on-demand manufacturing and Internet marketing. **On-demand publishing** includes promotions, retail sales, manufacturing, order fulfilment, accounting and collecting royalties on behalf of the author.

Suite 6E, 2333 Government St., Victoria, B.C. V8T 4P4, CANADA

Phone	250-383-6864	Toll-free	1-888-232-4444 (Canada & US)
Fax	250-383-6804	E-mail	sales@trafford.com
Web site	www.trafford.com	TRAFFORD PUBLISHING IS A DIVISION OF TRAFFORD HOLDINGS LTD.	

Trafford Catalogue #03-0683   www.trafford.com/robots/03-0683.html

10   9   8   7   6   5   4

Acknowledgements

Thanks go out to everyone involved in the making of this book but especially the following: Dr. Sherry Lynn Wien, Debra L. Rothenberg, Google, Chris Barry, David Mieras, Bob Makin, Al Muzer, Hal Selzer, Joe D'Urso, Bob Burger, Richard Barone, Michael J. Hoover, JPAT, Phil Marino, Rob Fuzesi, David March, Cheryl A. Wolcott, Frank Corace, Fran Smith Jr., John Pfeiffer, Maggie Powell, Chris DeCellio and, of course, Trafford Publishing. Special thanks go out to Billy Smith, WHTG, Y-107, Lee Mrowicki, the Beatles, Bruce Springsteen, Southside Johnny, Glen Burtnick, U2 and the Alarm for providing me with a love of music. And thanks to Melinda, Dawn and everyone at the Stone Pony.

The following photographers provided many of the pictures in this book.

Debra L. Rothenberg   www.rothenbergphoto.com
An award winning photographer residing in New York City. She earned a Bachelor of Fine Arts degree in Photographic Illustration/Photojournalism from Rochester Institute of Technology. Clients include the *New York Daily News*, *New York Times*, *People*, *Rolling Stone Magazine*, *Entertainment Weekly*, Columbia/CBS Records, EMI Music Publishing, Prudential, NYU, CUNY, and the Port Authority of New York/New Jersey among many others. For assignments, availability, and a list of the musicians/celebrities and stock photography on file please contact her at (917) 284-3738.

Alyse Liebowitz   www.goboss.com
A published concert photographer whose work has appeared in *Rolling Stone Magazine*, *US Magazine*, *People Magazine*, and VH1 and MTV productions. Her photos have also appeared in many fan magazines devoted to Bruce Springsteen, Bon Jovi, U2, the Black Crowes, and Hothouse Flowers. She has traveled extensively, and is now concentrating on landscape photography. For a list of available concert and travel photographs, visit her web site.

Kevin Papa   www.newjerseyrock.com
Visit Kevin's Rock & Roll Tribute Page to the Jersey (and NY) Rock And Club Scene from the 70s and Beyond...

Florence Mazzone   www.photoflo.com
Please visit her website to view a sampling of her work.

C.J. Photography   www.cjphotography.com
Please visit the website to view a sampling of their work.

About The Book

I can't imagine what would have happened with my career had I not lived at the shore, hearing and shooting some of the best music and musicians I have ever seen in these Jersey Shore clubs.

--DEBRA L. ROTHENBERG
PHOTOGRAPHER

Debra L. Rothenberg's Jersey Shore music career started when this photo wound up being included in the album art of Southside Johnny's *Reach Up and Touch the Sky*. Photo © Debra L. Rothenberg/rothenbergphoto.com

ABOUT THE BOOK

I can still remember being at Pat's Pub in Belmar with my wife, Sherry Lynn, when the band began to play. The lead singer's voice sounded so familiar, and then it came to me. He was the guy from Soul Engines, a band I used to see back in the early 90s. During the next break I went over to talk to the guys. That's when I began to wonder whatever happened to the other bands my friends and I used to go see.

Growing up, I was always hanging out with musicians or talking music with guys like Lee Mrowicki at the Stone Pony annex or Billy Smith from the Asbury Park Rock 'N Roll Museum. I first met Debra L. Rothenberg when my friend Dave March and I used to sneak into the clubs. At the time, Dave was an aspiring photographer and I had dreams of being a writer. We both managed to make a living out of what we loved to do, and I guess you could say Debra played a big part in both of our careers.

I still remember the first time I saw a photo credit for her in *Rolling Stone Magazine*. It was for a photograph showing Bruce Springsteen jamming on stage with Marshall Crenshaw at the Stone Pony. I was so amazed that somebody in the area was getting published in the same *Rolling Stone Magazine* that arrived at my door each week. We used to bump into each other at the Pony a lot and got to know each other a bit.

Years later, when I began working on this book, I contacted her to inquire about using some of her photographs. We met in the city and I was surprised that she still remembered Dave and I after all this time. I was even more surprised when she said she wanted to help out as much as possible with this project.

This book has been a true labour of love for me and I'm proud to include so many of Debra's photographs within its pages. She has truly covered the Asbury Park music scene from its founders to its near-misses; from those that can sell out stadiums to those who still pick up the guitar and play in front of a dozen fans in a cramped Jersey Shore bar. I can't thank her enough for all of the help she provided in the making of this book.

Her photos follow the trail of artists from the founders of the scene like Bruce Springsteen, Southside Johnny and Billy Chinnock to the next generation of "Asbury Sound" performers like John Eddie, James Deely and Glen Burtnick. They take you on a tour of the alternative sounds that made the Green Parrot special with artists like Richard Barone, Dramarama and Red House, and they show you some of the saddest moments like the day the Palace carousel was dismantled. Her photos were the perfect complement to what I was trying to show with this book. The following is Debra's story in her own words. Thanks Deb...

-Gary Wien
March 2003

BEYOND THE PALACE

I grew up in Fair Lawn, Bergen County (North Jersey) and the summer of 1978 was a summer that changed my life. As a sophomore, I had a bad case of mononucleosis and missed 3 1/2 months of school. In order to graduate on time, I needed to take a class during the summer. I took a printing class and the teacher was a young man right out of college named John Heyn who loved the music of the NJ Shore. The class met for 8 weeks, 4 hours every day. All day, everyday, all he would play on the stereo was Bruce Springsteen, Southside Johnny and the sounds of the Jersey Shore. Everyday I would complain. My musical tastes back then didn't stray past Barry Manilow, even though I grew up in a musical family with three older brothers and parents who had great taste in music. Mr. Heyn promised that by the end of the summer I would have every Bruce album and whatever bootlegs I could get. He was right. Within a few weeks I was hooked. Mr. Heyn was also a photographer and would bring in all the photos he took, and I was in awe.

I was always interested in photography since my father was an amateur photographer. On my 17th birthday I received my first 35mm camera. Shortly after I went to a Southside Johnny concert and one of the first photos I took from the first roll ever through the camera was used on his live album *Reach Up and Touch the Sky*. I had sent the photo to a magazine, and it turned out the editor was friends with Southside and showed him the photo, and they contacted me.

I graduated college in 1984 and worked as a staff photographer for newspapers in Upstate NY, and later Southern Pennsylvania. In late 1985, after living out of NJ for what seemed like a lifetime, I got a staff photographer position for a Jersey Shore newspaper and my life changed. I was spending all my free time at the Stone Pony shooting ANY and EVERY band that played that stage. It didn't matter to me if they had an album out or not. I went to college and studied photography but I perfected my craft with the musicians that graced the stage at the Stone Pony. During the summer of 1987, my editor told me if I could get myself into a concert, she would make sure the paper would use it. Every band that played the Garden State Arts Center that summer, I shot. In late July while shooting Marshall Crenshaw at the Stone Pony, Springsteen made a guest appearance and I was there, right in the front. Two nights later the E-Street Band played an unannounced show at the Pony and again I was there. These photos were used not only in the paper I worked for but in *Rolling Stone Magazine* and later the *NY Daily News* and *Backstreets*, the Springsteen magazine. Several more times that summer Bruce would appear at a local club and *Rolling Stone* would call for photos.

ABOUT THE BOOK

I found there to be so much talent in NJ that was going unrecognized and I wanted to put my talents together to try to make a difference. I was accepted to have a show at a local gallery and the title of my exhibit was "It's Only Rock and Roll: New Jersey Musicians." After seeing too many homeless people in the area, I then took this project a step further and produced a 16-month calendar with all the proceeds going to the NJ Coalition for the Homeless. I contacted local DJ's and music writers all over NJ to make sure that every county was represented with the best of musicians in NJ. Each month featured a band/musician who had a record deal while the centerfold was local talent from all over the great state of NJ. Before this project, I was not aware of the amount of talent in this state. I was until this time pretty much a Bruce/Southside/Pony girl and never went elsewhere. That project opened my ears to so much and I fell in love with the alternative sound and the Parrot and WHTG. The Parrot then felt like home where I once felt like an outsider. I always considered myself a "live" photographer but I wanted to learn something from this project so as often as time would permit, I tried to set up photo sessions with the musicians. I always made sure to get a tape of who I was going to photograph so I would know a little more about who I was going to shoot.

The bands that came out of, and played at the Shore are enough to make any music fan drool. People are under the impression that the shore is only Bruce Springsteen, Bon Jovi, and Southside Johnny. There was, and is, an alternative scene that so many people are unfamiliar with. There was also a metal scene over at the Brighton Bar in Long Branch where a man named Jacko, who fronted the band Dirge, ran the place and gave so many bands a break they never would have received elsewhere. Over at the Pony we had Bruce, Southside, John Eddie, James Deely, Mike Dalton, Joey and the Works, Mike Wells, the Smithereens while the same night over at the Green Parrot we had Dramarama, Richard Barone, the Blases, the Feelies, and then the Fastlane re-opened and we had a crossover where these bands would play there. I can't imagine what would have happened with my career had I not lived at the Shore, hearing and shooting some of the best music and musicians I have ever seen at these Jersey Shore clubs.

Debra L. Rothenberg
New York City
March 24, 2003

Table of Contents

FOR SHERRY LYNN,
MY MUSE

...and to all the hard working people like Kate Mellina and Tom Gilmour trying their best to bring Asbury Park back to glory

1 The Upstage

They used to call the Upstage the cheapest motel room in town because by the time you got out the sun would be coming up.

--BIG DANNY GALLAGHER

Margaret Potter of the Upstage is shown on stage with Bruce Springsteen.
Photo © Debra L. Rothenberg/rothenbergphoto.com

T his is where it all began. Musicians gathered each night at a club on the corner of Cookman Avenue and Bond Street that was set on top of a Thom McAn shoe store. The Upstage brought the sights of San Francisco psychedelia and the sounds of Greenwich Village together in an endless array of all night jam sessions, which attracted the best young musicians in the area.

"There was no place anywhere like the Upstage," said David Mieras, a regular at the club who grew up in Ocean Grove. "That place was totally in a league of its own. It was very, very different. It was a really avant-garde place, very art-oriented, individualized and where people found an identity. It was like your club. There was no liquor there, but you'd identify it as your club.

"Most people had passes to get in. It was no different than being part of a high school club. In Neptune, the cool kids belonged to their club, which was called the Centaurs. The Ocean Grove kids who had long hair and stuff like that and played music, they weren't cool enough for the Centaurs, but they had their own club called Upstage. That was the difference. We identified with music and stuff like that. We could care less about getting into a bar because we had the Upstage. It was the greatest place. I mean, we just had so much fun there it was incredible."

David Sancious, one of the original members of the E Street Band remembers the Upstage well. "You'd walk up this long flight of stairs and the next level was like a coffeehouse and they had folk acts in there, folk music, a small stage and some tables and a couple of coffee machines in the back. You walk up another flight of stairs and it was all done like a psychedelic club, you know. With a bigger stage, Day-Glo painting on the wall, no tables, no chairs, just a big open dance floor. There used to be a lot of bands that would play there and a lot of jams got started. In the early days, I used to go to Upstage to dance. I had some friends of mine from Belmar that used to go and dance and just be a part of the whole scene."

According to Big Danny Gallagher, the origins of the Upstage arose from a series of parties that were held by Tom Potter. "I had a job working at around four in the morning. One night my boss says to me, 'Wanna go to a party?' I'm thinking a party at four in the morning, what the hell's up with this? He told me to go over to Tom Potter's house. He lived over the top of Park Drugs, which was located two doors down from the Upstage. It turns out that these parties got so big that he decided to rent the building next door, which eventually became the Upstage.

"He sold memberships for two dollars. So, if you came and you had a membership it was a dollar and if you didn't it cost two bucks to get in."

"They opened this club, this two-story club above a Thom McAn shoe store in Asbury Park," explained Southside Johnny Lyon. "Second floor was folk stage and a kitchen where they made coffee and sandwiches, and the third floor was the rock and roll hall where they had built-in amplifiers and drums. All you had to do was bring your guitar or whatever. It was great. It was a college for us."

Third floor, or rock hall as it was sometimes called, was basically created for the purpose of jamming. John Mulrenan, a local musician that would later play in Lord Gunner with Lance Larson describes how the built-in amplifiers came about. "There was a hallway behind the stage that went into Tom Potter's office and the back of the stage was a plywood wall he had erected. He had a bunch of used guitar ampheads that he'd buy from kids. They'd tell him, 'I gotta sell my amp.' He'd say, 'Ok, I'll give you 70 bucks kid.' So he had about five of the old Fender guitar heads up there. And then people would bring him a speaker, like an old car radio speaker or whatever they wanted to sell to make a couple of bucks. He would take a saw and just saw a hole in the plywood, take wood screws, screw the speaker to the wall and then just jump it over to the other speakers with two wires. So you had this wall in back, it was all random speakers wired up to these ampheads with no rhyme or reason. And everybody would just come up and plug into the amps and play. The amps were hooked up to the back speakers with just wood screwed into the back wall. There was pieces of plywood just hanging there. It was speakers not being enclosed in an actual enclosure. All of these different weirdo speakers, half of them blown and stuff."

As haphazard as it may sound, there was a method to Tom Potter's madness and the sound, according to several sources, was excellent. Some people have described it as the same sound quality you might hear at a contemporary movie theatre. Although the sound would sometimes bleed from the harder sounding rock and roll from the third floor into the softer folk music of the second floor.

"There was this one time when Margaret had thrown a big spaghetti dinner," recalled Big Danny. "It was 50s night so everybody went with their sleeves rolled up and cigarettes inside them. And everybody was playing old rock and roll stuff. I don't know who it was, but somebody hung these mikes up and made a tape.

"The sound was just God awful good. Potter was like an artist that was way ahead of himself. He was doing double and triple exposures and making collages. I got a job working the door there and my whole life changed. I mean, rock and roll as a lifestyle had never come in front of me before. I saw it and said, 'Well, this is it!'"

The legendary jams at the Upstage Club involved many musicians that are well known around the world including many original members of the E Street Band and the Asbury Jukes. Guys like Bruce Springsteen, Southside Johnny, Garry Tallent, Billy Chinnock, Vini "Mad Dog" Lopez, Steven Van Zandt, Danny Federici, Kevin Kavanaugh and David Sancious all took their turns on stage. Local legends like Rich DiSarno, Billy Hector, Big Danny Gallagher, Tony Amato and John Luraschi honed their craft each night there as well.

Jams at the Upstage Club started around nine o'clock and ran from nine to midnight. The early show was largely for the younger crowd. Then, due to a zoning law at the time, everybody had to leave the building from midnight until one o'clock. The entire place would then clear out. Many people would head out to a bar and have a few drinks or buy a case or two and then return at one o'clock and resume jamming with the next show.

Southside Johnny grew up in Ocean Grove, the town that borders Asbury Park. He was a regular member of the Upstage jams. "I lived a half-mile away so I would go over there just about every night. Sometimes I'd go over right from work if I worked late at the post office, which I did for ten months, and I'd still have my post office stuff on. We used to do eight shows a night, eight sets a night, 40-45 minutes each. We were making songs up because we ran out of material. I mean, no matter how many songs you knew you'd do a week's worth of eight shows a night. And you don't want to repeat yourself, do the same songs over and over again - screw that! So we would make stuff up."

"I used to go there and want to sort of get in a jam and play, but I didn't really know any of the musicians in Asbury Park," said Sancious, who lived in Belmar at the time and was much younger than the other musicians. "Actually I knew Garry Tallent. We had some occasion to meet and work together. We'd done some gigs, maybe with Bill Chinnock. One weekend I was going to Upstage and I came in and Garry was standing at the top of the stairs next to Bruce Springsteen. They were trying to organize a jam session for the next show, that one to five break. I came walking up and saw Garry. He introduced me to Bruce and he asked me if I was interested in jamming. I said absolutely. And that was kind of the start.

"I think we played for hours. I think we went on forever. It was this long, long jam. People were coming up and coming off the stage. One drummer would come on for a while, he'd play for a while, then somebody else would come up. I guess it went on forever. It was a lot of fun. It was really, really fantastic."

Even back then, there was just something special about the guy from Freehold. The Upstage had already been around for a while before Bruce Springsteen made his first appearance there. But when he walked up the stairs to the third floor, it was clear that he wasn't intimidated by the local musicians.   And, in short time, they would find themselves slightly intimidated by him.

"One night, I walked up and there's this long-haired guy with a gold Les Paul," explained Southside Johnny Lyon. "He's telling this long involved story about going to Catholic school and how they mistreated him and all that stuff. But one day they had music appreciation and Sister Mary brought in a B.B. King album and the hook was that the nuns at Saint Catherine taught me the blues or something like that. He was just so charismatic and funny and good, playing great guitar and his lyrics were coming out and they were these tons of phrases. I thought who the fuck is this guy? Immediately I felt territorial! But it was like wow, he's really good.

"I mean, I kind of considered it my hang out, my club, because I was there so much and I was kind of the singer. Everybody wanted to be the guitar hero. Ricky DiSarno and all those other guys, they really didn't want to sing, they wanted to play. So I got to sing all this stuff. And I made a deal with a lot of them, I said I'll do all the Hendrix and Cream and that stuff as long as I get to do one blues song every night. I'll make it simple, I'll give you the chords and we'll play them. So it was good work for me. I got to practice my chops too."

It's somewhat amazing that many of the musicians at the Upstage can still clearly remember the day they first saw Bruce Springsteen play. He had that certain quality about him that made you know he was going to be a rock and roll star. It was only a matter of when.

"I think I was about 15 when I met Bruce and started jamming and playing with him," added Sancious. "I was like 19 for about five years, you know… I lied about my age to get into clubs. I remember that for years anybody ever asked how old I was, I was 19. I don't think anybody could have believed me. No grown up could have believed me."

"Tom Potter introduced me to Bruce up at the Upstage," said John Mulrenan. "The first time I sort of noticed him was when Southside Johnny was downstairs playing an out of tune 12-string guitar. So, I'm watching Johnny play this song, but I'm hearing great guitar licks coming out - lead guitar, beautiful melodies. I'm like what the hell is that? So, I walk around the back and Bruce is sitting on the steps, in back of the stage so nobody can see him, playing a Les Paul guitar. I was like wow! This guy can really play."

"One time I saw him at the Upstage and he just blew the crowd away," added Mulrenan. "He had real long hair, half-way down his chest and no shirt on. His hair was in front of his face so you couldn't even see his face and he looked like he weighed about 80 pounds or so. I was in the audience watching him. He was doing mostly Allman Brothers songs. And then I saw what looked like heat waves coming off of him like energy. Then I felt the crowd around me reacting to those waves. They were reacting to him in a way I'd never seen anybody react to anybody on stage before. That's when I really started paying attention to him."

Billy Chinnock was one of the musicians who was at the Upstage from day one. In fact, he even helped paint the place with its infamous Day-Glo colors. "I was there from the beginning," said Chinnock. "It was just an incredible time. It was kind of what Sam Phillips must have felt about Sun Records in the fifties. It was just a time that was incredible for music. People were just very open to it. It fostered and nurtured creativity. All of us nappy little kids growing up at the Jersey Shore were in an environment where there were tons of places to play. There was a huge audience for it. It was just a magical time. It enabled everyone to kind of develop their craft."

Most of the kids at the Upstage were from Asbury Park or nearby towns like Ocean Grove and Neptune. David Mieras, and his friends from Ocean Grove, used to sit at a table in the corner, all the way in the back, in the dark with their sunglasses on. As soon as they got to the club, they'd head straight for their usual table in the back. "It must have been cool or something," explained Mieras. "We'd sit over in the corner in the dark like little wise guys. I remember the first night Bruce came in. He must have seen all of us kids from somewhere before because he came in and he had these dark sunglasses on. It was so funny. I'll never forget it. He came up and his hair was real long, he had dark sunglasses on and he had like a fringe jacket, I believe. I looked at him and said wow, who is that? He just came up to the top of the stairs and stood there. It was like who's this guy? Then, I realized I had seen him a while before playing somewhere like Hazlet. He just kind of fit right in.

"The weird thing about it, and the cool thing about it, was that it was a place to get things organized. Like any kind of activist type of event. People would come from all over the place to Upstage and bring flyers, so you knew what was going on in New Brunswick. Back then, New Brunswick was the other music spot in New Jersey. And it was strange, you'd have Black Panthers coming over there and dropping stuff off. You know what's going on with them and things. Organizations that were anti-establishment and stuff."

A major part of the personality of the club was due to its owners, Tom and Margaret Potter. They were a pair of beauticians that owned a beauty salon next to the Upstage. With a bohemian attitude and love of rock and roll music, they brought their vision to life. Yet it's doubtful that they could have foreseen just how important their little coffeehouse would be to the history of the Jersey Shore music scene. Many great artists got their start at the Upstage and few have forgotten those days. Both Tom and Margaret have since passed on, but they are remembered fondly by the club regulars and the musicians who played there.

"I remember they were all crazy," said Southside Johnny. "We were crazy too. He was this wacky, big, burly, bearded, larger-than-life, profane man who was a hair dresser and I hate to have to say it but he wasn't gay. He was married to Margaret who was this gravel throated, chain smoking tough cookie guitar player. And they were just a delightful pair.

"Margaret had her own band and she would recruit us to play in her band and we'd come up and jam. Occasionally she had her own band with John Luraschi, I guess. He played bass with her, but if somebody wasn't there she'd come up and say, 'Can you play bass for me tonight?' It was standard material so we could do it. She was a real black leather kind of rock and roller and Tom was just a force of nature."

Tom Potter was the type of guy who could put a scare in you until you got to know him. Billy Hector, one of the best blues guitarists at the Jersey Shore recalls meeting Tom at the Upstage. "I went there when I was thirteen. I got up to play and was asked to leave. They had an open mike thing there and I got up there and we played a little bit. So I'm up on stage, tuning up, and he (Tom Potter) tells me to 'stop farting around and start playing some music or get out of here.'"

Skip McGarry, another regular at the club, remembers being with Greg Potter and meeting his parents, Tom and Margaret, for the first time. "What a trip!" recalled McGarry. "It was kind of like looking into a looking glass and seeing the future of what was gonna become Upstage. It was like Beatniks meet Hippies."

The second floor contained a life-size fluorescent green mermaid suspended from the ceiling along with a bunch of fish netting. This led to some people referring to it as the Green Mermaid Cafe. It was a typical 1960s coffee house. The room was dark with candles on the tables and kids too young for the Upstage crowd could be found hanging out there.

"In the beginning, the way it started out at the Upstage it was only the coffeehouse," said Mieras. "There was no third floor. No rock hall, that's what I called it. It was just a little, small coffeehouse.

"They had a stage that was built with curtains, nice velvet curtains and little stairs you'd walk up to. It was like a little stage that you would see in a school. It was small. And people would go up there and play folk music. We'd even put on little plays and things like that. You've got to understand, we were very, very young. When they opened Upstage, I think I was 13 years old. It was all under 21, absolutely. It was kids."

"Although a Day-Glo green mermaid hung from the ceiling, as some sort of gesture toward decoration, I don't know anybody who ever called the place the Green Mermaid Cafe," said Robert Lee Hefter, a guitarist who played at the coffeehouse.

"I was a solo guy, playing 20-25 sets per week on the second floor stage," said Hefter. "I did only acoustic covers - Dylan, Simon & Garfunkel, Beatles of course and some lesser-known artists including Tom Rush and Fred Neil. I never took part in the jams, but every now and then Bruce would take a break from upstairs and come down and back me up, taking leads and fills. He gave me one of his songs, 'The War Is Over,' to arrange for solo 12-string and it went over really well. It was obvious even then that he lived to play. I had a wife and a day job. Somebody once said that if you have something to fall back on you will, and I did. Music was always something I did for myself and while I did have some vague dreams of someday achieving big things as a singer-songwriter, I never put them above all else as most of the great ones seem driven to do."

Hefter believes that he was the inspiration for the line "Some Hazard from Harvard was skunked on beer playing backyard bombardier" from Springsteen's "Blinded By The Light." According to Hefter, he took a summer session course at Harvard in 1969. "Backyard Bombardier" refers to the fact that he once told Bruce that he had no interest in going on the road, but was "content to wow the crowd at the Upstage."

Tom Matthews was a regular patron of the coffeehouse. He remembers a unique dessert experience found there. "They served what was called the Orgy," said Matthews. "It was a sundae made with an entire gallon block of chocolate, vanilla, and strawberry ice cream. Supposedly if you could finish one by yourself, it was free. They also served a smaller version called Half an Orgy."

Around the country, the popular music of the time largely centered around the heavy sound of guitar heroes. The music at the Upstage reflected this as well and the jams included songs which sometimes went on for as long as 30 minutes. One of the local musicians, Tony Amato, found his calling at the keyboard because it was one of the few instruments in demand at the Upstage.

"You'd go to Upstage and there was like three keyboard players," explained Amato. "You had David Sancious, Danny Federici, and Kevin Kavanaugh, the original keyboardist from the Jukes. That was the keyboard players. Drummers you've got Bobby Williams, Vini Lopez, you had about fifteen drummers. You know, a thousand guitar players, five hundred bass players. Because at the time Led Zeppelin was big, Hendrix was big and power trios. It was hard to find a keyboard player."

Tony Amato, or Boccigalupe as he's known today, is one of the few musicians of that era that can actually lay claim to being from Asbury Park. He had a special relationship with the Potters' since his father was their accountant. "It was kind of hard for me to hang out at the Upstage and not get caught. It was like if you come home after twelve, I'm locking the door. So he'd lock the door and we'd go to sleep under the Casino over there or something or we'd stay up in the Upstage."

"They used to call the Upstage the cheapest motel room in town because by the time you got out the sun would be coming up," added Big Danny. "So, loads of people would come down from North Jersey, stay there all night and then go nod off on the beach all day."

"I used to do everything there," added Amato. "During the daytime, sun comes out, everybody's got to leave. They'd clean up and then you'd start all over again. It was just one big jam session. Most of the guys wouldn't show up until after their gigs were over. Like Bruce and his band, they'd be out about 9 doing some stuff and then they'd be done and come rolling in. Everybody gets to play. You start out with your bands and the bands playing, then everybody starts mixing and mingling. That's how we met each other. That's how we met everybody. Basically we created this, whatever you want to call it, sound of Asbury Park."

The Upstage had a very short but brilliant run. After the race riots hit Asbury Park, many places were forced to close simply because people were afraid to be there and the Upstage was no different.

"In 1970, Tom (Potter) made really good money, a lot of money for the time," said Mieras. "And the next year he went broke. A lot of people won't admit that that was the downfall of Asbury Park, but there's no doubt in my mind. We were the ones that were down here, we knew what was going on and what was happening. All of our parents shopped there. Suddenly, people just didn't go there anymore. They were scared. Who wants to go somewhere where they're scared?"

The Upstage lost its primary audience around the same time that the musicians and patrons were becoming of age to get into bars. The musicians would move to higher paying gigs at clubs like the Student Prince and Sunshine In.

"At the Upstage you didn't make any money," explained Chinnock. "You made fifteen dollars a night and you played from 9 p.m. until 6 a.m. It was a time when everyone could hone their craft."

The days of endless jamming were replaced with trying to make a living. Just as the riots had signaled an end to innocence throughout the town, the closing of the Upstage marked the end of an era. In the end, the Upstage will be forever remembered as a club unlike anything Asbury Park had ever seen and probably will ever see again.

"Everybody was there for the music," agreed Amato. "You had the hippies, the beatniks and the greasers. There was nobody better than this one or that one, or at least they weren't fighting about it. There wasn't all this other bologna that goes along with it. You know, like fighting for position."

David Sancious wishes there were more places like the Upstage where young musicians get a chance to work on their music. "It was great to have a place like that to play and the challenge of being good enough to ask to be in a jam," said Sancious. "It was a whole thing because back then it was all about practicing and getting better. What I remember about everybody back then, Bruce and everybody, was that we were all very serious about the music, about wanting to be good and wanting to be better and really do it for real. So there was a lot of work that went on just you in your bedroom at home, getting it together. And then you'd come out and want to develop that with somebody. You always wanted to be in a band or forming a band, jamming with somebody. It really tremendously helped me. It all helps. I mean, that's part of your history."

For all of us who grew up long after the Upstage had closed its doors, we can only imagine what that period of time was like. We walk past the building where the Upstage once stood and can only wonder what it was like to see these emerging artists at such a crucial stage of their development. Music was everything to them and this club gave them a place to experiment and grow as musicians. Who knows what their careers would have been like without such a place. Maybe the constant battles to be the best molded them into who they are today. To the musicians who played there and the regulars who came every night, there will never be another place like the Upstage.

2 Convention Hall and Paramount Theatre

It was just fascinating for my friends and I. It ended up almost being expected. It's like Asbury's the place to be if you like music.

--DAVID MIERAS

Convention Hall and Paramount Theatre have hosted some of the most popular acts in the world. Photo © CJ Photography

One of the most impressive buildings along the Jersey Shore has got to be where Convention Hall and Paramount Theatre converge on Asbury Park's boardwalk. The complex was built by architects Warren and Wetmore who were also the designers of New York's Grand Central Station. It opened on July 11, 1930 with a show at the Paramount Theatre featuring the Marx Brothers and Ginger Rogers.

Since its inception, many of the biggest names in music have brought their shows to either the grandiose Convention Hall or the more intimate Paramount Theatre. Convention Hall can hold up to 3,500 people, including a large standing room only general admission area, while the Paramount Theatre has seating for about 1,500.

In addition to concerts, Convention Hall has hosted many conventions, wrestling events and basketball games throughout its history. Recently, several of the area's top high school basketball teams took part in a local tournament here and Monmouth University (in nearby West Long Branch) played their first game in Asbury Park in decades.

"Convention Hall had major acts forever," said Lee Mrowicki. "Back in the 40s they had the big bands, the 50s had doo-wop rock and roll bands. I think the first concert I ever went to at Convention Hall was in 1966-67 and it was Vanilla Fudge. There was a major promoter named Moe Septee who always promoted the acts at Convention Hall."

Moe Septee was an incredible promoter who always managed to bring the top musical acts in the world to Asbury Park. Names like the Doors, Led Zeppelin, the Rolling Stones, the Grateful Dead and the Who are just a few of the bands Septee brought to the area. After a long run of booking the bands, Septee found himself in a battle with John Scher, who started booking acts at the Casino. Septee ultimately retired, feeling that rock and roll promotion was a young man's game and Scher took over as Asbury Park's main promoter.

The fact that Asbury Park was able to bring so many great bands to town is rather amazing when the size of the city is considered. Asbury's population is under 20,000, hardly in the same ballpark as the other cities found covered by the bands on their tours. Geography had a lot to do with it. Asbury Park's location in the center of New Jersey was a perfect place for a show in between dates in New York or Philadelphia or for bands heading up to Boston or down to DC. It was rather easy to get to from any of the other cities and the bands knew they could always draw well in Asbury.

"It was just fascinating for my friends and I," explained David Mieras who grew up one town over in Ocean Grove. "It ended up almost being expected. It's like Asbury's the place to be if you like music."

Shows at Convention Hall are still remembered by many of the fans in attendance. Asbury had a knack for catching bands on their way up. Many of the top acts in the world played Convention Hall during their first or second world tours.

"There were so many great shows there and a lot of them kind of run together as to who was the opening act for who," remembered Tom Matthews, who saw many shows at Convention Hall. "Led Zeppelin touring right after their first album came out was pretty great. I remember Jimmy Page playing the guitar with a bow during 'Dazed and Confused.' I think I was a bit dazed and confused myself.

"Emerson, Lake and Palmer I saw there a couple of times," continued Matthews. "Keith Emerson's synthesizer found all the resonant frequencies of that old building. And an unlikely combination, but enjoyable just the same, was Yes when Rick Wakeman was still with the group and the Eagles on their first nationwide tour as the opening act."

"My uncle Henry Vaccaro was on the City Council so I knew I had first row seats on the weekend," said Tony Amato. "I caught the Rolling Stones, the Rascals, Moby Grape. I think the first show I saw there was the Rolling Stones and Dave Clark Five. The best show was Led Zeppelin and Jethro Tull."

Tom Matthews and his friends didn't always have the money to get into the shows, but that never stopped them from trying to see the bands. "There were a few shows that I didn't actually see that were memorable just the same," said Matthews. "One that we tried to sneak into by elaborate means was Mott the Hoople and Ten Years After. We entered through a steel door in the sidewalk on Ocean Avenue. Then we climbed up from the basement of the Paramount Theatre and across catwalks above the ceiling until we reached the roof. Finally we ran across to the Convention Hall side and came down behind the stage just as Mott the Hoople were finishing their set. We were bumping into the band as we tried to make it down from the stage and into the crowd but several large roadies intercepted us and showed us to the back door.

"Then there was the Jefferson Airplane show a week or so after the race riots in Asbury Park," added Matthews. "I guess we wanted to show that we white kids could raise some hell too, so we spread the rumor that there would be a riot at the show. We assembled a few hundred folks on the north side of the hall. I think it was while they were playing 'Volunteers' inside that we tried to rush the place. The cops with their newly acquired riot gear were there to greet us. When they fired a shotgun blast above our heads, the crowd trying to climb from the beach back to the boardwalk ripped loose about a block or two worth of railing."

Of course, one of the most unusual aspects of concerts held at Convention Hall is that the sound can be clearly heard from outside the building. Lots of times crowds of people will hang out on the beach or the boardwalk and listen to the show for free. In fact, some music fans actually prefer being outside the building and listening to the show while relaxing on the beach during a hot summer night. When Bruce Springsteen and the E Street Band performed a bunch of benefit shows to rehearse for *The Rising* Tour, hundreds of fans that couldn't get inside hung out and sang along with the band as if it was a giant listening party.

In recent years, Springsteen has used Convention Hall and Paramount Theatre several times for benefits and rehearsal shows. His first Christmas Show benefit in 2000 attracted fans from all over the world. Bruce did his part in trumpeting Asbury Park's revival by encouraging people to visit the downtown shops. One fan that traveled all the way from Europe to be at the show was the music journalist, Maggie Powell.

"I was so lucky to get a ticket and the whole trip was totally last minute so I didn't really have time to think about it," said Powell. "The surprise element went through the roof! If anyone had ever told me that I would see all of my favorite Jersey Shore musicians playing together on the same stage in Asbury Park, I would never have believed them. But they were all there... Bruce, Little Steven, Southside Johnny... I mean, this was akin to seeing the 'Father, Son and Holy Ghost of Jersey Shore rock and roll!' And to hear songs like 'Kitty's Back' and 'For You' with Bruce at the piano... wow, it was awesome!

"I think the most poignant moment of the night happened when Bruce performed 'My City Of Ruins' for the very first time," Powell continued. "He dedicated it to Kate Mellina whose efforts to revitalize Asbury Park are an inspiration to everyone who knows her. I was standing about six feet away from Bruce when he sang it. The song quite literally moved me to tears and I felt so incredibly privileged to be part of an audience that was witnessing something so uniquely wonderful."

Although the glory days of Asbury Park shows are generally thought of as the concerts held during the 60s and 70s, the music never stopped. In the 80s acts as Peter Gabriel, the Clash and Elvis Costello came to town. And, in the 90s, such bands as No Doubt, Crowded House and the Goo Goo Dolls played here. More recently, shows by the Counting Crows and Jimmy Eat World once again made Asbury Park the place to be. In addition, Convention Hall and Paramount Theatre have been home to several festivals including those for punk rock and heavy metal bands as well as the first ever Asbury Music Festival, the creation of Tony Palligrosi, a former member of the Asbury Jukes.

3 The Student Prince

The Student Prince was great! The guy who ran the Student Prince was an interesting guy. We could con him and he kind of went with the folly.

--SOUTHSIDE JOHNNY

The Student Prince was once located in this building. Photo © Gary Wien

Historians and rock and roll fans will forever remember the Student Prince as the place where Bruce Springsteen and Clarence Clemons first met. As the story goes, friends of Clarence had been telling him to check out Bruce's band and so he did on a very stormy night. The wind was howling and blowing up and down the boardwalk. When Clarence opened the door, a huge gust literally ripped the door off of its hinges. Clarence saw Bruce on stage and yelled, "I want to be in your band." Seeing the very large man standing in the doorway that no longer had a door, Bruce replied something like, "Sure, you do whatever you want."

The Student Prince was located at 911 Kingsley Avenue. It was a major part of the music scene at the time. Many of the great Jersey Shore artists like Bruce Springsteen, Southside Johnny, Little Steven, Billy Chinnock and David Sancious were all known to play there.

"It was small," recalls Billy Chinnock. "The stage was on the right, and it was always jammed. You'd squeeze through the door and it'd be all you could do to be able to make your way to watch the band. The bandstand was really high like at the Fastlane and the Pony in later years. There were times when you couldn't even move when we played. Jammed!"

For artists like Southside Johnny and Steven Van Zandt, the Student Prince provided an opportunity and a venue where they could take some musical risks. It was sort of a bridge between the free-form days of the Upstage and the Stone Pony.

"The Student Prince was great," said Southside Johnny. "The guy who ran the Student Prince was an interesting guy. We could con him and he kind of went with the folly. I remember Steven and I put together a band, but we wanted to do a lot of blues at that time. I guess this was the late 60s. Bruce was on the West Coast, I believe. And we kind of formed a strategy that we wanted to do a lot of Elmore James and Muddy Waters, but he wanted to do reggae and we wanted to explore a lot of different things. And Ry Cooder was a big influence because he was exploring a lot of these kinds of music so we wanted to try some of that.

"Steven was the first guy I really knew that knew about reggae. I really didn't know that much about it, but he had found a bunch of wacky compilation albums. It was great! But we say we'll never get in anywhere. So we learned two Rolling Stones songs. I think it was 'Jumping Jack Flash' and 'Brown Sugar' or something like that. And we went in one night and a band was playing and we said, 'Can we audition?' There was like two people in the club. So he said, 'Sure, go play some songs.' We played the two songs and people went nuts. You know, Stones songs. So he said, 'Great! You've got a two week booking.'"

"We proceed to go in there and play all blues and these bizarre reggae and R&B things and we never did the two Stones songs," continued Southside. "He came over to me one night said, 'What happened to those songs that people really liked?' I said, 'We don't do those any more.' But we ended up having a following there. We started to draw fans from there, things like that. It's just that was what I was into. I forget what the name of the band was. Funky, Dusty and the Soul Broom or one of those bizarre Steven names."

Many of the musicians that jammed or hung out at the Upstage would play at the Student Prince. It was almost like a stepping stone for them into the world of playing in bars. One such band was Sunfield with Skip McGarry, who frequented the Upstage often. His band had a regular gig at the Student Prince. "We only played all original music and had five part harmonies, stuff like Crosby, Stills & Nash and America," said McGarry. "I think we were the only ones around doing anything like that. I remember times when Bruce and the E Street or pre E Street band would stop in for a cold one and listen to our band. Boardwalk musician Kevin Conklin was a member of our band. He was one of the best acoustic guitar players around. Unfortunately, he was killed by a car."

The most famous band to come from the Student Prince was, of course, the Bruce Springsteen Band. This band featured many of the members which would ultimately back Bruce as the E Street Band. Robert Salzmann, who remembers seeing the band for the first time.

"My best friend, Bob Strusz, went to art school in Plainfield with Vini Lopez's then girlfriend Beth," said Salzmann. "Bob's car had some problems and I gave him a ride to school one day. We ran into 'Mad Dog' (Vini Lopez) who was dogging Beth and we shot the shit and shared a joint. Vini raved about this band that he was playing in and carried on about the lead guitarist some Bruce fellow. Our musical tastes appeared to be similar and Vini was charming as well as very convincing so we agreed to drive down to the Student Prince in Asbury Park.

"The place was empty except for a couple of roaches. There must have been about 12-15 people, including groupies and friends of the band and the two of us. We sat at the bar about 15 feet in front of Bruce and Steven. They were fantastic! We requested songs by Chuck Berry and the Rolling Stones and supplied the guys with beer during the breaks. They were really good at covering the blues. The next day we spread the word up north (Metuchen area) and made arrangements to return with another group of people for the Saturday and Sunday shows. The word continued to spread through New Jersey and in the following weeks the audience started to snowball."

Salzmann would make the trek from Metuchen to Asbury Park often to see the Bruce Springsteen Band play at the Student Prince. He had a beat up old 1964 Mercedes Benz as his ride. The car had once been used as a dealer's loaner car, but was still a pretty cool car in the early seventies. Times being as they were, the smell of cannabis often replaced the smell of leather when you opened the car's door. It was like a "hippy mobile" designed to bring Robert and his friends to the Shore. Dressed like a bunch of rock and roll gypsies in their jeans, denim jackets and flannel shirts, seeing the Bruce Springsteen Band was one of their favorite ways to escape their daily lives. It certainly was the more legal approach.

"One night my friend and I were invited by the drummer to see the Bruce Springsteen Band perform," said Salzmann. "During the 30 minute drive down the Garden State Parkway, we got thoroughly buzzed. At the show we had several beers. During one of the intermissions we decided to step outside, walk around the block and get re-buzzed. We invited the drummer to join us on this quest for 'fresh air.' He accepted the offer and commented positively on the wisdom of the proposal. While sharing a joint outside the bar we were approached by Bruce Springsteen. We invited him to join the gathering. He looks over, smiles and gestures 'no thanks' by waving his hands back and forth. We shrug, smile back at him and continue to pass the thing around..."

Tom Matthews remembers going to the Student Prince a lot during the summer of 1973. That was the year New Jersey lowered the drinking age to 18. Tom, like many other 18-year olds, suddenly was able to see the Asbury music scene in action. He recalls seeing bands like the Bank Street Blues often at the Student Prince and watching guys like David Sancious take part in jams. "It was like a smaller version of the Stone Pony," he said regarding the club.

"The Student Prince was like this real sleazy little bar," said Sonny Kenn. "You went there because you could play there. They didn't pay much money, but you could play."

In later years, the area where the Student Prince was located became known as Club Xanadu, a popular bar in the eighties that hosted local and national acts, and more recently as Seductions Go-Go. It has not been in use for several years now, yet another abandoned building in Asbury Park hiding a wonderful musical history inside its walls.

4 Hullabaloo and the Sunshine In

That period of time was great. But I don't think we realized how unique it was for a small town like Asbury Park to have all of this going on. It was only in retrospect that I truly appreciated it.

--TOM MATTHEWS
FORMER SUNSHINE IN EMPLOYEE

You can get a pretty good idea of the wide variety of artists that came to the Sunshine In by looking at the pair of concert posters shown here.

I n the early 70s, Asbury Park was fortunate to have some of the biggest names in rock and roll come through town. The bands that had already made it could be found playing Convention Hall or the Casino. Those on the way up could be found playing the Sunshine In. Bruce Springsteen played here often with bands like Steel Mill, Dr. Zoom and the Sonic Boom and the Bruce Springsteen Band. But before it was the Sunshine In, it was one of several "Hullabaloo" clubs in the area.

"Originally if you look at old aerial maps of Asbury Park it was a bus garage," said Sonny Kenn. "They used to park all of the local buses in there and repair them. Then a television show called 'TV's Hullabaloo Scene' came out and they made it a franchise where you could buy your own club. So, all these clubs sprang up. They would all have the same pictures and would be decorated with the same orange and black Day-Glo paint.

"The original club, I believe, was in Boston. There was a house band in the Boston place called the Windjammers that would come down and open each new club. They were a nice bunch of guys, crazy guys. The Windjammers would play and they'd charge admission and the kids would show up. They'd promote it in the press. It was a big deal. We went there and we won the contest and became the houseband at the Asbury Hullabaloo Club. We used to rehearse there and we played the club once a week. Later they asked us to play some of their other clubs. So, we got an old '54 pickup, loaded up all of our stuff and went up to New York, Boston and Pennsylvania. We toured the Northeast Hulaballoo circuit at 16 years old!"

"The Beatles had just happened and kids were going out more," said John Mulrenan who used to play there with a band called Rasputin and the Mad Monks. "So there was no booze there. They decorated the places real nice. There was definitely a lot of money behind them. It's funny because I don't think they ever made a ton of money, but the opening night was always packed. I don't think it was a big moneymaker because it was like only a few years later that it became the Sunshine In."

The Sunshine In was an old concrete block building with a high wooden, open rafter type ceiling. The outside was painted a rather unattractive orange-yellow color. It opened as the Sunshine In sometime in the summer of 1970. The Sunshine In was an old warehouse type building, about a half block wide and two thirds of a block long, which was located on Kingsley Street. Although it has been called "Sunshine Inn" on bootlegs around the world, it was actually named after the Aquarius age.

"That was a horrible, ugly place," recalled John Mulrenan. "I played there with a band called Godzilla. There were cinderblocks on the floor that kids would sit on. I remember broken cement on the floor and lots of garbage."

There was no bar inside but since there was plenty of bars on the same block you never had to worry about missing a drink. Originally, it was standing room only for about 1,000 people or so, but in the later years ('72-'73) they installed some bleachers in the very back. The Student Prince was nearby so this part of town had great music each night.

"I lived at the Sunshine In for a while in '71," said Tom Matthews. "Everything was on one floor, there was no upstairs. We pretty much lived in the office, sleeping on the couches and floors. That is when we slept, which wasn't too often. I once stayed awake for nine days while staying there. In the beginning there was only a tiny dressing room, more like a large closet, but later due to demands from the bands, I imagine, they built a larger dressing room/lounge off the right side of the stage."

The Sunshine In was run by Bob Fischer. According to Matthews, Fischer was almost a caricature of the stereotypical rock promoter. "It was clear to everyone that he only was in it for the money. He was clueless when it came to rock and roll and the bands he was dealing with. Once, in a display of his great understanding of musical styles, he booked Kiss and Renaissance on the same bill. That made for quite a mixed audience. Probably my favorite show was one of the first I went to, Steel Mill, Black Sabbath, and the Chambers Brothers. It was typical of the somewhat eclectic mixes that Fischer in his ignorance was capable of putting together, but it was a great show nonetheless."

Fischer's tightness with money led to constant battles with the bands, according to people who worked there or knew him personally. He was always being chased up the street by somebody. "He used to like to pay the bands at the end of the show with the receipts from the door but he developed such a reputation for short changing the acts that several bands refused to go onstage until they had been paid," said Matthews. "One night he came staggering into the office after the show, bleeding profusely from the nose, and told us that his partner had slugged him and made off with all of the money taken in that night."

The legendary Jersey Shore rocker Lance Larson was a bartender at the Student Prince at the time. He remembers how Bobby Fischer was always a little short of money. "Bobby would always say, 'Lance you got any money to invest?'" said Larson. "He'd say, 'Put up $1300 and I'll give you the bill of sale to my yellow Cadillac.' So, I'd give him the money and he'd give me the bill of sale to his car. He used to do this all of the time."

"One time he didn't show up the next day with my pay back. This guy comes into the Student Prince and he asks me if I've seen Bobby Fischer. He's like, 'That guy owes me money.' I said, 'I ain't seen him.' Then he goes, 'Well, I know he won't beat me because I got this bill of sale.' And I say, 'I've got the same one!'"

In 1973, Matthews worked at the Sunshine In as a stage electrician. Basically, the job was to make sure that none of the wiring caught fire as it had during one of the Black Sabbath shows. He was paid $35 per show along with all of the beer he could drink.

"I remember our reaction when Kiss played there for the first time and were explaining some of their pyrotechnics," recalled Matthews. "We were horrified and thought that they would certainly burn the place down, the Sunshine In being a very old warehouse/garage with an old, dried out wooden ceiling. But they went ahead and all was fine and they played there several more times."

Lee Mrowicki, the long-time disc jockey at the Stone Pony saw a lot of shows at the Sunshine In. "One show really sticks out in my mind. It took place when I was in college. On the bill was a band from West Orange that had just gotten a contract, they were called the Truth and it was kind of like a jazz/progressive rock band. The headliner was Bachman Turner Overdrive. Truth was the second act so they went on before Bachman Turner. Nowadays, the opening act would be considered a shock, it was Bob Seger and the Silver Bullet Band. They were the absolute opener to a local band from West Orange and BTO on a triple bill."

Rich Robinson also remembers that show well. "The reason I remember it so much is because 'Taking Care Of Business' was the #1 song in the country," he said. "So, the night before they played the Sunshine In in front of 2,000 people they were at the Spectrum in Philly and the night after they were playing Madison Square Garden."

What makes that show even more amazing is that the band that played after Bob Seger was not even on the original bill. There was supposed to be a band from England in that spot, but they never showed up. So, Bobby Fischer was left scrambling at the last minute to find a replacement. According to Lance Larson, he came over to the Student Prince and grabbed the Truth, who were playing there that night, and put them on the bill in between their sets at the Prince.

"I remember the people went crazy over the Truth and they were playing across the street at the Student Prince!" said Larson.

"That period of time was great," added Matthews. "But I don't think we realized how unique it was for a small town like Asbury Park to have all of this going on. It was only in retrospect that I truly appreciated it."

5 Sonny Kenn

I remember sitting at a diner one time with Johnny and I just wanted to be the best blues rock guitar player. Then you realize that there's no best in anything.

--SONNY KENN

The first "star" of the Jersey Shore, Sonny Kenn, is shown performing live.
Photo © Debra L. Rothenberg/rothenbergphoto.com

S onny Kenn is widely regarded as the first rock and roll star of the Jersey Shore. In the early sixties, his bands Sonny and the Sounds and Sonny and the Starfires routinely played shows at places like the Eatontown Shopping Center (currently known as the Monmouth Mall), the Hullabaloo Club in Asbury Park and the Canteen in Belmar as well as high school dances throughout Monmouth County.

After playing rock and roll for many years, Sonny started playing the blues with the first incarnation of the Sundance Blues Band, which also included Southside Johnny. A little later on, the two would form a power trio called Maelstrom that was a regular at the Upstage.

Sonny Kenn is now known primarily as one of the Shore's finest blues guitarists. He can still be found playing in the area as well as in clubs in New York City. I caught up with Sonny in his Red Bank studio as he was working on his long-awaited follow-up record.

Was Sonny and the Starfires your first band?
Before the Starfires I had been playing with a group called the Blazers. There were only about two bands in my school at Manasquan. There was a band called the Galaxies and there was us. The Galaxies did mostly instrumental stuff like the Ventures. We came in and I was a big rock and roll freak so we were doing stuff by Chuck Berry and Little Richard. When the Rolling Stones came out we realized we were already doing about half of their first album so people thought we were doing Stones songs. We played a lot of dances and VFW shows. After the Blazers there was Sonny and the Sounds, and then Sonny and the Starfires.

I've heard that the Starfires had a certain look to the band.
Yeah, we had the gold suits. There was a place in Asbury which burned down in the riots called Fish's, we used to go there. It was in the black section of town and the greatest clothes in the world were there. So, we would go in there and buy the gold suits, Italian high roll shirts, Spanish boots or Beatles boots as they called them. We'd get black slacks or matching pants and shirts, whatever. And that's what we wore when we played. We'd sweat them up like hell and then Mom would clean them.

We played for about three or four years. It was until 1967. We used to play a lot at the Belmar Canteen there on 5th Avenue (currently Taylor Pavilion). They used to have dances every Friday and Saturday with live bands. It was a rental hall. The first version burned down but the second version is still there and they built it according to the original specs, so it looks exactly like the original. That place was a big deal because it was one of the few places in this area that teens could go and see a live band.

I remember a lot of bands coming through there. Usually they were a little older than we were. It was like God, if we could just play the Canteen, it would be so cool! So, one night this band didn't show up and the guy running it called us up. We got everybody there in an hour and a half and played the dance. After that we started getting work there. It was like one of those early moments where you've got five guys and you're playing rock and roll music with about 200 kids all dancing to you so much that you can hear the floor pounding. It was just very, very cool. It's one of those things that stays with you.

We used to play a lot of high school dances and stuff. I know we played at Freehold and Manasquan... we played a lot of places. It's funny when I look back it's like here we were 16-17 years old and we worked a lot!

What was the ultimate goal for you at that time?
The ultimate goal was just to play. At that point, it was just to play in front of people and to hear yourself playing this music that you revered so much. You take a normal bunch of kids thinking about girls and they're a little timid, then all of a sudden everyone's watching them and what they do is important. In the big scheme of things it means nothing, but it becomes a big deal in your little world and it leads to other things if it doesn't get too crazy. Some guys couldn't handle it and ended up dead. Sometimes the party becomes more than the music. For me, the music was always more than anything.

Sonny & the Starfires used to play a lot at the Eatontown Shopping Center (now known as Monmouth Mall) what do you remember of those shows?
Back then the shopping center wasn't enclosed and there was an outside area where the food court is now and they would bring in a small stage in front and put fencing around it. People would come into that and they would put on shows on every weekend at one o'clock in the afternoon and again at four o'clock to draw people to the shopping center because the mall had just opened. This guy, Frank Parr, started these shows. One of the first was a talent show. Our manager at the time came down and said, "Let's go to the mall they're having auditions for this talent show." And when you're 15-16 years old there's not a hell of a lot of places that you can play, so we jumped in his Olds 88 and went up there. We auditioned and got into the show. Then after that we started doing regular shows there. They would usually have an animal act or something for the little kids. The big one was Mugs the Chimpanzee. There was a couple of big chimp acts in the 60s.

Mugs had done the "Ed Sullivan Show" and had been on the cover of *Mad Magazine*. But that was what you did, you know? They put on these things and people used to come to them. On a couple of occasions they had the Beau Brummels who had the song "Laff Laff," which was a big hit. We opened for them and it was funny because they would set up on the first tier and we'd set up on the front tier. We started playing their songs and we had all the harmonies down and stuff, it was like a tribute to them. But we didn't know that one of the guys had just quit the band and they couldn't hit all of the harmony notes. So, they were all giving us dirty looks and thought we were trying to upstage them. But we weren't, it was just a tribute. They didn't sound too good that day.

One night we were supposed to play with Joey D & the Starlighters. He canceled for whatever reason. So, Frank Parr called up this promoter that he was working for and said that Jerry Lee Lewis was coming up through Jersey on his way to Connecticut to do a show and he would stop to do a pickup gig. He booked him to play both shows, but I think he only played the early show. I don't remember him playing the four o'clock one.

So, here I am 16 years old and Lewis is one of my idols. I told Frank, "Whatever you do, you've got to introduce me." He goes, "Yeah, okay. Just go in the dressing room and wait." I'm waiting in the back and Lewis is in his office. Finally it's about five minutes to showtime and I'm like we're not gonna see him. Then just before we were supposed to go on he tells us to go into his office. I'll never forget the scene... Jerry Lee had his feet up on the promoter's desk, there was a six pack of beer with four cans already gone and a bottle of Jack Daniels with about an inch left in the bottom; his eyes were bright red, he had this gold suit on and his hair was dyed blonde. I walk in and go, "Hello, Mister Lewis," and he just reaches out his hand and goes, "Howdy boy!"

Jerry had an album out at the time called *Greatest Live Show On Earth* and I asked him if he would do "High School Confidential," which was one of my favorite tunes. He said, "I'll see if I can squeeze it in." So we go on and then he comes on and we're sitting right down in front of the stage, I'm like five feet away from him. He goes through his Jerry Lee Lewis thing and I don't think that the people really got it because he was a little too old for the young kids and the people that remembered him pretty much thought he was a maniac. But he put on a good show and he did my song and looked down at me when he sang it, which was really cool. Then as soon as he was done with the show he just walked off the stage. In the back they had a Lincoln Continental and a U-Haul. He gets into the back seat and the band just packed up everything.

They got the organ, the drums, the bass, everything off of the stage and into the U-Haul within five minutes and started driving off. The last thing I remember was watching him drive off literally into the sunset. That was one of the first exposures you had of meeting somebody you had idolized and when you're that young with a band together and see somebody like that it almost validates your whole thing. It's like we're one of them!

Our manager ended up teaming up with the guy who did the promotions for the mall and they set up a little production company. We went up to the city in 1965 and cut a record. I didn't know anything about cutting a record. It was at this place called Variety Studios in Manhattan. I thought we would just go in and play. They were talking about "overdubs, mike placements and double tracking."

We went up there twice. I think we cut "Memphis, Tennessee" by Chuck Berry, "Just a Little" by the Beau Brummels, "Please, Please Me" by the Beatles, "Roll Over Beethoven," which was another Chuck Berry tune and "Oh, Lonesome Me," an old country song. We cut them and we got these lacquered dubs, which was cool. I remember going into that room. It was pretty advanced, one of the original eight-tracks in the city. When you were done they'd take the tape and run it through the cut. Then they would actually cut you a dub because cassette tapes weren't invented yet. So, they'd cut you a lacquered disc and you'd take that home to listen to. We thought that was so cool... man, we made a record!

At that time you could only cut one in real time, so we were there for eight hours to make about ten copies. I remember a couple of labels came down to see us. Now that I think about it they were probably all Mafia labels! At that time we were just doing covers. They all told us that the songs sounded great but what can we play on our own? So, all of a sudden, we went back and started writing material. Pretty feebly at the time, but it was a start. By the time we got that all together, people were graduating and either going off to the service or off to college and the band split up. When you're a teenager things seem to happen so fast. Just before that band split up, me and Johnny Lyon decided we were gonna form a blues band.

Johnny and me actually got a gig playing at a Good Guys Show at the Canteen in Belmar. I was giving lessons to this guitar player who was in a band that had gotten this gig and they wanted to know if I could come fill in as a guitar player. I said, "Sure, I'll do it." So, we rehearsed a few times and went there. I remember the bill was Children of Paradise, which was some band from the Village, the Dixie Cups who had the hit "Going To The Chapel" and Van Morrison who had just come out with "Brown Eyed Girl."

We all went into the back room and the promoter asks if we can back up the other bands. Van Morrison was trying to show me the chords to these songs and I was like, "I don't know all of these, I'll have to rehearse it." He goes, "Don't worry, I'll do it myself." So, he got the drummer from Children of Paradise and played with just him and the drummer. I remember he was still into the Gene Vincent thing. He had his hair kind of slicked back, a greenish gold suit with a jacket, tight pants and boots. It looked like some kind of Elvis/Gene Vincent knock off.

Then the Dixie Cups asked if we could do "Iko, Iko." I said, "Do you have a chart or something?" And she said yeah. Luckily the chart she gave me had the chords written above it so I said, "Yeah, I can follow this." We rehearsed it a little and then she's like, "Iko, Iko - it goes like this" and she snaps her fingers a bit. I'm like, "You mean the Bo Diddley beat?" She goes yeah! So we're just playing our Bo Diddley beat and they're playing "Iko, Iko" and it worked!

So, anyway we finished that show and I said, "Let's form a band." I met Johnny through Vini Lopez because they both went to Neptune High School and we got to be pretty good friends. Johnny, at the time, was just learning how to play harmonica so I got him in. It was me and Johnny, this guy Ronnie Romano, Steve Atwater and we began doing the blues thing because me and Johnny were really getting into the blues. So, that became the first incarnation of the Sundance Blues Band.

We both started getting into the blues together. At that point on Springwood Avenue there used to be a House of Hits right across the street from Fish's. You'd go in and there would be bins with Howlin' Wolf and Sonny Boy Williamson, Jimmy Reed and all of the Chicago cats. You'd go to Woolworths to buy a record and see Herman's Hermits but this place had all this other stuff that you didn't see in the regular record stores. So, every time we got paid from playing that night we'd go down the next day and buy four or five albums.

The Sundance Blues Band played at some of the Hullabaloo Clubs that were still left like the one in Toms River, we played at dances and started playing in some bars. We played for a while and then that band broke up. Led Zeppelin had come out and Johnny was into Zeppelin and Cream, Hendrix and stuff He said, "Let's put together a power trio." I'm like, "Sound's good." We called it Maelstrom.

Around this time we started playing at the Upstage Club. Tom Potter hired us to play downstairs because we were just a three-piece band so he figured we wouldn't make that much noise. Little did he know we'd be rolling in these great big amps. We were basically doing a blues thing but we were doing our versions of it with just guitar, bass and drums.

Then my friend Chuck came back from the Army reserves or something and started playing guitar with us. He was the guitar player in the Starfires with me. This let me switch off and play a little piano sometimes. People used to come and jam with us. I remember Carl Hughes, who was one of my first drummers in like 8th grade or something, brought David Sancious down and that's how I met Davey. He started sitting in with this little Wurlitzer keyboard. We'd play some Junior Walker, some Stones and some early blues. This was upstairs by now. We moved because the band had gotten bigger. I remember I had a '52 Buick and we would pile everything into the Buick and park right there on Cookman in front of the place. We'd play from 8 o'clock to about 12 o'clock and then take a break from 12 a.m. to 1 a.m. We'd go hang out on the Buick and then go back and play from 1 o'clock to 5 o'clock. Then we'd go home, ride down the beach and watch the sun come up.

Personally, I liked playing there but I remember seeing the scene change. You gotta remember I was an old greaser, I liked rock and roll, I liked the enthusiasm and exuberance of it. But it came to a point where we were playing "Shotgun" which is such a dance song and we used to do it pretty good... no matter what Johnny says he could play bass. And I remember one night looking out to the crowd and they're all sitting on the floor. I said wait, something's happening here. What happened to all the dancing? All of a sudden everybody got into that psychedelic thing where they were like, "Let's all get high and listen to the music." We weren't about just jamming away endlessly and I started personally feeling separated from it for the first time. It was because I never did any drugs ever. I've done my fair share of drinking but never any drugs. And it just seemed like everybody around me was doing it and I felt like a fish out of water. I either broke the band up or it might have just fell apart. I know that keeping drummers was a problem and Johnny didn't want to play bass anymore because he wanted to start playing harp. So, I just stopped going.

Did the genuineness of the blues steer you towards that direction?
Let me tell you something... when I was listening to WLIB, I heard music that I never heard before. It perks your ears up and you don't know where to go to get it. And then when Johnny turns me on to go to House Of Hits and he's like try this one... I go in and I'm reading the liner notes to a Stones album and they're talking about Muddy Waters and Howlin' Wolf. So, I said let's go see what these guys sound like. Now, I love the Stones but when you hear the originals it's like holy shit! They ain't talking about going out on a date... they're talking about screwing!

I remember when I was a real little kid living in Newark I used to listen to WLIB at night. They used to play a lot of this stuff. I remember the first time I heard Jimmy Reed, I didn't know what it was. I swear it sounded like this mysterious music... this weird stuff going through the air. It was like magic. I remember going to bed at 10 o'clock with this little Sylvania radio next to the bed. I'd turn it on and there would be this little yellow glow at night. I'd have my ear right next to it because I didn't want my mother to know I had the radio on. And I'd be listening to this stuff.

For a while, I did try the rock thing with my original stuff back when I was still trying to get a deal... the pie in the sky thing. I came close a few times, but it never happened because the stuff I did at the time wasn't like Bruce or Beaver Brown or Chinnock. It was different. I remember a guy from a record label calling me up on the phone. I'd submit stuff and they'd call me back. And it got to the point where I was like what the fuck do you want? Then I talked to some people who said that the problem is that they don't know what they want.

And now your son is giving it a go, right?
Yeah, well I guess once it's in the family... He's up in the city. They signed a deal with Ricon Records. The band's called Sunshine Flipside. They just finished recording a couple of weeks ago and they're in the process of mixing. If it happens it's good. If not, well that's the way it goes. We're hoping something will come of that. The record sounds good. It's a good rock and roll record. It's like a punk/psychedelic Beatles thing.

How would you like to be remembered?
I remember sitting at a diner one time with Johnny and I just wanted to be the best blues rock guitar player. Then you realize that there's no best in anything. So, now I just want to be able to play my guitar and write songs and have it affect somebody. I'm still having fun. I guess I'd like to be known as the guy that's still playing!

We play down at Crossroads in Asbury and McCann's in Belmar or BB King's in the city. I get up there and I still feel relevant. The minute that I thought I was becoming a lounge act. The minute it's like what am I doing here, I can't do this anymore. I mean, I've come close. You have to know where it is and temper it. You have to feel it and that's what makes you feel alive.

6 Billy Chinnock

> I sometimes feel less than politically correct to give the real history because my role in that early little part of Asbury, at times, has been quite overlooked.
>
> --BILLY CHINNOCK

Billy Chinnock, one of the Jersey Shore's premier songwriters, shown outside the Stone Pony. Photo © Debra L. Rothenberg/rothenbergphoto.com

B illy Chinnock just might be the forgotten hero of Jersey Shore rock and roll. Long before the E Street Band was ever formed guys like Vini "Mad Dog" Lopez, Garry Tallent, David Sancious and Danny Federici all played in bands with Chinnock. In many ways, the history of Jersey Shore music is incomplete without taking a closer look at Chinnock and his contributions to the scene.

A talented guitarist and songwriter, Chinnock was never quite able to shake the comparisons to Bruce Springsteen. He left the Jersey Shore and moved up to Maine where he was discovered by John Hammond Sr., the man who also discovered Bob Dylan and Bruce Springsteen. He released several critically acclaimed records but never achieved the success or recognition he probably deserved.

In recent years, Chinnock has spent much of his time with his company the Artist Group which produces everything from original scores for film and television to album projects and sound design on CD-ROM. He won an Emmy Award in 1987 for Musical Direction and Composition and was nominated the following year as well. He has also become a director and cinematographer for independent films.

Chinnock still performs once in a while and has been in the studio recording a new record due out in 2003. Speaking in a phone interview from his studio, Billy talked about his career from the Jersey Shore to Maine and everything in-between.

What do you remember about your early days at the Jersey Shore?
I was born in Newark and then my family and I moved to Milburn. We also had a little house in Avon-By-The-Sea on First Avenue. We formed our first little bands in the early 60s. By the end of the decade, I was living all over the Shore in places like Shark River Hills and I was caught up in the scene. The bands basically went Night Riders, Story Tellers into the Downtown Tangiers Band and then Glory Road.

I'd say probably the first record deal was in 1968 on KamaSutra Records. It was the Storytellers with a song called, "Cry With Me." That band's lineup included Danny Federici, Chippy Gallagher, Jimmy English, Bill Wolf and myself. Chippy Gallagher was later replaced by Vini Lopez. This was one of the predecessors to the Downtown Tangiers Band.

The Downtown Tangiers Band originally had a guy named Wendell John, eventually Wendell left and Garry (Tallent) came into the band. So that was Vini, Danny, Garry and myself. We played the great big Hullabaloo place in Asbury, the boardwalk and all of the little clubs. Wherever there was to play at the Shore, any place you could play, we were there.

The Asbury Hullabaloo was a huge room. It was just an amazing time. We were popular enough that we had a little van, a truck or whatever, and we were just playing continually with all original songs that I wrote. We also used to play the Hullabaloo Club up in Middletown.

Back in that time we weren't really as fixated on a deal as we were in playing live. We were really young and there were so many places to play in New Jersey and New York that I think we weren't totally focused on getting a record deal at that point. Although, Tangiers actually did cut an album for Koppelman-Rubin that was never released. It has a lot of those songs on it. I don't know where the tapes ever went, but I think Vini, Danny, Garry and I were on it.

Asbury Park was probably like an early Liverpool. It was a great environment, a great place for rock and roll. It just nurtured it and people absolutely loved it, enabling us all to grow as artists. If anything, I think that the shame or the disservice in the matter was somehow in the explosion that followed. When Bruce really came into his own, a lot of very valid artists got kind of washed in the backwash. Making albums and stuff for a long time, it was impossible to escape somehow being lumped into that kind of melee of the other artists in Asbury syndrome.

Two people that I think may have been sort of overlooked in Jersey Shore history are you and Steven Van Zandt.
I would probably say that too because Steve worked for a long time with some of the early bands like the Jaywalkers. Absolutely, Steve and myself. I would say that's a really good call.

I think at times, it's been very politically incorrect to kind of put my role with the band members and a roof in a real family tree there. People kind of raise their eyebrows, you know. It's like the environment surrounding Elvis, nobody really looked at the environment and the real players. The guys that were formidable back then. I mean, every member of the E Street Band except for Steve Van Zandt and Clarence, who I used to go hear at the Orchid Lounge - everybody that eventually migrated to that band, in the early days, had worked with me for a long period of time.

I lived at the Shore until around the time of the riots, but after that, I moved to New York for a while. We had been playing since we were little kids. I think that it was a little bit of a volatile relationship at times with Vini, but, you know, he's a drummer. And when I decided to move to New York, for the first time the band didn't have that guy in the center. Especially in that little circle of Danny and Vini and all of us. And then they advertised and they found Bruce, which was a blessing for them.

I sometimes feel less than politically correct to give the real history because my role in that early little part of Asbury Park has been quite overlooked. In the real reality of it... I mean, as God has things in life; in that very early period of time, it just seems like all of the boys were kind of in my band for three or four years. And when I finally left the area or kind of pulled out of the scene at 19, prior to the introduction to Bruce, all those boys played with me for years. Then when I left the Jersey Shore, Danny called me and said, 'Hey, we got a new guitar player his name is Bruce.'

But I went to New York and made a change and from there moved up to Maine. Just for a change of life, a cool place to live. It was kind of the Back to the Earth movement back then.

Did you used to play or hang out at the Upstage Club?
Umm, I helped paint the Upstage. I was one of the original guys who helped paint the walls. I think it was Day-Glo blue. It was Day-Glo whatever. It was really an incredible time and I was there for the whole duration, beginning to end, I know it all.

I remember big Bobby Williams playing the drums and David Sancious playing flute or guitar or keyboard. I remember the whole gang there, Johnny Lyon, everybody. I would just say that at the Upstage you didn't make any money. You made fifteen dollars a night and you played from 9 p.m. until 6 a.m.

What was it like going from Avon to Asbury Park back then?
It was kind of a treacherous walk because it was almost like the end of the fifties into the sixties. It was the era of James Dean so you had all these kind of greaser gangs and stuff that would hang out in Belmar. Sometimes while walking on the boardwalk you'd get chased. I remember one night I was walking back with Chippy Gallagher and we had a car following us up the boardwalk. People were running out and chasing us. We barely got home in time.

Which of your early bands did you think might go to another level?
I thought that either the Storytellers or the Downtown Tangiers Band might. Actually in 1991-1992 Garry Tallent, Danny Federici, myself and this drummer named Roger Cox, we actually did a reunion of the Downtown Tangiers Band and recorded three or four tracks in West Virginia. I don't know how hard we shopped it, but we couldn't get a deal. They were pretty cool songs. We were right on the same chord, it was like we were never apart. They're my friends till forever.

When you were in Glory Road with David Sancious, did you get the feeling that he was going to kind of go off to a different area of music later on?

I thought so with David. I mean, I thought that David was never purely a rock and roll, R&B guy. I always felt that we were not necessarily holding him back but perhaps not giving him as much freedom as he needed. David was a free spirit. It just seemed like he had his own journey. Not as a side man, not as an ensemble player in a band, but his own journey, which he did when he left and formed Tone.

You were "discovered" by John Hammond, Sr., what was that like?

It was fabulous, he's brilliant! He kind of oversaw things, and managed me a bit when I was very young. John couldn't get me signed to Columbia but when I did my first little cheapie album on Paramount it was John Hammond who did the liner notes.

You released your first two albums while living in Maine. Your third album, *Badlands* had interesting timing. It came out around the same time as Springsteen's *Darkness On The Edge Of Town*, which was originally going to be called Badlands as well.

Well again, it was one of those things. We recorded the album in Boston. My band was based out of New England at this point. We really weren't aware of what Southside or Bruce was doing at the time. We were kind of in our own space. We weren't like active peers living in Asbury Park watching Bruce and the band. So anything that happened was purely by coincidence. I didn't have any previous knowledge that Bruce had an album he was thinking about naming *Badlands*, which he named *Darkness on the Edge of Town*.

Bruce used to play cards at my house in Shark River Hills, but for some reason the relationship grew more distant. I had no idea what he was doing and he had no idea what I was doing. We just released an album called *Badlands* and he had a song called "Badlands." He changed his title once he became aware that we had an album out on our little local North Country record called *Badlands* - printing all of 3,000 copies.

Do you think that coincidence hurt your career at all?

That's a really good question. I only think it hurt my career because no writer, no musicologist, no journalist had the interest or foresight, at that particular point in time, to explore my career. To see if I was just this "Johnny Come Lately" who arrived completely after the scene or actually was one of the -

Founders?

Founders... That's a good word. One of the founders of it from the very beginning. And I think that if someone had actually done that they might have given the records a little bit more consideration. I always felt that if people really listened... we had a black sax player. I refused to fire him because there was Clarence in Bruce's band. I refused to do it! The record labels wanted me to, but I refused to not keep him in the band because someone would say E Street Band.

The music was so different. I've always thought my stuff came more from my roots. It came from that Newark, New Jersey R&B, bluesy Eric Clapton thing, and hopefully with good lyrics. Growing up in North Jersey about an hour north of the Shore, I used to listen to WNJR radio at night. I was around ten years old and it was the R&B station back then. You'd hear all the great R&B hits, blues hour and all that kind of stuff. That's how I got turned on to a lot of the bands like the early Paul Butterfield Blues Band and I got the fever. My father got me a guitar and as I started playing guitar I started working on writing songs. I always had the ability to do that. That was always my thing. I could always write songs.

I've always appreciated people like Don Henley and good writing. But I always thought that Bruce came much more from Dylan and Phil Spector and that real straight down the pike kind of Americana. That's "Born to Run" - great song, epic rock and roll. "Glory Days" - his stuff is really infectious, but if you listen to *Out On The Borderline*, my album in 1996, it's a very different place. The *Newark Star Ledger* did a nice story one time and they compared it more to Clapton. They said it was American in more that plan. That to me is always where it's been. It's just more R&B, just a little bit more R&B and its been darker.

Bruce has always known me. We've known each other since we were kids because I used to go hear him with the bands or he'd come up and hear me with the band. And I've always had nothing but just a whole lot of respect for him. He's always been incredibly talented.

Did the Jersey Shore comparisons really hurt your career?

I would say if it did anything they really kind of hurt my feelings at times because it made it hard to be heard. And, as an artist that's releasing albums and seeing good reviews here and there and getting FM airplay but not having big hits - it's like we were very successful and very lucky because of it. We had tour buses and houses and kept our families supported. Yet at some point in time you want a break and get that momentum going where you can bring your message a little bit larger. And that's really the deal.

I think that *Dime Store Heroes*, my goodness, I mean we used Sanborn. Will Lee, the guy that played in Average White Band. We used such an eclectic New York band on that beyond my own folks. Songs like "Streets of Paradise" I mean, they're just so un-Jerseyish. And yet, I don't think it got the attention that it should have.

What do you think was your best album?
That's a good question. I think *Out On The Borderline* probably was.

You've seen a lot of great local bands play around here. Was there anyone that stood out as someone that was going to make it?
I thought Bon Jovi was going to make it. He was my opening act and he did. He opened for me at Red Bank and at the Fastlane. Jon triumphed above it because he was so very different too. He was a true - I'm not going to say a glam rocker - but he was very different than what the rest of everybody from that kind of rooted R&B Jersey rock. You know what I'm saying? A very different place.

What have you been doing recently?
We came back from the Atlantic record deal in 1991, did an album for Atlantic with a group called Billy and the Suns. I did that album, which they really didn't promote and then I opened up this little multimedia company doing films and high-end websites, besides doing music. It's kind of eclectic stuff. And in 1991-1992, I did a stint with some members of the Doobie Brothers and did this reunion band with Garry and Danny. We didn't really make any money doing any of those things and by 1995 the Artist Group was just kind of booming, so I've been doing that. We released the album *Out on the Borderline*, did a duet with Roberta Flack on the theme to "Guiding Light." I've been producing films, documentaries and all kinds of stuff. Got some momentum going...

And you won an Emmy for the theme to "Guiding Light."
It really felt great. I mean, any time you're recognized for good work it really feels great.

Tell me about the movie, *Forgotten Maine*.
That was the first feature I did. I shot it, directed it and actually did the music score for it too. Even though it takes place in Maine, it's kind of a look at the changing face of America through the eyes of all these families and this kind of social network between the general store and the people who go there, the fishermen and farmers.

It reminds me a bit of a tone poem or a montage of images and stories. It shows you a part of America that we are trading away and devaluing, and it's going away for other things. I just think that we need to realize that perhaps we don't want to put a Wal-Mart in every town or perhaps we want to make sure that the little vendors like Mom's Pizza Shop or Joey's Haircutters - we want to make sure that some of that remains because that stuff has more value than we realize even on a commercial level.

Looking back how do you view your career?

I feel as if... if anything at all in my life looking back at my career, I've made some good records and I've made some bad records. There's no question about it. I've done some good work and I'm proud of some things. But I just think that perhaps it would have been nice if my role in it was in proper perspective.

I'm a huge Springsteen fan and I'm thrilled for the boys and the guys and I've been thrilled for everyone since I was 18. I'm thrilled for Bon Jovi. I'm thrilled for all of them because I know how much that the arts takes from you to be able to do good work. But I just think that the artist and the people that are part of that momentum or time, they all lend a certain amount of energy to it and I think at times that perhaps my work was discounted only because no one knew my proper history. I think if they knew that every band member played with me before joining with Bruce they probably would have listened a little more. Not being sour grapes, but if they think I came along seven years later, I mean, that's a very different perspective.

7 Steel Mill & Mercy Flight

It was like the sky was going crazy. I mean, the clouds were just mystical. It was the damnedest night. I'll never forget it as long as I live.

--DAVID HAZLETT
MERCY FLIGHT

Steel Mill shown in an early concert promotional poster.

Thing here was a time when Bruce Springsteen really knew how to rock. I mean really rock. Picture the best guitar licks from the *Darkness On The Edge Of Town* record and then multiply them by ten. That will give you a little bit of the hard hitting sound of Steel Mill, one of the legendary bands of the Jersey Shore.

Legions of Springsteen fans have since heard this material from scratchy bootleg recordings that fail to do the band justice. Their sound was intense from the powerful drum beats of Vini Lopez to the scorching guitars of Springsteen and heavy bass lines of Steven Van Zandt and the soothing, almost mystical organ of Danny Federici. The music was meant to be heard live where it takes on a life of its own. Like great jazz, Steel Mill sets had an often improvisational nature to its music. It was bluesy, hard rocking and it would go on seemingly forever lost in a myriad of jams that neither you nor the band ever wanted to see end. Solos flowed like the wind, vocals mourned with true heartache and the lyrics were always unforgettable. It was with this band that Springsteen really began focusing on writing his own songs. And he would prove to be a prolific songwriter even back then as every Steel Mill show featured new material.

The idea for Steel Mill came about after Bruce Springsteen discovered the Upstage. He originally formed the band Child with Vini Lopez, Vinnie Roslin and Danny Federici. They changed their name to Steel Mill after learning about another band called Child. Later, Vinnie Roslin was replaced by Steve Van Zandt and the band's lineup was set.

Steel Mill may have felt a friendly rivalry by the music of Godzilla, another local Jersey Shore band. While Springsteen was living in his manager's surfboard factory, Godzilla used to play the Pandemonium just down the street. According to John Mulrenan, a guitarist with Godzilla, they were one of the first really heavy bands in the area. "I think we were a precursor to heavy metal because that's what we were pretty much," said Mulrenan. "When we first started playing there our first set was at 9 o'clock and there was nobody there so we said let's just jam for an hour and get our chops together. It was like free-form, no key, no time just an open jam for 40 minutes and the funny thing was that more people would come for the open jam than for anything else. It was packed!

"So, Bruce used to come down with Southside Johnny and Steve Van Zandt after they got done rehearsing. They would come and sit in the back room and check us out, which used to make us nervous. We'd be whispering, 'What the hell are they saying about us?' I think maybe it was the first time they saw a band just jamming and not playing songs or covers."

Jamming at the Upstage provided Springsteen with the experience of performing in a spontaneous environment. Steel Mill took that experience and structured it a bit to form a sound that could take a rock song further than it had gone before and the crowds loved it. Every show became an event. Fans poured in to see the band in action. They routinely had several thousand fans at their shows - an unheard of feat for an unsigned band. In 1970, they went to San Francisco where they played a bunch of shows at the Matrix and were invited by Bill Graham to record at the Fillmore Record Studio. Graham liked the band enough to offer them a contract but Tinker, the band's manager, turned him down.

Steel Mill returned to the East Coast and continued as they had left off. They played up and down the Jersey Shore but those who really followed them knew that their fanbase spread out much farther than the borders of the Garden State. They had a second home in Virginia. In fact, Richmond, Virginia became one of Steel Mill's favorite places to play. Fans there loved the band every bit as much as those along the Shore. Part of the success had to do with a popular band from Richmond called Mercy Flight who would open for Steel Mill at nearly every performance.

"I think we complemented each other," said Tom Yolton of Mercy Flight. "It was a good combination. We might have been a little bit lighter in our sound than Springsteen. They had a heavy sound. We became friends, everybody liked each other. We were all in the same boat together, Springsteen wasn't famous at that point. He was really good, but he wasn't famous.

"We were all sort of comrades in the same predicament," continued Yolton. "We were trying to play music and do something with it and after we did a couple shows together I think it just became that it's not a complete Steel Mill concert unless Mercy Flight's with them. They'd go, 'What? Mercy Flight's not playing with them. What's wrong with that?'"

The two bands got along so well that Tinker invited Mercy Flight up to the Jersey Shore for a few gigs. They were shown around the local hot spots like the Upstage Club and opened for Steel Mill at a huge show at Monmouth College. They even played a high school prom where Steel Mill actually opened for Mercy Flight! And when Steel Mill needed someone to fill in on drums they turned to David Hazlett, Mercy Flight's drummer, who helped them out on several shows.

One of the most famous shows involving both bands took place in Richmond and was known as the 7th Marshall Street Parking Deck Show. Mercy Flight's manager was able to rent the space which might have been the biggest place to play in the area. It was the 7th floor, the top floor of a parking deck. Many of those in attendance that night remember it well.

"I swear to you if you could imagine a night that was just a magic night that would be it," remembers David Hazlett. "You're on top of the parking deck, you've got all of your friends and basically everybody that you've ever known through playing music up there.

"The sky was just wild," said Hazlett. "I mean, it was black clouds that were like - you know how at night when you look at the sky and it's like the clouds are moving real fast across? That's kind of the way it was. Everybody was just up there partying, having a great night, and the sky from the top of that parking deck was furious. I remember we played and then Brucie came on with that "Hail, hail resurrection" and "Sweet Melinda", songs like that. It was just like the sky was going crazy. I mean, the clouds were just mystical. It was the damnedest night. I'll never forget it as long as I live."

Yolton adds, "It was probably the biggest thing in Richmond that summer. It came off completely peaceful. It was like a mini-Woodstock. People were peaceful. People were friendly. I remember they had signs that they had put on the edge of the parking lot deck on the top floor that said, 'please, don't jump.'"

The crowds and the sky made for an unforgettable night. "Oh man," said Hazlett. "I don't mean agitated, but I mean that with the sky doing what it was doing and being on top of the parking deck and just the whole aura of the night - it was an anticipated night. The crowd was really into it. From the very beginning, even before the bands started, the crowd was wound up wide open. It was great."

After the show Springsteen asked Robbin Thompson, Mercy Flight's lead singer, if he wanted to join Steel Mill. Thompson would stay on as lead singer until the band called it quits and Springsteen headed in a different direction musically. Bruce would create bands like Dr. Zoom and the Sonic Boom and the Bruce Springsteen Band while forming the blueprint for the E Street Band. Mercy Flight added a pair of singers and continued on for a few years. Robbin Thompson returned to the band for its final round of shows and then launched a successful solo career.

Mercy Flight saw Springsteen at the time he was truly emerging as an artist. I was able to reach three of the original members of Mercy Flight for interviews which provide a look at a part of the Steel Mill history that is usually overlooked.

A Look at Mercy Flight

I think we complemented each other. It was a good combination. We might have been a little bit lighter in our sound than Springsteen. They had a heavy sound.

--TOM YOLTON
MERCY FLIGHT

Photograph of Mercy Flight taken at the legendary 7th Marshall Street Parking Deck Show. From left to right: Tom Cool Yolton, Robbin Thompson, Art Stacy, Jimmy Van Kueren, Dave Hazlett. Photo courtesy of Tom Yolton.

Tom "Cool" Yolton

former lead guitarist for
Mercy Flight

When did Mercy Flight actually get together?
We were all going to VCU (Virginia Commonwealth University). I had just
come down for my freshman year in the fall of 1969 and passed the word
around that I was a guitar player looking for a band. Somebody passed
the word to Robbin. I think, Robbin and the other guys had sort of
gotten the band a little organized. I came home one afternoon and there
was a note on my dorm-room door that said to call Robbin. He said they
had this band and they were looking for a guitar player. They were called
Mercy Flight. Robbin had been in a band in Florida, which was called
Mercy Flight and we all liked the name, so that's what we went with.

How long had you played before your first show with Steel Mill?
Not very long... If I remember correctly, we were a fairly new band. There
was this place in Richmond called the Free University. This was a
building down near the campus. It was the Vietnam War era and this was
sort of an university that would admit people so that they could get
student deferments from the draft. People that couldn't necessarily
qualify for regular colleges, they would join the Free University. Upstairs
was a concert hall. It was a college hang out place. We played a
couple jobs up there by ourselves and we did pretty good.

There happened to be an opening for this band coming in from New
Jersey and somehow or another they asked us if we wanted to open up
for them. We did and that's how we kind of hooked up. I think they had
played earlier that summer in Richmond at Monroe Park. They had done
something in Richmond. So this might have been their second time back.

Mercy Flight was a popular band, what were the crowds really like?
They were enthusiastic. Well, I still play music and I think music isn't as
important to them today. Back then, I think it was important to people and
it really showed when you went to these concerts. They were very
enthusiastic and a little more attentive back then.

It was pure rock and roll concerts is what it was, early rock and roll. It was just after Woodstock had happened. I remember Woodstock was in '69 and I went to VCU in the fall of '69. Woodstock had generated this thing about musical concerts of being peaceful happening events. So, when we did our concerts with Steel Mill, it was like little mini-Woodstock feelings going on in the audience. If that makes any sense.

We did a couple of shows in Monroe Park, which was the park by the VCU campus, and we did some outside concerts with them. When we did concerts with Steel Mill, it was usually in more of a concert setting. Mercy Flight did some clubs too. Of course, you're not going to get 2500 people in a club, but you would get a good packed house. We always packed the house, whether it was 200 or 300 people.

It was a pretty neat time, a pretty magical time when I think back. Of course, when we were there during it we never thought it was. We all thought that it was neat because we got to perform with Steel Mill and they always had great shows and were exciting. But when I think back on it I wish I had savored it more. You know what I mean?

You may not have savored it then, but you did you save all of the posters from the shows. Why did you do that?
Well, I saved them because they were Mercy Flight posters and I was in the band, and those concerts were pretty neat. I had been saving other posters of rock bands and concerts from Richmond, Virginia from that era. They aren't all Steel Mill posters, but they're neat posters artistically because the guys down there printing those posters were artists and they had neat artwork. If nothing else, they were neat artwork.

So, I was keeping them for the artwork value of them and because I was in Mercy Flight and those were Mercy Flight concerts that we did with Steel Mill. It was only later on that I realized I had done something right. One day, probably about three or four years ago, I came across one of these coffee table books, a real nice coffee table book on Springsteen. I was flipping through it and, in the back, they had pictures of posters of his concerts. One of the posters was one that I had and I thought I might have something here.

It's kind of strange that Springsteen really doesn't like talking about the Steel Mill days when so many people on the East Coast remember those shows so well.
Yeah, it's nice to know that. It was just that he was so much better than everyone else back then. He was just so much better. He came along and everybody just went, "Woh, wait a minute. Who's this guy?"

We had a song that me and Robbin wrote called "Train Ride" which was Mercy Flight's big song. When Robbin went on with Steel Mill for his time there, he took the song with him. There's a bootleg out where Steel Mill has a version of it that's nothing like the version by Mercy Flight. The words are about the only thing that's the same. But, I can always say that Bruce Springsteen actually covered one of my songs.

Do you remember anything about the time Tinker asked you guys to come up north and play?
Yeah, we did some jobs up there in New Jersey with them. Once, we did a high school senior prom out on the Jersey Shore in some hotel showroom. Steel Mill played first and we played second. Don't ask me how they happened!

We played Monmouth College one spring. That was a great concert. There must have been 3,000 people in that room. That was a magical night. We were like kids. You're a 20-year-old kid going up to New Jersey to play rock and roll with the big popular New Jersey band. It was exciting. We got to see the surfboard factory, where Springsteen lived on the floor in the office. We hung out there. We went up there once to do the Nothing Festival, which ended up not even taking place, but we spent the weekend there and hung around with everybody so it still was fun. The festival was just an excuse to get the bands together and have a festival to make some money.

We went to the Upstage, or Tom Potter's Coffeehouse. What was cool about that place was that they had built-in amplifiers on the stage. All you had to do was just plug into the floor and the amplifiers were already there, they were like part of the stage in the wall behind you. We jammed there a little bit. I remember one day Springsteen got up and jammed on something that I had never heard him play before. He had a conga player and somebody else was up there with him and they just blew the place apart. I'd never even heard the song he had played before and I had been listening to him for the last nine months or so. He wrote stuff every day, I guess.

Did the guys from Steel Mill ever talk to you about their trip to California when they were in the studio?
Let's see... I remember them talking about that when they got back. The part that sticks out the most to me was that we found out that Bruce actually drove. We drove the truck because, at that point, he didn't drive. So we were like, "Oh wow, Bruce drove the truck man! That's great!" That was like the big deal.

I remember them saying they had played the Fillmore East. I don't remember them saying much about not signing a contract. I think they said that they had done some recording out there. It sounded like it had been a successful trip, but they didn't come back with a recording contract or anything.

What do you remember about the show that has become something of a legend: the 7th Marshall Street Parking Garage Show?
I think that was the only time they ever did that. I guess the idea was to find the biggest place we could play. Our manager, Russ Clemm was quite a hustler and I think this was his baby. Somehow or another, he convinced them to do this and got the venue rented. Springsteen and Steel Mill were the biggest thing in Richmond at the time and this was on the 7th floor of a parking deck, the top floor. It held a whole bunch of people up there, a couple thousand people probably. They paid for the renting of the parking lot deck, advertised the show, got it all together and it was probably the biggest thing in Richmond that summer.

What was it like when Robbin told you that he was leaving to join Steel Mill?
It was pretty depressing. And, to this day, I would sure like to figure out who it was that instigated that whole idea. Did Robbin go to Bruce and say, "Hey, Bruce, let me join your band" or did Bruce go to Robbin? To this day, I really don't know what took place. It was a mystery... it was really an awkward time. The guys in Mercy Flight and a lot of the people in Richmond that were Mercy Flight fans didn't understand that either.

We picked up another singer after that. Unfortunately, we never did any more Steel Mill concerts after Robbin left the group. But we had done enough Steel Mill concerts to where we were very popular and well known, so when we played places we were still pulling in crowds and doing quite well. We were a high energy jumping around rock and roll band, just a fast-paced boogie, rock and roll band, and we were doing mostly all original songs. We were still playing some of the same songs. Me and Robbin were the main songwriters for Mercy Flight. We would get together in his apartment and come up with the basic core of the songs we played. So, we did those songs which was pretty cool for those times to be playing original stuff.

At the end there, we were sort of were hitting all of Virginia. The band even had two singers at one point in time and we were playing a lot of concerts at colleges in places like Charlottesville and Washington & Lee. We played several concerts at VPI (Virginia Tech) in Blacksburg.

I went to school for two years and then we moved what was left of the band up to Frederick, Maryland. We sort of resurrected Mercy Flight for a while and added two saxophone players. We had some gigs down in Washington, DC and then David Hazlett got married and had a baby, and it sort of slowly fizzled out.

There's a song on one of Springsteen's early albums with a line in there that goes: "the band was playing, the singer was singing something about going home." I like to think that he's referring to us in that line because we had a song called "I'm Going Home."

I kept close track of what Springsteen was doing. I heard he had gone up to New York and done the audition at Columbia Records and had some success. I remember, I went and saw him in Washington, DC with some friends of mine around the late part of 1973 at this little club called the Child Herald, one of the better places to play in Washington. They were there and they had the place packed. I remember that during the break we went upstairs to the dressing rooms and sat around and talked for a while. I asked Bruce, "Man, how did you do it?"

Did Mercy Flight ever pursue a recording deal?
Well, we tried to but we didn't stay together long enough. Once Robbin kind of bailed out we were like left holding the bag because here we had worked all these songs up with the lead singer and then the lead singer had left. We were kind of pissed off about it.

We did finally get back together again after Mercy Flight had decided to can the whole thing. We had gone through three singers since Robbin left the group, it was getting near the spring and a couple of the members were graduating from college at that point. One guy was gonna move back to Washington, another guy was gonna move up to Maryland. So we decided it didn't look like we're gonna be able to do this any longer, but we still had a couple of jobs left. We had fired the two guys who were our two singers and Robbin was back in Richmond, at that time, so we asked Robbin if he wanted to do these last couple of jobs that we had. And he did. So we did the last couple of jobs and they were fun.

I don't think very many people realize how much Bruce Springsteen was a part of both the Jersey Shore scene and Richmond back then.
Yeah, and you know I'll be damned if I can get anybody over here at my local paper to focus on me and my past on that. I've talked to the guy who's the music critic here in Lexington and that stuff just doesn't even mean a damn thing to him. Here I am in Lexington, Kentucky, I've had a great musical past and it's the best kept secret around.

David Hazlett

former drummer for
Steel Mill and Mercy Flight

How did you get involved with playing with Steel Mill?
Something happened with Vini, he got into a little bit of trouble down here in Richmond. So I went up to New Jersey to play some jobs with them while he was straightening some things out. It wasn't a real long time, I'd say maybe six months. We did a few shows, but there were a few weeks in between.

I stayed in the surfboard factory with Bruce. Everyone came over for practice and everything. Back then Danny and I were really close and I knew Garry Tallent's ex-wife here in Richmond so we knew each other a bit. Bruce and I would go to the beach during the day and hang out. Bruce and I were friends, we always had a laugh together. I kind of miss it, the guy's gotten so damn big that he's almost unapproachable.

We'd just kind of go to Upstage and play. It was pretty fun, but you have to realize that back then all the clubs were kind of the same. The Upstage, to me, was just a jam spot for a bunch of musicians to get together. But it was really a golden thing to do that Tom Potter did.

You were part of the legendary Clearwater Swim Club show. What do you remember about that show?
There was some sort of a curfew imposed on the audience there. I guess I should have known because there was a police or national guard bus parked across the road with lots of people in riot suits. I kept on thinking is this what this little town does for every job?

The band started playing and the people were dancing and screaming. I didn't give a damn about the cops, I was in that world where musicians go when everything is happening. Brucie was working the crowd just like he does so well. We played our set and everyone was going crazy. I was used to it from the times Mercy Flight and Steel Mill played together. It was just getting really good when it became time for the band to stop playing. The cops had started getting out of the bus about fifteen minutes earlier. The crowd was shouting, "Bruce! Bruce!"

There's no better compliment to an artist than to have the crowd loving you. So we got set to play a few more songs but the cops cut off the juice. Now Tinker was really good at getting things hooked things up and he was able to get the juice back on. As soon as we started playing again the cops moved in. They were trying to get on the stage from behind. All of a sudden the amps on the back of the stage fell over backwards. The amps almost fell on the cops. I don't know if the cops knocked them over or if we bumped into them but all hell broke loose. Danny and I kind of looked at each other and said, "Screw this!" The next thing I knew we were running off the stage and trying to load our equipment as fast as we could to get out of there.

What was it like after Robbin left Mercy Flight?
We hired another guy and he played for a little while. And then we found these two singers that were really awesome. Those are the ones that we took to Sigma Sound. They were really hot. They were singing hard and hit harmonies and everything.

You have to understand that Brucie is coming down here. Mercy Flight is the hot band to start with and we were practicing like hell. We were so tight it was just unbelievable. After all that we did, Bruce asked Robbin to go and he bagged on the band and went. And Bruce... I mean, back then, he wasn't where he is now or even close.

You've played with a lot of bands in your career, did Mercy Flight have a chance to make it?
That band should have been there. It's a damn shame that it didn't. We were doing the same thing that Bruce was doing, playing some clubs and promoting ourselves doing concerts. We had a real good following through Blacksburg and we were filling places up. We opened for a whole bunch of different bands. It was a great band.

Why do you think so many people remember all those Mercy Flight/Steel Mill shows?
I'll be honest with you. I think that the stuff Brucie was writing back then is the best he's ever written. Now, he's an excellent writer and he's been through many phases, but man when that guy first hit town and his hair was long (as all of our hair was long) and he was up there with that band going... I mean, it was just so hard hitting that it was unbelievable. You wouldn't have believed it, sitting there and watching it. It just blew people shit out of the water!

Robbin Thompson

former lead singer for
Steel Mill and Mercy Flight

You're originally from Virginia, correct?
Well, sort of. I came to Virginia from Florida and grew up in Melbourne. I was born right outside of Boston, Massachusetts but I moved when I was seven. I had attended college in Florida and I came up here to go to college at Virginia Commonwealth (VCU) in 1969. Actually, I came direct from Woodstock.

Did you start the band, Mercy Flight?
Yeah, actually the name was a shortened version of a band I had in Florida called Transcontinental Mercy Flight. And I just shortened the name and started a band up here.

What do you remember of that band?
Well, it seemed like we played a year or so and kind of became the band of choice or kind of the alternative rock band of that age. And, in Richmond, when Bruce came down we were always the band paired with those guys.

What type of musical influences would you say the band had?
We were kind of like a CCR type of band. We did a few originals and then were a kind of CCR, James Gang kind of sounding band.

The originals, were these some of your first compositions?
Yeah, I guess... I did two 45s when I was in high school down in Florida with a band called the Tazmanians. And they've since become, in recent history, actually kind of garage band classics. I mean, they're on some CDs called *Florida Garage Bands of the 60s*. And, actually one of them, the first 45 we did, is worth a lot of money.

How crazy is that to have a collectors digging back into your past?
It's real crazy.

You were in high school then, right?
Yeah, I was 17. Someone gave me like a lot of money for one of them within the last year. That's when I kind of discovered that it was valuable.

Did Mercy Flight ever come up to New Jersey with Steel Mill before the Nothing Festival? Was that the first trip?
We did come up there. I know, Mercy Flight played a club with Steel Mill but I don't remember what the name of it was. I remember going up there. Tinker said, "Hey, why don't you come up and play a gig with us?" And we went up there and played. It was before the Nothing Festival. The Nothing Festival... I'm recalling something put together to bail somebody out of jail or something.
  It seemed like we played. Our drummer came up... well, maybe I'm getting some gigs confused, but was it at a pool? Actually our drummer from Mercy Flight came up and played with Steel Mill because Vini was in jail.

What do you remember about going to Asbury Park and those clubs? Did you go to the Upstage?
Oh yeah, I'd go up and sing at the Upstage. I did that several times as I remember it. I know we played the Sunshine In with Cactus and Black Sabbath or something like that. I remember those guys. It was Cactus and somebody. I remember those two bands got in a fight, a fist fight, over who was going to play last. And I remember playing Monmouth College. One of my first gigs up there as a member of Steel Mill was with NRBQ and Canteen I think.

Did you play an instrument in Mercy Flight?
I knew how to play guitar and that's what I do now I play acoustic guitar, but I was basically a singer up until kind of after all that subsided. Although I did play and write on a guitar, I just didn't play in the band. We had two guitar players in Mercy Flight. I might have played some rhythm guitar or something in Steel Mill, though I don't really remember doing that.

Do you remember the 7th Marshall Street Parking Deck Show?
Oh yeah, you kidding? I've got the tapes of everybody. Yeah, I remember it a lot. Mercy Flight played that gig and it was us and Steel Mill - actually there were three bands. I can't remember the other band. They were down here and kind of stayed with us whenever there were those kind of shows.

After that show Bruce said, "Hey, you know, we were thinking about adding another singer. What do you think?" And that's when I went up and hung with them for about a week and kind of practiced with the band. You know, it was one of those where they all went into one room and talked it over and came out and said, "Yeah, let's do it."

You had opened quite a lot of shows for them before that, right?
It probably seemed like much longer than it really was, but we had played free concerts at the park together. There was a place here called the Free U (Free University) that we played together several times. We even played a Hullabaloo Club here together. We did a bunch of stuff. It seemed like we did a whole lot of gigs, but it probably wasn't as many as I'm thinking it was. Yeah, we became friends. Bruce and I actually had a mutual girlfriend. That was kind of strange and a problem.

Was this when you were in Steel Mill or in Mercy Flight?
Yeah, well, it kind of hung over from both.

What do you remember about being the lead singer in Steel Mill?
I remember it was a good time and that we didn't play a lot, but when we played we did well. That I always had the feeling that something was gonna happen with the band, but I always had a feeling that it might not happen with me in it. I mean, because it was really Bruce's band and I was always the kid from Florida or from Virginia or however you thought about it. Everybody was kind of scratching their head going, "What's he doing in the band?" I kind of got that feeling a little bit.

The good part about it was that I was a surfer kid in Florida. I moved to Virginia where it was far away, 100 some miles from the beach. But when I moved to Asbury and live there, and Tinker made surfboards, I felt kind of in my environment. I was a really good surfer and so I could go to the beach and I could fit in with those guys and be just as good a surfer as anybody.

Is it true that you didn't think Tinker really wanted you in the band?
Yeah, I didn't think so. I mean, Tinker's a great guy. I just don't think he understood what Bruce wanted another guy singing in the band for. It wasn't like he was standoffish to me or anything.

I think Bruce wanted to play guitar more and just concentrate on that. And I think he was also thinking I could maybe play some bass or something, which I don't think ever really happened. I might have played bass on one song. It probably was a disaster.

Did you ever write any songs while in Steel Mill?

Yeah, there's actually a bootleg out called, *Return to Rock and Roll,* that someone gave me, and I'm singing lead on a lot of the stuff. I don't think they knew that when they put it out, but there was a song called "Train Ride" that was on it and I wrote that. There was another song on that which I wrote but I can't remember what it was.

What did you do after Steel Mill broke up?

I came back and finished up college. I had another band for a bit called Robbin and I recorded a 45 with that band. We did it in Philly at Sigma Sound. I think I recorded another 45 actually after that here in Richmond, Virginia.

Then I started playing guitar more and writing more. I worked, I was in school for advertising communications and ended up working at a recording studio writing jingles at a place called Alpha Audio here in Richmond. That kind of subsidized my existence and I was able to do some other things. Some things I was able to not have to have a band. But then I started recording because I worked in a studio, I could record the stuff I wrote.

So writing the jingles kind of paid for those first few albums? Sort of covered you as you were doing it?

Yeah, it kind of helped me record songs that I was writing. Actually, I did an album that was never released with a group that I had. Then I wrote a song called, "Boy From Boston" and entered it in the American Song Festival and won that. And then, I don't think it was because of that, but I got a record deal on an Atlantic subsidiary that had guys like Jan Hammer, Lenny White, Andy Pratt and Tommy Bolin.

When did you get your first record deal?

Basically, I got my first record deal in 1975. I still worked in the studio but I did get to go to record the album in Los Angeles and used a whole lot of neat people like Steve Cropper, Timothy Schmit, Waddy Wachtel and Melissa Manchester. They all kind of came through different connections of James Mason, my producer. And that's how the first album came together.

And now you're the Vice President and co-founder of In Your Ear Studios. What does your company do?

We write custom music for commercials and do some film work also. We're a pretty big studio.

How did it feel years later during the *One Step Up, Two Steps Back* recording of Guilty?

I recorded "Guilty" in 1985. I had seen Bruce somewhere, then he came in and sat in at a Bayou concert in DC, I think. We had been doing that song, just playing it live and it was going over great. It was a great, long song. And so we played it as the Robbin Thompson Band.

I got a hold of him at one point. I remember, he came up to me after some show and said, 'Man, I really liked that song Guilty.' And I wasn't sure if he knew or remembered that he wrote it. But, anyway, I said, 'Look man, can I record that?' and he said sure. So I recorded it and put it on an album called, *Better Late Than Never*. I think that was the name of the album. So it was already recorded.

But that was still 15 years later, had you been playing it throughout the years?

No, I mean we just one day I said let's do this song. Everyone in the band knew the song. Everybody in the band was around during those times. And so we worked it up and it just started going over great. It was just one of those songs we'd do for an encore or last song. It was a great crowd pleasing song that I got off playing and singing so we recorded it.

Then Cheryl Powelski, the person that put together the record, *One Step Up...Two Steps Back,* called. I mean, I was amazed that she even knew me or knew of that song but she was familiar with my recording of it and wanted it on that album.

That band's legacy is pretty strong. It seems like wherever you go on the East Coast you bump into people that remember Steel Mill.

Oh yeah, especially here in Virginia. I don't think that Steel Mill played that much outside of Richmond. They might have played a couple of different places other than here. And we were the band here. It was a major event whenever Mercy Flight and Steel Mill got together for free concerts at Monroe Park here or something. It's probably the reason they don't allow concerts there anymore.

And you also had a song you co-wrote, "Sweet Virginia Breeze," nominated for the state song of Virginia?

Yeah, you know, that song's still alive. It's been on a couple of my albums and it was written in the 70s. It wasn't something that I really wanted to enter. People have tried to make "Sweet Virginia Breeze" the state song for a long time. Several times, in fact.

It got to be where every other year they were trying to make it the state song. It was funny because I knew Virginia doesn't like change, from a political standpoint anyway. So, they retired the old song and they decided to have this contest. And I didn't enter it and a newspaper in Virginia finally contacted me and said, "You've got to enter this song because we're getting letters and emails that want to know why isn't this song in it? It's the one that should be the state song."

I reluctantly entered under pressure a little bit. The record sold several hundred thousand records and to a lot of people it is kind of the state song. But I don't think they'll ever change or vote anything else the state song. I think that it's one of those issues no one wants to head up in government.

People have tried making "Born to Run" the New Jersey state song. How ironic is it that your career still somewhat parallels Bruce's?
Yeah, it's interesting... Not on the same financial plane, I might add.

What would you say was the highlight of your career?
Umm... you know, the highlight of my career is putting this studio together from a musical sense. I mean, that this is a big facility and I'm kind of a working class singer-songwriter and, not that the stuff I write is working class, but I don't expect ever to get real famous doing this. I just enjoy doing it, when I have enough songs to do an album I put one out.

Being involved with Bruce definitely has to be up there in the top five great things that I was lucky enough to be involved with. It never seems to amaze me the people that remember that and just the legs that it has. It's not like I dwell on the fact that I was in Steel Mill or that it keeps hanging around. And it's not a bad thing either. I mean, I'm honored to have been a part of anything with Bruce Springsteen.

8 The Asbury Riots

People just didn't go there anymore. It was like, "I'm not going to Asbury." They were scared. Who wants to go somewhere where they're scared?

--DAVID MIERAS

I was born right around the time the riots were taking place. Racial trouble was boiling in towns all across New Jersey as well as the entire nation. Asbury Park just happened to be one of the towns hit the hardest. The Asbury I knew and grew up with was very different from the Asbury pre-riot. A lot of things have to happen for a town to die, but the riots certainly pushed Asbury towards that end.

Growing up along the Shore you aren't told much about the riots, even though they basically took place in your backyard. People don't like talking about it much. I guess it's a period of time we all wish we could forget. But it did happen and it did change the face of Asbury Park forever. Redevelopment may come and the town may be rebuilt someday, but I doubt it will ever erase the memory of the riots.

Music, along the Shore, was profoundly affected as well. Asbury Park was the center of the music scene. After the riots, few people were willing to return to the clubs. The scene, which was so vibrant, started to wane quickly. Important clubs like the Upstage were forced to close. House of Hits, a record store in the black section of town, which was where many musicians went to learn about the great blues artists, burned down. The days of "going to musical college," as Southside Johnny described it, were over. And musicians were forced to move on as well.

-- Gary Wien

D avid Mieras grew up in Ocean Grove, the town that borders Asbury Park. Ocean Grove was basically secluded from the rest of the world. It's a mile square town, bordered by lakes with just five entrances in and out of town. On Sundays, they used to put a chain across. "It's a really protected onclave," said Mieras. "It's kind of like a fort. And when the riots did happen that's how they treated it. The townsfolk, not just the cops, were on the corner manning their posts with shotguns and stuff."

In 1970, Mieras was 17 years old. He was hitchhiking his way out to California when he changed his mind in Omaha, Nebraska and decided to come home. "I put my thumb out and I got a ride from Omaha, Nebraska and got dropped off at the Casino in Asbury Park, I swear to God," recalls Mieras. "Now that's a hell of a drive. I got to drive a little. They had a muscle car that was really fast. I got dropped off at the Casino on a Sunday. I got out and started walking towards Ocean Grove and looked up at the sky and was like what the heck is that? All this smoke was coming up. Must be a big fire somewhere, I thought."

He stopped by his house, but nobody was home. His first thought was that everyone must be hanging out down at the beach, so he dropped off his stuff and headed down there. Sure enough, the beach was packed with people.

"What are you doing back?" someone asked David.

"Aw, you know, whatever," I said. "What's that over there?"

He said, "You don't know what's going on?"

"No."

"There's a riot going on over there."

"Riot?"

"Yeah, they're rioting in Asbury Park. Race riot."

"You're kidding me." I said, "Hey Skip, let's go over to Upstage and see what the hell's going on."

Skip McGarry was a close friend of David's from Ocean Grove. They often went to the Upstage together. The two went over to Upstage, went upstairs and someone told them that everybody was up on the roof. So they went on up. There they saw John Luraschi and his brother, Fast Eddie, Vini Lopez and some other people. From the roof of the Upstage, they could see the destruction taking place.

"Buildings... Whole blocks of buildings were burning," recounted Mieras. "It was ugly. It was really ugly. We were the youngest out of all of them guys. They were more concerned with whether somebody was gonna blow up Upstage or the town or what. I said, 'Skip, let's go to the railroad tracks and see what's happening.'"

So the two took off again and headed towards the railroad tracks. This was the area where the riot was really in full force at the time. They were next to the Orchid Lounge on Springwood Avenue and Memorial Drive when they realized they were smack in the middle of a war zone.

"Man, there was people running around throwing shit," continued Mieras. "It was crazy. Then, all of a sudden, in comes marching all these police. They've got these shields and there had to be like 40 or 50 of them all lined up and marching like they were in the army. They came right up from Main Street to Springwood Avenue and when all the people who were rioting saw them they all came up to Memorial Drive. So there was a big crowd over there and the police were like in a face off – like a stand off. And did we see some crazy stuff.

"It was absolutely terrible. We're standing there and the first thing that we really saw that was bad was one of the New Jersey Transit trains came along and, I guess they didn't know there was a riot. They didn't have to worry about anything, they were a big old train. The train came, and all these people rushed it and started throwing bottles and rocks through the windows. They were destroying the train. It was unbelievable! And that got the cops going. The cops started marching towards the people. All of a sudden, out of everywhere Molotov cocktails start coming down. Cops were on fire. It was right in front of our face and we're standing there. It's like watching a movie. It was incredible."

Then, what might have been the most frightening scene of the day, occurred right before them. They saw a car pull up to the street. A woman was in the car all by herself. Apparently, she didn't realize she was driving right in the middle of a riot. The car stopped at a red light. A bunch of guys grabbed this extremely large piece of wood and rammed it straight through her window. There was a loud smash as the glass was broken. Somehow, the woman was able to get out of there.

"Well, I don't know how she did it but she got out of there," said Mieras. "It was like one thing after another. All of a sudden all of these rocks and bricks and shit started raining down on us. Skip got hit with a gigantic thing in his arm. It was like a big brick. I thought it was gonna kill him. That's when I said let's get the hell out of here."

Mayor Joseph F. Mattice ordered a curfew throughout the town and a state of emergency was declared at 3 a.m. Reports from the first day told of injuries to 6 policemen, 20 arrests made, damage to at least 75% of Springwood Avenue and considerable looting taking place.

The problems persisted and the next night saw another 8 buildings destroyed or seriously damaged in fires and the number of people arrested grew to over 100. The state police was called to provide help.

Police reported having human feces thrown at them, urine and hot water poured down upon them from upstairs windows and several police cars firebombed. Some people helped put out the fires while others hindered the efforts of firemen by bending their hoses.

Throughout the town graffiti spelled out messages like "fight for your rights." One said "pigs" and was painted by a pig's face. Boards covering a store on Springwood Avenue contained the messages "power to all black people" and "soul sister."

July 7th was the final day and by far the bloodiest. According to police records, the riot peaked at about 4:30 p.m. when hundreds of people were out of control in the area. The outbreak resulted in injuries to 56 people, including 32 who were treated for gunshot wounds. Police reported being shot at by snipers in the area. The devastation was unbelievable. From the railroad west to DeWitt Avenue (the heart of the business district) there was hardly a store window that was unbroken and the whole area looked like it had been torn apart from bomb bursts.

After three straight days of peace, the state police withdrew from Asbury Park. While the situation cooled there minor uprisings started in Red Bank and then Freehold. Bruce Springsteen described the tension of the time in the song "My Hometown."

News about the riots in Asbury Park could be found in the major newspapers of the day. Articles also appeared such publications as *Time Magazine*, *Newsweek* and even *TV Guide*, which wrote about television coverage of the race riots.

"There's no doubt in my mind," Mieras said. "After that happened people were just plain scared. They didn't want to go down there. A lot of people won't admit it that it was the downfall of Asbury Park, but there's no doubt in my mind. We were the ones that were down there, we knew what was going on, we knew what was happening. People just didn't go there anymore. It was like I'm not going to Asbury. They were scared. Who wants to go somewhere where they're scared?"

"I think that was definitely the beginning of the physical decline of Asbury Park," added Sancious. "Not just the club scene but the whole scene. Between that and the advent of shopping malls, it affected the whole downtown Asbury scene and boardwalk.

"Everything was difficult after the riots, anything to do with anything. It wasn't so much as the energy. I mean, things did cool out for a minute, but it wasn't like everybody sort of shut their doors and stayed inside. Some of the places were damaged in the riots, some buildings were burned or destroyed or partially destroyed, but it was more just the psychic energy of the times. Nobody got out of that unscathed, you know."

9 Dr. Zoom and the Sonic Boom

There were guys up there playing and they'd have the rug out and chairs and tables. People playing chess or checkers or Monopoly. It was some obscure shit going on. And it worked.

--TONY AMATO

SUNSHINE IN and GREAT BEAST present DR. ZOOM AND THE SONIC BOOM with BRUCE SPRINGSTEEN and SUNNY JIM SPECIAL ADDED GROUP CORNERSTONE * **ONE BIG SHOW** FRI. EVE. MAY 14, 8:30 PM admission 2.50

TICKETS AVAILABLE AT
UNSHINE IN BOX OFFICE

Tickets also available at
SOUND OF MUSIC
Monmouth Shopping Center, Eatontown - 542-4255
IGOR RECORDS

THRIFTY THREADS
100 Hwy 36, Keyport - 739-0258
Red Bank Mall, Red Bank - 842-8146
MEN'S ROOM

Dr. Zoom and the Sonic Boom played just three shows but each one was something special.

For a couple of months in 1971, Bruce Springsteen built a band unlike anything seen on the Jersey Shore before. The band was called Dr. Zoom and the Sonic Boom. Many people consider it to be a transitional band for Springsteen, who was moving away from the heavy metal sound of Steel Mill and towards the type of music the E Street Band would later play.

What made Dr. Zoom and the Sonic Boom so different was that the band was huge. At any given time there would be between 15-20 people on stage. The band's roster read off like a who's who of Asbury Park music. In addition to Springsteen, there was Steven Van Zandt on guitar, Vini Lopez and Bobby Williams on drums, David Sancious played keyboards, Danny Federici on organ, Southside Johnny played harmonica and a whole assortment of people were involved in the Zoom Choir. It didn't really matter if you played an instrument or not, there was a spot for you in Dr. Zoom and the Sonic Boom.

"It was a fun thing," recalled David Sancious. "I think that was a kind of maybe inspired by or had something to do with bands like Leon Russell and the Shelter People or Mad Dog and Englishmen. That whole Delany & Bonnie and Friends period. There was this whole group of large ensemble things with 12-15 people in the band - that energy, you know, I think that was his idea to put something together like that."

Bruce Springsteen has always been thought of as the ultimate professional. He's looked at as a very intense artist, someone that takes his music very seriously. But with Dr. Zoom, Bruce was able to just grab a guitar and have some fun. Band members showed up in costumes, members of the road crew sat at a table on the side of the stage and played Monopoly all night long and the crowd loved every minute of it.

David Sancious used to come to the shows dressed as a cab driver. "That was my thing, I'd show up with the work coveralls, some sneakers, and a cab driver's hat," recalled Sancious.

It was definitely a strange experience to say the least. Strange and rare because the band only played a handful of shows. They practiced far more than they ever played on stage. "We didn't have a huge catalogue of music," said Sancious.

"We played three farewell gigs that I remember," explained Southside Johnny. "That's with the whole contingent but Bruce at that time was trying to put together his big band with two horns too."

Officially, the band's three shows included one at the Sunshine In in Asbury Park, one at Newark State University in Union and one at Brookdale Community College in Lincroft.

John Mulrenan who played in Godzilla, a band that opened for Dr. Zoom at the Sunshine In, recalls seeing Springsteen with the Zoom Choir before the show. "There was this big dressing area in a corner of the club," said Mulrenan. "He's standing on a chair with all these guys and girls around him and he's teaching them real simple background harmony parts that they could all sing in unison. This is right before he's ready to go on. Then he goes on and he's got like 20 people on stage effectively singing these parts. And it was pretty good."

"Tinker (the band's manager) brought in the biggest PA I'd ever seen in my life up till that time," added Mulrenan. "These huge gigantic speaker enclosures, the biggest that anybody had ever seen. And these beautiful 400-watt Macintosh tube power amps which was the biggest power we'd ever seen."

"That was a silly goof," added Southside Johnny. "I mean, we had thirty people on stage, a Monopoly game, twirlers, a choir and I had fried chicken and a piece of furniture. It was fun. I think I sang one or two songs and played harp and stuff and I led the Zoom Choir.

"There were four musicians there that had an apartment on Suel Avenue. I had a little chair and a piece of my bedroom furniture that I brought and I put a bottle of champagne on one side and some fried chicken on the other. When I wasn't working I'd sit there and eat my fried chicken and drink champagne. It was all a spectacle. It was a very fun job."

Big Danny Gallagher believes the idea behind the band was to bring all of the friends from the Upstage on to one stage. "Bruce and the guys said, 'What do you say we get everybody we know together?'" he said. "There were guys at the door fixing a motorcycle, me and another guy playing Monopoly with a bottle of wine covered by a brown bag. We had twirlers and a fellow by the name of Bird (Kevin Conair) who's dead now, as the MC. He used to show up wearing a tuxedo and red Converses.

"We opened for the Allman Brothers for the first gig," continued Gallagher. "I remember Duane Allman was standing there and I had just come off of the stage because there was some serious music going on and you didn't need the Monopoly game. Duane Allman had been watching Bruce on stage, he looks up at me and goes, 'Who is that fuckin' guy?' I said, 'Man, he's the next guy!'"

Some of the songs were carried over from his Steel Mill days, some were covers and some were originals for Dr. Zoom and the Sonic Boom. As with Steel Mill, many of the songs clocked in at over seven minutes long. Although, the newer songs Springsteen wrote were much shorter.

"It was really good music, good-natured music, and it had this kind of zany energy," added Sancious. "It was just really light-hearted fun."

Tony Amato used to love seeing Dr. Zoom and the Sonic Boom. "I used to laugh at that band," said Amato. "There were guys up there playing and they'd have the rug out and chairs and tables. People playing chess or checkers or Monopoly. It was some obscure shit going on. And it worked."

With so many musicians it's a wonder if anybody ever got paid. Big Danny Gallagher believes that Bruce and Little Steven probably made a little back then. "They were the poor souls," said Gallagher. "They didn't have a steady day gig. Bruce's parents had moved to California and so he was out on his own. That's how we wound up living together. After Tom Potter left, he stayed in the apartment. One day the owner came and kicked him out. I was supposed to have my brother move in with me but he had just died. Bruce came up on his bike and said, 'Hey man, one time on the way back home from Richmond you said if there was anything you could do to help you would. Well, I need a place.' And so we lived together for about 9 months and then I worked for him for about a year."

"It was just a side thing," said Amato. "Back then, everybody was in fifteen bands. It was fun. It was just about playing. It wasn't about all this. No hype, no nothing. Yeah, the hype came and you're stuck with it. Then you've got to deal with people's jealousies because they want to be part of the scene. They were on the edge of it, but they weren't. You didn't have none of that back then. You're a musician, let's go play. End of story. Who gives a shit who's who? None of the musicians really screwed up anything for anybody. It was the media. This and that."

10 Bruce Springsteen

Everyone who saw him in the beginning agrees that he destined for stardom. The best guitarist who became the best songwriter, he always held the audience in the palm of his hands.

--BILLY SMITH
ASBURY PARK ROCK 'N ROLL MUSEUM

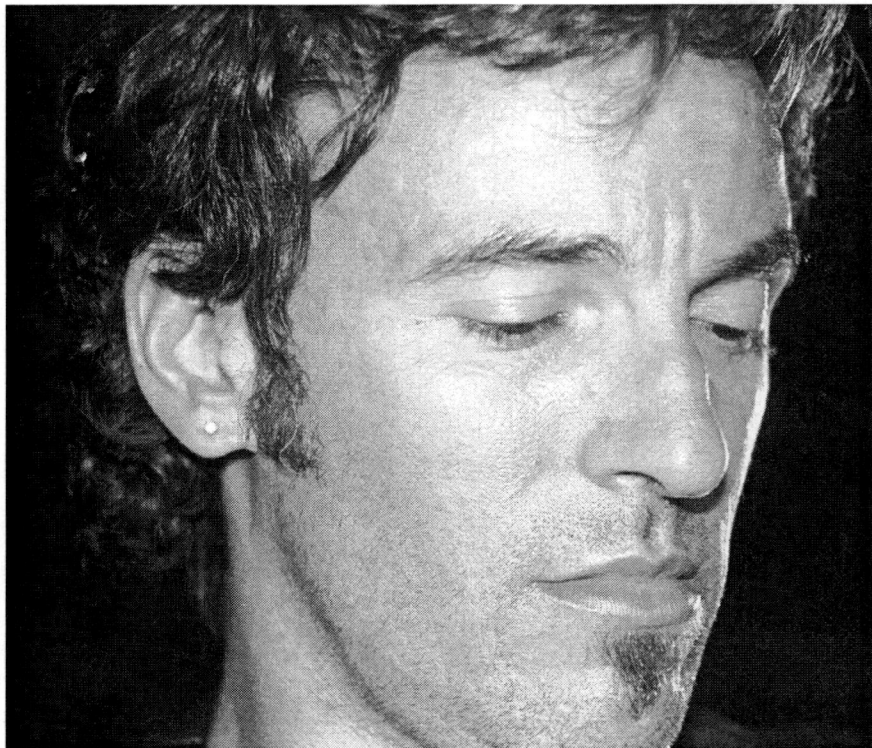

Bruce Springsteen, the man who put the Jersey Shore music scene on the map. Photo © Debra L. Rothenberg/rothenbergphoto.com

I t's safe to say that if Bruce Springsteen hadn't burst on to the national scene with *Born To Run* the history of rock music along the Jersey Shore might have been a rather short chapter or two. For years, New Jersey had not only lived in the shadow of New York City but record labels there couldn't care less about bands from the Shore. Even though Asbury Park is only an hour away from Manhattan, it was a world's away in their eyes. Until Bruce made it big, they wouldn't even bother come down to see what the area's biggest bands were all about.

The success of Springsteen changed everything. All of a sudden places like the Stone Pony were crawling with record executives hoping to find the next big thing. Not only that, but people growing up in the area were given hope that they could make it. After all, Bruce was a local boy.

One of the greatest things about Bruce Springsteen is that he never forgot where he came from. From making guest appearances at local clubs to performing benefits to support a myriad of causes, Bruce Springsteen has remained a major role in the area. And now that Asbury Park appears ready to fly again, Springsteen has stepped up his focus in the city. His performances at Convention Hall for the upcoming *Rising* tour brought the world's attention back to Asbury Park. It had been far too long since the city had been portrayed in a positive light.

There have been scores upon scores of books written about Bruce and his history. This book chooses to focus on the parts of his musical history that have somewhat faded away with time and with the rest of the Asbury Park music scene. Many of the artists in this book are friends of Bruce Springsteen's, and many have either been influenced by Bruce or feel as though their music is the direct opposite of Springsteen's, almost an anti-Bruce if you will. But one thing is for sure, the entire Asbury Park music scene really is focused around Bruce Springsteen. He's the reason many of the musicians live here, he's the reason many of the fans come to the shows and he's the reason Asbury Park is known as one of the greatest music scenes in the country.

One of the most important things that can be said about Bruce Springsteen is that he is still, above all else, an artist. *The Rising* was every bit as good of a record as he has ever put out. That an artist can create a work which defines a time period is impressive. That he continues to do so over a period of over thirty years is simply amazing.

It is my hope that people reading this book will take a look at and listen to all of the artists throughout these pages. Some clearly sound influenced by Springsteen and some do not, but all of them understand the role that Bruce has played in this area. There is no music history in Asbury Park without Bruce.

Bruce in Asbury Park

I think part of Bruce's genius is that he is able to portray places, people and situations through his music in a way that people can relate to no matter where they live.
--MAGGIE POWELL
MUSIC JOURNALIST

Bruce Springsteen and the E Street Band look out upon the crowd from Convention Hall. Photo © Debra L. Rothenberg/rothenbergphoto.com

I can still remember the night Dave and I were invited to the Asbury Rock 'N Roll Museum to hear an advance copy of Bruce Springsteen's *Tunnel of Love* CD. The guys from the museum, Billy Smith and Stephen Bumball, had managed to have a copy sent to them a month before it was scheduled to be released. They invited a bunch of their friends to a special listening party. There must have been at least thirty people cramped into a small room all anxious to hear which direction Bruce was going. Dave and I were the youngest in the crowd by far and we were kind of surprised to be invited. It was the first time I had ever been part of something like that and it would be a night I'd never forget.

When it was first released, *Tunnel of Love* didn't seem to register very high with Springsteen fans and I never understood why. Maybe it was because it was technically a solo record or maybe the legions of fans that joined up during the *Born In The USA* run expected something harder, more rock and roll. Whatever the reason, it received somewhat lukewarm reviews. But, for me, it was a great record from the very first note.

I remember hearing the unabashed honesty of "Ain't Got You" leading off the record. Here was Bruce, baring his soul in public in a way he rarely had ever done before, talking about personal problems and failures from the first person point of view. There was no need to hide under character names, no need to gloss over the production. It was bare bones honesty coming to you with nothing more than the sound of his guitar.

As I closed my eyes, I took it all in as if I was hearing him live in concert with a bunch of my friends. For true Springsteen fans, hearing his music with a bunch of people always sounded better. It was as if his songs needed to played in front of an audience. Bruce may have started out as a singer-songwriter but his live performances overshadowed that part of him. Ironically, even in a crowd of thousands, his songwriting always made it feel like he was singing just for you.

By the time the organ began playing in "Tougher Than The Rest," goosebumps were running up and down my arm. I could sense that this was definitely a new direction for Bruce and I was totally into it. As each song was introduced to me for the very first time, I knew that there was something special going on. The images of gypsies, amusement park rides and walks on the beach gave me the feeling that this was Bruce's return to writing about Jersey. Although the places weren't really mentioned by name, we knew where they were. Maybe this was his present to us, his long-time fans. Maybe it was his way of saying goodbye or writing a new chapter to his life. All I know is that it contained the last Springsteen songs to evoke such hometown memories until "My City of Ruins" was released.

The sparse production throughout the record seemed to make you focus on each and every lyric. Unlike *Nebraska*, the added arrangements made this a very accessible record even for those who weren't fans of folk music. It was sparse, but felt complete. By the time we had gone through the entire record, I felt I knew every song by heart. I can't remember, but I'm pretty sure that the crowd couldn't wait to hear it again and it was quickly started once more.

The Palace was always a wonderful place for me. As we called it a night and headed to our car, I remember staring at the tunnel of love sign along the building while the song replayed in my head. The neon lights were all lit up and shining, their reflection bounced over the lake. For one moment, it seemed like time had been turned back for Asbury Park. Nobody was thinking about the boardwalk being in bad shape or the graffiti stained walls. It was just a magical night. It's hard to believe that the Palace would be shut down the following year.

This was the second time that I had heard a new Springsteen record at the Palace. The first was for the live box set put out a few years earlier. The Palace had a general listening party and it attracted hundreds of people. It was the last time I ever saw the place packed. There were literally lines around the building to get in. They had the CD playing so loud you could hear it while you waited to get in. People had the same type of anticipation that they have before going to a Springsteen concert. My friends and I had been going to the Palace for years and never expected a crowd like this to show up. I finally had a glimpse of what Asbury was like during its glory days. Normally when we'd hang out at the Palace during the weekend there would only be a couple dozen people there. But this was like a Hollywood movie premiere party.

When *The Rising* was released, the official listening party was held at the Stone Pony. It was an exciting time as Bruce and the E Street Band would be playing live on the "Today Show" from Convention Hall in the morning. Once again, the boardwalk was visited by thousands of people. There were more people inside the bar that night than I had ever seen before in my life. It was right in the middle of one of New Jersey's worst heat waves in years. It must have been nearly 90 degrees at midnight when they started selling the record. All night long, the bar played selections from *The Rising* as sweaty fans took their turns answering trivia questions to win various prizes. The outdoor tent area provided little relief as that too was packed with fans. It was so hot that many people had to leave the club and return a few minutes later. Apparently, everyone knows that there's nothing in the world like hearing a new Springsteen record in Asbury Park.

It was very encouraging to see those types of crowds in Asbury Park again. Cars were parked all throughout the town leaving those just arriving to circle round and round trying to find a spot. There was definitely an energy in the air. Springsteen fans form a community. They love meeting other fans and telling stories about their favorite records and concerts they've seen. And there's no place better to do that than in Asbury Park.

The Rising contained lyrics every bit as personal as those found on *Tunnel of Love*. While he once sang from the perspective of a man struggling to deal with the problems of the adult world, the lyrics became that of a man struggling to deal with problems that he has no control over. Both records contain fear and love, hopes and dreams. But on *The Rising*, Bruce not only spoke from his own experience he spoke for everyone. He spoke for the people he saw on television. He spoke for the families he met after 9/11. And he spoke for all those who needed a voice, who needed to know that they weren't alone.

Nobody quite knew how artists would respond to the attack on America or who would have the courage to speak up or even what words could possibly heal the country. Somehow Bruce found the courage and he found the words. He delivered his best record in ages. And it couldn't have come at a better time.

The song "My City of Ruins" was first performed at Convention Hall in Asbury Park during a Christmas Show. It was dedicated to the hard working people like Kate Mellina who are doing everything they can to bring Asbury Park back to glory. It was a present to the town from one of its favorite sons. The chant "come on rise up, come on rise up" became the town's slogan as well as its mission. The words could soon be found on signs in windows throughout the business district.

After 9/11 the song took on a new meaning when it was adopted as a symbol of New York's resiliency. Bruce performed it live during the Concert For New York. What once was a gift to Asbury Park became a gift to the entire world. The music of Springsteen once again lifted itself from the beach towns of the Jersey Shore to the hearts and souls of people throughout the country. We realized long ago that we couldn't keep Bruce all for ourselves, he belongs to the world.

Thankfully for us, he continues to bring the world to Asbury Park. From his benefit shows at Convention Hall to taking the "Today Show" crew on a tour around town, Bruce Springsteen is the best spokesperson Asbury Park could ever hope to have.

11 David Sancious

Writing is my focus and I always personally thought of myself as a writer who plays well rather than a guy who plays the piano or the guitar or the synthesizer really well and kind of interested in writing.

--DAVID SANCIOUS

David Sancious, from Asbury Park, is one of the most talented and respected musicians in the world.

D avid Sancious may have been one of the youngest members jamming at the Upstage but he was one of the most talented as well. He played in several classic Jersey Shore bands including the Sundance Blues Band with Southside Johnny and Miami Steven Van Zandt and Glory Road with Billy Chinnock and Garry Tallent. He first played with Bruce Springsteen in Dr. Zoom and the Sonic Boom and when Bruce formed the Bruce Springsteen Band and later the E Street Band, David was there as well. In fact, the E Street Band was named after the street in Belmar where David lived.

In 1974 he left the E Street Band to embark on a solo career and formed the band Tone which would combine the various influences of jazz, rock and classical music that he had grown up with. Sancious has since released six solo records in his career. His most recent release, *9 Piano Improvisations*, was released in 2000.

Sancious is a highly respected musician that is constantly touring and recording with others. He has toured or recorded with such artists as Peter Gabriel, Aretha Franklin, Sting, Eric Clapton, Stanley Clarke, Jack Bruce and Santana. And he's easily played a part in the recording of over 50 records. In 1992, he found himself once again in the recording studio with Bruce Springsteen for the *Human Touch* record.

After what seemed like a endless game of phone tag for weeks and weeks, David and I finally were able to connect and take a few minutes to talk about his career. It was worth the wait...

You were born in Asbury Park and moved to Belmar when you were just six. One of the first things you noticed about your new house was that it had a piano.
Yeah, absolutely. That was the first time that I had ever really been around a piano much. Maybe I had seen a piano at school, you know, grammar school in the auditorium or something, but it was the first time I ever was up close and personal with one. I mean, we had one in our house... Definitely.

Did you start playing right away?
Yeah, well pretty much because my mother started playing right away. She had known how to play since she was a young girl. I had never heard her play for years because we weren't able to afford a piano where we lived in Asbury Park. We didn't have either the money or the space for a piano. But she was actually quite a good pianist. So she played instantly.

I guess what happened was that when my parents bought the house in Belmar, the owners wanted to leave some of the furniture in it and the piano came along with the sale of the house. So the minute she got in the house she sat down and started playing. I was fascinated right away. I watched a lot and then pretty soon after that I got into it right away.

Tell me about some of your early musical influences.
Oh, in general, early influences are kind of diverse, but they happened simultaneously, which was interesting. It was at the same time I was getting into music, I was really influenced by classical music, mostly from my mother but also from a few other sources. I was always fascinated by music in films and back in that time, in the fifties and sixties, most of that was kind of a classical nature.

My father was a huge fan of jazz music. He actually had a good friend who was a club owner in Asbury Park. He owned a club called the Orchid Lounge, a jazz club. My father and the father of one of my best friends from school were good friends with the owner and they used to sneak us into this club at night. We got to hear a lot of the great jazz talent at the time like Jimmy Smith, Jack McDuff and B.B. King. A lot of great players came through then. We were way under age to be in this place, but they knew we were interested in music and I think they were just trying to do something to encourage us or give us a little boost so they snuck us in to a lot of shows.

You got your start in a jazz band when you were still very young. What do you remember about that period of time?
I had my first band when I was about nine or ten. The good thing about that time was that we had a lot of support from our parents and older people. I think they recognized, whether they thought it was just cute or charming or whatever, that these young kids were playing this music and they really did support us. They got us some gigs and sort of helped set up opportunities for us to play. We played a couple of dances for older folks, wedding receptions, talent shows, of course. My parents were completely supportive. It wasn't like I needed any permission from them to go anywhere or play music of any kind with anybody.

Were you playing in bands with different musical styles at the same time or did you focus on one genre at a time?
I was playing classical music at home, jazz with my friends in Belmar, rock and roll with guys in Asbury Park and R&B on the other side of the tracks with guys like Ernest Carter. So I was playing all kinds of stuff.

That was the beauty of that time. There was all kinds of little quartets and quintets and different configurations of people that would get together and do something. It would be really interesting. You'd have some gigs for a while and have some fun, meet some other musicians and have some adventures then that would disintegrate and merge into something else.

See, partly because I'm black and partly because of the way things were at the time and partly because of where my interests was in music, I was really playing on both sides of the tracks, not just working in one genre of music with one bunch of guys. I did gigs... all the time that I was doing that stuff with John and Steve and Bruce, I worked a lot in Asbury Park. I mean, literally the other side of the tracks from Cookman Avenue to Main Street where it was all the black community and there were black clubs.

Unfortunately there's only a handful of white artists who ever got too much experience in that and saw it. It was a whole other scene, you know. And I was lucky to be able to sort of move back and forth between both worlds in a blink of an eye. Ernest Carter and I were in a lot of pickup bands and R&B bands that would get together and work the area for a while. Same thing, it would last as a quartet or quintet for a while. One personnel change and then somebody would fall out, somebody else would fall in, change the name.

We really played a pretty wide variety of music. And the fun thing was that it was really the beginning of the time when everybody was starting to really want to do their own music. It wasn't about being a cover band, you know. The real serious guys were interested in writing music and playing original music and working that out. But, at the same time, you had to know covers. You had to know tunes. So there were two scenes going on at the same time. And then there became a certain point when you really got serious and you stopped playing in cover bands. You only worked in bands that were playing original material. You only fell into that other thing if you needed the money or the work or you just wanted to do it because you knew the people and you dug the music and it was just fun. But the real serious interest at that time was creating music, being a writer rather than just playing whatever was on the radio.

After leaving the E Street Band you formed the band, Tone.
Well, Tone started as a trio. It was myself, Ernest Carter and Gerry Carboy then we got Alex Ligertwood, Gail Boggs and Brenda Madison. Ernest was with me way before Tone got together because we had a couple of versions of bands with different names and stuff. We had our own thing together for a while, but then we were also in a lot of different bands together with other people.

At one time, Bruce was ready to change drummers and I suggested Ernest. He came down and he came to two auditions with him, I think. And it was really good, the second one, especially, was brilliant. Bruce was really blown away. And he did that for a while.

Those kind of spin-offs were all things that went on. The thing about Bruce and his two bands was that he always had version of a band that he was working on or trying to get together.

Where did Tone play?
We played a lot of colleges in the Northeast. We probably played almost all of the state universities of New York. We played a lot of the places like Rutgers, Princeton, Fairleigh Dickinson, lots of colleges in New Jersey. Colleges, clubs and theatres.

How did Bruce react to the news that you were leaving the band?
Well, Bruce was… I won't say he was surprised because he knew that I was writing and had the interest the whole time. What he was, more than anything, was supportive. I mean, the whole thing was difficult because I always knew what I was going to do. I always had the intention to be a writer and make records and have a band and do a lot of different things in music. I wasn't looking for one situation to be everything.

What he was more than anything was incredibly supportive, really helpful, gave me some hints, and sort of guided me to some people in the music industry, people who might be interested in that type of music. What I was doing musically was quite different from what he was doing musically, but at the same time he very much appreciated it. Completely, completely supportive in every way, emotionally, any kind of guidance or support he could give me he was always there. And he really was very complimentary about it. He really dug the music.

Throughout your career you've played with so many great artists. Is that something you do because you love it or do you do it to satisfy your diverse musical tastes?
No, I definitely do it because I love it and I think I'm blessed to be able to do it. It sort of goes along with the pattern of my life from day one of music, it's really been about diversity. I really have naturally been drawn to and appreciated a pretty broad range of music. The people that have called me and asked me to do projects with them over the years, I mean, I think back on it and I'm amazed. If I really take a minute and look back at everything I've done since being on the Jersey Shore and playing in bars and stuff, it's a lot of good people and a pretty broad range of artists.

I definitely do it because I love it. You couldn't do it if you didn't love it. You couldn't live this life if you didn't really want to live it because it's wonderful – it's got a certain amount of glamour to it, got a lot of perks, a lot of fulfillment – but there's a whole other side that goes with it too. It's a lot of work, things don't always work out like you want, there's rejection sometimes and you don't get everything that you'd like to get. You have to deal with all kinds of things, but on the most part it's fantastic. But, like anything, to do it well you definitely have to love it, devote your whole life to it to be a musician.

You've toured with such great artists as Bruce Springsteen, Sting and Eric Clapton. Is there one particular tour that stands out as a great thrill?
That stands out? Well, it's really hard to have one, it really is. I couldn't say that there's one except, I'd have to say one that does stand out – I won't call it the best, but I'm starting to say that because part of me does want to say it was the best ever – I'll just say that one that definitely stands out in my mind as say a really fantastic time musically and personally, which was Eric's (Clapton) 2001 tour.

It was just a joy. We had a fantastic time. It was one of those combinations of where the combination of the music was fantastic and the people – the band and everything, the crew, the management, everybody involved in that project – it just had such a great aura, good vibes, good cooperation – that really stands out.

Are you constantly writing music? Would you say that being a songwriter was something you always wanted to do?
Yeah, pretty much. I would say I'm constantly writing. Writing is my focus and I always personally thought of myself as a writer who plays well rather than a guy who plays the piano or the guitar or the synthesizer really well and kind of interested in writing. For me... in fact, my whole interest in music is sparked by wanting to write music, to be a composer. And so, yeah, I'm pretty much always writing.

For example, last year I worked with Eric Clapton from January 2001 to late December. I did his last world tour that just came out with a live album and DVD. So I didn't... honestly, I can't say I wrote a lot of music last year. I wrote a few things, little sketches and things. Things I've either developed more since that has ended or I'll develop in the future. My normal thrust is if I'm home, I'm developing something. I'm either starting or finishing, developing some kind of musical idea that I'm working on.

You took a rather long time before your last record came out. Is it because you're so busy in the studio with everybody else or because you're rather demanding of your own work?

Umm, it's a combination of being busy and wanting it to be what I mean for it to be. I don't want to put albums out just to have an album out. Since my first album till present time, I think I've put out about six albums out over three record labels. The last record I put out is an album of solo piano music on my own label on the Internet.

It's a combination of being busy and doing things with other people. My life revolves around constantly touring for myself or other artists and session work. And, I really have to say, without it being intentional, it's not something that I think about. I didn't really plan to have so long of a gap in between projects, but it did sort of work out that way. I'm finishing an ensemble record that I've been working on in-between tours for quite a while and that'll be my focus probably for next year. Once that's out, I'll focus a lot of that, do live shows and publicity for that.

I'm literally working around the clock. I kind of stop to eat lunch, hang out and have dinner with my wife and stuff. I'm just keeping real odd hours. I sleep for about four hours and then I get up around 2:00-2:30 in the morning and I work. It doesn't make it good for promotional stuff.

Was it strange or did it feel a little different when, several years later, you recorded again with Bruce for *Human Touch*?

It was great! I love working with Bruce. I'd work with him anytime. I miss him terribly and any chance I have to work with him I would instantly do it. It was great being back in the studio with him and hearing the songs.

That was great because it was I think it happened over maybe three or four days in the studio. They called me about it before I left home, but I had been scheduled to be in Los Angeles to do another project, a recording session for about a week. And I just ended that project that I was called for, stayed out there for about three days and did some of that.

What do you like best about working with Bruce?

He's got this thing, you know, this sort of melodic hook, this kind of energy that comes in his music. The minute you hear it you know it's just going to be classic. It has this undeniable kind of vibrant, spiritual energy and this melodic hook that you couldn't possibly get out of your head and you wouldn't want to. It just really, really sticks with you instantly. The songs were all striking me as being like that and it was just a lot of fun.

Does it ever bother you personally that you're not mentioned more in the history of the Asbury music scene along with the other artists of the day?
Well, I haven't had a platinum record or a number one single or anything so my level of recognition with people on any level in the music industry is going to be different. If you know music and you're a fan of music and you know the artists I work with you're going to know who I am. But the average person who listens to radio or something and judges their artists by who's on MTV or VH-1 probably is not going to be as familiar with me.

No, I don't feel bad about that because I don't look at myself in that light and I don't even feel that way about it. I certainly have my share of recognition and I've gotten tremendous perks from what's happened in my life and what I've done and who I've been associated with. So, I don't feel left out or slighted at all by that. I don't think about it. I don't think about how much I'm being written about or how known I am in people's hearts.

Have you been back to Asbury Park in the last decade or so? If so, what were your thoughts on your former hometown?
I've been back a few times. I haven't been back there in a couple of years. The last time I was there it just struck me as how the whole Asbury scene, which used to be so vibrant, was like a ghost town. And it's been like that for a long time. I was really encouraged to see the "Today Show" when they had the premiere of the album and they did a thing from Asbury Park on the beach. It was really encouraging to see the plans and hear people talking about the plans to bring it back and revitalize that whole area because it's tragic that it should ever have gotten to that.

But Asbury Park is just one of a lot of places across America that it happened to. It's special for us, for me, because that's where I'm from, that's where we lived and grew up. But I was really encouraged to see it. I hope they actually follow through on the plans and build some of that stuff and get some vibrancy back down there. People need it.

12 Stone Pony and the Asbury Sound

Asbury sound... What Asbury sound? There is no way that the Shakes sound any way like the Jukes. The Jukes don't sound anything like Cahoots. Cahoots doesn't sound anything like the E Street Band.

--TONY AMATO

One of only a handful of clubs known to music fans around the world, the legendary Stone Pony. Photo © Debra L. Rothenberg/rothenbergphoto.com

Let's get this straight, there never was an Asbury Sound. It was simply a way of grouping the bands from the area into one category. It was probably more derogatory than anything. It gave the impression that everyone was trying to capitalize on a winning formula. To the musicians and people closely involved, each of the bands had a personality and style of their own.

"I think it was either the *New York Times* or *People Magazine*," said Tony Amato of Cahoots remembering an interview that took place during the height of the Jersey Shore scene. "The guy comes out and says, 'Well, with this Asbury sound...' I almost fell out of the woods. I said, 'Asbury sound... What Asbury sound? There is no way that the Shakes sound any way like the Jukes. The Jukes don't sound anything like Cahoots. Cahoots doesn't sound anything like the E Street Band.'"

The Stone Pony became known as the home for SOAP (Sounds of Asbury Park) music. In a way, this was where the evolution of the Upstage really reached its peak. While playing at the Upstage, the local musicians were able to hone their craft and develop personal styles. It was the perfect place for a group of young musicians hoping to make a living as artists. The Upstage was where they all pushed each other to be better than the day before. At the Pony, they were provided a stage and a venue to claim their own. It was here that they opened up their jam sessions to a much larger audience. One of their members, Bruce Springsteen, had already released two records and was becoming known nationally when the Pony opened in 1974, but fellow Upstage players stayed in Asbury and created a scene of their own. This wasn't easy, at first, because the Stone Pony wanted bands that played disco music.

Butch Pielka and Jack Roig, the original owners of the Stone Pony met as bouncers at a Jersey Shore bar called the Riptide. They took their savings and borrowed whatever they could to buy a club known as the Magic Touch. That bar was an out and out disco. At the time, disco music was sweeping the country and the Jersey Shore was no different. Except for the fact that the local musicians didn't want to play disco.

Cold, Blast and Steel was a four-piece band with two drummers, a bass player and a guitar player. The band was comprised of former E Streeter Vini "Mad Dog" Lopez, Rick DiSarno, John Luraschi and Steven Schreager. They wanted to play the Pony, but the Pony was a disco club. Butch told them they had to learn how to play disco. "Vini looks at him and says okay, we'll do disco," Amato said, retelling a story he's told a thousand times. "So, they wrote a song called 'Butch's Bump.' Well, they played that song one time and that was the end of that. Then the Pony started bringing in all these rock bands."

Steven Van Zandt was one of the main reasons the Stone Pony didn't go down in history as a legendary disco club. But more than that, he may have been the person most responsible for building the local scene. He was playing with Southside Johnny in the Blackberry Booze Band, which later became the Asbury Jukes. Van Zandt asked the Pony to let them play on one of the club's off-nights in exchange for the money brought in at the door.

"He was like we'll take the door," remembers Amato. "Everybody's like there's ten guys in this band what do you mean take the door? Well, the first week it was like three dollars. Second week was like six dollars. It kept growing and growing and the Jukes started getting going. Steve told us to bring our boys down there. So Shakes started playing and it started, started causing a scene. The three bands were getting lines around the block. There was already lines there before Bruce ever showed up.

"You'd have Southside Johnny & the Asbury Jukes playing, the Shakes and Cahoots. Bruce and the E Street Band never really played in the clubs, but Bruce would hang out, Clarence would hang out and Van Zandt would hang out. And whenever those three bands were there, Bruce would come down to the Pony. See, what actually brought Bruce to the Pony was those three bands. We had a thing where if it was say Cahoots and the Jukes, we'd play our normal set and by the end of the night Cahoots and the Jukes would both be on stage and Bruce knew it was Upstage time - time to jam."

Record executives in New York, who for years had ignored the Jersey Shore, finally realized that they had an emerging music scene practically in their backyard. They began paying attention to Asbury hoping to find the next Springsteen and the Stone Pony became the place to be. "I guess what happened is that Bruce made *Born to Run* and everything just exploded," thought Southside Johnny. "People started coming down to Asbury Park to see what was going on. And we (the Jukes) were the beneficiaries of that, of course. The Stone Pony benefited too because we played there so much. And the people who played Convention Hall would come over and jam with us. They'd just come over after hours and try to pick up chicks and drink and play. It was great because we were the kind of band that could play just about anybody's songs.

"I remember Boz Scaggs coming and playing," added Southside Johnny. "He had refused to do 'Somebody Loan Me A Dime' for years because he was too associated with it and he wanted to do new stuff. I said, 'Look, I think that's a great song. Will you do it?' And he did it at the Pony and it was great!"

It didn't take long before Southside Johnny & the Jukes caught the eye of Steve Popovich of Epic Records. "He was this complete nut from Cleveland," said Southside. "A complete psycho, he was like a 50s rock and roll record executive. Completely insane, loves the music and not really a businessman as much as an enthusiast. He said, 'You've got to make a record.' So we made a four-song demo. We used high school kids from Asbury to play from the school band. Popovich put out the demo and he gave it to a DJ in Cleveland named Kid Leo who started playing it. I was furious because it was out of tune. And that was the start of it. It was all very seat-of-your-pants kind of stuff. Nobody knew what was going to happen next. So, the idea of it being history it was more like a random history. But I guess all those scenes are like that. Nobody really knows what's going to happen next."

The Jukes held a record release party at the Pony with a live show broadcast on the radio. According to Lee Mrowicki, the long-time disc jockey at the Stone Pony, this was the night that brought the club national attention. Lee was working at WJLK, the local radio station in Asbury Park, at the time. WJLK was going to be the local outlet for the national broadcast of Southside's record release. "There were nine stations throughout the country, mostly in the East and Midwest, running it," said Mrowicki. "And, of course, that's when anybody who was in the music industry paid attention to what was going on."

Lots of special guests came up for the show. Ronnie Spector and Lee Dorsey, who were both on the first album were there. And two disc jockeys instrumental to the Jukes career - Kid Leo and Ed Schiaky, who was big in Philadelphia - made the trip. "It was just this wild scene with all these radio stations hooked up," remembered Southside. "It was great! That was a record company doing promotion. It was like it happened around me. It wasn't my idea, but it was really great."

The Jukes were always thought of as a great dance band. If a Jukes show didn't get you on out on the dance floor there must have been something wrong with you. "I was there when they played three nights a week," recalls Mrowicki. "That was a lot of fun because Johnny wouldn't play unless there was people on the dance floor. He'd say, 'You ain't dancing folks!' And the place would just get up and everybody would start dancing. You'd dance the whole night most of the time."

After the Jukes left Asbury for bigger and better things, bands like the Shakes, the Shots and Cahoots took over the scene. "Everything just carried on," added Mrowicki. "People who loved the Jukes loved those guys as well. Everybody was looking at them. They were supposedly the next big thing from Asbury."

Billy Hector, known today as a legendary blues guitarist, played in the Shots when the Asbury scene was still going strong. He recalled the impact WNEW had on the scene. Being so close to New York City, people on the Jersey Shore used to listen to New York radio stations and WNEW was the biggest of them all. "That was the rock station so anybody that was on that station had made it," said Hector. "Bruce played on that station live. I remember, I was with Tony Palligrosi at Drew University listening to it. It was a big deal. And then Tony was in the band when the Jukes were on the radio and they interviewed Southside. They were talking about Cahoots and the bands." Whenever one of the bands was doing well, the rest of the bands got a boost because they knew that they were all involved.

"It was a real scene," explained Hector. "It was buzzing. It was like Seattle was in the early 90s. Everybody was talking about it. The press would talk about it, people would talk about it, everybody was excited. The Pony was packed every night on the week. We were there, I think, Tuesday, Thursday and Sunday. We were there through the summer. The Jukes had made it so everyone's eyes were on that club and any band that played Convention Hall down the street would come to jam at the Pony. When the Jukes cleared out, the Shots and the Shakes took over and the scene was still going pretty strong. There were lots of record companies looking at the bands... well, at the Shakes anyway. We were more like the Commitments."

Fran Smith Jr., who went on to play with bands like Cats on a Smooth Surface and the Hooters, joined the Shakes in 1975. "Everyone thought that the Shakes were going to be the next big thing to break out of the Asbury scene," Smith remembers. "We had an exceptional amount of press at the time and many record companies were pursuing us. Bruce and the boys were always up on stage with us. The times were great and the fans were pumped. To say the least, it really was a magical time at the Pony. There were many rock stars coming in to catch Bruce and we were lucky enough to ride in the wake of his growing success."

According to Tony Amato, the Jersey Shore was loaded with bands getting signed by record companies. "We all had deals," he said. "Southside had their deal with Epic, the Shakes got their deal, then we had our deal with Columbia. Bruce and Jon Landau brought our tape to Mickey Eisner. We had the deal signed, sealed and then Eisner said, 'Get your boys ready, we're gonna meet.' That was like on a Tuesday. We played the Royal Manor on Wednesday. Columbia was supposed to come down with the papers on Friday. Thursday morning I get a phone call from George Theiss saying he quit the band."

It's possible that Theiss may have had a problem with Springsteen trying to help Cahoots out. Years before, Theiss had played with Bruce in the Castiles. A talented songwriter in his own right, George may have been adamant on making it on his own. Amato believes Bruce was simply trying to give his friends a chance at making it. "See what George didn't understand is that the man isn't doing anything," explained Amato. "What the man did is open the door to get us in. What I kept trying to tell people back then was look, 'Bruce ain't doing this for you, he's opening the door. He's bringing everybody in because this is our family. He's opening the door and once you go through the door it's up to you to stay there.'"

Some people think the record executives were looking too closely at bands with the so-called "Asbury Sound," hoping to find a carbon copy of Springsteen or Southside Johnny. In a scene filled with extremely talented musicians, it's a wonder why more bands didn't make it from the area. They had the crowds, but bands need more than that to make it. "None of them had the personality or the songs that Bruce did," said Mrowicki. "They were looking for hit songs, stuff that was going to be played on the radio. But Asbury was like an island on to itself. It didn't get affected a lot by what was happening in New York or with disco or punk music. It was always a little different throughout Asbury."

Looking back, Amato still believes that Cahoots was good enough to make it, but the band soon broke up for good. It was around this time that the idea of an Asbury scene had started to wane.

"After 1979, the scene sort of stopped," said Amato. "Anything after 1979 they're riding on what everybody had created acting like they did this. We sort of got out of it, you know. It's like there were four bands in the 'Asbury Park Sound,' that's all. There wasn't all these other bands that people think, they were after everything. The whole Asbury Park scene was actually from 1969-1979, a ten year span. That was from the days of the Upstage. The Upstage closed, so we just moved to the Pony and we kept doing what we did at the Upstage. What made the Pony something special was the bands playing and the impromptu jam sessions. That's what the Pony is noted for, that's what the people came to see.

"What the sound was I have no clue, but there was sort of a blood relationship," continues Amato. "It's like today if I'm in a room with me, Bruce, Little Steven or any of those guys there's no difference. It doesn't matter that you're Bruce Springsteen and you're a major star. There's no separation. It's the relationships that we had with each other, the kind of music atmosphere and the vibe we were creating - that's what it was. It's not a sound, it's an energy. We all had this certain type of energy that we were spewing out on the crowd. It was really never a sound."

Hal Selzer, a long-time veteran of local bands such as the Bobby Bandiera Band and Adrian Dodz, believes that the scene may have been created because of the level of the musicians in the area. "I don't know what it's like in other scenes that sprung up like with the Beatles, but around here I think it's got something to do with the quality of the players," he said. "To get into the scene you've got to be a good player. It's the quality of the players and the kind of music we play. You've got to be able to play with soul and feeling."

After Southside Johnny & the Jukes graduated from being a house band, the Stone Pony began booking national acts. According to Mrowicki, agents started calling the club to get their acts booked there. In the beginning, many were R&B oriented but the club eventually started taking chances with a lot of different types of music. Nowadays, the Pony is probably best known as a place where you can see national acts up close. It's an intimate setting that you don't find in too many places.

Mrowicki has seen his share of memorable shows at the club, but one show quickly comes to mind when asked to name the most magical night. It was the first time that Jimmy Cliff played the Pony. "The first time he played it was just... it was like seeing Springsteen because it had that same electricity," said Mrowicki. "The guy came out, looking like a boxer with a black hooded cape with a hood on and everything. Came out of the dressing room, threw it off and he was all white underneath. White in everything - white pants, white shirt, and everything. So it was a real contradiction. He was speaking very religiously, almost like taking in the whole crowd and saying we could move mountains. It was an electrical show and then Bruce played with him. They did 'Trapped,' which Bruce had been covering anyway."

Springsteen has jammed with many artists on the Stone Pony stage. "There was a time when we couldn't get rid of him," jokes Mrowicki. "Back then, he would just show up. Nowadays he'll call to send somebody in advance because it gets kind of nuts. But back then it was just show up and play. And there were times at that point he would say can we have the band play tonight?"

The spirit of the Upstage certainly is alive and well at the Stone Pony. It doesn't matter if you've sold millions of records or if you've never had a record deal. The comradery among the musicians is just as strong.

"Bruce said to me one night in here," added Amato. "I was walking out in the back, not paying attention, and he yells, 'Yo, Bacc... everything's different, but it's still the same.' Now everything is different but it's still the same. We're still doing the same shit. We're hanging, we're partying, we're having fun and we're playing.

"Money... greed... corruption and greed, it kills every town," said Amato. "Instead of getting back to what they should or try to keep what's going on. This town is known for that in that time and this in this time. And during our era it was known for rock and roll. Geez, at that time rock and roll... aw, drugs, alcohol, booze, rock and roll and sex, it was like too bad you got it. I mean, people would make pilgrimages here. What they should have done was capitalize on it, but they didn't really capitalize. They took the money that the town was making, put it in their pockets and walked. Even today they're still in trouble for that shit.

"I think before there was Asbury Park, Bruce Springsteen and all that bologna – Asbury Park was already a noted entertainment town. If you watch the 'Jackie Gleason Show' or 'The Honeymooners' they took vacations to Asbury Park. If you watch older movies, way before that, like movies from the 20s and 30s there's references to Asbury Park. Before Atlantic City there was Asbury Park. We're going to Asbury Park. And it was all about entertainment with the ballrooms and dance rooms. What they want to do now is make it a condoville. And, hey, it might work it might not work, but you're changing what the town was. You're changing the atmosphere of the town. People would rather come here for what it was not for what it's gonna be."

13 Southside Johnny & the Asbury Jukes

I didn't think they were gonna let me make a second album once they'd heard the first one because it wasn't like a lot of things that were going on and I thought nobody's gonna want to hear this shit.

--SOUTHSIDE JOHNNY

Southside Johnny & the Asbury Jukes as seen in 2002.

S outhside Johnny & the Asbury Jukes was the first band to make it from Asbury Park after the success of *Born To Run* by Bruce Springsteen. Originally the house band at the Stone Pony, the Jukes went national with the release of *I Don't Want To Go Home* in 1976. A record release party was held at the Pony with the band's live show syndicated on nine radio stations across the country.

The band played rhythm & blues music with the addition of a large horn section. Early records were produced by Steven Van Zandt and contained songs written by Bruce Springsteen. The band's third record, *Hearts Of Stone*, was once named one of the Top-100 albums of the last 20 years by *Rolling Stone Magazine*.

Southside Johnny & the Asbury Jukes have been touring and recording music for over 25 years. Through the years, they have built an extremely large fanbase around the world. Many of their fans have made trips to Asbury Park to see the town where the band got its start. Several hundred fans got together in 2002 for the first ever Jukestock - a Southside Johnny & the Asbury Jukes fan convention held at a hotel in nearby Tinton Falls. Later that year, the band released its latest record, *Going To Jukesville*.

I caught up with Southside Johnny during the band's annual summer shows in Point Pleasant. We met on the boardwalk in Asbury Park. It was a beautiful beach day, but the beach was empty. It was almost too quiet for a resort town, but a perfect time to talk about Asbury's past.

Tell me about the early days of Asbury Park.
Well, we weren't making any money, but there was an instinctual knowledge that what was happening with the Upstage Club, Student Prince, Stone Pony and all the other clubs and all the bands - all the jamming was just great fun and not everybody gets a chance to do this.

Nobody was thinking about getting deals. Bruce was still trying to figure out which way he wanted to jump, you know. He was writing songs way before anyone else and he had all those bands: Child, Earth and Steel Mill. He was just trying to figure it all out. Eventually he did. And I think we all were trying to find our way, but not to make earth shaking records but more to make it so we could have a career so we could continue. And that's a very difficult proposition. I know from my own personal experience with my father. I didn't know whether I had the stamina to do it, so I never took it that seriously as far as a career. But I took it seriously as I wanted to get it right. I guess that kind of tenacity stood me in good stead. But in the beginning it was just a laugh.

"Band of The Week" we used to call it. Garry or Steven or me would put the band up and we'd pick whoever was available. Big Bobby or Vini Lopez. Garry was usually the bass player but Vinnie Roslin was there and there was other guys. And there's a lot of guys whose names I don't even remember that I was in bands with. From a perspective of people who didn't go through it, it seemed like this crazy, verdant scene of wild experimentation and open arm stuff, but it really wasn't. It was a struggle to get anybody to do anything.

There's a lot of people that remember you playing bass back at the Upstage. How long did you play bass guitar?
I don't really remember. I was kind of forced into it. Garry played bass so I bought one. Sonny Kenn said come and sing in my band, which I never thought of doing really. He wanted to play blues after playing rock and roll for so many years. And he knew I played harp and sang because I used to hang around with those guys. But I never thought of being in a band or anything, just personal amusement. And then one time he said we need a bass player you're going to have to learn how to play bass.

So I bought a bass and Garry helped me out a bit. But it's very difficult to sing and play bass at the same time and I never really enjoyed it. I enjoyed the attitude of it. I love playing bass and I love singing, but doing them both together was just impossible. And so later, we got a bass player. We got this kid like 16 years old. He didn't have any idea of the songs we were playing we had to show him everything. But it's fun and that's the basic idea, it was fun. It wasn't this huge ambition like I've got to make it.

How did the Jukes come about?
There was a band called Blackberry Booze Band and that was David Myers and Paul Dinkler and Kenny Cutler. So these guys had this band. They did a lot of just jamming, you know. It was a four piece guitar/bass. A guy named Paul Greene, who was a friend of mine, was a harmonica player but he didn't want to sing he just wanted to play harp. And I was at a loose end. I was playing in a band called Bank Street Blues Band, which had a guy named Stu and he wanted to do all the singing and he just wanted a harmonica player. So I got to sing like two songs a night, and, of course, that's not what I wanted. As much as I like playing blues harp, I really wanted to sing. So Paul Greene and I one day decided, "This is stupid, we're in the wrong bands." So we decided to switch and we didn't even tell the other bands because he showed for one gig and I showed up for the other gig.

Eventually I took over that band and it was the nucleus of the Jukes. Actually, I only kept Kenny on drums. But I hustled a gig from the Stone Pony. I think they gave us Thursday nights or something like that for $90 bucks a night to split between the four of us. And that was the beginning of my run-ins with the owners of the Stone Pony. It was a constant battle to try to get enough money to actually live on. I tried to get more nights, but then I added Kevin Kavanaugh on keyboards. Steven was working jackhammer and playing with an oldies group, the Dovells but Chubby Checker was the band leader and he just got sick of the whole thing. He came and lived with me and my first wife for a while.

So, any way, the long story even longer... Steven and I started adding pieces. I'd always wanted a horn band. Steven was really into the idea of expanding the R&B and rock and roll combination that we had been exploring for a long time. So, we started looking for horn players and that was a nightmare. I mean, the weirdest people came and went. We found a sax player and he was completely insane. Found a trumpet player and he couldn't play. It was really tough, but we were determined to do it.

What was the hardest thing about that period of time?
We couldn't get booked. None of us could get booked in the big clubs like D'Jais. I had the owner from D'Jais come down to the Pony when we were doing 600 people there in the middle of winter.

I said, "Look, I know you don't know these songs." He sat down for two sets and said, "I don't know any of the songs you played. I can't book you."

"What's the matter? I got 600 people to come see me. Give me some off nights," which is what we did with the Pony. We could never get weekends.

"No, I can't take the chance that you're gonna alienate the people coming to see people do top-40 songs."

It was like that for years. There was no money to be made, no recognition, no real respect. So, to me, it's not like this wonderful thing, although I loved it. I'm so grateful that it was that way and I could do the things I wanted to do because there was always an audience for it. It just doesn't seem like Paris between the wars or San Francisco in 1965.

The early eight years of Asbury Park are what they are. And then when the Pony started booking Elvis Costello and all those different people it was because they needed a night to play between New York and Philadelphia. The economics of it was that every night you had off was a night you were losing money. You had to pay the hotel rooms, per diem for the band and transportation. So any place that was transitional between big cities that was a club you wanted to play and the Pony became the transitional club for a lot of people.

Music history kind of gets beyond what people can comprehend. You've got a couple million people taking vacations to visit a house in Memphis each year and people running around Liverpool looking for places where the Beatles once were.

Yeah, that's true. And they don't know the realities of that life. But it's just weird to be part of that because I just don't think of myself in that way. I mean, I'm always looking at what I've got to do next week. What do I want to do in the few months ahead.

What was it like when Steven Van Zandt left the band?

I don't really remember how the whole thing happened, but the transition was fairly smooth. In other words, Billy (Rush) was ready to go with that at that point. So he didn't just abandon us or anything like that, he made it very smooth. Also the year before that Bruce was going through all of this upheaval. Steven and Bruce always had their heads together as far as they had this kind of comradeship that made it them against all these other people that were trying to scrape off pieces of Bruce and all of us. And, they had talked about it and all this...

I said, "You know you've got to go. He needs you a lot more than I do. I mean, he's the one that's being hounded by all these fucking sharks and these monsters from the depths that were just trying to manipulate him and use him and you're the voice of sanity in his world. You both can figure it out." And it was more that than really anything else.

Tell me about making your first record.

It seemed a tempest in a teapot, you know. I didn't think they were gonna let me make a second album once they'd heard the first one because it wasn't like a lot of things that were going on, and I thought nobody's gonna want to hear this shit. I mean, here's this skinny white guy from Ocean Grove, New Jersey, a Methodist retirement community, singing blues with this horn section that we kind of cobbled together from Philadelphia.

Those were the days of guitar bands like Boston and Cheap Trick and all that. I looked around and went, oh, I'm gonna make a record... Big deal. To me, it was just something to do to say I did. And I figured I'd be playing in this area for the rest of my life although that's not what I wanted. I wanted to see the world. I wanted to travel, which luckily I got to do.

We went on the road. Once I got the chance I said, "Great - book me anywhere! I don't care how much money we lose." Which came back to haunt me too because you know how record companies are they charge for everything. But we did, we got to go over to England. We played with Graham Parker a bunch of dates in England.

Do you remember performing on the "Rockpalost Show"?

Yeah, we did "Rockpalost" at that time too. It was 1977 or something like that. The first one, I vaguely remember, there was a lot of different bands. They were all kind of predictable guitar bands. And we came on with the horns and everything and everybody was dancing. It was the kind of rock and roll that just lends itself to having fun. No hero worship. No deep cerebral activity. Just yeah, let's have fun and they really responded that way. And, I think, that's what people remember the most from that show is that there was an audience that really just kind of let loose. And that's what we've always done. I mean, that's what I started out doing.

It's funny all the different viewpoints you have of what rock and roll's become. You listen to the early Chuck Berry stuff, Bo Diddley, Little Richard - the real progenitors of rock and roll, other than the R&B guys that came before, and then Elvis Presley - it's all fun. It's all kind of wild, abandoned teenage nut-ball stuff. And even though that's not the only route I have, it is one that appeals to me greatly because I also come from Winonie Harris and Big Joe Turner and that's all fun. It's like this big party that's happening on your radio or your record player. That's what I thought I wanted to do. For all of my reading and all that stuff, really when I get on stage, I want to just blow my brains out. I don't want to be anything other than a conduit for emotion. I don't want people looking at me. I really don't feel comfortable. I feel comfortable on stage, but outside the stage I don't feel comfortable with that stuff.

Nils and I played a bunch of those shows together before he joined the E Street Band. He was one of those guys who really didn't fit in any niche just like us so they would put us together with all those kind of acts that nobody really knew who to put them with. He put on great shows. The music wasn't like what we were doing, but we really got along well and we did do "Rockpalost" a couple of times, I think.

What was your favorite album to work on?

Oh, I don't know, there's good memories in just about every one of them. Maybe not *Trash it Up*, but just about every one else. And there's tough times too, but that's alright. Those are the things you go through, you know. You look back and it all seems funny as somebody once said. But it wasn't funny at the time. It was a nightmare, but that's okay.

I'm not a big guy to stay in the studio for twenty hours at a stretch. I get bored. But the first album was fun. I mean, no one knew what we were doing. We hadn't a clue. Jimmy Iovine was supposed to be engineering and he had three projects going at the same time so he would sleep in front of the console.

Dave Thoner was the assistant engineer and he pretty much ran the sessions as far as making sure everything went to tape and all. And Steve and I, we knew what we wanted to do, we knew what most of the material was going to be, we just weren't sure how we wanted to record it. We ended up doing a lot of the stuff just live. Live vocals and everything like that. I don't really look back all that much. It just doesn't further me any to look back.

Could you ever have imagined *Hearts of Stone* making *Rolling Stone*'s list of 100 Best Albums of the Last 20 Years?
It was bizarre. That album came out and was doing well until I got hurt and we had to cancel the tour. The record company said screw it. They really weren't into us. There was a transitional period when top management like Ronald Luxonberg and Steve Popovich left. These were the guys who were on our side pretty much. New guys came in and they're never on your side unless you've already sold records because you're just a burden to them. And even though the album got some fairly good reviews and it was doing pretty well, 125 stations were playing it which is a lot, once that tour stopped they lost interest. Not that they had a lot in the beginning anyway.

So years later somebody shows me this *Rolling Stone Magazine*, says you're in the *Rolling Stone*. I said for what? And they show me this thing where they had - I guess we were next to a Doors album, I forget what one. One of the top 100 albums of the last 20 years. What a bunch of crap! You know, I can name... I mean, I like the album and I think Stevie did a magnificent job on it and I'm happy with a lot of my singing, but Tom Waits wasn't on that list. God, I could go down the list of people that weren't on that. There's a lot of albums I looked at and went, "Yeah, right, that's one of the top 100 albums of the last 20 years. It's a piece of shit!"

I've never been part of that. I've never been a part of the teen rock and roll scene. When everybody was digging the Beatles, I liked the Stones and the Animals but I wasn't a big hero worshipper.

Eric Burdon was a good singer. He did a lot of stuff, and the Stones too, that we were listening to. I mean, my brother and I were into rhythm and blues because of my parents. So we had R&B songs and we had albums by blues guys like John Lee Hooker. Then when these English guys started doing this stuff we went, "Hey, that's pretty cool." Same as John Hammond, Jr. and Paul Butterfield. Here are these white guys doing this stone black stuff. Maybe it'll be ok for us too, you know? And you felt like you weren't alone anymore at that point.

It's hard to believe a seashore town could ever get run down like this. Does seeing the state of Asbury Park today upset you?
Yeah, sure it upsets me. It's upset me for years since 1971-1972. I mean, when we were playing the Pony the place started to deteriorate and I thought what the hell's going on? They fought us tooth and nail. There was a lot of city councilmen that didn't want any rock and roll in Asbury Park. And I thought, we're the only thing on a Friday night that's open and people are here. It's insane. I mean, it's like they fought it off. And, of course, the theory was and I subscribe to it was that a lot of people bought up property cheap hoping that gambling would come in and they could cash in. So they really wanted to drive the city down as far as it could go so they can plead poverty and say we have to have casinos to save the city. Fortunately, they didn't get it. I hope they all lost a ton of money too.

Yeah, it bugs me. This used to be a great place. This is my childhood here. Ever since I was a kid I was coming to Asbury Park to get in trouble and play pinball and ride the rides, get people to buy us beer when we were 16. The Pony used to be Mrs. Jay's and my friend Buzzy, who was a nut, was fifteen years older than all of us. Buzzy Lubinsky, his father was Herman Lubinsky from Savoy Records. He was completely insane. And all of us young 14 and 15 year olds would hang around with him because he had music and he had a car and he would take us into all these places. He would say take this speaker and pretend like you're bringing in equipment. So there we were, we'd be hanging in these bars.

What do you see as the connection between Asbury Park and rock and roll music?
Well my perspective of it is that I've played so many cities like this with 30-50,000 people and I see the people going to the clubs and they'd be a thousand posters of all these different bands. They didn't have Bruce and Bruce broke it wide open. That's really what happened. If Bruce had not come... if the first two albums had been it and he sold 20-30,000 copies and settled into whatever life and touring and we made an album people wouldn't be coming here. But the fact is it's Bruce Springsteen and you get kind of attached to that.

I think the focal point is really that Bruce became this monster star. I mean the record company just went full bore to promote him and he was good enough to deliver. The thing is you can put that kind of promotion in front of somebody and then put them on stage but if they don't deliver they could be big stars for a couple of years and then be gone. And Bruce is just one of those guys that just will not be denied. So there it is.

I was very proud of Bruce because there was that little transition period when he was doing a lot of stuff in New York - and it was like, "Oh he's going to be the East Coast kind of New York/New Jersey." And they were trying to edge him into that. I think he just put his foot down and said no. *Greetings from Asbury Park...* And, of course, he's like James Joyce in that this is where his material is.

I think that we all, and Jon (Bon Jovi) is really adamant about that, and I feel that way too - it always used to piss me off to watch Johnny Carson or something and hear the jokes about Jersey. And, of course, in the early bands before Bruce recorded and all that stuff, Sonny and I tried to get booked in New York in some places like Cafe Wha? Forget it. "Where are you from? Jersey?" And it was like that for years. So when we finally got a chance to shove it in their faces we really wanted to shove it in their faces. After all those years of being the butt of the joke it was nice to be able to say, "Oh yeah, and by the way, I'm from New Jersey."

Do you think Asbury Park will ever come back?

Yeah, I think it will. I think in the next ten years you'll see a big change. I hope that's what happens. It seems like they've got a good plan. I mean, I know a lot of people say gee it won't be their honky-tonk town. Nothing stays like that forever.

Anything is better than this and what happens is... I had a film they gave me from the thirties about this area and north of Asbury Park and it was all residential, real nice. And this was very gentile down here. It descended into honky-tonk in the 50s and 60s. So they'll start as gentile again and in another 20-30 years it'll be honky-tonk again.

Memories of Being a Jukes Kid

by Kenneth Pentifallo II
(Popeye's Son)

I was 13 years old when *I Don't Want To Go Home* was released. I'm the oldest of three children, so I was "the man" of the house when Pop toured with the Jukes for six months at a time. I remember my friends didn't understand why Pop had to go Europe for six months to play in a band, but I knew exactly what was going on although I didn't realize the impact that the Jukes were having on people.

The Palace was like Disney World for children of musicians who played in Asbury. Everybody knew that my Pop was Mr. Popeye of the Jukes and that my sister and myself were the children of an Asbury Juke. We were constantly awarded with ice cream, stuffed animals and amusement rides by fans of the Jukes because we were with Mr. Popeye. I believe that by giving us presents the fans got a chance to meet a Juke up close and on a personal level.

I'll never forget the strong odor of moth balls backstage at Convention Hall. We always stayed backstage during the shows because Pop didn't want anything to happen to us. Since he was performing, he couldn't keep us under his wing....so it's backstage.

The Stone Pony...."Home of the Asbury Jukes". Seeing that sign on top of the Pony made me proud of my Pop! It's like he accomplished something that none of my friends fathers have done, almost like he left his mark on Asbury Park. I loved going to Jukes rehearsals at the Pony. It made me feel like a celebrity....free soda all the time and hundreds of people trying to look in to see what the Jukes were cookin' up next. Miami Steve (Van Zandt) made sure us kids had everything we wanted while the Jukes did their thing on stage. It became such a routine for me to be there at rehearsal (and I begged to go), I remember actually falling asleep in front of Pop's bass drum while the Jukes were playing. Alcohol was NEVER near us while rehearsal on. I'm not sure who implemented that rule....but booze, children and the Jukes never happened.

Just because Southside Johnny & the Asbury Jukes can now be found in the "bargain bin" at Sam Goody doesn't mean that these Jersey guys didn't kick ass in the 70s. It was impossible not to clap your hands, stomp your feet and dance when this 10-piece group took the stage! It was truly a musical and visual sight to see. My best musical memory is a tough decision, but I narrowed it down to two.

#1 - 1978, Count Basie Theater -- Southside Johnny & the Asbury Jukes performing on stage with Bruce Springsteen & the E Street Band. I don't recall the event but I do remember seeing three lead vocalists (Johnny, Bruce and Miami Steve) three keyboardists, six-piece horn section and Pop and Mighty Max, each on their own drum set playing in perfect sync....almost like one drummer aside a mirror!

#2 - 1978, Six Flags Great Adventure -- It was college senior night at the Great Arena. My family had on "JUKES" 3/4 length shirts walking around the park and everybody knew us! The show was dynamite and the crowd in a frenzy. The Jukes had out done themselves with this show! And it was the last Southside Johnny & the Asbury Jukes show I attended with Mr. Popeye on drums.

My favorite photo is of Southside and Bruce sharing a mike at the Pony with Pop in the center background on drums and the Stone Pony banner above. I'm a security officer for Jenkinson's in Point Pleasant and I see Bruce every so often on the boardwalk with his son. They love miniature golf and the aquarium. He goes undetected every time he's up there, blue jeans, tee shirt and a Miami Dolphins ballcap is the norm. Just a regular guy.

The main ingredient needed to make Asbury Park a resort again is already in place....a beautiful beach. If the boardwalk re-opens with arcades and shops, people will come. This will create a need for lodging and meals which should make Asbury Park "open for business." I know.....easier said than done.

It Ain't The Meat,
　　Popeye's Son

Talking with Rusty Cloud

former member of the Jukes

What bands were you in before playing with the Jukes?
Before Southside, I toured with Melba Moore from '77 through '79, played and wrote arrangements for the Cotton Club orchestra in Harlem, and freelanced as a studio musician and jazz and R&B sideman. Then late in 1980, a drummer named Mike Micara, who was in a little recording unit out in Brooklyn that I was working with called me about joining the new band that was being formed to back Gary U.S. Bonds. Gary was in the middle of recording *Dedication* with Bruce Springsteen and Steven Van Zandt. I ended up playing on over half the album and toured with Gary until April of '82. This gig was my entree into the whole New Jersey/ Asbury Park scene.

Who were some of your musical influences?
I loved jazz, blues and R&B growing up, and I still do. I guess my favorite influences would be Herbie Hancock, Ray Charles, Dr. John, Red Garland and Richard Tee. I love classical music as well, but never pursued it to any degree. I like a lot of classic rock and roll, but more individual artists than as a broad style. Most of the people I've toured with (including Johnny) have gravitated much more to R&B than rock and roll.

How did you first get involved with the Jukes?
I was first contacted about joining the Jukes by a guy named Pete Croken, who was then their tour manager. I was recording with Little Steven Van Zandt, for the *Men Without Women* album, and Pete was doing some production assistance on the sessions. He mentioned that Johnny was interested in adding a second keyboard player, mainly to be a piano specialist. I had recently left Gary U.S. Bond's band, so I was interested. This was spring 1982. I went out to Jersey to play with the band and shortly after that Johnny called to offer me the gig outright.

What I didn't know at the time was that Little Steven was planning to put his the Disciples of Soul together, and was planning to ask me to do that as well. I spent the rest of '82 jumping between the two gigs. At the end of '82, I chose to go with the Jukes exclusively. Alas, *Trash It Up* was my first LP session with the Jukes.

Would you say the *Trash It Up* recording session went about as rough as people were led to believe?

Yes, the *Trash It Up* sessions were very rough. Johnny and Nile Rodgers never got along and the vibes just got worse as the sessions dragged on. It was really Billy Rush's record rather than a Jukes record, and a lot of it was me on synth bass and various keyboards over drum machines. A lot of the guys in the band didn't get to participate much and the music was the worse for it. With some fleeting exceptions, it's just a lousy piece of work.

What was your best memory of playing in the Jukes?

My best memory? I can't name one! There was an absolutely magical show at the Grosse Freiheit in Hamburg that went on for almost four hours in '92. The Southside tightrope act worked to perfection that night. Every bizarre out-on-a-limb musical chance Johnny took panned out amazingly.

There was also a concert with the acoustic group in Holland in '95 in a sit-down, chamber-music sort of hall that I remember fondly as a really quality musical experience. Incredibly artistic in a way Jukes' shows seldom had a chance to be. Of course, the recording processes for *At Least We Got Shoes* and *Better Days* are very fond memories as well.

What was your worst?

As for the worst... well, that's easy! I got really drunk during a show in Germany on some bad vodka and blew my stack at Johnny for the way he was running the show. I left the stage, went upstairs to the dressing room and started wrecking the place. Johnny showed up, started screaming at me and I threw a half-sized metal stepladder at him. We kept screaming until we calmed down and talked things out. I had initially demanded a plane ticket home on the spot. We all had a tendency to booze it up in those days and that night I really hurt myself.

Your last recorded album with the Jukes was *Better Days*. What led you to leave the Jukes?

Actually, it's not quite accurate that *Better Days* was my last Jukes recording. I did a live recording with Southside In The Acoustic (Johnny, Bob Bandiera on guitars, David Hayes on acoustic bass guitar, and myself) in Paris in 1995 that was released as *Spittin' Fire*. I also played on a project that Johnny financed and released himself (it seems to have been the beginning of a trend for him that's still apparently going on) called *Ruff Stuff*. That mini-CD contains some of the most interesting music I'd ever done with Johnny, including a song of his called "King of the Night" that's my personal favorite of all his own songs.

I decided to leave the Jukes because I had just gotten serious with the woman who became my wife, and was already helping her raise her two boys from a previous marriage. She and I also had plans to make music together and I had a band called S'killit that had just been signed to a record deal. The deal went sour and I had to get out of it. The label was capsizing and it took us a while to figure that out. I had spent almost 20 years on the road in one band or another and I wanted to stay home now.

I recommended Jeff Kazee to take my place. He was the best cat I knew for the gig and I thought he and Johnny might click. Fortunately, they did. It seems to have turned out really well for both of them. How it happened is that I just called Jeff and asked him if he had eyes to do it and he said yes. Then Johnny agreed to take my word for it about him.

His first gig was apparently a typically chaotic Jukes Jersey extravaganza, but he hung with it (this guy is a man!) He's also subbed for me with the Blues Brothers' Band.

Is the music that you're playing now in a similar R&B style?
Some of the music is similar. The Blues Brothers Band, which is my chief "sideman" gig right now is, of course, pure R&B. My work with my wife involves a few different directions, as we do a lot of "affairs work" (benefits, weddings, parties, etc.) to make the bread and butter. I'm playing a lot more jazz now, which is where I kind of started, and much of the work I do with Claire falls into that category.

In 2000, you released *Every Little Dream*. How has it been to work and record with your wife?
It's been wonderful working with Claire. It's the ultimate in making a life together. We have the wherewithal to integrate work and family and that's very satisfying to both of us. She's a unique songwriter with a musical sensibility all her own, and writing with her has been a great process.

Would you ever consider being part of future Juke reunions or have you basically closed that chapter of your life?
I would always leave it open to participate in Juke reunions. I just haven't done so up until now because I needed the time away to sort of clear my head about the whole experience. I was contacted about bringing S'killit down to participate in the Jukestock event a while back, but I lost patience with some of the people I was dealing with and the process fell apart. I have very mixed memories about my whole association with the "Jersey" scene, but I made a lot of great friends over those years and you don't just "close the chapter" and walk away forever from something like that.

Talking with Joey Stann

longtime member of the Jukes

When and how did you first join the Jukes?
I joined the Jukes in 1980. What happened was that the tour player, Stan Harrison, had decided to leave the band and do something else so I got called to do an audition.

Did you leave after the live album *Reach Up And Touch The Sky* to join Gary U.S. Bonds for a while?
Yeah, because Southside broke up the band for a while at the end of 1980. He had decided to pursue a soap opera acting career, believe it or not. The band actually appeared on "All My Children" for a couple of episodes. So, he went out to California and was staying out there for a while and trying to do that. He came back about 3-4 months into 1981. By then, the Jukes horn section had been asked to play on Gary U.S. Bonds *Dedication* album. They asked the Jukes' horns to play on that record and we played on two cuts, but only one of them was released.

Basically after that they had the Jukes' horn section and they needed a tenor player. And from what I understood at that point Southside had broken up the band. He didn't say he was gonna put it back together again. So, I was asked to join Gary U.S. Bonds' band and I did. I worked for him for around four years from 1981-1984. Then in the beginning of 1985, the tenor player who had taken my place in the Jukes (Frank Elmo) got the offer to go in Julian Lennon's band and Southside gave me a call and asked me if I wanted to come back. And I said yes. I went back in the beginning of 1985 and I've been with him since.

Did you ever imagine being in a band so long?
Umm... I didn't think so, but I've enjoyed the band so much. He works and then he takes some time off. And when he takes time off I work with Bobby Bandiera, who keeps some of the rhythm section together. He has me and Muddy who play in the Jukes and Joe Belia on drums who used to be with the Jukes. So, it's almost like the Jukes band without Southside and a few other people. And I still do gigs with Gary Bonds whenever they don't overlap and I can do a gig with him I do.

The Jukes are going on 30-35 years now. Why do you think the band can keep going?

Well, because we have a good underground following, especially in Europe. We go to Europe and we can sell out. We went there last year, the year before and we're going again this year. The thing is that in Europe we sell a lot more records. Even when we came out with the *Better Days* album we had songs on the charts over there. So, we've had enough hit records in Europe to just keep the band going. And we have enough of a following through the East Coast and through part of the West Coast and, of course, Cleveland, which is our biggest center.

Speaking of Europe, what was Jukestock like? Lots of Juke fans from Europe made the trek to see you guys.

Oh, Jukestock was really nice. We had a great time with that. I know the fans want it to happen again. We got to mingle with the fans because we stayed at the hotel for about three days or so. We'd walk around and have breakfast with them, sign things, we were able to be a little more personal with them and that made a difference.

And I heard that Southside kind of gave you a little push to get your record, *Family Tree,* done in time?

Yeah, it was amazing because he was over at the house when I told him I was doing my own CD. He said, "Let me hear it." So, I brought him to my studio and put it on. He said, "Man, I really like this stuff. How many songs do you have?" I said ten. He said, "If you can get it together in time you can sell it at Jukestock."

I didn't think I'd have it ready, but I got it finished just in time. That's one thing about Southside he'll let you sell your products too, he doesn't have a big ego about that. Anything to help anybody in the band individually, like selling our records or promoting our stuff he's like go ahead and do it.

You've been with the band for a while now, have you noticed a difference with the shows nowadays?

The people seem to like the new songs a lot because a lot more of them are coming from Southside and what he really likes to do as opposed to what the record company tells him to do or somebody else's songs. I mean, the Jukes have been based around Little Steven and his songs but these last two CDs were what Southside wanted to do. He was in complete control of it for the first time ever and the audience really liked that. They liked that he decided to do a blues album because they were telling him to do one for a long time. He's really having more fun like this.

One thing that has always changed is the band's lineup through the years. How crazy is it to have so many musicians come and go? The Jukes are like a Jersey institution...

Yeah it is, but the good thing about that and one of the reasons why Southside does the changes is to keep it fresh. It's like if some guy starts getting bored or whatever and they don't give him 100% on stage then it's time for them to go. He's let a lot of musicians go like that. So, making the changes keeps everything fresh and it keeps everything fresh for him, which means he has more fun with the whole thing. If we had all the same players all of the time and they were just going through the motions and not getting into the music, it would be a drag for all of us. We bring fresh blood into the band and the songs become a little bit different, we feel a little bit different and everyone gets excited again.

Southside is into it more now, I think, than ever before. Especially since he's been doing his own music and just completely taking control of the band. He's mellowed out a lot and he's just having a lot more fun. I've seen him change from the times in 1980 when things were spinning all around. He's calmed down and seems to enjoy things more now.

You're from New York City, did the Asbury Park history mean anything to you before you joined the band?

I was not really aware of what was going on with that until 1980 when I finally joined the Jukes. Then I got the whole history of everything. That's when I started learning about what was going on here and I started playing in the Jersey places. Before that it was all New York.

Speaking of Jersey places, is it still special for you to play the Pony?

It's special to play there because of its history. It's the history of the Jukes and Bruce Springsteen. It's just been the history of the New Jersey sound. This was the center. So, it's a special place and it will always be a special place. Especially to the fans in Europe where they were like, "We can't let the Stone Pony go down." And they came over here and tried to get the officials to save it and Tillie.

Do you almost get the feeling that they care more about it over in Europe than people around here do?

I think they do actually because they feel a part of the history too. It's almost like bigger than life to them because they didn't experience it but they've heard so much about it that it's just grand to them. They really don't want to see it go down. It's just that whole history. It's more like a museum to them.

In addition to playing with the Jukes, you're also a regular member of Bobby Bandiera's Band. How are those shows different from Jukes shows?

I love playing with Bobby, he's great. It's just a smaller level of it because Bobby has the fans too and his fans really like the music. But when you're playing a club it's still a club. It's still playing two or three sets and it's the most fun for a band to play that doesn't have records. It's nowhere near what a show is with the Jukes because the Jukes play a 2 1/2 to 3 hour show and it's a lot more intense. The show with the Jukes are on a bigger stage with a light show and a sound man, it's a whole production. I guess the difference is in the way it's produced and the size of the audience.

Does it ever surprise you that Bobby kind of shies away from taking that leap?

Yeah, it does. I'm not quite sure why he's like that. Whether he likes to take the easier seat and just work with Southside and not be bothered with it or what exactly is going on with it completely. But he does shy away from it. He takes it to a degree, but he's also not a real businessman. It seems like he doesn't want to get a good businessman because I've said that to him. "Why don't you get someone to take charge of your career?" And he's like nah.

I guess for whatever reason he feels more comfortable working with Southside. He's been approached by people who could really do something for him and he just doesn't take it up. Musicians, in general, are not good businessmen. We're just not.

If you were writing a bio on the band, how would you describe Southside Johnny & the Jukes?

It's the same thing that a lot of people say, I think it's the best big-time bar band in the world. I really do. A lot of people love us for that because we don't just go ahead and play the huge shows. Southside, personally, likes the smaller situations where he can make better contact with the audience. He likes to feel the response of the audience on a closer, more personal level. And because of that he really likes more of the places that might only hold 1,000-2,000 people as opposed to doing the places that hold 10,000-20,000. He likes the smaller audiences.

That seems to be the big thing with him and that's why the Jukes are called one of the best bar bands going because he wants to feel the audience... to look into their eyes and get the direct reactions from them. He really enjoys that.

14 Steven Van Zandt

Steven actually created the scene. Well, not the scene, but he changed the Pony from disco to rock and roll.

--TONY AMATO

Little Steven, one of the most influential artists to ever come from the Jersey Shore scene. Photo © Debra L. Rothenberg/rothenbergphoto.com

Few people were as instrumental in creating the "Asbury Sound" as Steven Van Zandt. He was a lead guitarist with Bruce Springsteen and the E Street Band, a key member of Southside Johnny and the Asbury Jukes and basically left his fingerprints on the entire Jersey Shore music scene.

Steven Van Zandt grew up in Middletown and played in several of the area's most popular bands in the 60s. He was a member bands like the Shadows, the Source, Steel Mill and Dr. Zoom and the Sonic Boom. In the early 70s, he was part of the Blackberry Booze Band with Southside Johnny. Back then, everywhere you went you heard disco music and the recently opened Stone Pony was no exception. But Van Zandt talked the owners into letting the band play on the off-nights. Gradually, the band built up a large following. Eventually that band became the Asbury Jukes.

"Steven actually created the scene," said Tony Amato. "Well, not the scene, but he changed the Pony from disco to rock and roll."

Van Zandt joined the E Street Band for the *Born To Run* album, but continued to play a large part in the Jukes. He wrote, played and produced the band's first three albums including the classic *Hearts Of Stone*, which was once named one of the best records of the last twenty years by *Rolling Stone Magazine*.

In 1982, he branched out on his own as Little Steven and released his first solo record entitled *Men Without Women* with a band called Little Steven and the Disciples of Soul. As his career progressed, he became more and more politically active. He left the E Street Band after the *Born In The USA* tour to concentrate on his solo work and his emerging activism - something which, unfortunately, has kept him from becoming a bigger name in the industry.

Little Steven has been working to further human rights since the early 1980s. He spearheaded the hugely successful anti-apartheid Sun City Project and established the Solidarity Foundation in 1985 to support the sovereignty of indigenous peoples. He has been honored twice by the United Nations for his human rights achievements and received the International Documentary Association Award for his film *The Making Of Sun City*.

More recently, Little Steven has seen his career take a new turn when he landed the role of Silvio in the hit television show "The Sopranos." He also started a weekly radio show called "The Underground Garage." And as if acting and being a nationally syndicated DJ wasn't enough, he somehow found time to release *Born Again Savage* and returned to record and tour with the E Street Band for *The Rising*. Busier than ever, Steven remains one of the most important members of the Shore scene.

15 Lance Larson

The strangest feeling is not knowing who you are. For so many years, I wanted to get away from who Lance was. I hated Lance because he was such a clown. And then finally when I wasn't drugging up and when I didn't know who Lance was, I wanted to know him so bad.

--LANCE LARSON

Lance Larson, one of the Shore's most electrifying performers, is shown on stage in Asbury Park. Photo © Debra L. Rothenberg/rothenbergphoto.com

L ance Larson is one of the most popular artists to ever take the stage at a Jersey Shore club. An extremely talented singer and song-writer, Lance was the leader of Lord Gunner Group which developed a following from New Jersey to Maine and down to Virginia. The band regularly played local clubs like the Fastlane and the Stone Pony. They were close to record deals, but something always went wrong. Usually it was due to the "rock and roll lifestyle" of Lance that always seemed to crash and burn at the wrong time.

Lance has been through drug addiction, prison and an incident in which he was nearly beaten to death, but he's come out of it better than ever. In recent years, Lance has seen the release of his first record, *To Make A Long Story Short...* He's opened Lance & Debbie's, a bar in the former location of the Wonder Bar, and had a pair of his songs featured in the CBS television show "Hack." I was able to spend some time with Lance at his club where we talked about the wild ride he's taken through the years.

What were the first bands you had?

My first band was the Spartans. We were basically out of Red Bank. Our guitar player was Vito Genovese's grandson. That's Vito Genovese, the Godfather. I remember we always had to have our rehearsals be done by 2 o'clock on Saturdays because the family had to leave to visit their grandfather. It was like a religion. I remember asking my Mother, "Why do they always have to visit his Grandfather, what is he in the hospital?" And my Mom said, "His grandfather is a well known man."

I was always a solo acoustic guitar player. As far as bands go I had the Spartans, Cahoots, Cold, Blast & Steel, Lord Gunner Group, Lance Larson & the Heat, Travis Larson and Lance Larson & the Power. Travis Larson was a country band I put together. One time our opening act didn't show up for a club date in Long Branch, so they asked Travis to open. We actually had Travis Larson open up for Lance Larson! That's when you know you've made it. Travis played country songs that I had written. I wound up getting paid twice and, I'll be honest with you, Travis went over better than Lance!

What do you remember best about the Lord Gunner period?

I remember it was confusing as shit because we had been in some other local bands but Lord Gunner started getting on the mainstream. We took over the Jukes spot at the Pony and were playing there two days a week, but we were also working seven days a week touring from here to Maine. We started playing places in Maine, West Virginia, Washington, DC. We were touring!

It was confusing. No longer did we just play the Pony one night, wake up the next day and play a gig down the street. We were traveling. We were playing... We changed musicians as we went along whenever we had to. It was like a circus. And it was a circus. But it was a lot of fun and I'd never change any of those days.

How close did Lord Gunner get to making it big?
We were real close. We had big dreams, but I don't think my writing was... everybody thought I was a good writer and all this bullshit. But I didn't feel it inside me. I really didn't. I didn't feel like I was ready yet. Basically, I think that if you had handed me $200,000 dollars in those days I wouldn't be sitting here doing this interview. Because I was just a kid. We were enjoying it, I just wish I took what I did then and had more of a business sense. I wish I was more serious about my music... more disciplined. I was only writing because nobody else was doing it. I wasn't a great writer, I was just the only one who was writing.

One of your "undisciplined" times took place at a recording studio in New York City where you showed up late more than once.
That was with a very big producer. Now you've got to understand Sly Stone from Sly & the Family Stone was my roommate after Sly made it. I toured with him and then he moved in with me. Sly was the guy I looked up to and he's got the worst record of showing up to gigs, so I think the guy who I put on my pedestal was the worst guy in the world for me.

I hooked up with Sly as the opening act at the Fastlane, that's where I met him. Then we became very good friends. They went out on the road and we kept in touch and every time he came through Jersey he came to my house. We hung out and he did a lot of shows with me. I always respected Sly as a songwriter. He was a phenomenal musician. And I'm saying, "Look at this writer, how talented he is and how uncontrolled he is." He was a genius when it came to music. And I sort of respected guys like him and Warren Zevon... guys that lived on the edge. It just seemed that I saw eye to eye on things with these guys and they were the guys I respected.

What do you think of your songs from back then when you hear them now?
I hate my old music. A lot of the old stuff I listen to it and it's like, oh that was nice right there, but then I think I could have done much better with it. I still write. I'm a better writer now. I'm a better singer now. I'm more disciplined.

In a lot of ways it's rather amazing that you're still alive today. What do you remember about your accident back in 1993?

I was at a construction job. It was December 2nd, 1993. I was beat up real bad. I literally spent six months to a year in speech therapy. I lost my memory. Had a plate put in my head, I got beat up real bad. I was beat by four guys with my own hammer. The bad thing is getting beat by your own God damn hammer.

To this day, I notice that it's very frustrating for me to form words. I'm not as fast as I used to be. I'm a better writer now, lyrically and in forming things, but I can't give you something fast. Back in those days when we did those songs half of the lyrics weren't written. I made a lot of the stuff up on the spot. I'd have been a great rap writer back then like in that movie *8 Mile*. Today, I have a problem with my thoughts. Everything's got to go a little slower, but then once I've got it I'm good. I find myself frustrated because I can't do what I'm used to doing. Back then, I could be loaded or drugged up but I was still on the ball and everything was under control. A couple of guys have made jokes and said, "Lance, that has nothing to do with your accident it's all the drugs you took." No, it was my accident. I didn't know who anybody was. I didn't know who my Mom was. Bruce (Springsteen) had been calling me but when the nurses told me I didn't even know who Bruce was. I was very confused. I didn't know who my best friends were and I wasn't allowed to see any friends, although a few snuck up there.

The strangest feeling is not knowing who you are. For so many years, I wanted to get away from who Lance was. I hated Lance because he was such a clown. And then finally when I wasn't drugging up and when I didn't know who Lance was, I wanted to know him so bad. I didn't know who he was and I had to start from scratch. I had to start at the bottom like a baby and it was really frustrating.

Did the memories come back?

Oh yeah, they came back and they told me they were gonna come back, but they didn't want them to come back too fast. If they come back too fast you can't reason with it and you can really go into a deep depression. I had psychiatrists and psychologists - the whole nine yards. That's why they didn't let my friends talk to me for about a year and a half. They didn't want anybody to talk about old memories. I didn't know I played guitar. I didn't know I was a songwriter. I had no conception about what I even did. The strange thing about it was that while I was in there John Luraschi's brother, Eddie, was in the hospital. He was brought in because he got badly burned in a fire.

I had been there probably a month and a half when they wheeled me down in a wheelchair and I saw this guy who had bandages all over him. He looked like the "Invisible Man." And he said, "Lance." Now everybody's been calling me Lance for a few weeks so I'm starting to understand that I'm this guy Lance. He says, "Lance, you used to rehearse in my house with my brother Johnny and these other guys like Ricky D and you played keyboards." (I was a keyboard player back then.) I'm looking at him and he says, "Lance, believe me. I know you... You're Lance Larson." They told me to just go along with whatever my Mom said or anybody else said. So, I was just sort of joking with him and said, "Yeah, whatever you say."

The only person who even spoke to me was Eddie Luraschi. He talked with me every day and he wasn't supposed to. He'd tell me things like, "Lance, you left your organ and went to Las Vegas one time. You left your organ in my basement for so long that we were going to sell it." He's telling me stuff like this and all of a sudden I'm starting to remember. I'm remembering a little bit of Wall Township where we rehearsed back then. Man, that's weird! It's a weird feeling and you start getting depressed. And just when I begin to remember Eddie dies. When Eddie died I lost it because he was my memory.

I experienced problems after that too, drug problems, because I was on the pain killers and I had to deal with that. The pain killer was morphine and that didn't help me because it brought me back into it. You get very dependent on it. That was my life blood. Here I am finally getting my memory back and then I hear things we used to do. I ended up relying on the morphine. So all of a sudden they cut me off of the Percostats and no more morphine. I don't get to hit the button anymore and get that feeling which mellows me out. I was so confused and when I started seeing the past it worried me and I got so depressed that I needed that drug to help me forget. So here I am, I'm back to drugs and I went back to heroin.

What were you anxious to forget?
I'll be honest with you. I wanted to forget because I didn't feel like I was that Lance. I felt that those guys actually killed me. I really felt that I was killed inside. Whatever I had left in me, whatever dreams were inside, whatever I felt in my heart and my writing I didn't have that feeling anymore. I used to feel I had a connection to writing and I felt they took it away. In my mind, I couldn't write anymore. I didn't feel I was that Lance. I lost a big part of me. A victim of a crime is like a rape victim, they take away something from you.

It was a robbery, I believe on my boss. They thought I was him because it was payday and he probably was carrying about $3000. They just hit the wrong guy. It's not just the idea of getting your ass kicked it's that I had it kicked and I didn't get a chance to know who did it or how it was done. I had no idea. The only person who knew that was the old lady who saw it from her apartment four stories up. She called the police and when the police got there I was dead. Asbury Park revived me. The Asbury Park Fire Department saved me because I was dead several times. It's weird but at times I feel like I did die and this has already happened. I believe that you and me have already done this interview.

Do you think that you're still on the hospital bed?
No, the hospital bed is just another place. I believe that this is in my mind. I really believe that at times. The only thing that tells me that it's not is that I think God is showing me all of the good things I can still do. I feel that God has given me a second chance and that I can do some good. I don't feel like I was doing anything before. Since I've come out of this I've done benefits for things like drug addiction and I look at life differently. There are times I really feel scared because I think that at any minute I'll find out that this isn't real.

The only thing that lets me know that this hasn't happened is my girlfriend Debbie. She's been the most understanding person I've ever met in my life. That's why I know that this hasn't happened because I know I'd remember her more if this already happened. I guess if she wasn't there I'd still figure I was in some sort of maze. Debbie pulls it all together and then I know that this is really happening.

After I picked up a guitar and started writing again, I couldn't put everything together. But I felt I became a better writer. It was so easy. The puzzle was much easier for me. I now have control of that guy inside of me. It seemed like he needed to get the ass kicked out of him for me to control him.

What was it like when after all these years you finally had a Lance Larson record in your hands?
If felt real good. To me, it felt great to finally get something out. After so many years between Lord Gunner and playing. I was always so protective of my music. I always wanted to make sure that it was released by the right people because I know how this business can be. Then I heard about how you could put it on the computer and sell it through the website. I said to myself, hell I don't need a record company, I'll do it myself. And that's basically why I did it.

How did you choose which songs you were going to use?

That's a good question. I guess I wanted to give a variety of stuff. We recorded a lot of songs. I had so many from years of recording. I mean, there's so many Lord Gunner songs like "Soldier," and "The Way She Makes Me Feel," and "Passion and Pain" - these were the songs we were remembered for. And after Lord Gunner I did a lot of new stuff, but none of those are on this and everybody's asking me where's "Angel of Broken Wings" and others. Where are all the songs that I was pretty well known for as an original writer?

I wanted to show the other side of me, a different side of my writing which I did a few years after that along with things up to the current time. So, I want to release another one and bring back a lot of the older stuff. Just for the fans to have it, for the old Lord Gunner fans and everybody to have a piece of that music. That's my next record and I've got them in the can. It's just a matter of going into the studio and remixing them a bit.

One of the songs will be on the television show "Hack" on CBS on April 4th. It's the one with me and Bon Jovi called, "Listen To Your Heartbeat." And what's great about it is that they didn't pick it because of Bon Jovi, they picked it because of the writing. They didn't even know Bon Jovi was on it! I had to tell them that. So, that was nice. I left Jon a phone message two days ago. I told him as a joke, "Hey buddy, the things I've got to do for you to get you discovered!" Because I used to take him on as our opening act. It's always been a joke. In fact, when Tico left the band and told me that he was gonna go take a shot with Jon I said, "Good luck, but I think you're making a big mistake. We've been together for two years, don't leave right now because we're on the verge of it. You're making a big mistake." A few years later when they were playing in Miami, I saw Tico and the guys and they were all busting my chops. They were like, "Oh yeah, you made a big mistake Tico!"

Those guys turned out to be very supportive of me. They were my opening act and when Jon made it he came back and said, "Lance, what can we do for you?" Anything I wanted they'd be in there to help me musically. They're the greatest guys in the world. They never forgot about the home guys... no doubt about it.

I heard you once tried an interesting approach to getting a record deal and it kind of backfired...

Bon Jovi and Tico and the guys were always telling me how I should go down to Nashville. The Bon Jovi Band was in Nashville once and they saw how the publishers were all down there. They said, "Lance you'd be great down there."

I said, "I ain't got the money to go to Nashville." So what do I do? I look across the street from my house and I know those people are gone each winter. So, I say I'm gonna apply for a credit card and send it to their address. I applied for a card and they gave me one with a $10,000 limit. I applied under a false name and it was sent to the place across the street where I took it. I said, man this is easy... Two weeks later I got $20,000, then $30,000 then $40,000. I got all these credit cards under different names. I'm flying all over the country. I'm going everywhere flying first class and staying at the best hotels. I went down to Nashville and tried selling my songs. I actually tried getting myself discovered on a stolen credit card!

Then I got caught. The one thing is that I did a lot to help society when I came back. They held me for four months at Monmouth County and I got 3-5 years in a federal penitentiary but they released me. They didn't send me away because I told them how I did it and I paid full restitution. Westwood Music came in and gave me a publishing deal. I paid restitution for exactly what I spent and I never had to serve my time. I served my time by doing good things for society and that's better than being put in a prison cell. I learned from my mistakes. Between that happening and everything else it certainly gave me more to write about.

Since that happened and we've been doing benefits for Jersey Shore Addiction Services for other addicts, I've been clean and I feel great. I feel real good about myself. We still keep a night open for them at the club and it was packed last week. And these are the guys that I grew up with who were cocaine addicts and alcoholics. I'm looking around the room and seeing everybody feeling normal again. So, it's good that I didn't die. It's good to give back... and that is a reward to me. That's worth more to me than any dollar. It's living every day, living day to day and keeping myself as straight as possible and trying to do good. And I know my hits are right around the corner.

How would you like to be remembered?

Woulda, coulda, shoulda... did! I'd like to be remembered not for what other people remember me by - don't forget I've had this accident - I want to be remembered for what I can remember. I'm not concerned with what other people remember. But as far as for me, I want to remember that you've got to have your dream. With all of the woulda, coulda, shouldas there's always an "I did it."

16 Billy Hector

The thing is you have to play. You really have no choice. If you're singing when you wash the dishes and then you get done and say, "Oh shit, let me play that song" - it's a part of you.

--BILLY HECTOR

Billy Hector, one of the best blues guitarists along the Shore, is shown here. Photo © Debra L. Rothenberg/rothenbergphoto.com

Billy Hector has been a fixture on the Jersey Shore scene since the 70s. Now recognized as one of the best blues guitarists in the state, Hector once played in classic R&B and rock bands like the Shots, Paul Whistler & the Wheels and Hot Romance before forming the Fairlanes and his current band.

He continues to be one of the hardest working musicians on the Shore, and recently released his 11th record, *Out Of Order* that was recorded at the Pony. I spoke with him via phone about his long and historic career.

When did you first start doing gigs in the area?
Well, when I was sixteen, I started playing with Tony Palligrosi in Lavallette and he got us gigs like the Pancake House and the Yacht Club. We were underage. My father bought a house in Ocean Grove in 1968. So I was down here all the summers from 1968 on.

Tony also brought you into the Shots, right?
Yes. Tony got into the Jukes and when he left the Jukes he formed the Shots. He called me up. I was playing in bands in North Jersey. I was playing with any band I could play with at the time. The Shots were alright. We were a good band. We played the Pony, we played Sturfield Manor. The Shots actually played D'Jais for August of 1977. We played the matinee in the afternoon from 3-8. That's five sets, 40 on, 20 off. And then we'd do it again starting at ten. We were only there for a month. I think Terry McGovern was running the place at the time.

We definitely had it easier than Southside & the Jukes. They started from scratch. We came in and there was a scene already there. Tony just got it to last longer in a way.

Were you guys playing mostly covers?
We were playing mostly covers. Rhythm & blues, obscure covers that nobody still knows these days. Songs like "Lovie Dovey." I still play some of that. And D'Jais had ten beers for a dollar. So that was a pretty raucous month. And tiring, 10 sets in a day is a long time.

Back then everybody was paying attention to the Asbury scene. What was it like having the record executives at the club?
Well, I didn't see any of them. I think they were there. Yeah, I was in awe of the scene. I was like 21. I don't even think I was 21. I think I may have just turned 21, I'm not sure. Eighteen year-olds could drink then so it didn't matter. There were more people going out then too. It wasn't illegal to drink and drive, I guess. There wasn't stops and things like that.

It was exciting. You know, I was coming from small clubs and I was actually studying music at the time too. It was a professional thing and I could actually make enough money to live on. That was a big deal. Plus it was the scene that Bruce created and he came up and jammed with the band. He knew all the Asbury Park guys. They had all that hype even before I moved down here. But I knew Tony and that's how I could get into the scene. It was easier than just coming in from North Jersey.

I went to a few jams at the Warehouse when I was eighteen. A Monday night jam. I went to a jam or two there. They were pretty cold, you know. It was tough to break in there. It was like I was the new kid. I'd come in and everybody's got a bad attitude. "Get the hum out of that amp!" "What song are you gonna play? You better know how to play that song." That's what they were telling me. I'm like geez guys. That's where I met John Luraschi. I met him there and Stanley Steele was there playing. The guys from Daze, they were there playing. But you could tell it wasn't a warm and fuzzy scene. I don't know if it was competitive, but you couldn't just walk in. Something had to happen.

Then after a few years you were with Paul Whistler.
Yeah, then I went with Paul. Tony sort of got that together, got the Wheels together. Got me involved anyway. Since the Shots were defunct at that time, for a year or two, he got that together with Paul. I was there when the Wheels started. The Wheels used to rehearse in the Fastlane's basement because the owner of the Fastlane was sort of our benefactor. He said he was gonna get us all this work and stuff but we were just in that basement practicing every day. He was buying me Burger King hamburgers. That was a rough time there. The guy felt sorry for us so he'd give us odd jobs like when the club had a big show. I was a bouncer at the Rockpile show. I was a roadie for the Ramones when they came in. Things like that because the guy wasn't doing shit for us. We were just young artists, young musicians, whatever we were. Little street urchins just trying to get over. Those were strange experiences.

A little later on, you were part of Hot Romance, the house band at Mrs. Jays. What was that time like?
It was a biker bar that some tourists would go into. *(laughs)* It wasn't that bad then. Some days were worse than others. But I played there for a long time. Hot Romance played there and the Pony. We played Wednesdays with Lance Larson for a long time through the winter and that was fun because we liked Lance. We were friends and buddies and stuff like that. It was a really good time.

We played the Pony and Mrs. Jays. We played Mrs. Jays on Sunday when Bruce would show up to play with Cats. So basically everybody was hustling to get into the Pony so we got the overflow and folks that really wanted to hear us.

Was the Fairlanes basically the same lineup as your current band?
No, not really because we started out of the Renegade Blues Band that David Myers got together with him and Big Danny and Steve Schreager and Billy Lilly. They were all playing in there. The Renegade Blues Band was playing in Point Pleasant Beach and any other place we could get because nobody was really interested in that music. And really, not that many are interested in it now. But, in the early 80s, nobody really gave a shit about that and we were playing places for drinks.

There's a few more places because we stuck it out there. Plus Stevie Ray made it and Robert Cray and that definitely helped things out. But before that, that's why we picked the name Fairlanes. We definitely had to get the blues out of the name because that would squash your chances for getting any kind of employment, which is what I wanted to do. I wanted to work. I don't know why. I put the two things together.

Yeah, it's always harder. Especially now, people don't go out. The guys that saw me in their twenties are now in their thirties and they're just too tired to come out anymore. The demographics of the bar scene is very strange. It's a strange animal.

Where's your favorite place to play now?
My favorite club to play? Oh, I don't know if I can say. That's politically incorrect. The places where they dance and go nuts.

You play five or six nights a week on average, that's a pretty grueling schedule. What keeps you going every night?
Oh, I like to play. I gotta play. I play when I'm not playing. *(laughs)* The thing is you have to play. You really have no choice. If you're singing when you wash the dishes and then you get done and say, "Oh shit, let me play that song" - it's a part of you.

17 Cats: The Ultimate House Band

It's hard to believe that with such a multi-talented band of great performers and writers. Our biggest concern was who wants to sing "White Wedding."

--FRAN SMITH JR.

One of the many lineups of Cats on a Smooth Surface. The members from left to right include: Glen Burtnick, Fran Smith Jr., Ray Anderson, Bobby Bandiera and Peter Gagan. Photo courtesy of Fran Smith Jr.

The Stone Pony has always prided itself on being a great judge of talent. Ever since Southside Johnny & the Jukes put the club on the map, every house band at the Pony has been thrust into the spotlight. It's a hard job to acquire but one that instantly catches the eyes and ears of record company executives. The list of success stories include such bands as John Eddie & the Front Street Runners, Clarence Clemons and the Red Bank Rockers, the Smithereens, the Outcry and Highway 9 and, of course, Southside Johnny & the Jukes. Ironically, the band that just might have had the title of most famous house band in America never made that list.

Cats on a Smooth Surface arrived on the scene at the end of the 70s and held the title of house band for many years at the Stone Pony. They were the ultimate cover band, perfect for warming up a crowd and getting them in the mood for a great night. Cats could play the latest hits on the radio just as easily as classics from the 50s or 60s. Unfortunately, they might have been a victim of their own success. Cover bands were very popular along the Shore at the time. Since Cats did covers so well, it made it very difficult for the band to take it to the next level of performing original songs. After a while, band members would get frustrated and leave. Thus starting a revolving door of musicians for the band.

The band's lineup was constantly changing. In many ways, Cats was like the "Yardbirds" of New Jersey. Wave after wave of great musicians would sharpen their skills in the band and then move on to bigger and better things. Each time someone left, the band would bring in someone new, reload, refocus and keep going. They became an institution.

"Cats had a reputation of being a house band or party band," said Glen Burtnick, a member of the band in the early 80s. "Basically, they were like a training ground for Jersey musicians. You'd learn the ropes of being in a band, get disciplined and a feel for the job."

Lee Mrowicki, the disc jockey at the Stone Pony, said that, "Any musician that joined Cats instantly gained recognition. The band continued to have good musicians join because they wouldn't put anybody in the band who wasn't up to their standards. They always had tremendously talented people."

Burtnick was part of the Cats lineup generally thought of as the best in the band's history. His bandmates included Bobby Bandiera, Fran Smith Jr. and Ray Andersen. Each of the four would go on to very successful musical careers. At the time, Bobby Bandiera was clearly the leader. He had already built a reputation around the Shore from playing in Holme, one of the top acts of the day and was developing into one of the premier frontmen in the area.

Glen Burtnick was back in New Jersey after portraying Paul McCartney in Beatlemania and playing in bands like Jan Hammer Group and Helmet Boy. Fran Smith Jr. was already a veteran of the Jersey Shore scene from his days as a member of the Shakes, a former house band at the Stone Pony. Ray Andersen had been playing in bands in North Jersey when he was spotted by Bill Thompson, the sound guy for Cats at the time.

Ray had just left a club band called the Features, which mostly played clubs in the northern part of New Jersey. "Bill Thompson had told Bobby about me," said Andersen. "He goes, 'You gotta see this guy he does an amazing Billy Idol.' And Billy told Bobby, 'This is just the guy you need in your band, just the ingredient you need. He gets on the ground, he jumps around.' I remember there were people from Billy Idol's label at the time, Chrysalis, that used to come to see me and said I did a better Billy Idol than he did!

"So that was it," continued Andersen. "Bobby called me up. He goes, 'Hey man, I heard about you. My sound guy told me about you. Come on down for rehearsal so I can check you out, you know.' So I went down to Allaire Airport, the rehearsal studio there. I walked in and I remember doing 'Should I Stay or Should I Go?' by the Clash. I was like on the ground, crawling around and Bobby was looking at me like holy shit! He goes, 'Can you play the piano because we need somebody to play piano... to tickle the ivories.' So we started doing 'Great Balls Of Fire' and I'm not kidding I never really played like that type of showy piano, but when I auditioned for Bobby we did it and it was like all of a sudden I knew how to play it. It was the strangest thing. It's like I kind of lit up. The next day he called me and said, 'Alright, let's do it.' And that was that, I was in Cats."

The band found themselves in the news when Bruce Springsteen began showing up at the shows and jamming with them. In fact, Bruce enjoyed playing with the band so much that it became a regular occurrence on Sundays, which was Cats' regular night at the Pony.

"I don't think it was anything special but really the timing," said Mrowicki. "Sunday night was usually the night Bruce would go out and Cats would be playing on a Sunday night."

According to Stephen Bumball, one of the co-founders of the Asbury Park Rock 'N Roll Museum, Springsteen began playing with Cats around 1982. "Initially they were just a real good band which he would guest with to do cover songs," said Bumball. "He seemed comfortable with the band because they had musicians which had been around the scene for a while. He played with them consistently for several years. It became almost like a tradition, when he wanted to play he'd jam with Cats."

Jamming with Springsteen was quite an experience for these young musicians. "One time I saw Bruce walking on by and I was like telling him to come on stage," remembers Glen Burtnick. "It was the stupidest thing I ever did! Here I was jamming with him on 'Twist and Shout' and then he tells me to take over the vocals. And I'm thinking, how do you top Bruce?"

Ray Andersen compares it to playing on stage with one of the Beatles. "I grew up a Beatles freak," explains Andersen. "I still am to this day. I never got to jam with one of those guys, but years before I was on the same stage with Bruce I was also fanatical about the guy. I loved him. He just breathed passion in his music and in his words. And when he came on stage it was... well, what can I say? It was a dream for me. It's like if Paul McCartney were to call me down and jam with me. It was fantastic!"

Fran Smith Jr. jokes that Bruce may have "played more with Cats than some of the actual band members did. But it really was an inspiration to be on stage up close and personal with the Boss. I think it made me a better performer just singing on the same microphone and playing bass with him."

"One thing about the Asbury scene when you played the Pony and stuff you really had to be on your toes," added Andersen. "I cut my teeth at the Pony, man. Just being a musician it was so good for me. Even though I always wanted to be a front person myself, it was like rock and roll army for me. It was so cool."

Although it was happening quite often, each time Springsteen joined Cats on stage it made the news. At first it was just reported in local newspapers like the *Asbury Park Press*, but soon the news spread around the world. Cats found themselves in the pages of *Rolling Stone* and *Backstreets Magazine*, a publication devoted to Springsteen news. The band was even got mentioned on MTV, an unbelievable amount of press for a houseband. "It was crazy," said Andersen. "You get that and you say we've gotta use this... parlay it."

But, for the longest time, Cats never did make much of an effort to get rid of its cover band image. Even with a lineup full of fine songwriters and great musicians, the band continued to play few originals.

"It's hard to believe that with such a multi-talented band of great performers and writers," recalls Smith. "Our biggest concern was who wants to sing 'White Wedding.' Glen and I wrote a bunch of tunes in those days but, in all honesty, the clubs in the early 80s really did not want to hear songs they've never heard before. As fun as it was, it too was very frustrating not being able to play any originals, but I truly loved playing with those guys!"

Glen Burtnick was another member who felt limited by having to play cover songs in Cats. "It was a very talented group of players," said Burtnick. "Not only when I was in it but before and after. At the point I was involved I could tell it was a strong bunch of individual players but we were basically about doing cover tunes. We were a dance band. I had a problem with that. It was unrealized potential. Sadly, it was probably always that way. We each had to split up to create something original."

"My God, we had so much talent there," added Andersen. "I think we had too much talent. We just couldn't harness it. We had too many individualists. Not to say that we argued, but there was too much going on. The pot was just huge with so many ingredients. There was never really any talk about working on a record or anything like that. We all had separate originals that we brought to the project. And after we became kind of popular we started integrating those songs but we only did a couple because we really wanted to give the people what they wanted. Yeah, it's something. I don't know why we didn't really pursue it headstrong.

"But, even though it was a cover band we always jammed on things and I think that's what people really loved," said Andersen. "We were really diverse. We had so many people giving us so many different styles to the music. It was quite interesting. People were very entertained by us. There were always people jamming with us from notable bands."

Years later bootleg tapes of those jams with Springsteen are readily available from collectors via the Internet. Thousands of people have probably heard Cats on a Smooth Surface without even knowing it. They've seen pictures of the band jamming with Bruce but to them they were just a band that backed Bruce a bunch of times in New Jersey. Sadly, that's not too far from the truth. Once the word got out that Bruce had been playing with Cats, fans of the Boss started packing the club each night the band played - just hoping for a Bruce sighting.

"It was mostly exhilarating," said Burtnick. "But I gotta tell ya, there were times when the audience was awful. If Bruce was even rumored to be stopping by they'd crowd up against the stage and stare at us with complete indifference. We'd sometimes be the boring nobodies until the big shot got up to play with us. But Bruce was always solid and really on. He was always unforgettable."

Glen Burtnick was the first to leave the band. Shortly after leaving, he joined La Bamba & the Hubcaps and then embarked on a solo career. He would later become a member of Styx. Vinnie Daniele took over Glen's spot in Cats. Bobby Bandiera was next to go, replacing Billy Rush in Southside Johnny & the Jukes. Fran Smith Jr. joined the Hooters and Ray

Andersen would find success with Blue Van Gogh and later became a member of Meatloaf. He is currently performing as Mr. Ray and writing songs for kids in the Beatles style.

Just as it had before, Cats on a Smooth Surface went on. The band brought in new people and remained a very popular band. Vinnie Daniele, a talented songwriter, tried taking Cats to the next level. They put out a single and even recorded a demo. David Prater, who produced Burtnick's second record, did the production work. For the first time the band was trying hard to make it on their own rather than as solo acts. Unfortunately, the band never did get their break.

Cats will always be remembered for those special times at the Stone Pony when Bruce Springsteen would turn an average night into something magical. But, for a few years, the band had four incredibly talented musicians who all would wind up in highly successful bands. That's an incredible feat when you think about it.

The Stone Pony continued to have great house bands in the years after Cats. Bands such as La Bamba & the Hubcaps, the Outcry and Samhill (currently playing as Highway 9) were all house bands at one time or another. But the memories of that particular lineup of Cats are still strong for many fans along the Jersey Shore. When you saw them take the stage you just knew you were seeing something special. So next time you're at the Stone Pony waiting for the headliner to arrive, pay a little attention to the guys on stage. You just might be seeing a glimpse of the future as well.

18 Glen Burtnick

There are Styx fans out there who think of me as only a member of that band. There are Marshall Crenshaw fans who consider me his backup musician. I have a giant closet at home filled with hats. I wear a million of 'em.

--GLEN BURTNICK

Glen Burtnick shown in a publicity shot from 2002.

Glen Burtnick is a singer songwriter from the New Brunswick area that has been entertaining fans along the Jersey Shore since the early 80s. His first big break was when he auditioned and got the role of Paul McCartney in the West Coast production of Beatlemania alongside Marshall Crenshaw as John Lennon. From there he went on to stints in the Jan Hammer Band and Helmet Boy before returning to New Jersey where he married his high school sweetheart.

He joined the popular Stone Pony house band, Cats on a Smooth Surface and became a favorite of the Asbury Park crowd. After Cats, he played with La Bamba & the Hubcaps and then started a solo career which led to a record deal with A&M Records. Years later he joined Styx replacing Tommy Shaw and organized a bunch of musicians in the New Brunswick area into an all-star band called Slaves of New Brunswick.

Glen currently performs and records records both solo and with Styx. The year 2003 should see the release of the latest Styx record and a solo record by Burtnick. I caught up with Glen after one of his solo shows at the Stone Pony and he agreed to be interviewed via email. Apparently, the look at his past was therapeutic because he continued to examine his career in an issue of an online newsletter sent to his mailing list.

Many people still remember when you opened for Southside at the Garden State Arts Center and you lit your guitar on fire.
Growing up with Jimi Hendrix as my all time favorite rock performer, I used to be prone to occasionally pulling some of his stunts (I still do, actually, although on a much less risky level). The fire bit was one such wacky exercise. I used to buy cheap guitars and set them ablaze before smashing 'em up on stage. What a nut. It was probably more fun for me than it was for the audience…

I was always honored to open for the Jukes anytime I was asked. Being a Jersey boy, I feel a certain admiration for and loyalty to Johnny and his music. It ain't punk, it ain't super original, but it's full of heart. Besides, he's got a bit of an "underdog" appeal. I dig that too.

Years later, you returned to the Arts Center performing with Styx and rattled off a rather bitter monologue directed at the place.
The rant I gave at the 2001 Styx show wasn't as much bitter as an opportunity to rile up my hometown audience about the annoying currently popular habit of renaming familiar beloved venues (like the Garden State Arts Center) with some corporation's moniker (like PNC Bank) for a price. I also got to let off a little steam about the lies of politicians in the past regarding the Garden State Parkway.

And on top off all that, the PNC bank was actually giving me a hard time over something stupid that very week. Here's exactly what I said:

Anybody remember when this used to be called the Garden State Arts Center? This building was built and operated by the Garden State Parkway... Have you heard of that road?

It's kind of a little ironic...I gotta tell you a story - when I was a little kid my father told me about the Garden State Parkway...We got on the Parkway and we were tossing our nickels or something into the thing and he told me this was paying for the building of the Garden State Parkway and eventually the day would come when there would be no more tolls. That's what my father told me, way back when dinosaurs roamed the earth.

Like I said, so this is built and operated by the Garden State Parkway...but now, it's the PNC Arts Center, ladies and gentlemen. You know, I have a PNC bank account, right? I swear to God, three days ago I wanted to get some money out of this account, the man said you can take this money out of the account any time you want, it's your money, you can take it out any time you want. So three days ago I wanted to take money out of the PNC bank, I had to wait - he told me I had to wait like a week or something.

I said, "Wait - it's my money" and he says, "Well...you gotta wait a week to get it." I said, "Yeah, but I'm playing at the PNC Arts Center on Saturday night!"

I said, "Dude!"

Alright, so I got screwed by PNC. It's ok. It's alright. Just like I got screwed by the PNC bank, I got screwed by the Garden State Parkway, cause I keep putting quarters in the damn thing. The way I see it, you and I pay for this house every time we throw quarters in the goddamn machine! You know what I'm saying? Am I right? Is it me? It's time to take this place back!

I hereby declare that the name of this house is the Garden State Arts Center! At which point the audience was cheering, pretty explosively as I recall, and I felt somewhat vindicated.

Is it true that the Arts Center banned you after the guitar incident?
As much as I'm tickled by such a myth, the Arts Center never "banned" me. I'm not sure they ever noticed me at all!

How did you get involved with Styx? Were you a fan?
We were introduced through A&M Records, our shared label. I wasn't a fan, Tommy and I shared a manager and most Styx fans accepted me.

Let's go back in time... It's been written that your first gig was a "Be-In" in Johnson's Park. What do you remember about that day?
Wow! Your research is frightening! It was around 1967. I was such a teeny bopper. It was cold. Sunny. I showed up wearing denim and flowers, with an acoustic guitar. I sang a song I'd written to whoever would listen. I'm sure it was psychedelic and sucked.

What were some of your early bands like?
My list of bands runs long. In elementary school I was in the Ultra Reds. It was a very odd 4 man group - trumpet, accordion, clarinet and myself on drums! In junior high I was in Creeping Fungus Blues Band. In high school I was in Green Spit, Bonji and Otto. Out of high school it was Albatross, Phlyte Ensemble and Source.

Albatross had a rock opera called *Walls of Walden*. Was this based on Thoreau? Who did you think you were Pete Townshend?
I wrote it with Dusty Micale. We only performed it once. It was a story about cryonics and a family's dealing with it in the future. It was probably God awful. Yes, I was aware of Thoreau and probably did think I was Pete Townshend or something at the time.

Who were some of your favorite musicians and early influences?
Yikes! The small list of heroes is Hendrix, Dylan and the Beatles. The long list is from Aaron Copeland to Stevie Wonder to Pete Seeger to Aretha Franklin to Todd Rundgren to Oscar Peterson to Yes to Nirvana.

The first show I remember caring about was when my folks took me to the Latin Casino to see Ray Charles. Also, they took me to see Freddy and the Dreamers and the Supremes early on. The first concert I paid and made my own way to was Richie Havens.

How did you become part of Beatlemania? In pictures, you really did look like McCartney. What was that experience like for you?
I had seen advertisements in the *Village Voice*, looking for Beatle look alikes. Then a guy I knew (Joe Vadala, later of Joey and the Works) persuaded me to go audition. I had droopy eyes, a Wings era McCartney mullet and was left handed. For that, I passed the audition as Paul and began going to "Beatle College" - learning the music and the parts, particularly McCartney's. What a thing.

Having grown up under the profound influence of the Beatle phenomenon, putting on the clothes, strapping on the Hofner and becoming a fake Beatle was kind of a dream come true for me.

The two best things about the show were closely studying some of that ridiculously fantastic music's construction and meeting some wonderful people, many who I still consider dear friends.

You met Marshall Crenshaw through Beatlemania. Together, you guys recorded the single, "I Hate Disco Music."
That rare little chestnut was Marshall's song, filled with funny lines. We called ourselves the Sides. I wrote the B Side (it stunk). It was 1978. By then, many musicians our age had had it with the previous five or so years of that annoying, incessant bass drum rhythm shoved down our throats. Little did we realize that disco was a style that will probably outlive all of us.

And then you got involved with the Jan Hammer Band. How did that come about?
After Beatlemania, I answered yet another *Village Voice* ad. It went something like this: "Jan Hammer is looking for a lead singer/rhythm keyboardist." Having been an admirer of Jan's, I answered the ad and got the gig in the band called Hammer. We put out an album on Elektra's Asylum Records and toured a little.

A few years later, after having done a record as a member of Helmet Boy, Jan asked me to come work with him and Neal Schon on their second record for Columbia as a duo. In addition to working on other tracks on the album, I co-wrote the single with them "No More Lies" and played bass and sang back-up. It was great fun working with those two cats and it was the certainly most successful release I had been involved with up to that point in my career which ain't saying so much. They didn't tour to promote that record, and I didn't appear in the video, but my solo voice could clearly be heard at one or two points in the song.

Speaking of Helmet Boy, whatever happened to that band?
David Leon, another friend of mine from Beatlemania, called and asked if I wanted to join his band. They were managed by Freddy DeMann (who went on to manage Madonna). I enjoyed the short lived experience. We put out one album on Elektra/Asylum. Never got played. We musta been a tax write off for the label.

What was the first song of yours that you ever heard on the radio?
I live near New Brunswick, New Jersey, home of Rutgers University. One night I heard "I Hate Disco Music" being played on the Rutgers student radio station WRSU while in my car driving on Route 27, pulling into the Surrey Inn. It was a thrill, but I was all alone.

Now that I think of it, I had heard a recording of Otto, a trio which played my songs, on local AM station WCTC and I'd appeared on a Public TV show "New Art By Now People" both while in high school. But I knew when they were scheduled to be broadcast, whereas I bumped into "I Hate Disco Music" accidentally.

Is it true that you once turned down an offer to join Bon Jovi?
Jon and Richie came to the Stone Pony one night to inquire about me joining the band. They musta cut "Runaway" by then cuz they already had the record deal. I declined because A) I was stupid or B) I thought John was doing an impersonation of Springsteen.

After Cats, you joined La Bamba & the Hubcaps, another popular Stone Pony house band.
A while after leaving Cats, I wound up in LaBamba and the Hubcaps. Another great band. And another group Bruce sat in with. Richie LaBamba is a prince of a guy and very talented. I worked with a lotta cool players in that band, including Mark "The Love Man" Pender, Stan Harrison and Ed Manion.

Whatever happened to the band Manville?
It was a group of good friends of mine I threw together when I was going for my record deal at A&M Records. We never recorded, just played a few gigs and an audition (for A&M).

You had your first taste of solo success with "Follow You" from your second album. It wasn't long after that it appeared A&M had lost interest in promoting you. Did the falling out with A&M begin then?
My "falling out with A&M" began when the A&R staff was turned over. It's not an uncommon occurrence actually...
    What can I say? What happened, or didn't happen, is in the past. Perhaps I woulda been a household name given another situation. I've lived a good life. I'd rather not whine about it...

As with many of the New Jersey artists, you've been very involved with benefit shows. Tell me about your Xmas Xtravaganzas. Originally they were held at the Stone Pony but now they're in NY.
I think of New York as being more Christmasy than an old beach resort town, so I moved it. Musicians are suckers for charities. Usually entertainers enjoy getting up in front an audience, and even more so when it's for a good cause, which in this case is feeding the local hungry.

How did the Slaves of New Brunswick get started?
I approached Tony Shanahan about doing a weekly jam at the infamous and now defunct Melody Bar in New Brunswick... It was fun and it blossomed into this ambitious concept I had about writing an album about New Brunswick. It actually didn't come off horrible (no matter what the critic wrote in the local paper). It was named Album Of The Month in *Guitar World* magazine. We keep threatening to get back together and make a sequel.

When Patty Smyth took "Sometimes Love Just Ain't Enough" to number one, what did it mean to you personally and as an artist?
It felt great. There's nothing like achievement. I finally felt like my work was paying off. Not to mention what an honor it was having Don Henley and Patty Smyth singing a song of mine.

Here's something you may not know... the first time "Sometimes Love Just Ain't Enough" was performed before an audience was New Years Eve 1988/89 when Patty got up on stage to sing with me at the Pony.

Randy Travis had a hit with his cover of "Spirit of a Boy, Wisdom of a Man." Did you ever think you would top the country charts? What was that experience like for you?
I was blown away by the whole thing. When I think country, I think of a long line of rich music. To be awarded by that culture was an unexpected thrill for me.

I think that "Perfect World" just might be one of the best love songs ever written. It's been covered many times by various artists, but never really became a hit.
I dunno that it's one of the best love songs ever written, but thanks for the compliment. Yes, that's been probably the most covered of my tunes (6 or 7 times I think), and no, it's never really made it on the charts. Oh well!

In your opinion, what's the best song you've ever written?
The best song I've ever written is usually the last song I wrote (at this writing it's "Kiss Your Ass Goodbye"). But I'm extremely proud of "Liars Club", "Spirit Of A Boy, Wisdom Of A Man," "Watching The World Go By..."

What song of yours did you think had the best shot of being a hit?
The song I think that coulda/woulda/shoulda had the best shot? Maybe "Spinning My Wheels" or "I Should Be Laughing." I don't know... that's hard for me.

Your last few albums have been released on indie labels. Does it feel better not having the pressure you had on you while signed to A&M?
Each situation has its advantages and disadvantages. My solo albums on A&M were fun cuz the label spent some money on videos and got me time on TV and radio. But it was often a frustrating drag, to be honest. Not only were my records dead before I ever released a note of music, but I had to face direction and opinions from a million different departments - all clueless know-it-alls. In hindsight, it seems it was an exercise in obscuring my own vision.

As an indie, I am afforded control of my music, which is all I know, really. I don't understand promotion and image and advertising and marketing and positioning. Now I am free, in a sense, to do what I know how, without answering to the politics of a zillion different department heads. Of course, I do miss that support at times. *Palookaville* was probably my best hour, and worst distributed.

Ageism in the music industry is pretty much a given, so I have no delusions about becoming the next Britney Spears at this point.

Your son, Beau, has grown up and plays in his own band called Dibs. A few months back they opened for you at the Stone Pony. What was it like seeing Styx fans in one area, long-time Glen Burtnick fans in another area and Dibs fans in another area?
I think it's awesome. I'm happy to have any audience at all! And to see my son's band get attention is a good thing. And just like Beau's better looking than his old man, I wouldn't be surprised to learn his audience is probably more attractive than mine.

What's it like to have your son join you on stage?
It has to be privately one of my life's landmark moments, to be honest.

You really belong to both the New Brunswick and Asbury Park music scenes. How does it feel to have two musical homes?
Hell, I feel like I have my foot in many more doors! There are Styx fans out there who think of me as only a member of that band. There are Marshall Crenshaw fans who consider me his backup musician. I have a giant closet at home filled with hats. I wear a million of 'em.

The community of Asbury Park related musicians is working musicians. I see something noble in that (of course, there's something a little shoddy about it too, but no more than any other careers). There's somewhat a bit of comradeship among us. I'm proud to have played some part, however small, in any such noteworthy musical scene.

19 Fran Smith Jr.

It really was a magical time at the Pony. There were many rock stars coming in to catch Bruce and we were lucky enough to ride in the wake of his growing success.

--FRAN SMITH JR.

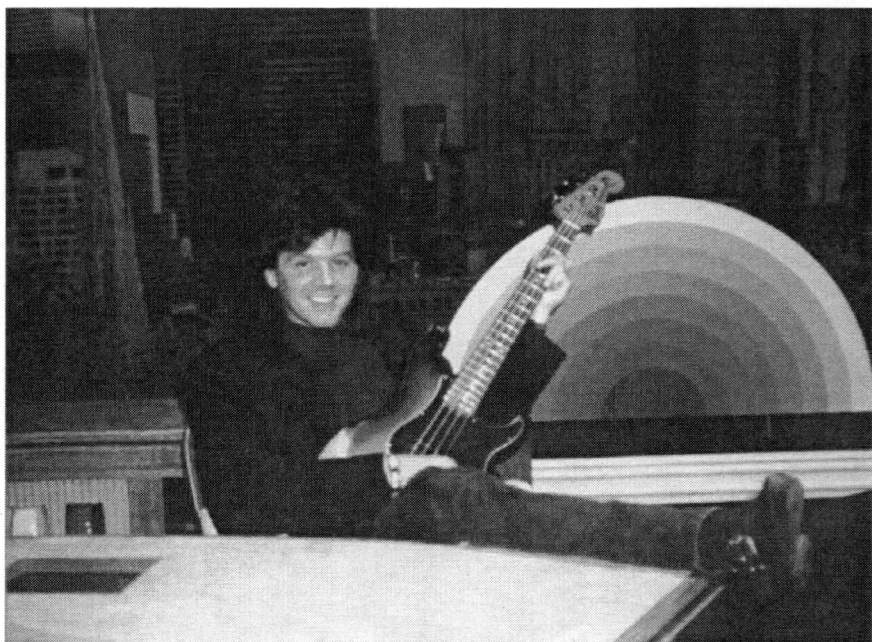

Fran Smith Jr. shown on the set of the "Today Show." Photo courtesy of Fran Smith Jr.

F ran Smith Jr. has been part of the Jersey Shore music scene since the mid-70s. He was a member of the Shakes, a popular Stone Pony house band that was once looked upon as the next big thing to come out of the Jersey Shore by record executives. After leaving that band he joined Johnny's Dance Band, a legendary group in the Philadelphia/Trenton area that had a record deal with RCA Records. Eventually Fran returned to the Jersey Shore and back to Asbury Park where he was part of the famous Stone Pony house band, Cats on a Smooth Surface.

He's probably best remembered as a member of the Hooters, a band that enjoyed its best success in the 80s but remains extremely popular outside the United States today. He's traveled around the world with the Hooters and has toured and released his own records under the name Rory Kunkle. I interviewed Fran via email to see what he's been up to recently and what he has planned for the future.

When were you in the Shakes?
I was in the Shakes from 1975-1977.

Lee Mrowicki from the Pony said that the Shakes was the band everybody thought would be the next to break.
Yeah, Lee was right, everyone thought that the Shakes were going to be the next big thing to break out of the Asbury scene. We did get an exceptional amount of press at this time. Bruce and the boys were always up on stage with us. The times were great and the fans were pumped. Many major record companies were pursuing us; however, it was my first taste of huge disappointment when the band started to go south.

What was it like playing the Stone Pony at that time?
To say the least, it really was a magical time at the Pony. There were many rock stars coming in to catch Bruce and we were lucky enough to ride in the wake of his growing success.

Any particular memories from your days in the Shakes?
I remember playing at the Capitol Theatre and Bruce walked in with the E Street Band. We had just finished our show and the Jukes were on. I was on the phone calling a bar I used to play at to wish a happy new year to a friend. Bruce walked by and grabbed the phone and commented about how he liked the Shakes, then people on the other side of the phone heard Springsteen was on the phone and lined up to wish him a happy new year.

Needless to say, it was a pay phone and my dime was quickly running out. Bruce reached in his pocket and took out some money and asked me to run up to the ticket box for more change. I think I made three trips...

Why did you leave the Shakes?
The band started to spin out of control. Huge egos ultimately were the demise. I was afraid it would be a mistake to leave, but I was getting very frustrated staying in the band. I was a writer and I felt I had nowhere to go in this situation.

How did you get involved with Johnny's Dance Band?
A band from Philadelphia called Johnny's Dance Band had a record deal with RCA Records and, in the middle of a whiffle ball game in my parents' backyard, Nan Mancini called and asked me to join the band. I went on to write the title track for our next album *It's A Man's World*. I had made the right decision to leave.

How did you get involved with Cats on a Smooth Surface?
If my memory serves me right, Bobby Bandiera and Glen Burtnick came to my home in Clementon, New Jersey, knocked on the door and asked me pretty much what I was doing and would I be interested in joining.

Do you miss anything about those days?
Without a doubt, I don't think I have laughed that much since... I miss the people that used to come see the band also.

What are your thoughts on the Stone Pony?
The Stone Pony really was a second home to me. I had an apartment down the street and the cook and I split the rent.

Tell me about your former bandmates in Cats:
Bobby Bandiera -- great musician, cool fellow, made me laugh a lot.
Glen Burtnick -- a wonderful songwriter... my Beatle soul mate.
Ray Andersen -- Ray gets my most spiritual maturity award, great musician too!

Isn't it funny that you wound up playing to huge crowds with the Hooters just like Ray Andersen did with Meatloaf and Glen Burtnick did with Styx and Bobby Bandiera did with with Southside Johnny. Did you ever imagine that everyone would all find such success?
Well, it didn't surprise me. It was great to see everyone get their due!

How did you get involved with the Hooters?

Well, it's a pretty funny story. It was Thanksgiving week and my sister called me and told me she had a dream I was in the Hooters. I pretty much laughed it off. A few days later, Glen Burtnick called and invited me as his guest at the Spectrum in Philadelphia. He was opening for the Hooters on Thanksgiving night. I took my daughter along, and after the show she asked if she could get her Hooters t-shirt signed by the band. I sort of chickened out and said, "I didn't think so." Glen heard this and said, "Come on, let's go talk to them."

We went into the Hooters meet and greet room, which was packed with other fans. As I was in line, the drummer Dave said, "Fran, I can't believe you are here. We were trying to get your number. Andy King just informed us he is leaving the band!"

The Hooters had an incredible run for a few years. With hit records and worldwide tours, what were some of the highlights for you since joining that band?

Well, actually lucky for us, except for the US, the rest of the world still sees us as a viable music source. Highlights include playing "The Wall" with Roger Waters of Pink Floyd. When the wall finally came down in Berlin, Germany we played the largest concert in the history of Europe.

Besides being blessed with so many great highlights, meeting some Beatles while doing a show with them in London's "Tops of the Pops" was mind-blowing. And the Hooters did not break up. We will tour this summer in Europe and continue to play.

In addition to the Hooters, you're also doing a solo thing as well. Tell me about Rory Kunkle.

Rory Kunkle is my alter ego, just a little more twisted. If you ever want to hear a cool CD, pick up *For No Apparent Reason*. That's me singing, playing bass, sitar, piano and writing all the songs.

What are your plans for the future?

New CD, I just wrote 30 new songs. Just getting ready to record, can't wait.

20 Ray Andersen

I really learned to play with other musicians, to listen to other musicians, to play off of them. That's what I learned from being in Cats.

--RAY ANDERSEN

Ray Andersen back when he was a member of Cats on a Smooth Surface.
Photo © Debra L. Rothenberg/rothenbergphoto.com

R ay Andersen started out playing in bands in North Jersey and moved down to the Shore when he joined Cats on a Smooth Surface. After Cats he had his own band for a while called Ray Andersen and the Fire. Then Ray and his wife, Patti Maloney, created the popular alternative band Blue Van Gogh which had success on a major independent label. While touring Europe in support of Matchbox 20 a side project called Mr. Ray suddenly took off. Mr. Ray features Andersen singing original songs for kids in the Beatlesque style.

After a wild ride as a member of Meatloaf, Ray is focusing on Mr. Ray full-time now where he has a major record deal with a label focusing on kids music. In a phone interview over the summer Ray talked about his career and the incredible journey he's had and continues to have.

Before joining Cats you were in bands like the Features. Where did that band play?
Oh, places like Motions in Irvington, more Northern Jersey clubs because I'm a northern boy - East Orange and stuff. So I was playing at those clubs up north more even though we ventured down south a few times.

I had never really ventured down to the Shore much. Then I moved down to Long Branch and became a Shore guy like overnight. It was great!

Bruce Springsteen loved to jam with Cats. Did you guys know when Bruce was going to show up?
Yeah, we did a couple of times. Most of the times we did because Terry McGovern, his right-hand guy, would come in and we'd get the word. But there were a couple of times, like at the Tradewinds, he would just show up. He would always use my guitar because the other guy in the band with the other lineup had a fancy Kramer guitar or something. He didn't like them. I had a Fender Strat, good old Fender American Strat. He'd say, "Ray, let me use your guitar." I used to tune it up for him. He'd bang the shit out of that! He loved it.

Did those early days with Cats help everyone with future bands?
It all helps, brother. It all helps. On my website now I still have pictures of me and Bruce. I mean, I had the wonderful distinction of jamming with a lot of cool people like Chuck Berry. When I was on tour with Blue Van Gogh in South Dakota, I saw a special with Bruce talking about how he and the E Streeters backed up Chuck Berry and how that's something he can tell his grandkids. Well, I had the distinction of jamming with both of these guys. So for Bruce to say that about Chuck and I'm saying it about Bruce, you know what I mean? It's very reciprocal. It all helps.

What have you been up to since Cats?

Well, I had my own thing called Ray Andersen and the Fire for a while. Just a solo artist thing with a band in back of me, but my wife and I were like we should pool our resources together. We started writing songs, we always wrote songs together, but we started writing songs for this specific project called Blue Van Gogh. And then we got a deal when we had the whole band intact.

How did you go from being there to singing Beatlesque songs for kids? Tell me about becoming Mr. Ray.

In 1994, my wife was temping at a daycare locally and one day she was like, "Can you come in? The kids are really going a little crazy today, they could use some soothing music." So I went in. I never did this before. I started strumming like "Twinkle, Twinkle Little Star" and "Yellow Submarine" and the director goes, "Hey, you want a job coming here on a regular basis to sing for my kids?"

The first thing I think is you mean I could get paid for this? Just singing to kids? What a cool job, you know. So then I started coming every week and I started writing my own kid songs. You know how you expect kids songs to be Rolly Polly kind of things? I always wrote with a rock / pop sensibility. By the way, Mr. Ray... I never wanted to be Mr. Ray, but when you work in a day care you're mister this or miss whoever. I wanted to be like Rocket Ray or something cool but I got stuck with Mr. Ray. So that's what the kids call me and I don't want to confuse them.

So then I started writing my own songs and the parents were like, "Ray, what is this dinosaur song my kids running around singing 24/7? You gotta come out with a tape." So I'm like alright, maybe I'll throw these songs on a little 4-track. Well, mister ambitious here booked 24-track studio time and I made a CD. I've got kids singing on every song. It's like full band renditions, rock band renditions. It's not folky, not that I don't love folk, but it's very British pop.

So then I started doing that and I released my own CD and Patti, we still had BVG - we call Blue Van Gogh, BVG - and we got a call to do Germany. I had never been to Europe before and here I was in Germany doing a whole European tour opening up for Matchbox 20 with just me and my wife on acoustic guitar. It was awesome! That was in the middle of my Mr. Ray thing. When I got back, I released the CD on my own before I got the deal with Carol King's daughter's company, Sugar Beats. And I sold boatloads! I sold thousands on my own because parents are starved for quality kids music. I found this untapped market, you know? So that's how Mr. Ray came to be.

And that was about when you joined Meatloaf, right?
Then I got a call from Meatloaf's bass player in '98 to join his band. I was like blown away because I don't consider myself a musician's musician. I'm not a virtuoso on any instrument. In Cats, I was known as the utility guy, just like a baseball dude - guitar, keyboards, percussion. And that's what Meatloaf needed. I went on a tour with him. I was out for like 3 1/2 years coming back and forth, major European tour, Jay Leno, David Letterman. It was unbelievable!

Did you see the Meatloaf episode of "Behind The Music"? Next time it's on VH1 watch the "Storytellers", I'm on the whole hour. That was my first gig with Meatloaf. Can you imagine how nervous I was? First gig, it's not like the Melody Bar in New Brunswick. It's VH1 "Storytellers". My heart was racing. What an experience that was.

Had you done much live TV before that?
Before Meatloaf? Zero, zilch. I mean that was it. I did Letterman, bro. I can't tell you, being a Beatles freak... to be in the Ed Sullivan Theatre where they tape Letterman. Playing on that stage, down in the bowels of that building where the dressing rooms are just like when the Beatles and all those amazing pop stars in the 60s and 70s were. It was unbelievable! So that's stuff I'll always treasure. Great experience.

Are you still touring with Meatloaf?
I just left the band in April because I wanted to devote my whole time to Mr. Ray. And with Meatloaf, he's bigger in Europe so you're always on the road. But it was such a rewarding experience playing with these guys. In Europe, you're on TV there and they have variety shows. Remember the variety shows we used to have here like Ed Sullivan? In Europe, they still have that. We'd be on a TV show with us, Hootie and the Blowfish, REM, Sinead O'Connor. It was amazing.

How is the Mr. Ray thing going for you?
I have a record out now that I signed with Carole King's daughter. The label's called Suger Beats and it's all original music for preschool kids. It's not like Barney or anything, it's very sophisticated pop rock for kids one to seven. Trust me, their ears are much more sophisticated than people give them credit for. And the music is really for the classic rock parents of these kids too because they've got to sit through those long car rides. It's not condescending at all man. Imagine Beatles songs like "Maxwell's Silver Hammer" and cool songs like that. Songs that you would think sound like kids songs. That's how my music is.

It's selling wonderfully. It's a national release. It came out April 2001. I'm working on the next one. It'll be out next spring. And I can't tell you my life right now it's totally singing to kids. And it's not like I'm doing this because nothing else worked out. It's like I have Barbara Walter's producer trying to get me my own TV show. I have major meetings with PBS about all this. We're coming out with a DVD and a video. It's just unbelievable what's happening.

Everything else is pretty much on hold right now. This Mr. Ray thing it's totally what I'm doing 24/7. I mean, I play museums in Manhattan. People fly me to Orlando to play at their daycare center's opening.

The funny thing is I grew up in the house where Carole King and Jerry Gosselin lived in West Orange, New Jersey and then I'm signed to her daughter's label. She lived in a house where her doorbell rang, "Will You Still Love Me Tomorrow" and that was my doorbell. Growing up as a kid, we moved in there in '68. Jerry Gosselin and Carole King wrote a lot of their hits in that house. A lot of *Tapestry* was written in that house. "Pleasant Valley Sunday" by the Monkees was all about my neighborhood there.

Pleasant Valley runs right through West Orange. "There's Mister Green, he's so serene, he's got a TV in every room." Mr. Green, he lived down the street. I kid you not. That song is totally my suburban neighborhood. Isn't that wild?

I always thought that was California or something?
No man, West Orange.

And you can dress normal as Mr. Ray, right? There's no costume?
I dress in black. Kids don't care. The whole thing with Hawaiian shirts and suspenders... That's the whole thing. I brought all my pop/rock sensibilities, everything about it - the image - I've brought it right over to the kids thing but the only difference is the lyrics I sing are written 99% of them from the perspective of the kid, the child. Like when I sing about the colors of the rainbow I talk about red being the color of the bouncing ball we play.

When you hear the name Stone Pony, what do you think about?
It's like rock and roll high school for me. The bands I was in before, like the Features up north, that was junior high. It was like high school for me and I mean that in a very loving, wonderful way. I really learned to play with other musicians, to listen to other musicians, to play off of them. That's what I learned from being in Cats.

I remember playing at Club Xanadu around the corner. It was basically what they would call a disco - real glitzy. Just a block away, but it seemed like a world away. I mean, as far as the ambiance inside. Cats would play that place sometimes. It was just such a dichotomy, such a paradox.

Just what a rewarding experience, you know? What a time to be at this mecca of music in America, what I consider Asbury Park. I was there from around 1982 to 1988. Unfortunately, I wasn't there in the early years when it was really hopping, but for a while it was like the place to be. People from Manhattan, what do they call them? Bennies? They were even coming down to party and stuff. We knew there was something cooking when that happened. So that's what I got out of it. And I have lifelong friends, musician friends. Bobby and I are still great friends and we still see and talk to Glen. My wife and Glen are really good friends.

I met my wife at the Stone Pony. She was in some other group, I can't remember the name right now and we met backstage. So, it's a very, very special establishment for me. Great memories.

My wife Patti Maloney was good friends with Patti Scialfa. Patti was pretty much on stage with us with Cats on a Smooth Surface. She would come up and jam with us. We were the jam band. We were like Paul Schaffer is on Letterman. In fact we ran into Bruce and Patti three years ago. You know that big cluster of antique stores in Red Bank? We just sat down and talked for like an hour, the four of us.

It was just a great window of music in that time, the whole "Asbury Sound." Whenever I heard the "Asbury Sound" I always thought more of Southside with horns, things like that. It was just because Bruce loved the Pony and people associated him with the Pony. I never really called Bruce Asbury music. For me, it was just passionate music, soulful music, rock and roll music right from the heart.

21 Bobby Bandiera

I seriously doubt there would be a Jukes today without Bobby. He made Johnny want to play again. Super nice guy, loves everybody and everybody loves him. Who else from New Jersey can sing Roy Orbison songs perfectly?

--BILLY SMITH
ASBURY PARK ROCK 'N ROLL MUSEUM

Bobby Bandiera shown playing at at the Stone Pony during the 80s. Photo © David March

B obby Bandiera has long been considered one of the Jersey Shore's best secrets, but he's really not a secret anymore. He's been Southside Johnny's right hand man since the *At Least We Got Shoes* record, has released a pair of independent solo records, has played with Jon Bon Jovi for his solo concerts and has backed up Bruce Springsteen on numerous benefit shows. No longer a secret, the real question may be why isn't he a household name?

Bobby has been heavily involved with the Jersey Shore music scene since his days in the popular band, Holme. Back then Bobby was just a part of the band instead of its leader. According to Lee Mrowicki of the Stone Pony, "He was one of the members, but it wasn't really his band. There were other people before Bobby and after Bobby too. And, in fact, we sometimes talk about it as the first musical baseball trade. Bobby had been in Holme then went to Cats, went back to Holme and then back to Cats and he was traded for Joel Krauss and a guitar to be named later."

Cats on a Smooth Surface was his band. He was the leader of what has been called by many as the band's most talented unit. Back then, Bobby Bandiera was clearly a star on the rise. He helped bring in the rest of the band, always finding the best musicians in the area. The result was a band that everyone wanted to see including Bruce Springsteen who joined Cats on stage dozens of times. Many people believe that Bruce guested with the band so much because he enjoyed playing alongside Bandiera. In fact, Bobby was once rumored to be the E Street band's new guitarist (as the replacement for Little Steven), a rumor that even found its way on to MTV News.

Since joining the Asbury Jukes in 1985, Bandiera has become one of the band's most popular members. He's not only a great guitarist but he's an incredible student of music as well. There's rarely a song that he doesn't know how to play. "Garry Tallent used to call him the human jukebox because he knows every song ever written from 1974 back," said Hal Selzer. "When I was young, I used to be one of those guys that wanted to show off and play fast and everything. Playing with Bobby I learned that it's all about the groove, just creating a groove and sending a groove. It's not about playing a million notes. It's playing the song."

"I remember Max Weinberg telling me that he never takes his eyes off of Bruce and Bobby was the same way," said Ray Andersen, one of Bobby's bandmates in Cats. "Bobby got a lot of that from Bruce. He was like the ultimate front person. You never wanted to take your eyes off him because he would be the one to cue us when to stop on the downbeat and all that stuff. I really learned so much from being in a band with Bobby Bandiera."

22 Jon Bon Jovi

It amazes me that to this day, he can be played on Z100, WPLJ and WDHA. Artists his age don't usually have that kind of success anymore.

--JIM MONAGHAN
FORMER WNEW DJ

Jon Bon Jovi started out playing in Asbury Park clubs like the Fastlane and Stone Pony. Photo © Debra L. Rothenberg/rothenbergphoto.com

J on Bon Jovi grew up in Sayreville, just up the Garden State Parkway, but he made his name in the clubs of Asbury Park. Early in Jon's career his band used to open for Lance Larson and many of the national acts that came through Asbury Park to play the Fastlane. It was a great opportunity for Jon to play in front of the demanding Asbury Park crowds and he became a great performer because of it.

Jon started out playing the Asbury Park area in the late 70s with a band called Atlantic City Expressway that he formed with his friend Willy Herceck. David Bryan, then known as David Rashbaum, was also in the band. Their sets were comprised largely of R&B songs. As with many Asbury Park bands, they had a horn section and were inspired by the songs of Bruce Springsteen and Southside Johnny & the Jukes.

The band split up soon after David Bryan left to study at Julliard School of Music. Jon soon joined up with the Rest, a popular punk band led by Jack Ponti. This move didn't last long and Ponti ultimately fired him from the band.

Other bands like John Bongiovi and the Wild Ones began playing more and more of his original music. While playing in the Rest, Jon developed into a great frontman and became something of a local sex symbol. His band opened for many of the national acts that would come to the Fastlane. Lance Larson, a popular local performer took a liking to the band and had them open for him on numerous occasions as well.

When Jon was just starting out record companies had almost given up on New Jersey. It was largely believed that the local music scene had run its course with Bruce Springsteen and Southside Johnny. Many labels were reluctant to sign anybody that sounded "too New Jersey." Fortunately, Jon's uncle Tony owned the Power Station, a famous recording studio in New York. This gave him the opening he needed and he made the most of his chance. Originally hired to do menial tasks for the artists, he got his big break two years later when Billy Squier agreed to produce his demo tape.

One of the songs on that tape, "Runaway," was played on many radio stations in the New York metro area and appeared on a local music compilation album. The success of that single led him to a record deal with Polygram/Mercury in 1983. Jon then changed his name to Bon Jovi, created a band and was on his way.

The core of the band was Tico Torres (who used to play with Lance Larson in Lord Gunner) on drums, Richie Sambora on guitar, Alec John Such on bass, David Bryan on keyboards and Jon Bon Jovi on guitar and providing the signature sound of Bon Jovi through his unmistakable vocals.

The first thing many people noticed about Bon Jovi was his boyish good looks and his hair. The next thing they noticed was that the band's sound, comprised of melodic metal/hard rock, sounded nothing like Bruce Springsteen. The band's first two albums, *Bon Jovi* and *7800 Fahrenheit* sold well, but the third album truly exceeded all expectations.

With the release of *Slippery When Wet*, he was able to do something that few New Jersey artists have been able to do. He not only escaped the shadow of Bruce Springsteen, but he became one of the world's most popular artists. In doing so, he proved that the world was ready for another rock star from the Garden State.

Slippery When Wet, released in the summer of 1986, contained hit song after hit song and was the biggest selling rock and roll record of 1987. It sold over nine million copies in the United States alone and included the number one hits "You Give Love A Bad Name" and "Livin' On A Prayer" along with the top-10 hit "Wanted Dead or Alive." Bon Jovi then embarked on a world tour which vaulted them among the most popular bands in the world.

Glen Burtnick, a Jersey Shore musician who was once asked to join Bon Jovi describes Jon as "another obviously potent performer. Hard worker. A bit of a Bruce take off, but it sure has worked. It's a very strong band, a well oiled machine. I also think 'Livin' On A Prayer' is about as good as a pop song gets."

Following this success, the band showed that they hadn't forgotten their roots by releasing the record *New Jersey* in 1998. The hits kept coming for the band as the record spawned two more number one singles and a trio of top-10 hits.

"You know what? I never thought there was any more room in New Jersey after Bruce," said Joe D'Urso. "Jon Bon Jovi, being as brilliant as he is, pulled that off by his music being different... for another generation. The fact that Jon has turned into what he has turned into blows my mind. The guy is absolutely brilliant. He came out from the most recognizable music star from New Jersey, which was Bruce Springsteen. And Jon Bon Jovi puts out a record called, *New Jersey*. The guy's got balls and I applaud him for those balls."

During a brief hiatus, the band members were free to work on projects that may not have fit in with the band's traditional sound. Jon recorded a solo album containing ten songs inspired by the film *Young Guns 2*. The record, with songs mainly dealing with cowboys and the wild west, featured the popular singles, "Blaze Of Glory" and "Miracle." The following year, Bon Jovi guitarist Richie Sambora released his own solo record entitled *Stranger In This Town*.

After a few years off, the band came back stronger than ever with the release of *Keep The Faith* in 1992. They followed that record with a greatest hits collection called *Crossroad*, and then returned with *These Days* in 1995.

The mid-90s saw band members taking another break. Keyboardist David Bryan became the latest to release a solo record with *On A Full Moon* in 1995. Jon Bon Jovi, Richie Sambora and David Bryan would release additional solo albums in the next few years.

In 2001, the band returned once again with *Crush*, an album that produced the band's biggest hit ever in "It's My Life." While on tour the band enjoyed a wonderful homecoming concert at Giants Stadium that July. Just a few months later, the members of Bon Jovi found themselves deeply affected by the September 11th terrorist attack. Jon Bon Jovi, always heavily involved in charitable causes, played several benefit shows in the Monmouth County area to help raise money for local families that were directly affected by the tragedy.

Almost exactly one year later, Bon Jovi released *Bounce* containing several songs inspired by the tragedy. Kicked off by a free concert in New York City, the band launched into another world tour and fans eagerly grabbed up tickets.

Lately, Jon Bon Jovi has really stepped up his participation in local causes, such as his role in the Benefit for 9/11 at the Stone Pony and the Alliance of Neighbors of Monmouth County show in Red Bank. The development of Jon's social conscience comes as no surprise to those that have known him for years. "They're the greatest guys in the world," said Lance Larson. "They never forgot about the home guys, no doubt about it."

In recent years, Jon Bon Jovi has split his time between an emerging acting career and his musical career. He has appeared in such films as *Moonlight and Valentino*, *The Leading Man*, *No Looking Back*, and *U-571*. He also had a prominent, recurring role in the hit television show, "Ally McBeal."

Even though Bon Jovi has become one of the most popular bands in the world, Jon can still be found performing around the Jersey Shore. He routinely lends a hand by playing benefit shows and can be found guesting with local bands throughout clubs along the Shore. In fact, he seems to jump on local stages a lot more these days. Maybe he's more comfortable with his fame or maybe he's just out there having fun, but he still has the ability to turn an ordinary night on the Jersey Shore into something you'll never forget. And he no longer has to worry about any shadows, his own looms just as large.

23 **John Eddie**

A cross between Bruce Springsteen, Elvis Presley and Hank Williams. Great on stage, lots of fine original songs but his two albums didn't sell well. Should have went country.

--BILLY SMITH
ASBURY PARK ROCK 'N ROLL MUSEUM

John Eddie, always an explosive live performer, is shown tearing it up on stage at the Pony. Photo © Debra L. Rothenberg/rothenbergphoto.com

John Eddie may have been born in Richmond, Virginia but he's got Jersey Shore blood flowing in his veins. A long-time favorite of local music fans from the Shore to Philadelphia and back down to Virginia, his live performances embody the definition of Jersey rock and roll music.

"It has that classic Jersey rock and roll sound I love," exclaims Kris, a fan from Sewell, New Jersey. "You can hear it in John, Bruce, Southside Johnny & the Asbury Jukes and Little Steven. It just feels like home. It can be a ballad or balls out rock and roll and it's always perfect! These guys work harder in their live performances than anyone else and it shows in their music. I never get tired of it."

One early fan of John Eddie's was Bruce Springsteen himself. Bruce joined John on stage numerous times at places like the Stone Pony and Big Man's West. The relationship between John and Bruce always seemed like a friendship based on a mutual love of music. In 1984, John Eddie even cut short a show of his at the Stone Pony so Bruce Springsteen & the E Street Band could kick off the start of the *Born In The USA* tour. That's the kind of guy John is.

In the early 80s, the Jersey Shore music scene needed a kick in the pants. The glory days, when bands like Southside Johnny & the Jukes, the Shakes and Cahoots lined crowds up along the block, had passed and Asbury Park was no longer seen as the place to be. John Eddie proved that Asbury Park still had plenty of life left in it. John and his band the Front Street Runners became yet another Stone Pony house band to gain national attention. And after several years on the club circuit, John released his self-titled debut album on Columbia Records in 1986. The album contained the hit song "Jungle Boy" which shot John into the spotlight. Unfortunately, he was hyped up as the next Bruce Springsteen - a label that would stick with him throughout his career. Later that year, John Eddie had the distinction of being the opening act at Amnesty International's show held at Giants Stadium in East Rutherford, New Jersey. He went on tours supporting acts like Bob Seger and the Kinks and gained fans around the country.

John Eddie released a second album on Columbia called *The Hard Cold Truth* which didn't sell as well as hoped. After his contract with Columbia was finished he signed a new deal with Elektra Records. He recorded his third album for Elektra but the label chose not to release it. Ironically, a few years later, John would score a minor hit with his cover of the Cure's "In Between Days" which was released on Elektra's 40th anniversary compilation album *Rubaiyat*. That cover remains a popular favorite of John Eddie fans.

Even though John routinely packed the house in clubs throughout the

East Coast he wasn't seen as a commercial success. Some people feel he may have gotten lost in the comparisons to Bruce Springsteen. Others feel he should have gone the country route. Although his influences were similar to Springsteen's, his songwriting and vocals are very different. But John never let anything slow him down or stop him from doing what he does best which is get up on stage and put on a great show. He continues to tour regularly throughout the country with a heavy concentration on the New Jersey and Pennsylvania areas.

"Probably the best show of John's I've seen would be the CD release party for *Guy Walks Into A Bar* on June 2nd, 2001 at the Stone Pony in Asbury Park," said Jeff from Westminster, Maryland. "It was his first show after a break from touring, the crowd was unbelievable and the band was as good as I've ever seen them. Lots of new songs which was a real treat. Not to mention the best version of 'Judy's Party' and 'No Surrender' I've ever heard.

"Truth be told," continued Jeff. "Probably the thing I like most about John's live shows is that he gives his all whether it's for a small crowd of less than 50 or when he's the opening act in front of an unfamiliar crowd that's never heard of him or playing before a packed house that's been waiting just for him. Nothing is taken for granted and there's no better time to be had. His sense of humor and great personality come across in his performances and I've never seen anyone be disappointed by his shows."

Kris from Sewell thinks all of the John Eddie shows are good but if any had to stand out it would be the two shows at Trump Marina in Atlantic City over the summer of 2002. "These were both free shows and held outside," said Kris. "The sound system there is perfect and it's a nice bar-deck on the marina. The first show in June was awesome! The weather was perfect, the crowd was into it and the band was hot! It's cool to see the younger kids and families all dig the music too, you don't get that in the bar. The later show was in August and it rained most of the show but that didn't stop John or the 'faithful' from rocking it out. It almost made the show a little special."

After his ups and downs in the music industry, John Eddie now appears more at peace on stage and his recent lyrics show a maturity from those on his first two records. "He writes about topics that mean something to me, whether it's fun and light-hearted or serious," said Leslie from Hummelstown, Pennsylvania. "I love his early stuff but musically the newer songs are more 'mature' and complex. You can sing along, dance and genuinely feel the music. I've seen a tremendous number of live artists in the last five years and nobody has hit it with me like John's music has."

A few years ago, John started his own record label called "Lost

American Thrill Records." Releases on this label include his own *Seven Songs Since My Last Confession*, *Happily Never After* and the live album called *Guy Walks Into A Bar*. The label also has acquired the rights to John Eddie's first two albums and now offers them as one double CD.

Recently John Eddie has been crisscrossing the country playing shows with such diverse acts as John Hiatt, Ryan Adams, the Jayhawks, Five For Fighting, John Mayer, Ian Hunter, Graham Parker and Big Head Todd and the Monsters. His record label made a deal with Lost Highway Records of Nashville so his last record released in May, 2003 - was once again put out on a major label with distribution across the country.

As with many of the Jersey Shore artists there's a strong community of fans that have supported and continue to support John wherever he plays. "The faithful" as they are called are sure to be found whenever John takes the stage at the Stone Pony in Asbury Park or the Conduit in Trenton or wherever John is up on stage performing his good old-fashioned rock and roll music.

"Yes, I would definitely consider myself one of the faithful," said Leslie from Hummelstown. "I'd imagine I've topped 75 shows by now and John plays private parties for a group of us fairly often. There's a song I think he told me he wrote when he was 17 called 'I Want A Kiss' - it's hysterical. He won't play it live except at the private parties."

John's humor has never been more apparent than in the song "Fuckin' Forty" where he talks about surviving and growing old in the music business. In the song John knows that he'll most likely never be the giant superstar he once might have hoped to be, but that no longer matters. Besides he's still ten years younger than Bruce Springsteen!

John Eddie likes to make fun of his lack of recognition with the slogan "Who the Hell is John Eddie?" Well, to fans of Jersey Shore music that question is pretty easy to answer. We've known who he is for years and years. He's a great performer. And, above all, he's a great guy.

"I have to say that John Eddie is one of the nicest, funniest and most sincere performers I have ever had the pleasure of meeting," said Jeff from Westminster. "He is genuinely concerned about what the fans want, humble to the point of almost being insecure and incredibly grounded. Maybe part of this is due to being so close to grabbing the ring and then having it snatched away a couple of times, but I really think it comes from within him. He is always willing to spend some time talking with fans, joking but also giving insight into the man and the music."

24 The Smithereens

We are like a family. We virtually learned to play together and like playing together. People like our music and we make our living doing this. As long as there's an audience that comes to see us there's no reason to stop!

--DENNIS DIKEN

Group shot of the Smithereens, a popular 80s alternative band that is still releasing new records and touring across the country.

The Smithereens are one of the most successful bands to come out of the Jersey Shore scene. Based in North Jersey, the band played some of its first gigs at the Stone Pony in Asbury Park. Lance Larson, a favorite of the Shore crowd, invited the band to open his shows there. With influences ranging from the Kinks to the Who to Buddy Holly and the Clash, the Smithereens developed a sound a bit like punk mixed with Beatlesque melodies. Deemed "alternative music," it was very different from what the Asbury Park crowds were used to but the band ultimately won crowds over.

It's been over 20 years since the release of their first record, an EP called *Girls About Town*. Since that time, the band has had a string of hits including "Blood & Roses," "Behind The Wall Of Sleep," "Only A Memory," and "A Girl Like You." They were one of the first rock bands to form a bond between the New Brunswick and Asbury Park music scenes. The band continues to stay busy, touring the country and releasing new records. Pat DiNizio, the band's lead singer even ran for the New Jersey Senate a few years ago. I was able to interview the band's drummer, Dennis Diken, via email to get his thoughts on the band's history and its incredible longevity.

How did the Smithereens first get together?

I met Jimmy Babjak in Earth Science class on the first or second day of freshman year in September of '71 at Carteret High School. I introduced myself after spying color pictures of the Who that he'd plastered on the inside cover of his looseleaf notebook. We became fast friends and began playing together that very week. We explored all the possibilities and limitations of our drums/guitar lineup during our high school stint. We were hard-pressed to find a compatible bass player and vocalist. All of the other players we met in the area were more into the Grateful Dead or fairly pedestrian fare. We were pretty determined to form a band in the spirit of the Who, the Kinks, the Beatles, etc. As popular music was becoming more slick and formulized, we dug deeper into the likes of Chuck Berry, Eddie Cochran, Buddy Holly and other seminal rock'n'roll for our inspiration. Jimmy and I clung to our original vision and waited for the right guys to make themselves known to us.

Shortly after we graduated high school in June of 1975, our schoolmate Mike Mesaros picked up on the bass guitar and got real good on the instrument in short order. Our group was now a trio but we lost some momentum when Mike attended college in Maine. Plus we were still in search of a lead singer. We eventually did some gigs (at Mike's apartment in Perth Amboy and at Carteret Park) with Paul Mulligan (also from Carteret) on vocals.

We ran an ad in the *Aquarian* in search of a lead singer. At the same time I answered another ad in the *Aquarian* and teamed up with Pat Dinizio's combo called the Like. We rehearsed for several months in Scotch Plains and played one gig in New Brunswick. Mike, Jimmy and I continued to play together sporadically. Then Mike and I joined Mark Mazur & the Targets (Mark was formerly in Holme, a popular Jersey Shore band).

After the Like split up Pat started to write songs. He and I kept in touch and he eventually asked me to go in the studio with him to play on some of his original tunes.

When we talked about starting a new band together I brought Jimmy in and Mike eventually joined up with us. The Smithereens first gig was at Englander's in Hillside in March of 1980.

Who were some of your musical influences while growing up?
There were so many, mostly what was played on WABC and WMCA; the Beatles, the Beach Boys, the Four Seasons, Motown, Stax, the Lovin' Spoonful, the Turtles, the Kinks, the Who, the Rascals, millions of one hit wonders. I can go on and on...

Do you remember the first band you ever played in? The first time you ever performed in public?
The first musician I ever played with was John Hornak, a classmate at Lincoln School in Carteret who was learning the guitar. This was early '69, I think. We played an all-Creedence repertoire in my basement. I believe we had one or two sessions.

My first real band didn't have a name. We got together in 1971 during summer vacation between my 8th grade graduation and the beginning of freshman year of high school. Our family newspaper delivery boy heard me practicing in the basement of our Carteret home and asked me if I wanted to join him and his bandmates who were seeking a drummer. We played around town that summer, and one gig was an outdoor political function. I forget if it was Democrat or Republican! I think that was my first public performance. I quit this band later that same year.

What were the names of the bands you played in before the Smithereens? Did any of the bands include future members of the Smithereens?
What Else (70s, 90s); Richman T. & Taylor ('73-'75?); Pix ('76-77?); Empty Set (late 70s); Toby Mug   (probably 78); Snappy Hawaiians ('78-'79); The Sensational Coupons ('77 or '78); The Like ('78-'79?); Mark Mazur & the Targets '79-'80); Zoo Crew ('84-'85).

What Else was the name that Jimmy Babjak and I used when he and I played together. We actually did a track for a Sonny Bono tribute album in the early 90s under this name. Jimmy and I started playing together in high school. The Like was a cover band with Pat Dinizio and Bill Rozar. Played one gig in New Brunswick.

Mark Mazur & the Targets had Mike Mesaros on bass, Mark Mazur on guitar, Dave Cogswell on keyboards. We played NJ (including Shore gigs at the Stone Pony, etc) and the NYC club circuit (Kenny's Castaways, Max's Kansas City, Great Gildersleeves, Snafu, etc.)

Some of the first shows the Smithereens ever played were at the Stone Pony in Asbury Park opening for Lance Larson.
It's funny, I remember being sick with a bad head cold or a flu for most of those shows! We played on a certain weeknight for several consecutive weeks. Pat's good friend and former bandmate Sam Lindley was the drummer with Lord Gunner and I shared his kit. I recall he had blue Evans heads in his drums. Sam got us the gig.

Lance and Lord Gunner had a devoted following and he always gave a good show. We were and are grateful to him for letting us play not one, but numerous gigs with him when we were totally unknown and just finding our way as a band.

Did you get the feeling that your music was a little different from the standard Jersey Shore music usually found at the club?
It did feel that we were the odd kids on the block. But we stuck with it. Through sheer persistence we made a go of it.

The Smithereens have lasted for over two decades. Why do you think the band has been able to keep going for so long?
No matter what happens, we're dear friends. Our roots run real deep. I've known Mike since 1966 and Jimmy since 1971. I've known Pat for 25 years. We are like a family. We virtually learned to play together and like playing together. People like our music and we make our living doing this. As long as there's an audience that comes to see us there's no reason to stop!

Although the Smithereens have had several songs get substantial radio airplay, the band is still kind of considered a cult band. Does that ever bother you?
Only if I let it. If there's anyone out in that big old world that responds to what's in your heart and soul at all then it's a blessing.

Is there a particular song that you never get tired of playing?
I don't tire of any of them. It's always a challenge to do the best you can and keep things as fresh as possible.

What's your personal favorite Smithereens records?
Especially For You and *Green Thoughts.*

In recent years, you have been an extremely busy guy. You've been part of several bands and recorded records with many, many artists. How do you find time to play with everyone?
People ring me, I check my book and schedule the gigs in! I still get the charge I got when I received my first drum kit in January of 1968. Plus, there are always new things to learn so playing never gets boring. You get to tap into your kid heart and explore your adult mind.

How is working with Jim in Buzzed Meg?
Buzzed Meg is really a lot of fun. We get together so rarely but when we do it's a very no pressure situation. Jimmy's got a load of great songs and he keeps on writing them. It's a fun "boys club."

The Smithereens were recently included on a George Harrison tribute CD called *Songs From The Material World*. What did Harrison mean to you?
I always had a special spot in my heart for George as we share a birthday. This was big deal when I was a kid. When *The Beatles Anthology* came out it was reported that a mistake was made somewhere down the line and his actual birthday is 2/26. Well, to me it will always be 2/25! I like a lot of his songs ("Don't Bother Me," "I Want To Tell You," "Long, Long, Long," etc.) on the Beatles albums and I always dug *All Things Must Pass*. I liked his vibe and spirit in the Beatles.

You've also been doing some writing. Tell me about the *Encyclopedia of Record Producers* and your work with liner notes.
I got a chance to write about some of my favorite musical figures like Bob Crewe and the late George Goldner. I also interviewed Mitch Miller who was 86 at the time and still working!

The most recent liner notes I've done were for two Lovin' Spoonful reissues, *Daydream* and *Hums of The Lovin' Spoonful*. They were always one of my very favorite bands. I didn't have nearly enough money to buy all the albums I wanted when I was a kid but I always had theirs when they came out. Their long-players are solid works and never got their due.

I was thrilled to make the acquaintance of Zal Yanovsky, who is one of my biggest rock'n'roll heroes. I was shocked and deeply saddened by his untimely passing. I wrote some notes for a Del Shannon compilation and a piece on "The Amboy Bowler" for *Weird NJ*. I've got several recording projects in the works, one of which is to finish a Sleeping Giant album.

After 9/11, the Smithereens participated in a benefit for the Alliance of Neighbors of Monmouth County at the Count Basie Theatre in Red Bank. What do you remember about that show?
It was a very exciting time. The Smithereens were very well received and folks have been very kind with their praise of our sets at the show. In addition, I met so many wonderful players and people. One of my biggest thrills was to play with Felix Cavaliere. The Rascals were a big inspiration to me and still are. I was stoked to play the big drum fill at the end of "Shannon" with Henry Gross. I always dug that moment on that record! And of course, hanging with DJ Fontana and Sonny Burgess was the most! I was very happy to get the call from Garry Tallent.

You played drums while Springsteen sang one of the most memorable songs of the night - "My City of Ruins."
It was a very special moment. Remember, the show took place just five weeks after the attack in NYC so the whole event was pretty emotionally-charged and because of 9/11 that tune took on a special meaning. I was mostly concentrating on remembering the song and doing a good job! I hadn't heard it 'til rehearsal for the show a few days earlier. Bruce gave me a big hug on the second night so I guess I didn't screw it up too bad.

Where were you when you heard the news about the 9/11 attack?
I was reading the paper and having my morning coffee. My Mother-in-Law called from Florida to give me the bad news. I was shattered by the loss of thousands of fellow humans. We were all in those towers. By that I mean that it could have been any of us. My wife and I could see the NYC skyline from a few blocks from our house. This happened in our backyard.

What does Asbury Park mean to you?
I've been going to Asbury Park since I was a young kid. The first trip I can remember was around 1963. It's always been a special place for me and has represented positive feelings and what is great about New Jersey. Thanks to Bruce it's a mecca for music fans around the world. I'm hoping it can see the renaissance it deserves.

25 In Between Dreams

We got to be a big fish in a small pond, but we literally didn't know how to take it to the other end. We didn't know what to do with it.

--JOHN PFEIFFER

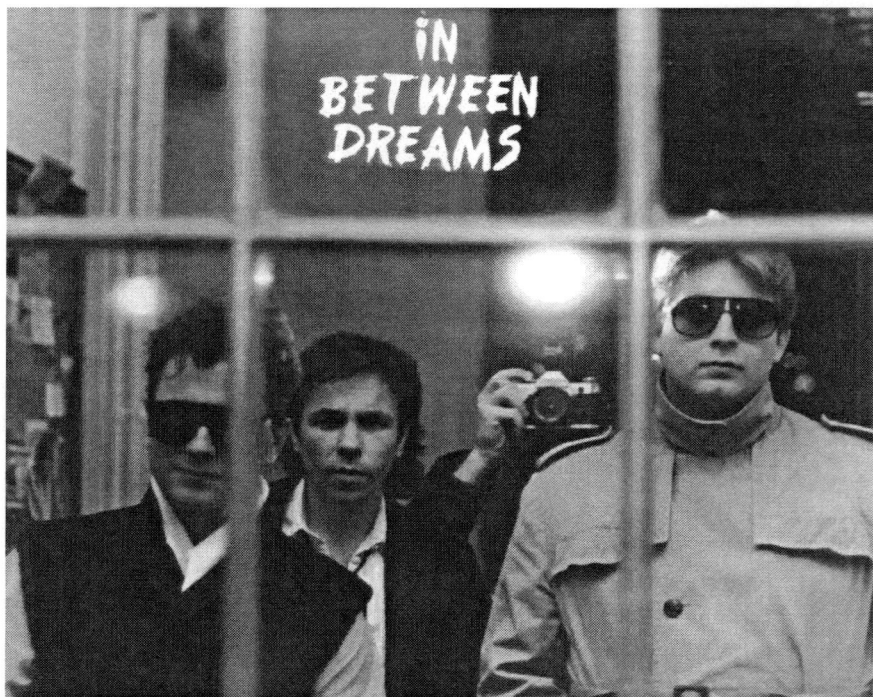

Members of In Between Dreams from left to right: John Pfeiffer, Gordon Gunn, John Hoenge (with camera) and Al Spector.

I n Between Dreams has been called one of the most influential punk bands of the Jersey Shore. The band started out at the Brighton Bar in Long Branch during the early 80s and then went on to play many of the legendary clubs in the tri-state area like Maxwell's, the Stone Pony, the Green Parrot, CBs, the Loop Lounge, the Court Tavern, the Melody Bar and the Limelight.

The band was comprised of John Pfeiffer on lead guitar and vocals, Gordon Gunn on lead vocals and harmonica, Al Spector on bass guitar and vocals and Joseph Quinto on drums. They were influenced by bands like U2 and REM and took pride in having a sound that was not typically heard from a Jersey Shore band.

In Between Dreams released their one and only record, *A Different Life*, in 1987 with a release party at the Limelight in New York City. Unfortunately, that would be the highest point the band would ever reach before splitting up later in the year. I had the chance to talk with John Pfeiffer via phone to learn more about this influential band.

When did In Between Dreams play?
From 1981 to 1988, we were on the scene in '81 at the old Brighton Bar when the Brighton Bar was cool. We did fairly well. The band got popular quickly and we wound up opening for bands like Blue Oyster Cult, Julian Cope and Big Country at the Stone Pony. We never played with any famous bands at the Green Parrot, but we would be the headliner with two or three other bands.

We played the Brighton Bar, Loop Lounge, Court Tavern and Melody Bar in New Brunswick. The band played throughout the tri-city area. We played CBs and started on a Sunday then worked our way to a Thursday. We did some showcasing at Maxwell's in Hoboken, and, of course, we played the Stone Pony. I should have my picture on that God damn wall for spending so much time in there and bringing so many drinkers to the place, but what are you gonna do. It's kind of funny because I'm in the booking business now and I book the bands next door at Jimi's.

How many records did the band put out?
In Between Dreams did one record. That was done in '87.

What did the band sound like?
It was like a punk U2. We had the echoey guitar and our singer, Gordon Gunn, had that whole Bono, big dramatic thing going on. It was cool. I would call it more of a hard edged U2, kind of eclectic and airy, but some of the stuff was very heavy.

The band played most of the places that booked punk acts around then. Were the crowds different at each place?
Yeah, people were almost like gangs where they have their different colors, people were different at each place. The Court Tavern crowd was cool, but the Brighton Bar crowd was real cool. They would hardly even clap for you because they were all too cool. It was great! We would yell insults from the stage like, "You're all a bunch of fucking posers!" Then after we started bringing people in people would clap because it was more fashionable.

Each club was different. The Stone Pony just had regular people that wanted to go to the Stone Pony or friends of yours that you could get out. The Brighton had its own punk scene, the Court Tavern had its own punk/fashion scene and the Melody was totally different as well.

As for the Green Parrot, I hung out there a lot and got used to it but it always reminded me of a restaurant. In the time period that we were there everybody hung out and knew each other. I always went and hung out with the Dervishes because we were friends. I was actually in a side project with Bob Ardrey. We had a band called the Summer Nationals with Karen Mansfield, me, Bob Ardrey and the drummer from the Dervishes. So, I'd go see them, I'd see the Wallbangers who were great, Surface From the Future, Fatal Rage - Jacko's Band. There was probably a ton of bands I'd go see.

What were some of your favorite shows by In Between Dreams?
We opened up for Blue Oyster Cult with about 4,000 rednecks there. We played the Limelight in the height of the Limelight's fame. In Between Dreams actually played the Limelight twice, you only played the Limelight if you had something to say. I still have the full page ad for our record release party at the Limelight that I cut out from the *East Coast Rocker*. I remember us thinking, "We've got to get in the *East Coast Rocker*, we'll be famous."

In Between Dreams has been called one of the most important early punk bands in the area. How would you like the band to be remembered?
I think it was best remembered like the old Brighton that was owned by Big John. Loud, drunken - just fully rocking. There was no image problems, there was no talking about management. The bar was packed, everyone was having a great time and your energy level was super high. That's probably how I'd like to be remembered... back in those old Brighton days. It was a big deal back then.

What ultimately led the band to call it quits?

In Between Dreams was playing constantly. No lie, we were playing 4-5 nights a week. We got to be a big fish in a small pond, but we literally didn't know how to take it to the other end. We didn't know what to do with it. There was a guy who was our manager who tried to change the way we dressed and like make us smile on stage. I swear we had the Bradys' managers! We actually had guys telling us how to talk... It got to be a lot of pressure.

You know what it was? It was four guys who thought they knew everything but really knew shit. So, you have the egos and stuff and we just broke up one night on stage at the Brighton. The guitar player just threw his guitar against the wall and that was it. We all kind of walked off. I said, "Let's get our shit together, finish the set and then we're done." So, we came back and finished it and everybody loved that. That was it, we were done. There was simply nowhere for us to go. We had given it a shot, but we didn't have the right people. And looking back at it, we weren't ready anyway.

In Between Dreams broke up and I started a band called Fall From Grace. It was an acoustic project with a bass player and Mitch Wilson from the Blases. We used to open for the Dervishes and stuff. It was during that whole late 80s thing when acoustic music was big. We saw the band Mr. Reality and we were like let's do that. We lasted about six months. Then Tom Kanach found out that I was available and we'd known each other for a long time. His band, Mischief, used to open up for In Between Dreams at a bunch of places. Actually, the night we opened for Julian Cope was kind of funny. Those guys (Joe DeLorenzo and Tom Kanach) wanted to get in to the show. They were like, "We'll pretend we're your roadies." I'm like, "So you'll help me carry my stuff in there?" And they're like yeah. So, we got them in as our roadies. And the minute they got in the door they were like, "Fuck you!" and took off!

I remember going out with Chris Barry one night when Well of Souls was playing the Fastlane. I was thinking about joining them so I went to see the band and that's how I met the rest of the guys. So I joined the band and we did a few rehearsals and then went right into the studio because Tom had won some studio time. About a week or two later we had our first gig in Ambler, Pennsylvania and that was it, I've been in ever since. Tom and I started writing together. I came in and I was more of a songwriting guy, so I immediately wanted to start writing with him. I liked what he was doing, I thought he was talented and I had my own ideas. We split things up and it worked. The band got popular and it went pretty far.

Which band - In Between Dreams or Well of Souls - did you think might have been closer to making it?
Well of Souls was real close. We sat in that big room that Elvis Presley sat in when he signed his contracts at RCA and had lawyers telling us that we were the next big thing. But it never happened. It was a strange situation. We had expensive lawyers, great songs, people that were helping us out as management and we couldn't get signed. I was always scratching my head going what the fuck? We came into the city a few times and met with label people and lawyers who were very enthusiastic, I guess they just couldn't figure out what to do with us. We didn't get signed, but I thought we were gonna for a while. I still can't figure that stuff out.

How frustrating was it to go from one of those meetings in the city to a club gig the next day?
Oh, what's even worse is going from that meeting in the city to a day job the next day. I didn't mind as much with the regular shit. I was very excited about that stuff and wanted to take it further. We were right on the outskirts, it was really like people didn't know what to do with us. Tony Palligrosi used to book us a lot. He would literally have us open for everybody you can name that was famous in the nineties that came to the Pony. We did Live several times, another show with Big Country and even Julian Cope again. I was like great, another time I'm opening for this guy and he's making more money than me. We would actually outdraw some of the bands. After a while we started making some money playing at the Pony. And Tony was great. he was a businessman, but he knew we had something going. He'd say, "Ok, I'll put you in front of Live. You have to set up in front of their gear, draw people, be good, keep the audience amused then get off." And that's what we did for 3-4 years at the Pony. It was a lot of fun, we got to meet a lot of people. It honed us. We became pretty tight.

What band would you have compared Well of Souls to?
Oh, that's a tough one... A combination of Foo Fighters and Soundgarden.

A lot of music fans in the area really dug that band.
It's funny because one time Chris Barry, as a joke, said there was going to be a Well of Souls reunion at the Broadway Central. The writer from the *Two River Times* showed up and Al Muzer showed up and somebody else from another paper came. So, these three writers all showed up and he had to tell them that he was just joking!
It's funny that there's still people that know about it. We really haven't

stopped. We kind of went off and did other things. Tom did a solo thing and I did a solo thing, for whatever reason. We still have a songwriting deal with George McMorrow from Cinecall and we're trying to write for TV and movies now.

After we did the Well of Souls thing we became Grimace and then we became Lustre, which was just me and Tom. In fact, we did all kinds of weird stuff when we were Grimace. We had an audition once for a Wendy's commercial so we jumped in the truck and went to the city. They needed a band in the video, but they said we weren't punk enough. Lustre did a studio record called *Holiday City*, which was the latest thing we've done together. It never got released, but Cinecall took it and is pushing it towards record companies and movie houses. We'd love to be songwriters and have other people do our stuff.

Do you ever see yourself getting back into playing live shows?
I don't know. I'm older now. I have different priorities. But it wasn't bad, I didn't mind it. You get to the point where you're like what am I doing this for? Am I doing this because I have something to prove or am I doing it for a reason? Now, I don't feel the need to be in a bar five nights a week playing in front of 20 people. That's not to say I wouldn't do it if somebody asked me to, but for the most part I'd rather stay home and watch television.

What was the best thing about the rides with In Between Dreams and Well of Souls?
The feeling of accomplishing something and moving forward, just knowing that your hard work led to results for you and the band and that they were genuine. I think that's the most important thing. It's like you get girls and stuff like that, but the most rewarding thing is hearing people clapping or cheering for you after something you had done yourself.

And you're like a booking scout now.
I work with Chris Barry. He's got his World Beyond Network and my company is Lustrevision. I still do some recording and stuff, but I'm mainly trying to find new bands now. I've got a couple of bands I'm high on like the Brian Mackey Band and Ton of Bricks.

Being a performer, you see it from a different side. It's actually better for them because I'm looking out for the bands. I'm not trying to rip them off or trick them - all the shit I went through. They trust us and that's the way it should be because I know what I'm doing, I've done this before.

26 Secret Lovers

I don't really think about this stuff that much because so much has happened since. Unfortunately, there is a big prejudice against women that are not 26 in this business. And so that's the problem. My history can only go back ten years.

--ALICE LEON

Secret Lovers with Scott Nagrod (left), Alice Leon (center) and Dave LaRue (right). Photo © Debra L. Rothenberg/rothenbergphoto.com

S ecret Lovers was a popular band along the Jersey Shore in the mid-80s. They released an EP in 1986 which contained the hit song, "Desiree (I Know You're Home Tonight)." That song would be played heavily on radio stations throughout New Jersey and Philadelphia.

Around 1990, the band had pretty much run its course and lead singer Alice Leon was looking for something new. The result was a band called After Alice that would have brushes with fame from two appearances on "Star Search" and songs featured on "The Guiding Light." But by 1995, After Alice was finished and Leon had pretty much given up on a music career. That's when she was discovered by Sony and signed to a development deal. She's currently leading the Alice Project, a band that has just released its third record and shows her growth as an artist.

I was able to talk to Alice Leon via phone to find out what it was like being one of the few female rockers along the Jersey Shore in the 80s and about the twists and turns her career has taken since then.

When did Secret Lovers actually get together?
We started in 1984.

I noticed that this stuff is kind of omitted from current biographies...
Of course it is! Well, first of all it's hard to say that I'm 27 when I started in 1984! I did an interview with the *New York Times* a few years ago when they reviewed my album and the guy was like, "How old are you?" And I said, "I'm not gonna tell you how old I am, that's ridiculous! How about if I tell you I'm in my extremely late 20s..." Anyway, the guy was so bent on finding out, he actually found out and put it in the newspaper. Let's just say I was young... I was younger than the rest of them.

What was the most difficult thing about playing back then? It seemed like the scene was pretty isolated regarding female led bands?
That's right! Isn't that strange? It was very isolated, I can tell you. I've even tried finding other female players to work with and they're really hard to find. Of course, few have stuck it out as long as I have, most have all thrown in the towel.

There were a couple of things going on at the time because I was the only woman. I'm trying to think back as to how I used to feel. I definitely felt younger than all of the other players. I was just coming up, I felt like a kid. There weren't a lot of women I could draw off of either, so my style was being formed without having anybody to bounce it off of and that was different.

The changing room situation was always a pain. The Pony just had that one room, so I had to go back there or change where the ice machine was. Back in the 80s, the clothes you wore were a big deal and you never came to the club in what you were going to wear on stage. I used to wear things like lace gloves and crazy jewelry. Actually, I still have some of the clothes that I wore in the eighties because I just couldn't get rid of them. Nowadays, people show up at a club with the clothes that they're gonna wear. They look like they just fixed their car and then go on stage. But they didn't do that in the eighties. I remember La Bamba used to go to Chess King, which had nothing but shiny clothes. He used to always bring his clothes in a Chess King bag and we'd make fun of him!

Asbury in the eighties was a great place! It was nearly all original music at the time and people really came out to the clubs. It was just a different vibe than I feel there is now. You almost have to pry people out of their armchairs to get them into the club. The club scene has changed dramatically overall, but I think Asbury was a great place to play. We even did a really neat show with WNEW back when the station was really supportive at the Shore. We did a live outdoor morning show with the Asbury Jukes. It was such a scene down there! In my opinion, the scene's just not there anymore.

Secret Lovers had a song "Desiree (I Know You're Home Tonight)" that found its way on to a WDHA compilation of New Jersey bands. Did the band also release a record?
We had a 5-song vinyl EP.

Did that find its way on to any radio stations?
Yes, in 1986 or 1987, "Desiree" ended up on WPST, which was the big Philly station. It actually ended up on their charts. We were a top-5 most requested song for about half a year. We sold thousands and thousands of copies of the EP. So, that was kind of neat. But I think all of the money from the sales just went back into paying it off. I know it cost us a lot to make the record.

We ended up doing a lot of big opening shows, a lot of these 1000-seat college shows with guys like Glen (Burtnick), John Eddie and Tommy Conwell. We did all of the cabarets in Philly. We even did a show at Convention Hall in Asbury with Burtnick, Bon Jovi and us.

Was that a benefit show?
Yeah, I think it was a benefit. Everything was a benefit, I don't think I ever got paid... Someone was benefiting! *(laughs)*

Where were some of your early shows?

Oh my gosh, every club that there was. It's probably easier to ask me which clubs I didn't play. We played just about every club that would have us in New York from the Bottom Line, the Bitter End, the Palladium and Kenny's Castaways. We played Joe Pop's and all the Jersey Shore clubs. At one point we were playing every Thursday at the Stone Pony with the Front Street Runners. John was recording his record for Columbia and so they had other people fronting the band, usually it was Bobby Bandiera.

A couple of nights, Springsteen showed up. That was always good for us because we would go on first and then Bruce would show up. So, we'd play, break down the stage and then Bruce would come on and whoever was to go on after us didn't get to play.

Is it true that you didn't really play live until college?

Right! I didn't play at all. My freshman year at Rutgers, I was playing my guitar a lot and writing lots of songs. I used to play in my dorm room and my roommates thought I was good. So, I just got inspired and went up to all of those open mike nights in the Village. I wound up getting a steady gig at this one club called the Dugout, which is now the Peculiar Pub on Bleeker Street. I played there three nights a week from 1-3 a.m.

One thing led to another and I started doing background vocals for bands at school. I ended up meeting Scot, the guitar player, who told me he was looking for a girl to sing on a record he was doing. It turned out he didn't even have a band! So, we put together this band with Dave LaRue and we got this pretty cool band that became Secret Lovers.

I don't really think about this stuff that much because so much has happened since. Unfortunately, there is a big prejudice against women that are not 26 in this business. And so that's the problem. My history can only go back ten years.

How did Secret Lovers bleed into the band After Alice?

I think our band member changes always revolved around spending a lot of money on band pictures. So, every time we would do a band photo someone would leave the band. Finally at one point, I think it was just the guitar player, a keyboard player and me left. This was around 1990. By then, I really wanted to have the focus put a little more on me because I was writing the music, I was the lead singer, I was booking the band... I was basically doing the whole thing. We ended up going with After Alice, which kind of changed the focus. That was when women were starting to make the scene.

After Alice was on the TV show, "Star Search."
Yeah, we were. It's so weird because recently I've been starting to feel like I've been in this so long. We were there in '93 and '94. In '93, we were doing a show in New York at Cafe Wha? A scout saw us there. It really wasn't what you thought, you didn't submit your stuff to them they actually had scouts for the show. They asked us to come for an audition and we set up at some studio where they videotaped us. I remember we didn't take it very serious because we thought it was a pretty cheesy show, but it ended up being a lot of fun. They sent us down to Disney World for a week with all expenses paid and cool hotel accommodations, and then we played on the show.

We were supposed to be in the live band category, but we ended up going against six guys that were doing acrobatic rap stuff without instruments or anything and they apparently won. The next year "Star Search" called us again and apologized for the category mix up and asked us to come again. So, we did it two years in a row. And then we lost again! We lost to these women who sang "I'm Every Woman" from *The Bodyguard* soundtrack. They sang to a pre-recorded track. I don't know what's happened, but it's almost like the karoke market has taken over. It's harder and harder to find places to play that will let you do what you do. They're like, "We know you have a record, but what kind of covers do you do?"

It was around that period of time that you had a brief soap opera career wasn't it?
Where did you find this stuff out? Oh my God, that's right... I forgot! There's actually another Shore guy that I did this thing with... It was Mike Dalton. They had called me completely separate from Mike because I had submitted some stuff to the guy that does all of the music programming for the "Guiding Light" and they ended up using a lot of After Alice stuff. So, I was on the payroll.

They didn't know what I looked like, but somebody told the music director that I looked okay. He wanted me to come re-record the theme song and actually sing it on the show. So, I said, "What do I wear?" And they told me to wear what you'd wear at a wedding. Of course, I had never played a wedding before. So, I went out and got a dress and had it fitted. I showed up on the set and they ended up giving me all kinds of primetime! It was just one episode, but they were originally going to give me only one shot. They ended up giving me a lot of shots... I basically sang the entire song. Mike Dalton didn't get to be in it because he doesn't look as good as me!

Was it with After Alice that you were able to get a development deal?
Yeah, actually After Alice had finished. Everybody sort of started drifting their own ways. I guess the big push was done. This was in '95 around the time I was doing the "Guiding Light" thing. I was pretty much done. I didn't know what I was going to do, then I went on the professional women's tennis tour for two years as a coach. In doing so, I started writing a musical. I came back and did the show in New York. And, after all those years of showcasing, when I really didn't care at all a Columbia representative was there and offered me a deal and I said no. I said I wasn't interested and that's when they really pursued me. The secret was don't give a crap at all!

Honestly, I wanted to get out of that weird chasing a dream that you have no control over. I didn't want to have to worry about showcasing or appealing to A&R people, but they set me up with some producers and I gave it a shot. By 1999, we pretty much knew that they weren't going to pick up the option. So, we released our first CD on our own. We went and recorded everything completely again for *The Big Number* by the Alice Project. I really liked the record and it got some airplay. Then we did the second, *Traveling With Lady Berlin,* which was critically acclaimed, and now we have *Overnight Success.*

What are your plans for the future? What are you trying to do?
Well, I just signed a licensing music deal with Westwood Music, which is based at the Shore. And we're hoping to get a licensing deal overseas and get some placement. I've also been asked to do some writing for some pretty big artists. Jimmy Leahy and I are co-writing now, and that's basically what we're hoping to do. We're trying to make our mark as writers, but we're also not giving up on what we're doing. We're still recording and promoting this new record. I now have a young son, so my days of being out four or five nights a week are decidedly over.

What would you like people to remember about Secret Lovers?
It's funny because I feel that the whole process for me has been kind of a development and learning experience. There's been some wonderful moments with Secret Lovers and After Alice and with the Alice Project. I just hope that they thought I was really good with what I did.

We played a show up in Vermont last week and there was a guy in Killington that looked at me and said, "God, I feel like I know you from somewhere." He thinks about it a moment and goes, "Did you ever play the Pony?" I look at him and say yeah. He's like, "I remember you... you were hot!" And then he goes, "I mean, you're still hot!"

27 WNEW
On the Beach

Bruce and Southside certainly put the town on the map, giving it an international spotlight. Without those two, Asbury Park is just another town with a good music scene. With those two, Asbury Park took on a kind of romantic notion.

--JIM MONAGHAN
FORMER WNEW DJ

Every Memorial Day and Labor Day, WNEW-FM sponsored an all-day free concert on the beach in Asbury Park. Photo © Gary Wien

I n the mid-80s, Asbury Park had already become largely a ghost town even during the summer season. The Palace was still open but most of the rides along the boardwalk were long gone as were many of the restaurants and shops. The once crowded beach was largely abandoned in favor of nearby towns like Belmar and Manasquan. But for two days each year, WNEW-FM of New York made Asbury the place to be again.

Every Memorial Day and Labor Day WNEW-FM took over Asbury Park with a free all-day concert on the beach. The show took place in front of the old Casino and was broadcast live on the radio. Tens of thousands of fans from the tri-state area used to take the Garden State Parkway to exit 102 (as in 102.7 FM) and come down for the day. Crowds of up to 80,000 were not uncommon. And, since school was still in session for the first show, it became the local "cut day" for students from the area. "The fact that it was free didn't hurt," said Jim Monaghan, a former DJ at WNEW-FM.

Boardwalk vendors that seemed to be closed every day of the year sold pizza, hotdogs, hamburgers and soda. WNEW-FM hats were given out and the station had promotional giveaways throughout the day. Each show was more than just an event, it was a celebration of music in a town with an incredible musical legacy.

"Bruce and Southside certainly put the town on the map, giving it an international spotlight," said Monaghan. "Without those two, Asbury Park is just another town with a good music scene. With those two, Asbury took on a kind of romantic notion."

Monaghan believes the Springsteen connection was a factor in why WNEW chose Asbury Park. "WNEW-FM had a long history with New Jersey listeners and at the time there was still a pretty vibrant Jersey Shore music scene," he said. " I would also imagine that the station's relationship with the Stone Pony had a lot to do with the decision to have the shows there. Asbury was also convenient to get to and had an area of beach and boardwalk large enough to hold a significant amount of people."

Shows featured such local artists as Southside Johnny & the Jukes, Glen Burtnick, the Smithereens and John Eddie. National acts included Joan Jett, the Fabulous T-Birds, Robert Cray Band, Georgia Satellites, Nick Lowe and Roger McGuinn of the Byrds.

Monaghan's own band, Bums In The Park, was a regular member of the lineup as well. "There was always a feeling of celebrating the sense of community that the station had always tried to develop with its listeners," said Monaghan. "Some very cool national artists played those shows with me... I was always on the lookout for good local bands that we could help break on the air because that had long been a big part of the station's history."

BACKSTAGE STUFF...

WNEW DJs Carol Miller and
Pat St. John hang out backstage.

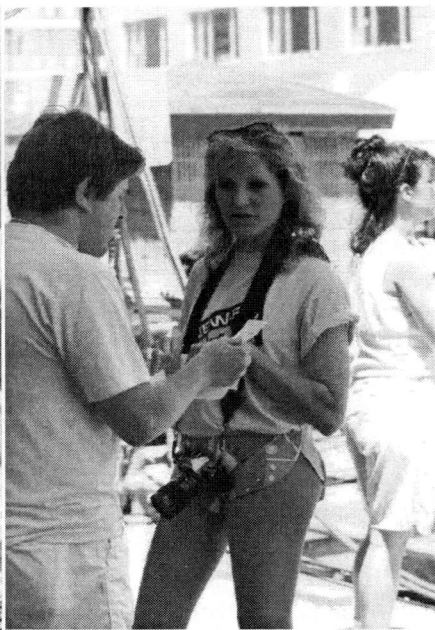

Program Director Mark Chernoff
and Newscaster Donna Fiducia.

The beach in Asbury Park is shown packed with music fans. Between
50-80,000 people used to attend the concerts. Photos © Gary Wien

Glen Burtnick. Photo © Debra L. Rothenberg/rothenbergphoto.com
Georgia Satellites, Joan Jett and Roger McGuinn. Photos © Gary Wien

Mike Mesaros of the Smithereens performs at a WNEW summer concert.
Photo © Debra L. Rothenberg/rothenbergphoto.com

Above: Southside Johnny greets the fans. Below: Shot of the WNEW crowd.
Photos © Debra L. Rothenberg/rothenbergphoto.com

28 Jersey Shore Photo Section

We ain't great... We're just some guys from Jersey.

--SAL AMATO
EDDIE & THE CRUISERS

Debra L. Rothenberg (second from left) is shown among a crowd of music fans and performers that include James Deely, Bob Makin, Lance Larson, Bobby Bandiera, the "Italian Springsteen" Graziana Romano and Sonny Kenn. Photo © Debra L. Rothenberg/rothenbergphoto.com

Above: A carousel used as part of a movie set. This shot would show up on Springsteen tour t-shirts and the *Tracks* record. <u>Below</u>: The first shot of hers to land in the pages of *Rolling Stone* - Springsteen with Marshall Crenshaw. All photos © Debra L. Rothenberg/rothenbergphoto.com

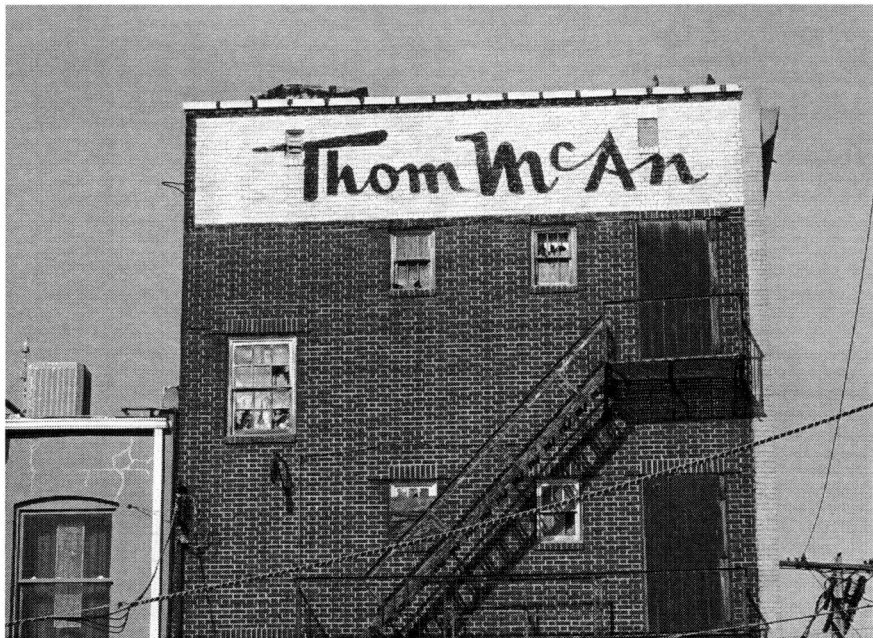

Within this building stood the Upstage, the place which started it all. The club was located above this Thom McAn shoe store. Photo © Gary Wien

Two veterans from the Upstage days: Vini Lopez and Big Danny Gallagher. Photos © Debra L. Rothenberg/rothenbergphoto.com

Bruce Springsteen and Steven Van Zandt, from the Upstage to around the world. Photo © Debra L. Rothenberg/rothenbergphoto.com

Levon Helm and Bruce Springsteen at the Stone Pony in Asbury Park.
Photo © Debra L. Rothenberg/rothenbergphoto.com

Jimmy Cliff is joined onstage by Bruce Springsteen. Photo © Alyse Liebowitz

Bruce Springsteen takes a break from rehearsing and gazes out from Convention Hall. Photo © Debra L. Rothenberg/rothenbergphoto.com

Above: Southside Johnny and Bon Jovi. Photo © Alyse Liebowitz
Below: Clarence Clemons, "The Big Man." Photo © YUWADEE

Above: Bobby Bandiera and Billy Rush (left) and John Eddie (right).
Below: John Cafferty from Beaver Brown Band with Southside Johnny.
Photos © Debra L. Rothenberg/rothenbergphoto.com

That's Bobby Bandiera underneath those glasses with Glen Burtnick at Club Xanadu in Asbury Park. Photo © Kevin R. Papa

Southside Johnny and Bobby Bandiera. Photo © David March

It's hard to say which may be wilder in this photo: Glen's shirt or his guitar?
Photo © Debra L. Rothenberg/rothenbergphoto.com

After Well of Souls there was Grimace shown here.

John Easdale of Dramarama (left) and James Deely of the Valiants (right).
Photos © Debra L. Rothenberg/rothenbergphoto.com

Above: Carolyn Mas (left) and Tom Kanach of Well of Souls (right).
Below: James Deely, Bruce Tunkel, Tony Stives and Paul Ford.
All photos © Debra L. Rothenberg/rothenbergphoto.com

Above and bottom right: Richard Barone in photos taken during the last night of the Parrot. Photos © Debra L. Rothenberg/rothenbergphoto.com
Below left: Richard Barone. Photo © Florence Mazzone

Left: Jon Leidersdorff and Blow Up. Right: Singer-Songwriter, Danny White.

Formerly the Whirling Dervishes, the band now continues on as Everlounge.
Photo © Ed O'Brien

Mr. Reality. Photo © Debra L. Rothenberg/rothenbergphoto.com

Above: A cartoon illustration of Highway 9
© Butch Suhoskey
Left: Peter Scherer and Gordon Brown
from Highway 9 (the band formerly known
as Mr. Reality and Samhill)
Photo © Gary Wien

Above: Albie Monteressa of DeSol. Below: Nicole Atkins & Josh Zandman.
All photos © Gary Wien

Above: Shot of the Asbury Park boardwalk leading up to Convention Hall.
Below: Madam Marie (left) Baronet Theatre (right). Photos © Gary Wien

Top: Sandy's Arcade, which once held punk/hardcore shows.
Middle: Empress Motel, former home of Club 101 & Club 66. Bottom: The Casino.

Pictures inside the Palace Amusements building, one of the last indoor amusement parks in the country. All photos © Cheryl A. Wolcott

Pinball was very popular with the musicians of the day. In fact, Southside Johnny was known as the "pinball king." Photo © Cheryl A. Wolcott

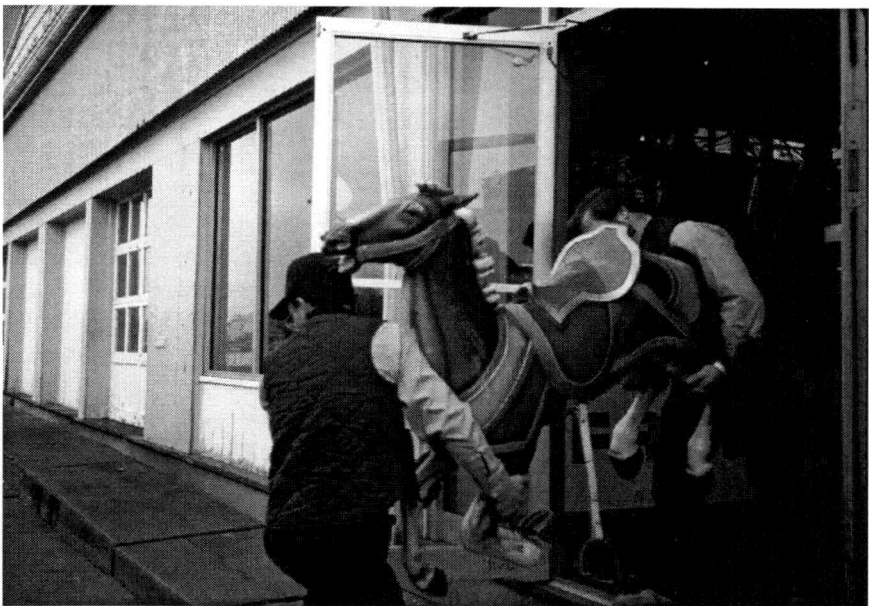

Workers remove a carousel horse from inside the Palace Amusements building. Photo © Debra L. Rothenberg/rothenbergphoto.com

29 Joey and The Works

Joey and the Works was tough in respects that we weren't a metal band, which was very popular in the late 80s. We were more of a melody, Beatlesque folk type of band. We couldn't find anybody that would grab it.

--JOEY VADALA

Joey and the Works, led by Joey Vadala (center bottom row), in 1990. Photo © Debra L. Rothenberg/rothenbergphoto.com

J   oey Vadala is a talented singer-songwriter from the New Brunswick area. He played in several bands with Glen Burtnick while they were both teenagers and actually replaced Glen in La Bamba and the Hubcaps years later when Glen left for a solo career.   After La Bamba, Vadala fronted Joey and the Works, a popular band along the Jersey Shore. From there he went on to the band Poetic Justice, which changed its name to Big Sky after a movie by the same name came out.

In addition, Joey had a song publishing contract with Polygram who published over 75 of his songs. He currently performs in small clubs in New Jersey and Pennsylvania and has released a solo record called *Eleventh Hour.* He plays both acoustic shows and shows with a full band.

In a phone interview, Joey talked about his days in Jersey Shore bands and his future plans. Although he hasn't performed in the area much in recent years, he still looks back fondly on those days that clearly helped shape his career.

What do you remember about your days with Joey and the Works?
Oh, gosh. We did the Stone Pony on Sundays. It was basically playing all originals on Sundays. The original unit of Joey and the Works was together from late 1986 to around 1989-90.

Did you guys give it a go to try getting a deal?
We had some management for a while. What had come out of it was the band at one point just got frustrated at the industry itself and we just went our separate ways. I wound up getting a publishing deal with Polygram.

At the time, a lot of the bars were really into cover music. Did that hurt you at all?
I think what hurt us was the change had come involving the Seattle sound. Grunge came in and songwriters of melodic melodies were kind of discarded. Joey and the Works was tough in respects that we weren't a metal band, which was very popular in the late 80s. We were more of a melody, Beatlesque folk type of band. We couldn't find anybody that would grab it. Then, in the early 90s, groups like the Gin Blossoms and stuff came out, which we had a sound similar to.

So, if you could only have held out a little longer...
Yeah, exactly. But it's so tough. It's like what am I doing wrong? You try something new when you probably should have stuck to your guns. You live and learn.

Did you know there was a group of people that taped every show.
Yeah, I know. (laughs)   You'd look in the back of the *Aquarian* or
East Coast Rocker and you'd see ads from people trying to sell our
bootlegs or trade them off. I found it amusing. It was flattering in a lot of
ways. Actually, in the past year, a couple of those people showed up at
some of my gigs. I was like, "Wow, I haven't seen you in ten years!"

Before that you were played with La Bamba and the Hubcaps.
I remember I joined the band March 7th, 1985 and a week later we were
playing the Brendan Byrne Arena opening for the Kinks. That was
amazing! But immediately after opening up for the Kinks we played a
Ground Round on Route 46! Same day, same night!

Was La Bamba still a house band at the Pony at that time?
Yeah, we were playing either Wednesdays or Thursdays.

What did you think of Richie (La Bamba)?
He's a genius! I mean, he's a really nice guy. Unbelievably musical. He's
very talented, a great trombone player. He's a guy to hang out with.   I
never had a problem with Richie. That horn section was a treat for me to
play with because they played so in tune with each other. I've played with
a lot of different horns, but that unit in itself, they were like locked into
each other so well.

You grew up near Glen Burtnick in the Brunswick area.
I've known Glen since I was about 12 or 13 years old. We met in a friend's
basement.   He played guitar upside down and backwards.
I looked at him and said, "You play guitar weird, man."

Glen told me that you pushed him towards Beatlemania.
Wow! He said that? Well, thank you Glen. Yeah, I was playing in New York
with a guy named Buzzy doing gigs around Manhattan. I guess I was
about 18 years old. The guy who was producing Beatlemania at the time
used to come in all of the time to see us. I said, "I've got the guy for you."
And I kept telling Glen, "Go try it, you're perfect. Just go for it."
    Glen was always a talented guy growing up. He was a guy I would look
at and go, "Wow, I want to be like him."

Did you guys ever play in bands together?
Yeah, we played in several bands in our teen years. When I moved back
from Florida in 1984, Glen and I did some duo gigs here and there.

He had already left La Bamba by the time you came, right?
No, actually... I would go in and just jam when Glen was in the band because we were hanging out together. I'd go down on Wednesday nights and they'd call me up for a couple of songs. Glen told me he was going to leave to pursue his own record deal. He said, "They really like you, you should try out for it." At that time, I had started another band with someone else and I said I really couldn't back out of it.

One morning Gene had called me to join the band and I said I couldn't do it, but on the way to rehearsal that night I lost two hubcaps. I said this has got to be a sign because the rehearsal with the other band was horrible. I said these hubcaps are an omen to call Gene. So I called him up at about 3 in the morning. And then, at that time, I had to audition for it because they had already called up several other guitar players to come down and audition. But, as it came to be, I became the guitar player.

What have you been doing since then?
I was in a band called Poetic Justice. We changed the name to Big Sky because the movie had come out. I had a publishing deal as a writer for a couple of years back in 1993 and Polygram published about 70-75 of my songs. I'm still writing and doing that whole thing right now. I have a band and I do some acoustic shows in South Jersey. I released a record called *Eleventh Hour* about two years ago. Actually, I'm in the process of putting a release out - a single - that will probably be out in about a month.

What does the Stone Pony mean to you? Good memories?
Oh, great memories. The Pony, it's just one of those clubs that will always be a part of my life because of the times I've spent there. I think the people that go there were generally into music. I mean, they went there to hear music. It was like play me some good music. Don't give me the latest cover song, play me something that's different. Give me something that has substance to it. Don't be a clone of somebody else. I think that's what the Pony was really good for. It was one of those launch pads for people who wanted to expose their talents and originality.

What would you say has been the highlight of your career?
Hopefully the highest of highlights hasn't come yet. The highlight of my music career would have to be the Stone Pony days and all of them together because there were so many highlights it would be hard to say one thing really stood out. Things like Bruce coming in and jamming or just sitting in the back dressing room just talking. We opened up for Beaver Brown Band, Cyndi Lauper - those were just special nights.

30 Asbury Park Rock 'N Roll Museum

I guess we were way ahead of our time, because recently the new leaders in Asbury have begun to understand and appreciate that Asbury is a mecca for music fans, and a potential source of much tourism revenue for the city. We tried to point that out 16 years ago.

--BILLY SMITH
ASBURY PARK ROCK 'N ROLL MUSEUM CO-FOUNDER

Stephen Bumball (left) and Billy Smith (right) of the Rock 'N Roll Museum.
Photo © Debra L. Rothenberg/rothenbergphoto.com

I n the eighties, two memorabilia collectors named Billy Smith and Stephen Bumball had a dream to create a museum that would be centered around the Jersey Shore's top acts like Bruce Springsteen, Southside Johnny and Bon Jovi but also include lesser known bands and artists of historical significance. The museum opened during the summer of 1986 in the Palace Amusements building. It gave music fans a place to go to learn more about their favorite local artists.

The museum contained photographs of Bruce Springsteen from early bands like the Castiles and Steel Mill to *Born In The USA* shots, there was a large collection of concert posters promoting shows at local clubs like the Sunshine In and the Student Prince, original lyric sheets written on pieces of notebook paper, signs from venues like the Capitol Theatre in Passaic and the entrance to the Upstage Club, rare buttons and promotional items and even a copy of the Castiles single was on display.

For the first time ever fans of the Jersey Shore had a place to go in Asbury Park to take in the history. During the short time it was open thousands of visitors from around the world came through its doors. And this was during the time before the Internet. These people came largely from word-of-mouth or from seeing the museum on MTV or the article in *Rolling Stone Magazine*.

I used to hang out at the museum and bug the guys to tell me about the early days. It was there that I first became interested in the history of the music from the area. Many of the artists that were played on their stereo were long out of print by the time I was introduced to them. Hearing them at the museum was my only exposure to this new world recently introduced to me. Personally, I don't think that it was just coincidence that they wound up being housed in the Palace. It was probably destiny.

The Palace just might be the very essence of Asbury Park. When people hear Bruce Springsteen sing the opening stanza of "Born To Run" they instantly know where those words come from. If the Palace is destroyed I wonder if the next generation of musicians from the area will really understand just what it meant to people around the world. Asbury Park has already lost many of the buildings involved in its illustrious music history. It would be a shame to lose the biggest of them all. Some people see an ugly, decaying building. Others see what made the city great and what could be once again. I wonder what Asbury Park will look like beyond the Palace?

Early in 2002, I ran into Billy Smith at a "Save The Pony" rally. It was the first time I had seen him in years. It was great to relive old times and he sent me this brief history of a museum which is sorely missed.

--Gary Wien

I had started collecting memorabilia relating to Springsteen in 1975 and soon began collecting everything relating to the local musicians and clubs. The collection had become quite large and several articles were written about it in the local papers. I always thought that it should be publicly displayed, because visitors to Asbury didn't have much to see when they arrived. I felt that the town's rich musical past was its biggest tourist attraction, but the city did nothing to promote that.

Around 1983 I was introduced to Stephen Bumball, who was also an enthusiastic music fan and collector. We began to search for memorabilia together, and we'd split up our findings. We were both looking for a "side job" that would be enjoyable and satisfying, so we started to discuss the possibilities of combining our collections for display in some fashion.

Our original idea was to buy or rent the historic site of the Upstage Club, restore it to its former glory and fill it with the memorabilia. We envisioned a combination of a nightclub and a museum. However, upon closer inspection we realized the structure was in very poor condition, having been closed for 14 years. The costs of a renovation would have been too great for our budget, so we thought about other possibilities.

We thought that the museum concept was still a good one, because Springsteen fans were then flocking to Asbury during this period of *Born in the USA* mania. We thought it was a good idea to go public with our idea, and then see what might happen. A friend of mine was a reporter for the *Asbury Park Press* and she thought we had a winning idea, and managed to get a large story about our concept on the front page of the newspaper, complete with a color photo of us surrounded by our collection. We received a great deal of attention due to that article, and we considered several different ideas and offers. Then we were contacted by local developer Henry Vaccaro, who owned the Palace Amusements building at the time. He offered to clear out a large portion of the Palace on the Cookman Avenue side, and to build us a structure to house the collection. We would help design the building, and he would receive rent based on the admission money we collected. Besides receiving our rent money, Henry realized that we would attract both a great deal of publicity for the Palace, and a great many patrons to it.

Things progressed nicely, and while the structure was being built, we were gathering more items for the display. The local musicians and fans were very supportive and the collection continued to grow. We set an opening date of July 4th (1986), and we spent many long days and nights getting it ready. But we opened on time, the mayor cut the ribbon, and the publicity was overwhelming.

We found ourselves on MTV, in *Rolling Stone Magazine*, on dozens of TV news shows and in countless newspapers and magazines.   Our visitors included Bruce Springsteen and most of the E Street Band, Jon Bon Jovi and Southside Johnny.

We successfully operated for three full seasons, having thousands of visitors from dozens of countries. Even though our museum was more successful each year, the costs of keeping the Palace operating was far exceeding its income. It was decided that the Palace would not re-open for the 1989 season, and that obviously meant that the Asbury Park Rock 'N' Roll Museum would be without a home.   So we packed up in November of '88 and put the collection into storage, which was provided for us at no charge by Max Weinberg, our biggest supporter from the E Street Band.   We looked into relocating but that did not materialize.

I guess we were way ahead of our time, because recently the new leaders in Asbury Park have begun to understand and appreciate that Asbury is a mecca for music fans, and a potential source of much tourism revenue for the city.   We tried to point that out 16 years ago.

-- Billy Smith, 2002

31 WHTG 106.3 and the Green Parrot

Until I did my calendar of New Jersey musicians in 1990, I was pretty much a Bruce/Southside/Pony girl and never went elsewhere. That project opened my ears to so much and I fell in love with the alternative sound and the Parrot and WHTG. The Parrot then felt like home where I once felt like an outsider.

--DEBRA L. ROTHENBERG
PHOTOGRAPHER

Nick Celeste, Jane Scarpontoni and Richard Barone perform on WHTG with DJ Chopper. Photo © Debra L. Rothenberg/rothenbergphoto.com

B y the mid-80s, the Jersey Shore music scene was pretty much running on fumes. Cover bands were the rage, original artists were no longer getting record deals and the drinking age had been raised, forever changing the face of the bar crowd. Things certainly looked bleak until a small radio station in Eatontown decided to change its format and wound up creating a music scene of its own.

WHTG (106.3 FM) was a radio station that played beautiful music, something akin to elevator music, but the disc jockeys really wanted to play anything else. According to Rich Robinson the station was far from a success back then. "It was going absolutely nowhere," he said. "I could tell we were losing our shirts. We would have hours without any commercials."

Robinson was attending Monmouth College at the time and had an interesting project for marketing class. Each student was to choose a business, deconstruct it and then bring it back up again with a complete marketing plan. Robinson chose WHTG for his project. Together with many staff members from the station, they handed out surveys dealing with radio listening habits to people at the Monmouth Mall. Roughly 1500 people took part during the three days surveys were handed out. The end result was that people wanted a rock and roll station.

"The owner made us go really slow with it, but I started infiltrating more and more music in," explained Robinson. "We had this guy who did a Sunday night rock and roll show called 'The Friendly Stranger in the Black Sedan.' It was the anniversary of 'Rock Around the Clock' by Bill Haley. I pulled him aside and said, 'It's the anniversary of the record that everybody thinks was the birth of rock and roll, why don't we do something for that?' And his eyes lit up. So we did a whole night of rock and roll like Bill Haley, Chuck Berry and that kind of stuff. The phones lit up and the owner realized what happened. I was like, 'See the audience wants to hear rock and roll, here's what the research says to do, we're starting to infiltrate it anyway so let's just bail on this stuff and do it.'"

If people didn't recognize the changes at the station they found out soon enough when JT, one of the disc jockeys that stayed on after the changeover, came on for his big band show. The show always opened with the song "Jersey Bounce" by Benny Goodman. On this particular night, the song didn't last very long. "He let it play for about 30 seconds and then killed the turntable," said Robinson. "After the song died he cued up 'Party Out Of Bounds' from the B-52s where it goes 'Surprise!' And as soon as the word 'surprise' came out he had 'Rock and Roll' from Led Zeppelin come on. When it went into Zeppelin the phones lit up and people thought JT was on drugs! I told him to go ahead and have some fun and he just started playing rock and roll for the rest of the night. And that's how it started."

In the beginning WHTG was similar to the progressive FM radio stations popular in the sixties. But over time the station began building its identity as a source of new music. The station took chances on artists that the more popular, mainstream stations were largely ignoring. WHTG became the commercial version of a college radio station. It not only was one of the first alternative rock stations in the nation, but it launched the careers of several influential alternative rock disc jockeys. People like Matt Pinfield, Mike Marrone and Loretta Windas got their professional starts at WHTG. Each would go on to highly successful careers. Pinfield would go on to MTV as the host of "120 Minutes" for several years, Marrone and Windas both would DJ at major market stations. Today, Rich Robinson and Mike Marrone can be found worldwide through the dueling satellite radio services Sirius and XM Radio, respectively.

Passion for music was one of the ingredients needed to be a disc jockey at WHTG. According to Robinson, the station's Program Director, many of the disc jockeys hired had never even seen the inside of a radio station before, they had only been disc jockeys at clubs. "The original reason for hiring all these people was I wanted them to be real music nuts," explained Robinson. "I wanted them to be able to mix music like you heard in a club. I wanted that to be on the radio. I didn't want anybody that had all these preconceived commercial radio notions and all that crap. They were to bring that kind of club vibe on to radio.

"Everybody that worked at that station had an undying passion for music and they knew about all this local music and they were all excited about bringing in a new record whether it was on a major label, an indie label or their friend's label. It was like, 'Here, you've got to listen to this.' We had everything in the world going against us. That's what made the whole event so spectacular because if you had everything there and were successful it would have been expected."

"We just played stuff that we liked," said Mike Marrone. "It was the old concept of progressive radio. In the very, very beginning it was more like WNEW but we played what would become alternative music. And when you're doing anything different like that you're going to attract the musicians in the area."

Musicians took to the new station quickly. The Jersey Shore has long lived in the shadow of New York City and radio was no different. New York stations like WNEW and WPLJ dominated the Jersey audience but were far too big for local bands to gain any airplay. WHTG gave budding artists a chance to be heard. "A lot of these guys cut records and probably sent them out to stations thinking they would never get played," said Loretta Windas.

"When WHTG started doing the alternative stuff I think they were just happier than pigs in shit," said Windas. "I remember when I did overnights and 2:30 a.m. was album side time. One time, instead of doing a regular album side I decided to do both sides of the EP put out by the Whirling Dervishes. I remember getting a call from this girl Eve who was a friend of the band. She said, 'I can't believe that you're playing these guys on your album side. I think that's great!' She was just tickled pink that I was playing her friends as an album side. I think that the way Eve felt probably epitomizes how most, if not all, of the local bands felt to be getting their records played on a commercial radio station. The really great thing about what we were doing at the time was we really felt we had made a mark in some people's careers. It was like we helped them get there."

Mike Marrone remembers the first time he ever heard Red House, a band from Union County that would become an WHTG favorite. He was working as the disc jockey at the Melody Bar in New Brunswick when the importer from GEM Records came in with a test pressing of the record. "He said to me, 'Hey Mike, you gotta hear this you're gonna love this!'", recalled Marrone. "And I put it on the cue phones while I was spinning Cure remixes for the Melody Bar crowd. I heard 'Rain' and I was like, 'Oh fuck, this is going in!' I was gonna put this on the air and we started playing it from the acetate tape. So whenever you start to play that stuff in an area, it takes a while, but eventually they'll be a room or a club that will have live music and that's how the bands started to come to play there."

Local alternative bands found that club in the Green Parrot. Located just outside Asbury Park on Route 33 in Neptune, the club was literally designed with WHTG in mind. Tom Ackerino, the owner of the Green Parrot, wanted to create a club that went hand in hand with WHTG. He wanted the club to play the music heard on WHTG and wanted to book the bands that were being played. Together the station worked out a deal to have the WHTG disc jockey become the club's DJs.

"I'll never forget my first night walking in there to DJ," said Windas. "None of the staff knew me. They were like, 'How is this going to turn out?' I don't think they really knew the music at the time. I mean, a couple of them did and they were really psyched about it but they were dance music types. The crowd was okay numbers wise, but it was really fun. Within a couple of weeks we were all buddies and they were psyched because it was very successful."

Night after night, the Green Parrot brought the feeling of New York club's like the Ritz to the Jersey Shore. It gave people a reason not to leave for the city anymore. It became a home for many local bands and was host to many classic performances by upcoming national acts.

WHTG did everything they could to make Ackerino's club a success. They sent him the station's playlist, they told him what the new ads were, they would talk about the bands being played and let him know which bands were getting requested and which had record labels willing to promote them. "I looked at the Green Parrot as a very cool, cheap way of getting as much free publicity as humanly possible," said Robinson. "So, it was to my benefit that Tommy was really successful."

"The Green Parrot was really the perfect size," said Marrone. "Because it was small enough that it was very intimate, but it was big enough where you could get a decent sound and get a nice sized band on the stage. And that was a room where we could bring bands in and we had some great shows there, just unbelievably great shows. I have a lot of them on videotape because we had video cameras set up in the DJ booth and tape decks up there, since I would run cartoons and video art while we were playing music. In fact, Springsteen himself even showed up one night to play guitar with Jah Love and the Survivors because one night of the week was reggae."

Tons of great shows took place at the Green Parrot. There were nights like Faith No More and the Red Hot Chili Peppers for 3 bucks. Shows with national bands like the Bolshoi, Flesh for Lulu, the Del-Lords, Social Distortion and Husker Du. And local bands like Red House, Dramarama, the Blases and the Whirling Dervishes made a name for themselves there. It was truly a club unlike any other along the Jersey Shore.

One of Rich Robinson's favorite memories of the Parrot was the night that Living Color played there. "We were the only station playing them," Robinson said. "They had put out the album and the record label went after a track that was like the worst song on the album. We started playing 'Cult Of Personality' and it just blew up the phone lines. People just went rabid over the song. So, Tommy booked them into the Parrot for two nights.

"I remember the first night going there. The place was so packed I had to sit on the ledge by the windows and all of the windows were wide open. It was dead of winter but the windows all had frost on them because there was so much sweat going on inside and it was so cold outside that the windows had fogged over. I got seasick from watching everybody jump up and down when the band took the stage. The whole building was shaking. The place must have been oversold that night. It was just a madhouse. When they broke into 'Cult Of Personality' I thought the building was going to come down. And that's when I knew... It was the first time that I looked out and thought, holy shit! This is a mob scene and it's all because of us! It had nothing to do with any New York radio. They had no exposure anywhere, it was totally us. It really worked."

The combination of WHTG and the Green Parrot succeeded in creating its own music scene apart from the traditional world of the "Asbury Sound." They succeeded so much, in fact, that bands that had routinely packed the house at the Green Parrot would struggle to sell out shows down the road in Asbury Park. The Stone Pony and the Green Parrot were about as far apart as two clubs could be. Part of the reason why was that the Pony had always had relationships with New York stations like WNEW and didn't want anything to do with WHTG.

Many of the people involved with WHTG believed that there was an undercurrent of resentment from the Stone Pony because the radio station didn't play Bruce Springsteen, a charge that Robinson says was misleading. "We used to play 'Candy's Room' and stuff like that from Bruce," he said. "The funny thing is we used to get requests all the time from Julianne Phillips, his first wife. We'd get calls all the time from Julianne from Rumson requesting songs. And two others who used to be big fans of the station was Dorothy and Jon as in Bon Jovi and his wife. All these people that the Pony hated us for not playing used to listen to us all the time because we weren't playing them."

It took years before the Stone Pony ever let WHTG sponsor a night at the Pony. Mike Marrone says the first time was when WHTG presented Julian Cope at the Stone Pony and even that night had its share of WNEW-related problems. There were people outside the show handing out WNEW hats and bumper stickers. "That's how much they hated us," said Marrone. "Of course, that all changed years later when the alternative became the mainstream. That all changed and then WHTG and the Pony had a good relationship."

The success of alternative music along the Shore prompted many clubs to start booking WHTG-related acts. The Fastlane became home to acts too large for the Green Parrot to hold. This actually brought the Fastlane back to its roots as the premier place in the area to see New Wave bands. In the early 80s, the club was host to shows by such legendary bands as U2, the Police and the Psychedelic Furs.

The radio station also helped alternative bands get booked in other Asbury Park clubs like Club Xanadu and Visions, a short-lived club located next to the X-Rated movie theater by the Palace building. Rich Robinson recalls seeing the club change before his very eyes. "It went from a gay bar to our club to a gay bar almost overnight as the bands were playing," he said. "I think they changed it to a gay bar as the bands were changing sets. When they came back in everyone was special and everybody's wardrobe looked so much better than when I went outside for a cigarette."

The Green Parrot days were special to everyone involved. "It was such a scene that we were a part of and I'm grateful that I was part of such a happening hip thing," added Windas. "People could not believe it, this club just fell from Heaven. All of a sudden there was a club in town playing the music that they loved to hear and booking the bands that they wanted to see so they didn't have to schlep into New York all of the time. It was too much fun, it was incredible!"

Unfortunately, the club's history was short and sweet. The last artist to play there was Richard Barone, former frontman of the Bongos. Even Barone had no idea the club was closing until after he had completed his set. The last three songs played at the Green Parrot were the encores of "I Belong To Me," "Barbella" and finally "Numbers With Wings."

"It felt like something had been ripped out of me," explained Windas. "Because nobody knew it was closing until that night. The management had their reasons for not telling the staff that it was closing. So, we all found out after the show, although rumors had started going around while the band was on. People were upset. We were crying. That had been such a huge part of who we were. Not just the fact that it was this happening scene-making place to be, but it had just ingrained itself into ourselves. It was a humongous part of my identity. I felt like something was ripped out of me and I know other people felt the same way."

The memories of the Green Parrot became tales of lore that WHTG disc jockeys passed down to the station's new blood. Long after the club was just a memory, the stories of those classic shows were told and retold often. Mike Sauter, a disc jockey that joined WHTG after the Parrot had closed recalls the last days before the station was sold to Press Communications near the end of 2000. "The power of the Parrot was such that by the end of WHTG we had an hour-long show on Friday night called 'HTG Old School' which played nothing but classic WHTG artists," said Sauter. "The host of the show, Tod Lewis, was fresh out of college, and he was inundated week after week during with calls from listeners asking him, 'Hey, remember the Green Parrot?' Despite the fact that he was probably about 12 when the Parrot closed."

Even after the Green Parrot closed, WHTG remained a force in the local music scene. One night, the band Dada was playing at the Stone Pony. Although they were originally supposed to be the 2nd or 3rd opening act, they wound up being the headliner when the others were forced to cancel. They had just released their debut record and figured nobody had heard of them, but WHTG had been playing their music for a while. When they took the stage they were surprised to find a huge crowd of people that actually came just to see them.

The Fastlane picked up most of the slack and became the leading place to see alternative shows. There were concerts with such WHTG favorites as Concrete Blonde, Matthew Sweet, the Connells and Material Issue. Meanwhile, WHTG continued to be the area's leading source of alternative music, a position that confused many people who thought the Jersey Shore only listened to Springsteen.

"In 1992, when Springsteen released his *Human Touch* and *Lucky Town* albums, some reporter somewhere else in the country came up with the brilliant idea that he would write a story about an Asbury Park radio station playing the new music from the Asbury scene's most famous cultural export," recalled Sauter. "He called up WHTG, which despite being physically located in Tinton Falls had an Asbury Park mailing address (Tinton Falls has no post office, so its mail is routed through Asbury), and spoke with our Program Director at the time, Mike Butscher. Butscher patiently explained to this reporter that we were an alternative rock station, and we didn't play any Springsteen. I don't know whether it was because grunge hadn't really taken hold of the cultural zeitgeist yet and this reporter simply didn't understand what alternative rock was, or perhaps he was just dense or he just wouldn't let go of what he thought was a really good angle on a story, but he spent 20 minutes on the phone trying to convince Butscher to play Springsteen just so he could write his story. That's the strength of the Springsteen legend - the power of the Asbury Park mythology.

"We always knew that his reputation was clouding the waters of what we were trying to do at 'HTG, but even so, we always were glad to have a rock and roll mailing address. There are only about a dozen towns in the country that are closely identified with a rock scene - Nashville, Memphis, Detroit, Austin, Woodstock NY, Seattle, Athens GA. Cities like New York, Los Angeles, Boston, Chicago, Philly, and New Orleans have so much going on that their rock and roll heritage gets diffused. But Asbury Park ranks up there, and it's largely due to Bruce."

Rich Robinson thinks that many people forget that WHTG played a wide variety of music, including many bands that people wouldn't normally associate with an alternative radio station. "A lot of people when they look back at WHTG may have selective memory," he said. "They forget that we played a lot of mainstream rock acts but it was within the context of this music that we were playing. We'd play the Smithereens and follow it up with the Kinks or play a Jane's Addiction and then an off-Zeppelin track. What other alternative station anywhere would think of playing a John Lennon song or a Chuck Berry song? But it all fit within the flow of what we were doing and that's what made WHTG special."

"It depended on the set you were playing," added Windas. "It was all about the flow of the set you were doing. That's what our listeners appreciated, the open-mindedness."

WHTG was far more successful than many people realized. The station helped launch the careers of local bands like the Smithereens, Dramarama, the Whirling Dervishes, Red House and the Blases in addition to dozens of national acts like Living Color and Dada. Fans plastered street signs with FM 106.3 bumper stickers throughout Central New Jersey. According to Robinson, during one 3-month period of time the station distributed 250,000 bumper stickers. Many of those can still be found on signs throughout the Jersey Shore.

"I can't think of a better feeling than watching Dramarama when they did that big outdoor tent show at the Pony and there were several thousand people there," said Robinson. "They had the big stage and the big logo behind them. The scene was packed and when they broke into 'Anything, Anything' to see the rush of people and fists in the air and people singing... Just to know that we helped them get there, there was no better feeling in the world."

Unfortunately, radio, as with all businesses, has to deal with a bottom line and the station constantly struggled to sell enough advertising space to compete. The station's Arbitron ratings were always subpar and never seemed to reflect the true audience along the Jersey Shore. A secondary rating system, Scarborough, provided a much clearer look but was largely ignored by advertising agencies.

"I remember one time we didn't get creamed by Arbitron, but we had our usual so-so numbers," recalled Robinson. "We got the Scarborough report and came in as the number one rated station in the county. Our average listener was a 30-year old white guy making over $50,000 a year, which was like the prime advertising demographic. We had the longest time spent listening of any station in the New York Metro area. We just kicked ass and took names, but none of the advertising agencies would look at the information so we couldn't get the kind of national buys that we needed to make any money. It was like a great compliment that didn't do us any good. But we knew what we were doing, we knew we had the audience out there."

The audience stayed with WHTG even as the original disc jockeys moved on. Early DJs like Bart, Chopper, Mike, Rich, Matt and Loretta left the station after staying about five years each, a remarkable number considering that the pay wasn't very much. But WHTG was a special place, the disc jockeys all hung out together. They were like a family. Even today many of the disc jockeys stay in touch with one another.

"That passion for music was our common bond and it was so strong that we're all still friends," said Windas. "These guys were like my big brothers that I never had back then and they still are."

Nowadays, WHTG appears to be in a constant state of flux. Ever since the station was purchased by Press Communications in 2000, it has become more and more like a traditional chart-reading, strict playlist type of station that turns its back on the local music scene. Each day it looks a little less like the station which once was voted the best small-market radio station in the United States by *Rolling Stone Magazine* readers. The station now bills itself as "G-106.3" in an apparent break from its history as well.

"I've heard it, yeah, it's frightening!" said Marrone. "It's just a joke and the thing that gets me is that we created that place and I underline the word we – meaning the entire staff – out of pure love for the music and nothing else. We weren't making any money there. We had to work at clubs to survive, and then you get a bunch of people afterward who either used it as a stepping stone or just totally trash the history of the station."

Mike Sauter was the last DJ on the air with the "old" WHTG. The station pulled the plug after a two-hour edition of "HTG Old School" filled with highlights from throughout the station's history. According to Sauter, the station will never be the same. "The era of WHTG under Press Communications has seemed like any other corporate radio approach," he said. "They nurture few new bands except those on major label agendas. They don't support the local music scene. They appear to care little except for the bottom line."

Many of the disc jockeys from the second era of WHTG like Jeff Raspe and Mike Sauter can still be heard in the area on the public radio station WBJB ("The Night" 90.5 FM) from Brookdale Community College. The memories of the Green Parrot and that period of time was evident at a recent Peter Case show at Brookdale Community College, which was sponsored by WBJB. Cheers from the crowd were heard when Jeff Raspe introduced Case and mentioned seeing him play back at the old Green Parrot club. WBJB is the station that a lot of the old WHTG fans listen to now. Unfortunately, its signal does not reach that far.

Memories of the old WHTG are still strong. WBJB fills the void somewhat, but there was nothing like that period of time, before playlists took over, when that little station from Eatontown played one great song after another. Many former WHTG disc jockeys have rediscovered that freedom with the Internet and satellite radio. Rich Robinson is now with Sirius and Mike Marrone is with XM Radio. Both can now program their shows the way they want... the way radio was meant to be.

32 Dramarama

Every time we played in New Jersey it was so much better than any other show we ever did in California or anywhere else in the country. There was something just wonderful and heartwarming. It felt like being at home. It felt like going home and we were welcomed like the prodigal sons.

--JOHN EASDALE

Dramarama is the classic example of a band that should have been a household name but never quite reached that level. Photo © Jay Blakesburg

D ramarama was an explosive live band that recorded several brilliant records during the late 80s and early 90s. The band was formed by a group of guys from Wayne, New Jersey who moved out to California around the time they were signed to their first record deal. Even while they were living on the West Coast the band played a major role in an emerging alternative rock scene along the Jersey Shore. With sold out shows at clubs like the Green Parrot, the Fastlane and the Stone Pony, Dramarama became one of the most popular bands of its day.

Unfortunately, the rest of the country (with the exception of California) never took to the band the same way. Although Dramarama songs have reached near classic levels in the alternative music world, the band never achieved the success or recognition they were due. But to the fans that packed each show along the Jersey Shore, Dramarama will always be one of the greatest bands that nobody knows. I was able to talk to three of the original band members Chris Carter, John Easdale and Mark Englert via phone to go over the band's history.

Talking with Chris Carter

former bass player for Dramarama

Are you one of those people who hates talking about the past?
I would, but I think it's all about where people are now. It's all about how you're doing. If you're doing real good or if you're happy in life, you don't mind talking about the past. Maybe if you're really bumming out with what you're doing... But the past was really fun and a lot of good times. So, I'm more than happy to talk about it.

Tell me about Looney Tunes. Is that really where the band started?
Oh yeah, absolutely. It was a record store I opened. I had gone to the Connecticut School of Broadcasting to be a DJ and, at that point, you had to get a third-class license. So I was doing that and those were my two dreams: To have a record store and to be a DJ. After going to broadcasting school, I realized that it was kind of tough because you had to stick to playlists and play things people wanted you to play. I was all about my own thing. So I opened a record store.

It was an old head shop in Wayne, New Jersey and we turned it into a record store. It was like a mini-Bleeker Bob's of Wayne. We were trying to have imports there, and this is 1979 so imports were like GEM Records and there was a lot of progressive records imported at the time. It wasn't like the way it became. We had lots of bootlegs and hard-to-find things. As '79 turned into '80 and '81, the whole new wave thing and independent 45s really started to become a big thing and we were pretty much the only store in the area that had them. So, we had people come from all over.

We got hooked up with Uncle Floyd. We were actually the Uncle Floyd headquarters, the only store where you could buy Uncle Floyd merchandise. So we had guys coming from all over, these kooks... We had all of his records and the records of all the characters and the wacky guys who had their own visions of getting off the "Uncle Floyd Show" and becoming a "Saturday Night Live" cast member. They all had their own line of products and we sold all that stuff. As a result, we got the Ramones and the Plasmatics, Ian Hunter and Mick Ronson - everybody came to our store and did in-stores because we had the connection to Uncle Floyd.

At the time, whatever those guys were doing be it David Johansen or Ian Hunter, we got them to come to the record store and we had huge lines. It was just a little store in an outdoor mall. I remember when the Plasmatics came they pulled up in an all-convertible Cadillac and the windshield was busted and Wendy O. Williams was sitting in the back seat with her tits hanging out. It was classic! Fucking Wayne... this little town. It was really weird.

So we really made our mark there as a record store and, throughout the whole course of the store, John Easdale used to come in and hang out and he used to work there. He was younger than me and Tommy. We graduated in '77 and John graduated in like '78 or '79. John was always younger, but he played football with Tommy so we all knew him and we let him hang out there. That's how me and Easdale hooked up. We then proceeded to go down to the basement of the record store, began bringing instruments down there and started making tapes. It was me and John and Mark. Mark was John's next door neighbor and he was younger as well so those guys had been in lots of bands together. I had been in bands before with Tommy. I didn't know Mark very well, other than I knew he played guitar. And the three of us started playing. I don't know why Tom didn't start playing with us. I guess he had to watch the store.

So, yeah, that's how it really started with me, John and Mark in the basement of Looney Tunes.

What do you remember about those first shows?

Our first show was on the "Uncle Floyd Show", of course. I think we did three Uncle Floyd shows. I guess the first one might have just been the three of us with a different drummer - a drummer from Asbury Park, actually, who was in this band called Max. This is all coming back to me now. That was our first appearance and then we played our first real big gig at the Meadowbrook, which was a big place to have a first gig.

That place was huge and, in the early 80s, it had bands like Duran Duran and Billy Idol play there. When they didn't have a big-time band, it was a dance club. It was packed! I remember we were standing in front of the sign and it said "King Crimson, Dramarama and Billy Idol". That was our first gig and that's where it all started.

We're all from Wayne, New Jersey and we came out to California because Rodney Bingenheimer, infamous DJ on KROQ out here, was playing our record and our record became a huge hit on KROQ. So we came out to play one gig at the Roxy. We had round-trip tickets and we never came back. We just stayed there.

And now you're producing a documentary about him called *Mayor of the Sunset Strip*.

I owe it to him to do it. We'll finish the movie and it's going to be a big thing. We're going to the Cannes Film Festival... We got everybody from David Bowie to Courtney Love, Cher to Brian Wilson, Oasis and Alice Cooper - it's amazing.

It's going to play at whatever the cool theatre you go to that plays the cool movies. Wherever *Crumb* or movies like *Punch-Drunk Love* played, those cool little theatres will have it. It'll be out probably at the end of 2003, by the time it's all sold and everything.

And you've got your radio show, "Breakfast With The Beatles." How's that going?

It's great! It's probably been a dream of mine for the last 15 years to host a Beatles show. The way it came about was kind of sad. The host died. It's not funny, but it sounds like a black comedy. Everybody was really sad when she passed away, but the first thing I thought was who's going to do the show? They had this big contest and they voted for the DJs who had filled in all year long. Anyway, I got the gig. It's probably the greatest thing that ever happened to me. I'm thrilled!

It's just great, just to play the Beatles and the solo music. I get to do whatever I want. Come up with all these different shows, just any angle to keep it fresh because it can get old playing the Beatles every week.

I just try to make it real interesting with mono shows and solo shows. It's a lot of fun. The show is so successful it's the number one show in Los Angeles for any station on the weekend. Not that it has anything to do with me. It's the music, but it's really fun.

What was it like on the way up with Dramarama?

Well, it was weird for us because it started before our first album. We started with an EP and sent it off to France. Our first record was actually on New Rose Records in France and we went to France before we went anywhere. We had a following there. The record was somewhat of an underground hit in France, so that was kind of cool.

We just had really good breaks, you know? It was like wherever we aimed the cannon we went for specifically like France. We said, "Ok there's this label called New Rose. They have the Replacements and Johnny Thunder, Willie Alexander and all these wacky people we like, let's go with this label." And they put the record out. Same thing with California. We got played in California and went and moved out there. We just went after it, you know?

It was cool, but it was really weird to be in California because the kids out here put us in the same league as the Smiths, Love and Rockets and Depeche Mode. They thought of us as one of those bands. We, of course, knew the difference. We knew when we left California that we weren't going to go sell out the same places as the Smiths or those guys. But the kids in California didn't know that. They saw Dramarama as the headliner for the Palladium and playing with the Psychedelic Furs at Irvine Meadows. So, it was kind of a goof for us. It was a bit surreal in that we were so big in California and we knew when we left it wasn't going to be that way. We had to work on the rest of the country and we slowly started to do that from 1989-1991. By '92, we were considered pretty much a good, strong B-level alternative band in places like Chicago and Texas. But New Jersey and Los Angeles, those were our two big spots.

And we didn't know about the Jersey thing. We forgot about Jersey for a while. Then we realized that the DJs like Matt Pinfield and Jerry Robino and those guys, who had been supporters of us from the beginning, they were hip to what was going on in California. They were like, "Hey man, we played you guys first!" And they stayed on us on all those stations. It was cool that when we would come home -- we were used to coming home and telling everybody, "Hey, we just played the Palladium" and they'd go, "Yeah, sure." Then as things went on we started actually doing good in New Jersey, which was nice for us because you always want to do good where you come from.

Why did Dramarama break up? Did you guys just get tired of being so close for so long or was there one incident in particular that sort of ended it?

It was a succession of bummers in a row. My recollection is that we were going to end the tour at the Hollywood Bowl, which was our biggest thing ever. Duran Duran and the Cranberries were going to play. A weird bill, but it didn't matter because we were playing the Hollywood Bowl. In a two day period, we got a call that says your Hollywood Bowl show is cancelled with Duran Duran because the guy has strep throat and they're not rescheduling and then a couple days later we found out our label Chameleon, who had been hooked up with Elektra, was splitting. We were finally on a major label and something happened between the presidents of both labels and they got into a fight.

John and me were just like, "Aw man, we're not playing the Hollywood Bowl, we have no record label... this sucks." We just got real depressed. I think the band was at its height at that time with Clem Burke on drums. We were just finishing a semi-successful tour, we had a big tour bus, we were finally doing the things we all wanted to do. But it's weird because when you get to where you want to be, sometimes you realize that that's as far as you're gonna go. It's like well, that's it. We're not gonna ever be U2. We're not going to play stadiums. Next year, we're probably going to play the same places we played last year. I think you reach the point where it's not getting better and then if things go wrong they kind of affect you more than they might have affected you in the beginning where you're used to bad things happening. Once you get to a certain point you want things to keep going better for you instead of worse.

I think we started having a couple of setbacks like our manager might have left at this point and we had a new manager. It just wasn't a warm feeling of love. Plus, we had been together since high school, which had been about 12-13 years. Guys were getting married and having kids. Even if you're making the same money you were making three years before it's different now because you're getting older and you need a little bit more money and you have a little bit more responsibility. Not all of the guys were in the same situation. Some weren't married, but it just made for an easy out when things really started going wrong.

I think that's what happened. And, I'm not going to lie, there was some substance abuse problems. There was some personalities that were getting a little altered here and there. So, I think the combination just ended up the way it did.

What did you do after the band broke up?

I got really depressed! *(laughs)* Because I never realized that I didn't have anything else going on.   When you're in a band, it's like you're in Disneyland every day. Everyone's kissing your ass, everyone loves you. Even if they don't, they'll tell you they do. Everything's free, everybody gives you everything and it's wonderful. You get used to that and you don't realize that the reason everybody's doing this is because you're in a rock band and they feel that they're supposed to treat you this way. Then once you're not in the band anymore, all that kind of ends.

It's not all superficial, it's not just the free things and the ass-kissing I miss. I miss the actual business of doing business as a band. We were professional musicians and we were treated that way. All of a sudden, you're not that guy anymore and you're not in that band and you realize your self-worth. I was a bass player in Dramarama... big deal. What do you do? What do you do with that? Do you start another band? I don't know if I want to do that. You don't know what to do. So, I got really depressed.

I thought originally that John and I would continue as a team and it almost worked the opposite way in that it was like this Paul McCartney/John Lennon thing.   It was like, "I'm going to do things without Chris because Chris gets so much credit for the band and I'm writing all these songs. Maybe Chris shouldn't get as much credit as he's getting, so I'm gonna go out on my own without him." Because basically John had a raw talent that I picked up on real early at Looney Tunes. Believe me, I would always want to be the songwriter in the band or write lyrics or music, but he was so damn good, he impressed me so much, that I felt he had that covered. I didn't even have to go in there and do that. It's like, I don't even have to try because he's so good at it. I knew that from the beginning and he knew I knew that.

But John also has limitations. He doesn't necessarily know what to do with his songs. Sometimes, I felt he didn't know how to express them to the band as well as I did.   So, I felt, I was very important in his song writing process. I would get the producer or pick the studio. I would pick the guitars we would use on certain songs. He was definitely a partner and we worked very well together, I think he just wanted to go off and do some stuff on his own.

Do you play anymore?
Umm... my last gig was with Mike Myers as Austin Powers on the MTV Movie Awards. I played bass. I just do some weird, little things. I just produced an album by Stew called The *Naked Dutch Painter*.
What would you like people to remember about Dramarama?

Geez... I just think that we were consistent and every album, I felt, was listenable from beginning to end, which is really not the case with most rock and roll records you get. Those records are very listenable. They hold up really well production wise with the exception of *Box Office Bomb*, which sounds dated. It's weird because the album before it still holds up.

I think *Vinyl* is like a classic to me. I almost listen to it from a third party perspective. The other records I really hear everything we're doing and I really put myself back into it and I know what's up. But when I listen to *Vinyl*, probably because we had an outside producer, I can actually step back from it and listen to it like I listen to some Stones records. That's a nice record on a whole bunch of different levels, whereas *Hi-Fi Sci-Fi* or *Cinema Verite* I was in the thick of the record production so I know them better and I can't look at it the same way. I think *Vinyl*, of all of our records, is a good one. It really holds up nicely.

We're in between deals right now. Rhino had a license for our records for five years and that's over now, so we're in between labels. Hopefully, we'll be able to put these things back out in the next year or two.

Looking back do you view Dramarama as an alternative band or a regular rock band?

Well, we were an alternative band because when we were making records that's what they called it, but we would consider ourselves a rock and roll band. Our influences weren't the Pixies, you know? Although it may have been if you listen to "I've Got Spies." *(laughs)* See, a lot of the alternative bands when we were around were really rock and roll bands that we liked, bands like the Replacements and Hoodoo Gurus. The bands that we liked were rock and roll bands. I didn't give a shit what they called them.

Alternative was a way that you could get on a chart, you know? There was no rock and roll chart in 1985, but there was the alternative chart, the dance chart and the whatever chart. So, yeah, I guess we were alternative, but we never thought of it that way.

Talking with John Easdale

former lead singer for Dramarama

Let's start with today. What do you do at Network Magazine Group?
I am the senior editor here.

I guess that takes up a lot of your time...
Unfortunately, it does. After the band played what proved to be its final show at the Stone Pony in 1994, I took about a year off, I kind of stepped away from being in a rock group. Then I got back into this place by producing a radio show for the company that was hosted by Johnny Rotten called "Rotten Day." I produced that show for about two years and then saw the writing on the wall for that to be going away. So, I kind of like jumped into editing and I've been here a total of nearly eight years.

And you still have the John Easdale Band. Is that basically whenever you feel like doing a gig?
No, it's way more about when people ask. For the last few years we've actually been, I guess, playing on our popularity in the Central Jersey region. We've played every May... the first weekend in May.

That's the Surf Club in Ortley Beach.
Yeah, opening the season for them for a couple of years.

You've also come back for some birthday shows...
And I've come out for several birthday shows. What really got me back into playing or even considering playing was doing a show for the station down there, which I always consider an Asbury Park station, WHTG. For years that station played music and was very influential on things that were going on down in that area.

WHTG listeners have consistently voted songs like "Anything, Anything" and "Last Cigarette" among their all-time favorites.
Wow! I wasn't sure because I knew they had gone more right of center. I haven't been in contact with them since the new people bought it. That's fantastic! That's certainly very flattering and gratifying.

224

How are the shows with the John Easdale Band different from the Dramarama days?

Umm, I don't think the crowd or the artist is different except that maybe he's not drunk off his ass anymore!

Little older... little wiser?

Yeah, that's the thing. As far as the crowd out there, whenever we've played and whenever there was a place to play in Asbury Park we've always continued. The John Easdale Band played there as well. I was calling my band the Newcomers for a while. The last few times I've been out there I've been using Jersey guys to play with.

I used to go to concerts down the Shore in the mid to late 70s. All kinds of great shows were down there after the Springsteen era when the boardwalk was still open and it was still happening. Then when we started playing there with Dramarama it became a decidedly quiet town, more like Bruce Springsteen's video for "Atlantic City." A really kind of dark and scary place. We were down there on the 4th of July one year at the Pony and it was empty. The entire city was like a ghost town.

The good thing is that it's finally showing signs of coming back.

Well, I certainly saw last year's big Bruce send-off and that was refreshing. I didn't watch the whole "Today Show" so I don't know if they actually focused on the positives or the negatives of the city. It really is a bizarre kind of thing. It had such history and was such a cool place with the boardwalk and the rides. I think it had a lot to do with narcotics and stuff.

And corruption...

Yeah or lack of corruption, you know? No one was paying to keep the place clean anymore. And that's me using my "Simpsons" kind of logic. It's like the boys moved out of town, go ahead it's a free for all! Because the boys run the boardwalks, the coliseums, the stadiums, the jukeboxes and the pizza boxes.

What do you remember about those early Fastlane shows?

I remember everything about them. They were always very well attended, great crowds. When we were growing up in New Jersey we never played down in Asbury Park. It was at that point when the Springsteen thing had passed and the originals thing hadn't taken off. It was more of a cover band scene when we were growing up. We were an original band, so we played up in North Jersey in Passaic and any dive that would have us, places like the Dirt Club.

When we moved to California our record came out and WHTG came on the air. We came back and first played a place called the Green Parrot. That was our reintroduction into New Jersey via California after we started making records. Originally, the Asbury Park scene was closed to us if you will. It was far away and it wasn't a thriving original scene in the early 80s.

What did you think of the Green Parrot club?

We had a wonderful, wonderful time there. We had magnificent shows, always well attended and enthusiastic crowds that wouldn't let us leave. We had to keep coming back. That was one of the few places where we would get called back for encores that weren't planned. We loved it!

It was like a house, you know? Actually, it was like going home. You'd go upstairs and go into the little rooms. That was a different kind of club than the Pony or Fastlane.

Did you guys feel a part of that local music scene at the Parrot?

I was stunned and shocked. It had a lot to do with a guy named Matt Pinfield and Mike Marrone and the guys who worked at WHTG. Obviously, they made us a part of that scene by including us because we were from Jersey. Even though we lived in California we never became an L.A. band, I don't think. We always felt like we were from Jersey. When we lost a guy we tried to get somebody from Jersey. It's very much always been a part of us. It's where we're from and it's what we're a part of. I have a very warm spot in my heart and I love it dearly. If I hadn't come out here and married and had four children I would be back there.

What is it like for you to come back for a birthday show?

It's heartwarming, it's delightful - those cliche words that they use on television shows. It's the most wonderful kind of feeling because everyone's really just so welcoming. I like the relationship that I have with the people who like my music. I'm very fortunate that there are people like that.

I try to be as non-showbiz as possible because I'm so aware of it, especially working at the trade magazine and seeing all the stuff that goes on in the business. Coming here to work I didn't so much learn a lot as have a lot of my suspicions confirmed about the way things go. As much as I felt what happened to our band and our story was very unique with our battles with the labels and the ups and downs - the fact that we had a career at all, much less that we did accomplish as much as we did and the fact that 20 years later you and me are talking about it and that they're playing it on the radio is so miraculous. I often say that it's easier to win the lottery than to make a living playing guitar.

For people in NJ and the LA area, it's hard to fathom why Dramarama didn't become a bigger band. The albums still stand up.
That's very kind of you to say. What's funny is that we're gonna be like the New York Dolls, a band that never sold any records but influenced a lot of people. Everyone loves the Dolls. Everyone loves Dramarama. But when we made records no one really went out in droves and bought them, which is not all bad. Sometimes you're ahead of your time. And I've got to think that was the case rather than we just sucked or something.

Why do you think Dramarama never reached that final level?
There are hundreds of reasons, thousands of reasons, and none of them have anything to do with the quality of the music. First and foremost, most of the time we were totally independent. The first three albums we released basically on our own. The 4th and 5th albums were released through Elektra but through a subsidiary called Chameleon, which was owned by this really rich guy who had bought the independent record label we were part of and dropped every band but us.

I mean, your book is about New Jersey and Asbury Park. You know what? New Jersey and Asbury Park never let us down and we always had extreme popularity there. I can still go there and get a crowd of people to show up. It's fantastic! The rest of the country was a couple of years behind. They started listening to rock music in the early 90s when Nirvana came out. Whether it was the Cure, Depeche Mode or anything else it was considered old as far as radio was concerned. Very few bands that were having hits in the 80s survived the cresting of that wave.

I'd much prefer to think about the amazing thing as to why we did what we did. I think it's the music. Luckily, we based everything we did on our music. We weren't really of a time. It's not like you listen to that record and say, "Oh, that sounds so much like 1985 or 1989 or whatever." Not that it sounds so great or so modern, it's just not dated so much hopefully.

What do you think of the label alternative music?
Well, it meant a lot more then. None of that stuff had any outlet in New York City. Bands played shows there but there was no radio station playing that music except for college stations and WHTG. So, every band would come to New York and then take a ride to Asbury Park to visit Matt Pinfield or whoever was on the air. That's why Asbury Park had such an amazing spotlight on that scene that a lot of the rest of the country didn't get. A lot of those bands had an entire North American tour consisting of a gig in Manhattan and the Pony or Fastlane. That was their trip. There was no reason to go anywhere else because no one knew who they were.

One other thing about alternative music was you had a radio station that was unlike any other radio station in any major market in the country except for KROQ. KROQ was unique for many years until Nirvana came along and then all of a sudden there was 100 modern rock stations. You had people listening to that music and that influences people in an area.

I think alternative itself was alternative until grunge came along. Alternative meant something that wasn't popular particularly, something that wasn't mainstream. Something that was an alternative to the mainstream. Now it's become a branding/marketing tool that is targeted at the mainstream. It's a word that they use that doesn't mean the actual meaning of the word because I don't know how you could be less alternative than U2 or No Doubt doing the Super Bowl halftime show. What's that the alternative to? Jazz music? Classical music? I guess it's not alternative anymore at all.

Dramarama had a pair of final shows, which have been called the band's funerals. What do you remember about those shows?
Every show Dramarama did in New Jersey except for the tent show was unspeakably hot. It was ridiculous. I remember having to stop that particular show in New Jersey and go outside and breathe for two minutes because I was suffering from dehydration and heat exhaustion, I think. I almost passed out. We were all soaking wet as was the crowd. It was a wonderful thing. Actually, that was the first time I had cut my hair. I had short hair at that show for the first time in God knows how long. I'd been long-haired forever!

Every time we played in Asbury... every time we played in New Jersey it was so much better than any other show we ever did in California or anywhere else in the country. There was something just wonderful and heartwarming, it felt like being at home. It felt like going home and we were welcomed like the prodigal sons. That show, in particular, was pretty much our last show and we knew it was gonna be. The other one in California I don't know that everyone knew it was going to be the last show at that point. We were still trying to do something at that point. It was like our last effort. The California show was in April. The Jersey show was in July and by that time we had pretty much called it quits and knew it was going to be our last hurrah. So, that had a lot to do with that final show being maybe more of a funeral. Well, more of a wake I hope, more of an Irish wake than a very dark thing. They're always celebrations and always really cool. The only time I ever crowd surfed and ever stage-dived was out there. It had been the type of experience to enable me to do that. I'm just so lucky to have been able to experience all that shit.

Why did Dramarama break up?

It was way more to do with the industry than it had to do with the music or the people in the band. It seemed as if the time had come. We had discussed it before, when we were on our last tour and we were still our own record label, about how we were fighting a losing battle. And realistically we got more of a shot than most bands get because we did it ourselves for so long.

Our first major label record was our 4th album and we got to do another one after that. But we ran into the same kind of things that a lot of bands run into when they deal with major labels. And also because we had been spoiled by doing it ourselves for so long that we had our own ideas about how things get done.

My recommendation to any band that ever gets signed is shut up and let the label do what they want. You write the music, deliver the record, the greatest record you possibly can, and then just sit back. Don't say "I don't like that pick for the single" because maybe the record company can't guarantee that they can make it a hit but they can sure as hell guarantee that it won't be a hit.

Do you have a particular favorite album by Dramarama?

No, not really. I like them all. There's certain ones that are more embarrassing than others and certain ones that I wish I could go back and fix. They're like photographs of a time. You can remember entire periods of your life just as with anybody's favorite and I can remember parts of my life from looking back at those albums too. We always tried to have different styles on every record. We never wanted a sameness from beginning to end, never wanted a sound that was the sound.

What would you like people to remember about Dramarama?

It's all about the music ultimately. It'll be 18 years this year that we released "Anything, Anything" on an album. It came out in 1985 in November in France on a little label. That was all it was ever going to do and we were so thrilled about that. And the idea that 18 years later it's still on the radio is just ridiculous and it has to do with the music. People don't remember our haircuts or clothing. People don't remember anything about us except for our songs, which is pretty cool. I'll take that over being remembered because I had a funny haircut in the 80s or wore some goofy clothes in a video. I don't mind not being part of that whole 80s nostalgia wave. There's all these 80s albums that come out we're not on them and I'm thrilled about that. The greatest compliment and the greatest reward is that anybody still cares. It's just so cool.

Talking with Mark Englert

former guitarist for Dramarama

What have you been up to lately? Tell me about Phat Boris.
Oh boy, that's the big record label I launched. I just had a bunch of songs and I wanted to put them out on a label. So, it's kind of like it's my mock record label if you will. I don't really do that much with it.

Basically, I just play with a lot of different bands. I'm kind of like a guitar player have gun will travel for a lot of singer-songwriters. I'll just come out and do a lot of solos for them and stuff like that. I'm better as part of a team than I am as a solo guy.

And you're a member of the John Easdale band, the Newcomers?
Exactly. Well, we've been called everything. The Newcomers are kind of going through another incarnation. Basically, whenever John gets back into it again. He's been writing and recording lately, which lucky for me I get a chance to work with John in a big studio. It's great in that way.

What are the John Easdale Band shows like compared to the old Dramarama days. How do they differ?
They differ because back then it was more like a career choice or sort of a life choice. We were putting out records and that was basically putting food on our tables. So it was like this is what we do, this is our job, this is our life. Now it's more like I'm just a regular working guy, you know what I mean? So, it's more like vacation. It's more fun. And, in a way, it's more of a free style. A lot of it is free form. We don't even have set lists with this band.

You basically stick to your NJ and LA now. You're not really hitting the country and playing a spot that doesn't know you very well...
Gary, I worked in the Whiskey A Go-Go for five years. I've watched bands say, "Could you guys buy our demo so we can have gas to get on to the next town?" I'm not really into trying to get to that point.

I was doing sound and lighting there. I'm more like a white collar guy now. But back then I was more into sound engineering. I did that for a long time though.

Dramarama was first signed by a French label. Did you tour there?
Yeah, we were out there for six weeks. It's something that you're not going to get in a cruise or from a travel agency. Go tour France in a rock band in the back of a meat wagon where the only way you can see is by looking straight out. It was like a converted meat refrigerator truck except all the stuff is completely in the back. The guy in the front can barely understand what you're saying and they're calling you Marky Ramone because they say you sound too much like the Ramones for them to understand you. That's what they called me.

France was amazing. It was really a fulfilling thing. Even our band was like laughing at them in a way. A lot of the guys in the band were really nervous about traveling around in places that didn't understand any English. But once you got into the whole thing, it was like, "Wow what a trip! This is great!"

Talking with fans on both coasts, it really seemed the audiences were just so electric for those two areas.
Oh, it was pretty much like you say. I think if we had better radio airplay or a solidified promotional thing we probably could have gone farther. But we were just hanging on by our pants a lot of times. And, of course, we had our secret weapon - Chris Carter. Honest to God, if everyone said Mark we want you to plan the way we were going to get out to California we'd all still be living in Wayne! But Chris, he was a promotional guy. He really was. I kind of provided the product that was my end of the deal. John wrote the songs. It really was a team effort in a lot of ways.

You grew up right next to John, right?
Two houses away.

Were you two in a lot of bands together growing up?
Oh yeah. Well, the first memory I have of playing with John was in junior high school. We were doing this stage band thing together and he was playing drums. The thing about John is that if he had a set and it was set up in his house he'd be one of the best drummers I've ever played with because his sense of rhythm is so there.

There was our punk rock band, Department of Public Works. Well, I worked for the Department of Public Works in Wayne, New Jersey so it was easy to get a bunch of township t-shirts and that became the bands uniform. John played bass. Later John said, "I'm not really thinking this band's going to do a whole lot." I'm like, "John, we're playing the Who as good as the Who. What are you talking about?"

It almost sounds like the punk version of the Village People...
Yeah, except their dancing was way better than ours.   Their
choreography was a lot better than ours, that's for sure.

**What do you remember about those early Dramarama shows on the
"Uncle Floyd Show"?**
Just that it was interesting. It was a first time experience and being a
little nervous around the TV cameras. But you knew it wasn't like being
on CBS so you could relax a little bit.

A different level than Letterman, right?
Letterman was a total trip for me. The whole thing of that just came about
quickly. Thursday it's like, "What are you doing this weekend?" and we'd
say, "Oh, we're flying to New York to play on the 'David Letterman Show'
and then going back on Sunday."

**It's strange. At the Shore, we all knew you guys were in LA but we
also knew that you were from Wayne. There was a little alternative
scene during the days of the Green Parrot. Did the band feel any
connection to that or were you an LA band?**
No, you can take the guys out of New Jersey but you can't really take the
New Jersey out of the guys. Even when I go back now I realize how
amazing New Jersey can be in the sense that there's a lot of bands out
there. There's a lot of talented people and they all play as good as you,
but the thing is you were lucky. You kind of did things at the exact right
place at the right time as far as that goes. I would have to say I just felt
like coming back home a lot of times.

Do any of the shows stand out?
I remember an Asbury Park show in which the owners hated the opening
band that were friends of ours from Wayne, New Jersey. Basically, after
they played the crowd hated them. Every time the singer said something
the crowd got uglier. After they left the stage the owner said, "Take your
stuff. We're putting your stuff on the sidewalk right now. Pack your stuff
and get the hell out of the club. I never want to see you here again!"

It's stuff like that. I remember the circus tent in Asbury Park. I think we
were the first band to actually do that. We were outside under a circus
tent and going look at this. And what you were saying about polarizing
was really true. We could go 90 miles west of Philadelphia and have
about a third of the people there. That radio station down there helped an
awful lot.

We had our funeral show. It was funny, we had two funeral shows. One was at a place called the Coach House in Orange County and the other one was in Asbury Park at the Stone Pony. One person wrote about it like it was an obituary. I was thinking come on it's not so bad. For me personally, I was kind of happy when it was done because in a way it was kind of like we had taken this as far as we could go. Maybe it was a good idea to get off.

What did you do after the split?
I played with one band up north thinking I have all this knowledge from Dramarama, I know what I'll do I'll put out an independent record. Except at that time everyone had an independent record and you don't say you're from California, trust me. That's when I really became the guy from Jersey and reinforced it by ordering six packs of Bud in cans, which always freaked them out up there.

But after that I just came back down to LA, put myself through college, worked at the Whiskey A Go-Go, worked at E-Entertainment doing journalism stuff and now I'm kind of doing my thing in LA with different bands. The thing to me is that music is just part of existing, a part of life. Whether there's a record deal or not a record deal it's kind of pointless in a way, especially when you study what's going on in the industry.

Speaking of the industry, did you see Dramarama as an alternative band or a regular rock band?
Well, that's an interesting question. What is alternative music? I always kind of looked at us as a square peg in a round hole if you will. We were always kind of out there on the outside. But when you look at bands like Soul Asylum or the Replacements, I didn't think we were that much different than those guys. It's just we were a song band. We really based ourselves on our songs and not our crazy lifestyles or anything else.

Looking back, what would you like people to remember about Dramarama?
Good songs, good records... At least you knew we had a sense of humor. I like to think at least we had some brains. Maybe not so much in the way of the cash department.

Any chance that Dramarama will ever record together again?
You never say never, that's the whole thing. If it comes together it won't be a planned thing, I'll tell you that much. That's the way I picture it. But there's always the chance.

33 Red House

We put a few years into playing really hard, we became very close like a family and we worked as a band and played constantly. It's funny how quickly it was dissolved by being a part of the industry.

--BOB NICOL

Red House was a favorite of the Jersey Shore crowds during the late 80s. Photo © Debra L. Rothenberg/rothenbergphoto.com

Red House was formed by a bunch of guys in Union County in the early 80s. They became one of the most popular bands along the Jersey Shore and one of the leaders of the alternative scene taking place in clubs like the Green Parrot and the Fastlane.

Success came quickly for Red House after the release of an independent record in 1987. The band found themselves on the cover of the College Music Journal (CMJ), an unheard of feat for an unsigned band. Record companies were soon bidding against each other to be the one to sign them. Red House ultimately signed with SBK and released a CD featuring the alternative hit "I Said A Prayer."

Unfortunately, problems with the label surfaced after the band's first tour. A second record was recorded but never released. The band ultimately called it quits and headed their separate ways. I was able to conduct phone interviews with all four of the original band members of Red House, a band that always deserved a better fate.

Talking with Ron Baumann

former bass player for Red House

The band started out as Toys. How did that name come about?
We had some trouble coming up with a name back then, and it was a bunch of different names. So that's how it started.

I think we didn't really start heading down to the Asbury area until, I guess, we got good enough to start playing at the Stone Pony and the Fastlane. I guess those were the kind of places that we always thought if we got there, we're really doing something. You know, get on the stage of the Stone Pony.

There was something special with the Jersey Shore scene at the time with 106.3 and bands like Red House, Dramarama, Whirling Dervishes and the Blases and clubs like the Green Parrot.
Yeah, I think probably it was a combination of the live music scene between the Pony and the Green Parrot and the radio station, which was local to the area. There were a lot of different bands that were around at that time doing a lot of good stuff. So the whole combination really did make it feel like there was something special going on there besides Bruce Springsteen.

What do you remember about the Green Parrot?
At times, I felt that maybe other bands might have resented the fact that we had kind of taken over the Green Parrot in a sense. It seemed to me the doors were open to anybody, but evidently I think it was just monetary because we could bring in more money than anybody else.

And, it seemed like the DJs really liked you guys and the place was pretty much run by 106.3 employees.
Yeah, that's right. So, maybe some folks felt it was a little too incestuous and it wasn't fair to other bands. I always felt that, on one hand, it was nice that we kind of had a shoo-in, but, on the other hand, I felt there might have been some resentment with other bands because of that because we were too comfortable there.

Could you notice a difference in the crowd between the Green Parrot and the Stone Pony?
There was a whole different crowd at the Green Parrot. That was a younger crowd, maybe a more college-oriented crowd. The music was more on edge, more fresh. I mean, I saw the Ramones at the Stone Pony and more established bands like that. There was a little more attitude there. They didn't allow as much new music in there, and didn't experiment as much as the Green Parrot did.

The Stone Pony crowd was certainly... well, it wasn't as alternative. I guess, at that point in 1988-1989, the definition of alternative music was really the Red House for lack of a better definition. Because we weren't playing anything that you could hear on the radio in the area. I don't know where REM was classified at the time, but the so-called alternative has turned into something that is completely different than what we were doing. But, if I remember all the tags that were used to describe us, alternative was always used. We were in the alternative press - CMJ was alternative.

Red House was from North Jersey. Did the band feel like they were a part of the Jersey Shore scene?
Yeah, I think we did. We'd been playing there so long and I don't think there was too many bands from that area. I mean, the Smithereens were from up north and Dramarama was from up north too. So there really weren't too many bands doing originals at that time in the area that were making any noise. As far as I know, we were the first ones to really get an independent record on WHTG and Mike Marrone was the champion of that.

When we put out our first LP, our first independent, that really started the ball rolling for us in that area. Of course, we couldn't get on the radio anywhere else. We did dabble with some college radio, but there was really no coverage as far as the college stations were concerned. So WHTG was really the one that started everything. They gave us a much wider audience than we would have gotten otherwise.

Did you notice anything right away when the CMJ report came out?
Oh yeah, that was a big thing. We created that first album, which we recorded in the basement and then it wound up on the cover of the College Music Journal. Partly due, I guess, to Mike Marrone being the champion there and party because, I hope, the merit of the music.

I think it was maybe a week or two after, that we got mail from RCA Records and they wanted us to come in. We were getting phone calls because they wanted to check it out, see what was happening, find out why we're on the cover. So that was pretty exciting when it happened. And it was all because of champions, people who really believed in the music like Mike Marrone and others. I guess that was also the time when WHTG was new so they were able to take chances. They didn't have the format or weren't as formatted as they are today. I guess they weren't making as much money as they are today so that probably has a lot to do with it. I think we also sent our first record to WFMU, but it wasn't the right kind of music for WFMU.

Do you remember your first show in the Asbury Park area?
I would say that the very first place we ever played as a band in the Asbury Park area was probably the Stone Pony. I think we were playing there before T-Birds was even open. We played T-Birds a lot. See, we used to play down in a place in Seaside called the Chatterbox. We played there once, it was a battle of the bands. It was in the dead of the winter, January or something, and we were all excited because we got to play down at the Chatterbox. I bet that place burned down. All the places we played burned down.

The Green Parrot was our second home. Our first home was a club called Mingles in South Amboy. That one burned as well, and after that we had to find a new place. So then, I think truly between '88 and '89, we really felt at home in the Green Parrot. We were comfortable with the people who worked there and we pretty much had gigs whenever we wanted. Because of our record coming out and the radio station, we started to sell out the club on a Saturday night. So, because of that, it really did feel like something special.

How did you guys get involved with your manager Rich Stanley?
He was booking the bands there at the club and we didn't have a manager. We figured we needed someone to handle that kind of work; the managerial, bookings and all that kind of stuff because nobody in the band wanted to do it. So we met him there and asked him. He refused for a while, but I guess as things started to progress he thought maybe it was a good opportunity.

And we stuck with him all the way through, even in the demise years. There was talk about maybe we should get a new manager, but I'm glad we didn't jump ship. We stuck with everybody who was there from the beginning regardless and although we didn't turn out to be a big success, at least I'm confident that we did the right thing with everybody.

Was it disappointing that the record label didn't really seem to push you guys as much as they could have?
What happened was they claimed the single was doing okay, but it didn't perform as well for the money they were spending on it. They've got some kind of mathematical ratio showing the money they should spend and the response they should get. And they didn't get the response for the money.

The record label paid for everything: the videos, the albums, traveling... And that was nice. It makes you feel kind of good. We spent all those years in the Green Parrot moving all of our own equipment and now we were able to grow up a bit and go out on the national scene and we did that around 1990.

Adam Schlesinger from Fountains of Wayne, played keyboards with us for a while. He recorded with us when we were recording our third album. We recorded our third album, but it never got released. They dropped us before they would release it. That was a real toughie because things were going very poorly with the record company. They had brought in people to write songs with Bruce. They brought in this guy, Frankie Previtt, who wrote the big single off the *Dirty Dancing* soundtrack and then they brought in the guy who wrote "Eye of the Tiger" for Survivor. As a result of the Memphis session, it was just a big mix of what we thought the record company wanted to hear and what we could tolerate.

In hindsight, that was the beginning of the end when they started doing that. For us, it was like a last gasp. We tried to do what we wanted all of the time. All through our career through Asbury through all the places we played and everything we did. At that point, in our careers, when they started bringing in the songwriters everything fell apart because everybody started second guessing. And that was the end.

Talking with Bob Nicol

former drummer for Red House

I know you're still playing, what's the name of your new band?
Brother Eye. We're playing the South by Southwest show in Austin. So, that's pretty exciting. We've been together for quite some time. Since 1993, I guess. We put out a record called *Soapdish Antennae*.

So, it wasn't that long after Red House broke up?
No, it wasn't. I started playing with Tony (who was in the Red House) and Adam Schlesinger (who played keyboards with us and now is half of Fountains of Wayne). The three of us started playing in a band right after Red House split up. We only played one show at CBs. Luckily though, Steve Garvey of the Buzzcocks was there and he saw us and got in touch with me. He was producing this band from New Hope and it turned out to be Brother Eye. I've been playing with them ever since really.

When we first started playing we played a lot of shows in New York. Now, everyone's got a job and got responsibilities. So, I think every show we've played over the last couple years has almost always been at John & Peters in New Hope, Pennsylvania.

Did you guys feel a part of that Jersey Shore/Green Parrot scene?
Definitely. I haven't experienced anything like that scene at that time since. It was really great and we were lucky to be a part of it. I always hoped to find a little community of bands that sort of all go see each other play and have a small string of clubs that can accommodate all of the bands. Something like a cross breeding of the fans and stuff. It was really nice.

What did you think of the Green Parrot as far as a rock club?
Well, it wasn't soaked in atmosphere like a CBGBs. So, physically it didn't have a great atmosphere, but I think it was just the combination of WHTG and all of the DJs who were really eager to meet all the bands and get you played on the air. That always made you feel like you were doing something a little more than playing in your basement. It was so great that you could be driving around and hear yourself on the radio.

The combination of WHTG being involved and the really steady loyal clientele to that place made the atmosphere, in general, really energized and just a lot of fun.

So the combination of WHTG (106.3) really helped it?
Absolutely, that was key I'd say. And we were lucky that we had good timing. We had just recorded our first record in the basement, and we had all pooled our money and got copies pressed. All of a sudden here's this little station and someone said you should give it to these guys. Mike Marrone over there took the record from us. He really liked it and all of a sudden we had about four songs in rotation at the station.

Around the time that you guys released your indie record not many bands were doing that. What led you guys to take the chance?
Umm, I don't know. We didn't really feel that it was taking a chance. All of us in the band were interested in recording and the process of recording, especially Bruce and I. We used to read all these magazines like *Musician* and stuff and pick up all these miking tips. Then we'd go to Radio Shack and buy whatever mikes we could afford. We spent a lot of time in his parents' basement setting up a little makeshift studio and we recorded everything. Then we started doing some multi-tracking things on a cassette four-track. Later on, Bruce finally went out and bought an 8-track 1/4 tape deck by Fostex.

Anyway, we just liked the process of recording and we thought the best thing for us to do would be to make something to put into someone's hands that we thought completely represented the band and what we could do. Maybe it would have our picture. We just thought it would just be a big help to have something like that and if we could get it distributed and on to some college radio. I guess we had a lot of confidence that we were doing something that people would be interested in at the time, which was good because it really was a lot of positive thinking that we used.

Could you ever have imagined landing on the cover of CMJ?
No, again it was just a wonderful little gift. Yeah, that was the record and it got some sort of basic distribution. I forget through what service, but that's how they got it. It was just amazing because we found ourselves being able to cut out all of the begging and pleading and whatever you have to do to try to get yourself listened to at record companies. They just all started calling us asking for the record. We'd take orders and then just send them out. It was amazing.

Who came up with the album's symbol, the red Monopoly house?
Oh, I guess I did that. I'm an art director now at an advertising agency and I've always been an illustrator. I just always drew and stuff. So, I did all of the band things like that. I think it was a combination of me and Ron who sort of planned out what the record would look like. We thought it would be cool if there was no writing on the cover and we just put the house because it basically was the name of the band. When you looked at it someone would say its Red House.

Did you come up with the ideas for the photos like the famous one with the band pictured in front of the Eggomatic?
I think that was Ron. I think it was something that he used to pass. I believe it was in Scotch Plains, which is where I live now actually. It's not there anymore. It's been featured in *Weird New Jersey* as a landmark of the past that was unexplained.

Around the time that you had the labels fighting for you and you did showcases. What was that like for you? Was that the first time you guys played places like CBGBs?
Yeah, I guess it was. I don't know, I guess the Red House wasn't the kind of band that fit in nicely at CBGBs. But it was exciting to go and play at a legendary place. It was fun. Most of the entire experience was just a lot of fun. As soon as things like major labels or organized business transactions started becoming a bit more part of what we were doing everything always got to be a little less fun.

We always tried to remain true to ourselves. We sort of looked up to bands like REM, U2 and the Waterboys who we felt always sort of just did what they did and seemed to not be too pressured by the record company. So, we just tried to always keep that attitude ourselves.

How difficult was it after that first major label record when you really did start having them pressure you in certain directions?
Well that was ultimately and stereotypically the end of the band. It was really sad. We put a few years into playing really hard, we became very close like a family and we worked as a band and played constantly. It's funny how quickly it was dissolved by being a part of the industry. It was really rough. We felt we had a really strong follow up to the first album. We thought it was a little truer to what we envisioned ourselves to be. It was a little less anthemic than the SBK CD that came out. None of us over the years felt it really represented the band. I always felt that little record with the red house on the cover was a lot closer to what we were at our best.

Anyway, we got the typical runaround. I mean, it's just so predictable it's even boring. It was like, "Oh yeah, this is nice but we don't hear a single. Give us some more and work on a single." And we kept doing what we do, which was just writing songs. But then it got sticky in that they started to try pairing Bruce and all of us off with other songwriters. Most of the people that were sent our way were ridiculous!

I heard one was the guy from *Dirty Dancing*...
Yeah, Frankie Previtt. Unbelievable, surreal even that we were sitting around in Bruce's apartment working on a song with this guy. I guess we always had a good attitude. Ok, we'll try this. That was the attitude.

And the guy that wrote "Eye of the Tiger."
Yup! The guy from Survivor. Well, at least that guy left us with a good story because we invited him to a party at our friend's house later that evening after we worked with him during the day. He wound up literally running out of the party afraid. He just left. We found out later that he was very religious. He might have been born again or something. I guess we really scared him, which I was kind of proud of.

What was your experience of the first tour? I know a lot of the shows weren't really supported well.
Every aspect of the Red House after we put out the record with SBK and even to a point of making the record was sort of mishandled by the label. They really didn't know what to do with us. It was a bad time to try to break out. Classic rock was still real big. Few bands that were new were getting the kind of radio play that SBK was trying to get us. It was bad timing.

It was almost like we had great timing all the way up to then and then the timing just turned sour. So, we went around and we did some touring. I still had a blast. I always did. Even if there was only 20-30 people at some of the venues, it was still always great to play. It was fun to be traveling as a band and have that be your only job. I enjoyed it and some of the shows were supported well.

Are there any shows that stand out on that first Red House tour?
I remember the last show of the whole little road trip was in Appleton, Wisconsin. It was packed! It might even have been sold out. We were almost looking at each other like what is this all about? I don't know, maybe there's absolutely nothing else to do there, but it was packed and we had people in line after the show bringing CDs up for us to sign. So, that was nice that we ended it on a high note.

The shows that we went and did with the Moody Blues, another strange mismatch, were a lot of fun in the big places like the Garden State Arts Center and other outdoor venues like that along the East Coast.

Was the band still in good spirits when you were recording the second record in Memphis?
Yeah, we were. We were very positive, especially at the start. The more you bang your head on the wall the more it hurts. It started to feel like that, like the door just wasn't going to open and we were pounding on it with tons of songs. We always had a lot of material. It was frustrating, but we stayed in good spirits even to the point when we dissolved our relationship with SBK. We stayed positive. I remember doing a new photo shoot. We were sending out new press kits and setting up showcases again. We still stayed positive. At some point, I guess, Bruce just didn't have it in him to start over. He just wasn't up to it.

Did you guys have the rights to that second album or did SBK?
That's a good question. I don't think they have the rights to that stuff. I think it was only submitted to them on cassette. I doubt that there's anyone existing that could find out if that material is owned by them. They were just a branch of EMI. I'm sure some of the people are around, but I'm sure they don't remember us.

What would you like people to remember Red House for?
It seems to all of us, the people who really did like the band liked the band a real lot to the point where they were very detailed about reading the lyrics and stuff. We never slouched off on any aspect of the music. We worked our butts off from the words to the arrangements to the live stuff. I'd hope we'd be known as a fun band... energetic. We used to do some unpredictable things on stage with covers and things like that. I guess it would be nice if anyone remembers us to remember us as guys that were just honestly trying their best to make music that we thought was good and not for any other reason.

Talking with Bruce Tunkel

former lead singer of Red House

In the beginning Red House was originally called Toys, right?
Uh, yeah. Wow! You're sneaky with this research, Gary. That was a pretty short-lived name. When we first got together we started off playing covers, although I think that lasted a couple of gigs. And we were called Toys for a very short amount of time and then I guess it became Red House at some point.

Was this your first band?
No, I think we all were in different bands in high school and stuff. I think basically the short story is we met through mutual friends. I used to play in a band with Ron prior to Red House, a high school band that we were in with some other guys. And Bob and Tony playing in another band in their town. I think Bob and I met, through somebody else, and we started playing for a short amount of time. And then that fell apart and then we decided, well we each know these other guys, and that was kind of the genesis of it.

Do you remember where you played your first show?
Yeah, I think the first place we ever played at was a place in Elizabeth. I think it was called the Rock Lounge. It was a pretty scary place.

Now, what was it like after your self-released album and before the national release - trying to get the crowds at the Shore to accept an alternative sound? Did you have trouble getting gigs?
Well, it was never really hard to get a gig. It was probably hard to get a good gig. But there were a handful of places to play. When we first started playing around doing originals we would just read the *Aquarian* find out where other bands were playing, send tapes and all that stuff. And then it kind of evolved after we did the self released album, *There is a Window*, and that started getting airplay on WHTG at the time. Right around the same time we started playing at the Parrot. I guess through the airplay and whatever and we just started drawing pretty good crowds at the Green Parrot.

244

There was a period of time where whenever we played there we'd sell out the Parrot, so that was very cool. It didn't necessary translate to other places, which was weird because, even at the same time, if we'd go play at the Pony it would be like a different crowd entirely.

Right, even though it's almost right up the road.
Yeah, it's weird. I think it probably had something to do with us and probably something to do with that the Parrot was becoming a little bit of a scene.

I guess you guys were together a couple of years, probably 4-5 years, before you released *There is A Window.*
That sounds about right. I believe we pressed 1,000-2,000 of the records.

It was recorded in your parents' basement, right?
The indie record, yes. I'm very into home recording. And since the SBK thing, I've recorded all my stuff in my basement. It's hard to find now. There aren't that many and really we never intended to sell them. The whole idea was we'll make this record and we'll send it around and people will take us seriously. It was that kind of thing and oddly enough it did kind of work.

I mean, there's certainly a lot of luck that goes into that kind of stuff too. But what happened was that when we put the record out we sent it to a lot of radio stations and a few, notably WHTG, picked up on it and they were playing it a lot. And so we kind of got a bit of a following down at the Parrot and the next thing you know there gets to be a little buzz about it. We actually had a period of time where the record companies were calling us.

And you guys were the first indie to land on the cover of the College Music Journal (CMJ).
Right, and that, I think what happened at the record companies was people were like, "Who the hell is this? What is this band?"

How come I don't know these guys...
Right, exactly. So, it was weird for a period of time. I'd come home from work everyday and there'd be a message from somebody at Capitol or whatever label. And then there was a long period of time where we kind of went back and forth with talking with a few different labels, but that was very cool, you know. It worked out well for us.

Red House did a lot of showcase gigs. What were those like?

Umm, they were always a little bit of a drag because I guess, especially at the time, it was hard to be as natural in performing as you would normally be. It was like a gig, we did a number of those at CBGBs, usually going to the city. And you'd get people in there and they'd go away with whatever opinion they had of it. So it eventually came down to a couple of labels who got to the point where they were interested enough in wanting to do something. And then we stupidly signed with SBK.

How did you guys decide to sign with them?
I guess the gist of it was that SBK wanted to do a deal and there was a smaller label, it's alluding me which one - it's an indie label that was pretty known at the time - but we just thought, in hindsight probably the wrong way, that okay SBK is going to have more money to get behind us and we'll be able to do more with them. So that was kind of the line of thought.

You guys met one of your first managers at the Green Parrot.
Yeah, this guy, Rich Stanley, who ironically I just saw the other day actually. He was involved in running the club and over time he started helping us out and eventually became our manager. I think he was involved with booking the bands and stuff.

What was it like shooting the video for "I Said A Prayer?"
It was cool. A little weird too. It all kind of happened very fast. We went out to Los Angeles to shoot the video. We shot it with, the guy's name is going to elude me but he had done a video for Michael Penn that we had all liked -

The "No Myth" video?
Right. I remember that video was on at the time we were recording our album, and we were all into that video. We're like we want to get that guy. And so, that was fun. It was a long, one-day shoot and then we flew back like the next day. It was kind of weird, but it was a lot of fun. I mean, a lot of the things individually that we got to do as part of the SBK thing were a lot of fun although the whole overall experience really wasn't that great, you know.

It was must be nice to tell your friends that you're on MTV.
Oh, yeah, that was awesome.
I remember you guys got some pretty good reviews. I remember

seeing something in *Billboard Magazine*, I think.
Yeah, I have all the clippings.

Well, it's got to make you feel good, I mean, most of the clippings I remember really talked about you being a songwriter.
Yeah, that was definitely gratifying. It was very satisfying to see. Yeah, we got a lot of good press, which was nice. And it felt good because we felt that we really did try hard to do something of quality, so that was very cool.

What was the first tour like?
Umm, the tour was really kind of shitty. It was kind of like we were doing a combination of promotional tour kind of stuff where we'd go and visit radio stations and play a song at the station on acoustic guitar or whatever and then we would do shows in clubs and things. So again, it varied a lot. We'd go to one town and play for nobody and another town would be great.

But we were kind of all fighting at the time. Like no one was really getting along and I think we were getting on each other's nerves. It's no fun being in the car for a thousand miles with people that are pissed off at each other.

What broke first? The deal with SBK or the band?
The SBK thing ended before the band did although not by far apart. I think the nutshell version of what happened with the band was SBK was kind of pushing us with we don't hear the hit song kind of thing. This was when we were getting material together for what would have been our second album. And that kind of pissed us off a lot and we really weren't willing to do what they wanted as far as creating whatever they thought was going to be this hit sound or something.

So, anyway, we just ended up doing a round of demos and things with them. I think that a lot of the stuff is good, which will be unheard, I guess.

So the unreleased demos... did any of that stuff make it on to a Bruce Tunkel CD?
Not directly. I think I did use maybe a couple of songs here and there that I liked or reworked them. I've since made CDs for the guys in the band. We have all the stuff archived and it's fun to listen to. We'll see, it might be interesting to make it available for charity.

What was it like when you made your first solo record?

That was kind of a weird time for me. Actually, I started working on stuff while I was still in the band. I guess the band hadn't split up at the point when I started working on it. I think what I was trying to do at the time was rediscover why I liked music. The SBK thing really left a bad taste in my mouth. I wanted to just get back to basics to use a cliche.

There were certain things when you're in a band that function as a democracy, which is always how Red House worked. There tends to be compromise and sometimes that compromise works to the benefit of the music and sometimes it doesn't. And so, this was like a chance where it was like I can do whatever I want kind of thing. But it was fun.

I was living in Cranford at the time and it was recorded in my apartment there. It was fun. I like methodically worked on it and got the songs together and recorded them. That was mostly done by myself. A few people played on a few tracks but otherwise it was a very indulgent thing. But, the whole point was just to get back to this is why I like to play music. I'm not doing it for any other purpose. I'm not trying to sell it to anybody. I just want to write songs and play them.

Was it definitely much better doing that independently than with the pressures of a label?
Yeah, because, at that time, I probably still had some aims in thinking about it. I certainly did play that stuff, when it was done, for some people at record companies. But ever since that time I've never really pursued that seriously any more.

What is it like now playing with all the original Red House guys in the studio?
Well, I'm trying to finish up this project that I'm working on now. It's taken a lot longer than I thought, for a variety of reasons, but I'm pretty much recording with everyone I've ever recorded with before. So all the Red House guys and all of the guys I've played with since Red House are on it. I guess the final product will have 15 tracks on it.

What do you have in store for the future? Are you just having fun writing the songs?
Yeah, pretty much that's where my head's at with it. I've got kids now, and I don't see myself going on the road at all. I have a regular job and all that. And that's fine, you know. If I'm in a writing mode, I try to write. It's not really on a schedule. When I'm really in a writing mode I try to write all the time. But it's a little different than it used to be.
You definitely sound like you've had pretty bad experiences with

record companies. If a label approached you, what would you do?
I guess I would just say that it would take a lot to make me interested in something like that. It's a lot of hard work to make it in music. And guys that have gotten there, including us at the time, and lots of other guys... if you talk to anybody I'm sure they would tell you. It's a lot of work. And you have to work. It's a level of commitment that a lot of people don't understand. It really requires it to be your top priority. And so, at this point I'm really not up for that kind of commitment. I mean, I still will create music and do it, but as far as getting involved with the music business it's just a whole other thing.

Would you like to be more known as a songwriter? Have others cover your songs?
Well, that would be great. It's not something I've really pursued. It's probably something I will pursue at some point. Right now, I want to get the current project done. It's definitely something I've thought about that I'd maybe like to shop some of the songs around. Maybe for a publishing kind of thing. But again, it's premature now. I haven't really thought about it. And, to be honest, I'm probably content to just do it for my own enjoyment now. I mean, I like people to hear it and I like to play gigs occasionally, which I do, not that often anymore, but I'll do it.
   I'm somewhat cynical about the music business now. In fact, not just somewhat, I'm extremely cynical about it. But, I still enjoy playing it a lot. I love to write music. So, that's what I do. I enjoy what I do a lot.

Is it strange when you find yourself linked to the Jersey Shore?
Umm, no, I think it's very cool. I'm a big Springsteen fan and it's a great tradition of Shore music. There's a lot of cool people that we've met over the years that play and still do. I like feeling part of that community as much as I am. It's very cool. I like the whole lineage. There's nothing weird about it. I think it's a good thing, you know.

Do you find it special to play shows in Asbury?
Yeah, but it's hard to say why. It probably is just the tradition of what's come before. It's the same with Yankee Stadium and baseball. On one hand it's just a place where they play baseball and the other it's the history that goes along with it. You're aware of it when you're involved there. And so it does make it a little more special.

Talking with Tony Stives

former guitarist of Red House

Let's start with what you've been up to lately. What have you done since Red House broke up?

I played around with Bruce Tunkel for a little while and then started recording with a friend of mine from South Plainfield, NJ. We did a bunch of demos under the name of Wormwood. It was power pop combining influences of Jesus Jones, Faith No More and Rush. We ended up recording a somewhat crude CD with the help of Bob Nicol and Ron Baumann. Didn't get too far, still have plenty of copies sitting in my closet.

Tell me about the band Brother Eye.

I've been playing with them for over three years now under the name Leslie St. Ives. Two Tony's in a band gets very confusing.

Are you hopeful that the band will go to the next level or are you just having fun playing now?

Hard to say... I would love to get some kind of recording contract. I feel we've been writing some great material lately. As far as going further than that, I do have a mortgage to meet every month so it would be a little difficult to go at it full strength.

How much would you say the radio station WHTG played in the success of Red House?

Mike Marrone gave us the biggest break ever. I remember the day he played us for the first time. He put us on a light rotation, but it was strong enough to start bringing people out to the clubs.

What do you remember about the Green Parrot?

The Green Parrot was our home. The cleanest club I ever played, very comfortable. The Parrot was still relatively new at the time for a rock club and it seemed more laid back, the Pony had more history and an attitude. I guess it was obvious that we were part of the scene, but I never personally felt I was a part of it. I used to leave after we played. I wasn't much of a club person.

There Is A Window **certainly opened doors for you guys. What do you remember about making that record?**
I just remember it being a lot of fun. There was no pressure, we did what we wanted.

What was it like landing on the cover of the College Music Journal?
It was fantastic. I can remember being more excited about that than actually getting a record deal. We did a lot of showcasing. SBK tried to give us some kind of image. We never really got one. I think we had signed some kind of a contract on a trial basis until they were satisfied with the final result. Then we signed the real deal.

What do you remember about that album's tour?
Mostly the venues and the fans. The traveling kind of sucked and by then the band was starting to get split apart.

During the recording of the second record the label started sending other songwriters to work with? Do you remember any of that?
Sure do. One guy won an Oscar, not for us though. We were certainly not the band that we used to be. Although I feel some of the best recordings came out of those sessions. I wish we recorded the first album under the same watchful eye of Producer John Hampton. We recorded it in Memphis and he got such great sounds.

Looking back, did you think SBK gave you guys the support needed to make it?
Absolutely not. They didn't know what to do with us. They had their minds occupied with Wilson Phillips and Vanilla Ice anyway.

If the band could do anything different, what do you think would have been changed during that period?
We would not have signed with SBK. Before we got signed we seemed a lot more focused as a band. It would have been great to re-record *There is a Window* with some strong production behind it. I believe that *There is a Window* should have been our first release. There were a lot of great songs on that record.

How would you like Red House to be remembered?
As a band ahead of its time.

34 James Deely & the Valiants

We had a great time, we didn't get the big record deal but look at what we did do. We were on the radio! I mean, not only was WHTG playing us but we were getting played on WMMR in Philadelphia and Y-107 in Long Branch.

--JAMES DEELY

The members of James Deely & the Valiants are shown with WHTG DJ Loretta Windas. Photo © Debra L. Rothenberg/rothenbergphoto.com

J ames Deely was born in Washington, DC, but he grew up in New Jersey. After studying music in Los Angeles and a brief stint in the LA based pop-rock band the Palisades, Deely returned home and put together the Valiants.

James Deely & the Valiants was one of the few bands to bridge the gap between the alternative world of the Green Parrot and the "Asbury Sound" of the Stone Pony. In the mid-80s, the band became known for great songwriting and raucous shows in clubs from Long Beach Island (LBI) to Asbury Park, including regular shows in Philadelphia and New York City. The band released three albums (*Beyond The Beaches*, *Set The Night On Fire* and *Custom Made*) and had steady airplay on radio stations from Philadelphia to the Jersey Shore. When the run was over, Deely joined the Disco Rejects, led by Vini Lopez, for a brief while. He moved to Florida and formed the Big Show before heading out to California. Deely currently lives in Los Angeles and continues to write and record songs. His last record, *El Corazon Negro*, was released two years ago. I spoke with James via phone about his memories of playing along the Shore.

The first band I remember you from was James Deely & the Valiants. Did you have any bands before that?
No, that was pretty much it. That was the start of the show... the long journey. *(laughs)* We started playing right around '84-85. I had just come back from music school in California. We were playing in the DC area, I was living with my folks down there. Then we started to realize that to really get something going we had to go up to New York. I had lived in New Jersey for a long time, so I moved back to Long Beach Island and that's when we started playing clubs. We had a few newspaper articles written about us and then we did our first recording.

It all kind of came out of Long Beach Island. There was Joe Pop's, the Tide, backyards... anything we could to play back then. We had a kind of built-in audience, which was good. And then we started making money and it was like what's the point in going anywhere? We can drive 4-5 blocks and make some cash here! Soon other bands figured it out and started going there. LBI was a place to go in the summertime and make some money rather than just play. I mean, you could actually make some real cash there. It had a built-in audience and a built-in bar scene, we couldn't resist. We loved playing there. It was almost like we stumbled upon it. But then we realized that we had to get in touch with people like Chris Barry and start playing the Pony. We started going to Philadelphia and New York because we knew we had to. Our first album was called *Beyond The Beaches* because we knew we had to get past LBI.

We put that one out on cassette at Garry Tallent's studio, Shorefire. The radio station said, "We'd love to play it, but we can't play a cassette." So we had it made into a vinyl and actually I've recently been in the studio transferring that vinyl into a CD. The whole thing was like a bunch of kids running blind. We didn't know what the hell we were doing. Here we were after just starting out in these back yards in Beach Haven. The next thing we know we're in Shorefire Studios and we did two albums there. That was kind of neat.

Your band was definitely a mainstay of the Long Beach Island scene, did you guys feel a part of that Asbury scene as well?
Yeah, they definitely opened their arms to us. It felt great too because that whole scene with the Green Parrot was really cool. They were just awesome and we had a blast over there. There was this weird thing going on with bands - you either played the Green Parrot or you played the Pony. Somehow, we managed to do both. We kind of slipped in and out of both places, sort of flew under the radar. There was the whole "are you with Springsteen or not with Springsteen" thing going on. The Stone Pony was Springsteen and the Parrot was more of an alternative scene.

What was your first show at the Stone Pony like?
It was Chris Barry's World Beyond on a Tuesday night at midnight. I remember when we got our first gig there we were all excited. We didn't know then that there'd be about ten people there. But then we ended up playing there later on and got a little thing going there. It was one of the first places outside LBI where we started to get something going.

Then the Green Parrot came along and that was really nice for us because they had the radio station built-in and they would just coordinate the radio station and the club. It worked out great! That one DJ there, Loretta (Windas), she was playing us all the time. I think that they had to tell her to stop playing us. The program director was like, "Are these guys paying you?"

One thing people always seem to remember is that your live shows didn't seem to transfer the same way as your records did.
Right, well we were heavy drinkers! There was a lot of things happening back then. That's why it was kind of good to stay close to Long Beach Island because we couldn't get into too much trouble there. If we got drunk we could just stumble home. Those were some dangerous days. I ended up getting an apartment in Asbury because I was spending so much time there.

I think looking back on the whole thing, I was really serious as a songwriter but as soon as you put me and these guys in the element of a bar with a lot of alcohol and a lot of women our attention span was very limited. We started thinking more about the women and the booze than going out there and putting on a great performance. I don't regret a thing that happened. We had a lot of fun. But as far as that place where commerce meets art, we kind of chose the bar over that. We wanted to have fun and we wanted the people to have fun. That didn't always involve a perfect sounding set.

The live stuff used to sound much harder than the records.
Yeah, we were all jacked up on some booze or something! We were really heavy drinkers. As a matter of fact, that's why I had to stop playing. I got a bit older and it became too hard on my body. I got to that place where you either quit drinking or you calm down.

Even with the inconsistent shows, lots of people were paying attention to the band. How close were you to signing a deal?
We came close, but I think the word that came back to our manager was how people would see us one night and think we were the greatest fuckin' band in the world and then come back two nights later and we were all drunk and sounded terrible. That was one of the things that plagued us. There were bands like Red House that were really disciplined and had their shit together. They got the record deal. They approached it like a business where we really didn't. We approached it like it was an opportunity to meet women.

That may have been our downfall as far as a long term way to make money in the music business. But when I look back now, I think the way things happened really happened for the better. I had a good time and everything... We did some great music and I didn't get killed. I'm still alive to tell about it. It's a little scary to think what would have happened if we actually had some money back then aside from the $80-90 bucks we made each night. If we had some real cash rolling in we would have ended up in therapy or Alcoholics Anonymous. It was out of hand.

We had a great time, we didn't get the big record deal but look at what we did do. We were on the radio! I mean, not only was WHTG playing us but we were getting played on WMMR in Philadelphia and Y-107 in Long Branch. We were getting played almost as if we had a record deal. The band was recording in Garry Tallent's studio turning out 24-track masters. It was like the only thing missing was the record deal. We were just young and crazy and wild. We wouldn't listen to anybody.

Did you ever imagine doing this for a career?
Yeah, that was the intention. It was kind of like a paradox. We intended on doing it but we also lived by that credo of the Replacements and that whole Charles Bukowski drunken artist type thing where you think you need booze to be creative. We lived in that kind of world.

It's kind of hard because you want to do the right thing with music. You want to be a songwriter and stuff, but there's this element of the bar. Lots of people have had to quit drinking. It's part of the business. You've got to be responsible.

Everybody knows this going in from when you're 15-years old and starting out that there's no guarantee no matter what you do that you're going to be on the cover of *Rolling Stone*. You've got to take the good, hope for the best and play your ass off!

What did you think about the constant comparisons of your music to Bruce Springsteen?
That was fine, I guess. The thing was by sneaking in through the Green Parrot we didn't get as much of that. The other thing was that I had a pair of guitar players who played like Peter Buck of REM. So when you contrast those two things against each other - me having that heavy Jersey influence and the REM sound - it kind of offset a little bit. It worked out good for us. I wanted to do everything, to write all sorts of songs not just Springsteen type stuff. When people heard me singing and doing my writing it kind of came off like a Bruce thing, but it was a little different.

So the Bruce comparisons didn't really play a role in you moving away from the scene?
I think I went to Florida more or less because I thought I had kind of played my hand out in Jersey. It was kind of hard to re-invent myself in Jersey because people had seen me for so many years. It just didn't go over the top, didn't click into that big record deal. So, I was trying to figure out a way to re-invent myself a little bit and I went to Florida. I met up with this keyboardist and we started doing more keyboard-oriented arrangements.

In this business, there's that window of opportunity and the only guy I've seen that has really expanded it is John Eddie. He's got another deal now with Lost Highways. That guy's had more record deals than anybody I've ever seen! It's just amazing the longevity of that guy without ever really going over the top. He came really close to exploding a bunch of times, but he never went to that next level where Southside and Bruce went. But he's still around... still banging away.

What would you say was the highlight from those days?
Getting played on the radio and hearing yourself on the radio. The first time I heard myself on the radio was down in Philly on WMMR. Later on driving through Neptune or Asbury and hearing us on 106.3 or Y-107 you just felt like pulling the car over, turning the speakers up and dancing on the hood! It's incredible to think of being a songwriter and having a song go from my parents' house in Brant Beach to a little tape deck to a little studio to Garry's 24-track and then to the radio station. It was really a great thing. I knew that if we were gonna have any future at all our future was getting on the radio somehow. And we did it.

You released your last record a few years ago. What are your plans for the future?
Yeah, *El Corezon* was released about two years ago. I did that one out here in California. We did it all through the Internet and kind of networked through the Springsteen fanzines and sold a bunch of them. I've got another one ready to go actually, in my little brain here, but the main thing I want to do before releasing another one is get my website organized. I also have a whole bunch of outtakes that are pretty cool that I'd like to get together and put out somehow. Just some recordings that are pretty good that never made it on any albums.

The first thing I want to do is try to get a whole multimedia thing going with the website. I want to make it a place where people can go and look at the stuff I've done in the past, and then we'll move into the future. I have another album called *A Harder Road* that I've already run through demos, but I really feel like I've got to get the stuff I did in the past organized first before I start pushing something new.

Any regrets at all about not making it to that next level?
We made it baby! Believe me... We did everything we set out to do except land the big record deal and all that stuff. I have no regrets at all. We had a hell of a time, met a lot of great people and had a blast. See, I think that's where some people forget about things. They look at what they didn't get as opposed to what they got. What I set out to do was make some great rock and roll records. If we got signed and made some money, whatever happened after that it was fine. And, if we didn't get the big record deal we still had a blast.

35 The Blases

"We're not in the Wailers, we're in the warmup band."
They're like, "Oh, what's the name of the band?" We said
The Blases. And they go, "Oh, you're that band that gets
so fucking drunk that you can't even stand up when you
play, right?"

--ROB WAGNER

The Blases wanted to be the Jersey Shore version of the Replacements.
Photo © Debra L. Rothenberg/rothenbergphoto.com

The Blases were formed by Billy Donahue and Rob Wagner while they were high school students in Union County in 1980. They were originally called the Hernia Boys and also included the bass player, Paul Virdon, who died after being hit by a train. This experience provided the basis for the songs on their only released CD, which came out in 1989.

The band was a favorite of the Green Parrot crowd and WHTG DJs. Band members became as semi-legendary for their partying and raucous stage shows as they were for their fine songwriting ability. With influences from bands the Clash and the Replacements, it's not hard to see where their "rock and roll from the edge" lifestyle came from.

The band's CD was released on Permanent Rave Records, a small independent label that had national distribution. One of the cuts, "Time Walks Away," became a modern rock hit and was played regularly on MTV, but the band never quite made it to the next level.

I was able to speak to the original two Blases members, Rob Wagner and Billy Donahue, via phone to talk about the story of this great band.

Talking with Rob Wagner

former lead guitarist of the Blases

Can you tell me about the band you and Billy Donahue had before the Blases - the Hernia Boys?
I'd hardly even call it a band because we didn't even have a drummer. We just sat down and wrote songs, Billy on upright piano, me on acoustic guitar and Rock, our bass player, writing lyrics and singing along.

Rock (Paul Virdon) was killed after being hit by a train. What do you remember about the day he died?
We were all abusing drugs in those days. He was spending the day at my place and I knew he was tripping. He was on mescaline. At that point in our lives, that was like a routine kind of deal. It's like hey, it's the weekend... which one of us is going to trip? The other guys would watch out for him instead of the current rave routine where everyone all gets together and does that shit.

He was acting very strange and said, "I'm gonna go for a walk." Our drummer, George, was there too and we were cool about it. We sort of decided to let him go walking around and follow him. He appeared fine. He was just wandering down the streets making turns every couple of blocks. And so we just said, "Hey what the fuck. Let's just go home, drink some beers and watch some TV until he comes back again." But he didn't come back. So, we went out looking for him and when we saw that train parked there it was like, "No fuckin' way." We walked up and the cops right away were like, "Do you know this person?" We were like yeah.

To this day, I don't know whether to blame what happened on drug abuse or his depression. After he died we went through all of his personal belongings. He was an avid journal keeper and he was writing about how depressed he was and how he wanted to kill himself. So, honestly, to this day, I don't know whether he was so fucking whacked out that he thought he could walk in front of a train and not get hit or whether he said, "The time is right," and did himself in.

The Blases CD was full of songs about Paul and his death.
Yeah, I mean what else is on your mind when something that tragic happens? We were all looking to do a little musical venting and Billy Shields, who was a good friend of Paul, was also looking to play. It was only about eight months later that the Blases were already out playing.

So the reputation for hitting things a bit hard was right on?
Oh yeah... We were big Replacements fans and we wanted to emulate those guys. I remember one time we had a gig warming up for Bob Marley's Wailers. It was one of those outdoor gigs sponsored by Rutgers. About two weeks earlier, we played the Court Tavern. We were semi notorious for doing some heavy pounding before we played, still surviving and getting through it. But at the Court Tavern I honestly didn't drink that night, besides the usual one or two beers to lubricate the vocal chords.

We started playing and I was excited because the place was packed. I wasn't paying attention to where I was standing on the stage and three chords into the first song I took a step back and wound up stepping on the monitor. So, I trip and fall on my back and I think it's the most hilarious thing in the world. I just keep playing the song laying on my back. And Bill, without missing a beat, takes the microphone and sets it up so that I can keep lying on my back. It was a small stage, so I was like literally stuck into a fetal position and I proceed to play the first six songs like that. Finally it's time to take a real break and that's when I stand up and we finish the set.

Anyway, we show up at this Wailers show about two weeks later and we're getting out of the car and there's a whole mess of college freshmen standing around asking if we were in the band. "We're not in the Wailers, we're in the warmup band." They're like, "Oh, what's the name of the band?" We said the Blases. And they go, "Oh, you're that band that gets so fucking drunk that you can't even stand up when you play, right?"

What does Asbury Park mean to you?

First of all, before we could even drive we would go down to Asbury for no other reason than it was a major city on the rail line. One thing I've learned over the years just watching New Jersey grow and change is that whatever's left of your rock and roll cultures are always in the vicinity of train hubs. Whether that's because, like in our case, people were too young to even drive or whether it's because nowadays everybody's too paranoid to have a couple of drinks and go out, it seems to me that all best venues are somewhere near a railroad station. And that's what led us to Asbury. We lived in North Jersey and just wanted to get the hell out of the suburbs. Springsteen was already popular so we went down on our days off to see the boardwalk, Madam Marie's and just hang out.

During that time we were doing the Hernia Boys thing and writing our own material. We were like freshmen or sophomores in high school and wanted to get out there and show people what we could do. But we knew there was no way in hell anybody was going to want to hear original music from us. So, we had to do cover music and the hottest thing at the time was Bruce Springsteen. We learned every single Springsteen song and we put a band together in those high school days that was just emulating Springsteen. We had a sax player and played a lot of Springsteen music and the kids loved it. We were the only local high school band that was playing Springsteen music. We made more money being a high school band than we did all those later years bopping from club to club playing original music.

Around the time we were graduating from high school all three of the bands being inducted in the Hall of Fame - the Police, the Clash and Elvis Costello - were all playing Asbury. Those three bands were barely bringing in a crowd because it was something new, but for us it was like a second British Invasion. Our influences at that point were the Ramones and the Cars simply because they were writing music that was so simple that it made us think we didn't have to do covers. To see these bands whip out these three chord songs and have such an emotional impact was an epiphany. Exactly at the time when those three bands came here, our musical sensibilities just totally changed thanks to seeing them in Asbury.

Are there any Blases shows that stand out for you?

Pretty foggy dude. The one that stands out in my mind was when we expanded from a four-piece band to a five-piece band around 1987. When Rock died, his best friend took over as bass player but he had asthma which was getting worse and worse. It got so bad that he couldn't play in smoky bars. And it wasn't like we were going to play in libraries, so we needed a new bass player. Bill came up with the idea that instead of just getting a bass player we should go out and get a bass player and a second guitar player. So he took the job on his own and hunted these guys out, Joe DeLorenzo and Mitch Wilson.

We first met them at the Green Parrot on a Monday night two weeks before we had a gig lined up. We meet them at the bar and they buy us drinks so it's like alright we already like them. Joe looks like a rock star. He's got his hair bleached completely white and it's like down to his ass. Mitch doesn't look too much like a rock star but everybody I talked to swore up and down that he was a really good guitar player. So that's it, sight unseen, conversation, couple of drinks and we hire them. We figure what's the worse case scenario? We play this gig, they suck and we kick them out.

So, we have a few rehearsals and they're fine, they're really great. They learn the music quickly and everything's cool. We're totally set. It's the last rehearsal before the gig, we get through the set twice, finish and want to go out and celebrate. Mitch says, "Wait a second, there's one more thing we have to talk about." And I'm like, "What? It was great." He goes, "But what about what we're gonna wear." At this point we're all Clash fans and we're like, "What are you talking about?" Both Joe and Mitch are just wearing jeans and a t-shirt to the rehearsals so I didn't understand. I'm like, "It's not about clothes."

The following weekend we were playing our first gig at the Green Parrot. Bill and I are late because we have to go out for some cocktails first, as part of tradition. We fuckin' walk into the place and these guys have makeup on! They both have eyeliner on, Joe has lipstick on and wearing something I can only describe as maybe "a march of the wooden soldier uniform" made out of plastic. Mitch's guitar strap has batteries powering it and little lights going on and off on the strap. It was too late to do anything. Frankly, I personally was too embarrassed to say to them you can't wear that. So, we just let them wear it and, in hindsight, it was great because it was sort of along the lines of Cheap Trick. You know how they had the two goofy guys and two regular guys? Well, you can figure out for yourself which ones were the goofy ones and which were the regular guys.

What are you most proud of with your music career?

All through the years our video guy was always the same guy, Paul Devlin, because we were high school buddies with him. He also makes independent movies, one of which Bill and I actually did the music for. It didn't do very well but it's my proudest thing. It was called *The Eyes of St. Anthony* and it was released in 1992. There's a scene in the movie where a guy is just looking through his old baseball cards and he sees how his life has just passed before his eyes and he's just sobbing. Bill and I with straight piano and real clean acoustic guitar - I tell you man, it will bring tears to your eyes. I swear that's the thing I'm most proud of... Just a short two-minute piece. The two minutes in that movie that didn't go anywhere. All because I can still watch it and it will still bring tears to my own eyes.

Why did the band break up?

You know it's a strange thing because we didn't do the Beatles' thing and sit down and say, "Ok, as of today we're not going to be a band anymore." It was just that time of our lives between Rock dying in March 1985, in June 1985, I graduated college and in September 1985, I started a full-time high school teaching career. We got back into it around the time I started my career so there was some stress.

I was always more into recording than anything else, but you've got to get the money together and sponsors together. If we shelled out our own money it was fine but if we got a sponsor the sponsor always said, "I'm going to pay for this recording on the condition that you guys are going to promote it with at least an East Coast tour." And that was always very iffy for me. I could do it as long as it was during the summer months, but let's say there looks to be a serious possibility here. Come September, don't put my back against the wall and ask me to quit my job so I can take this 1 in 75 chance of actually making it big like our idols. So, there was a little tension happening from that.

Talking with Billy Donahue

former keyboardist of the Blases

When did the Blases first get together?

Wagner and I started the Blases in 1979, while in high school, when we were both 15. Rob Wagner, the guitar player, and I would write the songs for the most part. We started writing songs together even before that with a band called the Hernia Boys. It's funny because once we actually had a video on MTV for this "Battle of the Bands" contest and Billy Crystal was the host. He gave a history of the band and mentioned the Hernia Boys and we all got a kick out of it. We almost won but we didn't.

Anyway, we've been around for a long time. We played all the high schools in Union County back then. We started as a cover band playing a lot of Springsteen. We had a sax player and a trumpet player. We'd do songs like "10th Avenue Freeze-Out" and "Thunder Road" along with tons of songs from the Clash and the Ramones. The Blases started as a cover band in Union County, where we grew up. We released our first single in 1983 or so. Guys like the Smithereens inspired us to start putting our own records out. And what happened was that we gravitated down to the Shore scene because the clubs were there.

The DJs at WHTG were incredibly helpful to us. There was a compilation that came out of New Brunswick called *Mental Floss* that WRSU put out. The song "Firefighter" was on that compilation. That's when WHTG sort of noticed us and that's when we started becoming big down the Shore.

Did the record take you guys anywhere?

We did the video and we charted all over the country. It was great! The video for "Time Walks Away" got on MTV but there was reluctance to tour because of lack of support from the label. Not really out of lack of will but out of being too small of a label. We probably could have... Well, we didn't know what we were doing.

It was a local indie label with nationwide distribution. I've even been in record stores and seen the record in subsequent years in vinyl shops across the country, college towns, of course. When the video got on MTV that sort of helped too.

Did you guys ever talk about going with a different label?
No, we didn't. We started to... you know what happened? I became frustrated because we weren't going to tour. I went to California for a while to see what I could do out there. When I came back we tried to put everything together but we just never got it together again.

So, you never really recorded a second record.
Well that's not true actually. We were in the process. There's probably a whole album's worth of stuff on an 8-track pre-production that was recorded with Joe Crowley and I think Karla Crowley was still involved. Then we recorded stuff with Brad Morrison, who is a friend of mine. We probably did about five tracks with him.

We were continually starting a new thing. It just never came to fruition. There's probably at least 16 tracks that are sitting somewhere that we never released. It's always like that. Back then there was more of a tendency to try to get things perfect and you had less control. We were relying more on people to help us out. I think because of the way technology is now there's more of a "do-it-yourself" attitude. The technology's more manageable with recording to disc and things like that.

You said you wanted to tour more. Did the band tour the East Coast? How far did you guys get?
That was the problem, we didn't. I'd say we went between Philadelphia and Boston. We didn't do anything else. That was kind of the conflict at the time. We just did colleges and small clubs.

Did the Blases feel a part of the alternative scene at the Green Parrot?
Oh yeah, of course. I mean, we would do the Parrot's Memorial Day shows, 4th of July shows, all their big weekends. We played with the Dervishes all of the time. We felt incredibly a part of that. That was our stomping ground, our home. Tommy (Ackerino) made us feel incredibly at home there. That dressing room was like our clubhouse.

WHTG DJs tell stories of the band's partying that are kind of legendary...
Yeah, well I don't know if we were trying to do it or if it's just our nature, but we kind of carried it to our middle-adulthood. The Blases weren't blase about partying. The DJs from WHTG loved hanging out with us, I think. We enjoyed their company. We just had a great time together. If you get any specifics out of people I won't deny anything!

When I was playing with John Cale, Mike Marrone was working for Rykodisc at the time. At our show in Boston all of the Rykodisc people came to see us and backstage Mike Marrone was telling stories about me that had me afraid I was going to get fired from the Cale gig. And that was a great gig to have.

How did you wind up playing with John Cale?
I was living and playing in the city. A friend of mine was the manager of a studio that put out a record that got on a compilation and we did a show at the Knitting Factory. The little band started to do pretty well. Then Dave got a call from a guitar player that had worked with Cale before. I was in Dave's loft rehearsing with him at the time. The guitar player was putting Cale's band together for that 1997 tour. He had two compilations out and a new record so he needed a touring band. Dave reluctantly recommended me because he knew he was going to lose me. I played with him in 1996-97.

What was the Green Parrot like for you?
To me, the Parrot was like our clubhouse. It was like our home because when we weren't playing we went there. We were younger and we kind of got away with acting ridiculous. We were forgiven for a lot of behavior that wasn't atrocious but was a bit stupid.

Who would you go see there?
Whoever was in town at the time. Dramarama was a band that we'd go see and talk to afterwards. Matt Pinfield would always be at those shows. We'd basically go see whoever was in town. The Blases played with a lot of the other bands then go see their shows. It's like you'd be at parties or birthdays and things like that afterwards. People hung out with each other.

The band has had a reunion or two in recent years, is that basically the same lineup?
Yeah, the one we did at the WHTG benefit was the band lineup from the album. That, for me, was the most fun to play. We've done a couple of other ones with older lineups in New Brunswick as well. I'd like to do that more often.

You're currently in Speedsters & Dopers, what's that band like?
It's actually Greg Di Gesu's band. We play in the city. We've recorded an album. It's Greg's project, I'm happy to help him out.

I don't know how to describe Greg's stuff. We would have been more up tempo and poppy while Greg's stuff has got that Velvet Underground side to it. Guys like Nick Cave have been mentioned too because we have the piano floating underneath the guitar.

What would you like people to remember about that band? Do you ever look back and think it could have been something big?
I probably always will. I don't think that the band ever wanted to take itself seriously out of self-consciousness. Either that or the fear of putting all of your eggs into one basket... something like that.

The irony is that now that I'm actually married and more settled than I've ever been, I just started writing again for the first time in years. I've written some stuff that I'm very, very happy about. It's funny because after all these years, what do you do with it?

What kind of direction is the new stuff?
It really isn't that dissimilar from what we were doing except it is a bit more piano based. I hate to make comparisons, but when you write something that's good you know it's good.

Do you think you and Rob Wagner might do some shows together in the near future?
I wouldn't count it out. I mean Wagner and I will know each other for the rest of our lives. I also wouldn't count out something silly like trying to get some cover gigs.

Are you thinking of trying to make another push with the new material?
I'm probably going to because I have the opportunity to and very few people have that opportunity and I know that. It's one of those things like if you have the inspiration and you're lucky enough to be able to react to it and you're talented enough to do something about it, I think you really should take the chance.

I'm lucky enough to have studio space always offered to me. And just to have some songs again... to go and do that is a great thing. I think you'll hear from either Rob or me or both of us because we're also not getting younger and we want to still rock while we can rock.

36 The Whirling Dervishes & Everlounge

The thing gets played every year all across the country. I have people calling me to say they heard "The Grinch" in Hawaii or in Philadelphia or in Giants Stadium. I just wish we wrote the fucking thing.
--DON DAZZO

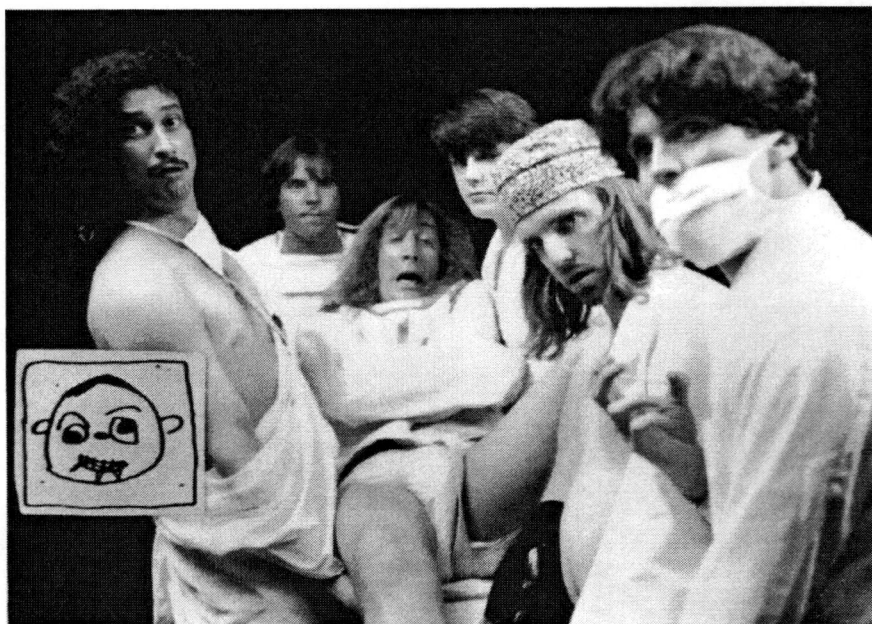

The Whirling Dervishes were a popular quirky alternative band. Their cover of "The Grinch" still gets played every Christmas. Photo © Phil Leo

The Whirling Dervishes was a classic alternative band. They were the typical popular band, always drawing large crowds, always on the brink of success but never quite getting there. During the 80s, the band was part of the emerging music scene along the Jersey Shore in clubs like the Green Parrot and Fastlane and was a favorite of the alternative rock radio station, WHTG.

The band released a pair of independent records and had a brief renaissance in the mid-90s before morphing into the lounge band, Everlounge. They continue to play throughout the area today and have released two records as Everlounge.

The band's name is based upon a spiritual offshoot of Islam that can be traced back to the 13th century Ottoman Empire. The Dervishes, as their fans called them, can still be heard each Christmas with their classic version of "The Grinch."

I caught up with Don Dazzo, the band's lead singer, for a phone interview one night to talk about one of the strangest and most interesting bands in Jersey Shore history.

How did you guys come up with the name Whirling Dervishes? I know what the actual name means, but you don't see many bands named after ancient religious rituals.

Uh, Bob Ardrey, our guitar player... Bob and I were the principal songwriters in the Dervishes. He came up with it. He was reading about it when he was in college and thought it might make a good name for a band. I went to Rowan, which was Glassboro, and he went to the University of Delaware. We were both from Westfield, New Jersey.

When we first put the band together it was more of a cover band and it was called Johnny Bravo and his Whirling Dervishes. Then when we decided to write a bunch of songs and go the all-original route, we shortened it to Whirling Dervishes.

When did the Dervishes get together?

Well, we really started playing in clubs in 1983-84. It was around 1984-85 that we put out our first record and WHTG started playing the record. I'm not so sure of the dates, that's when I remember it starting to happen for us. We just happened to release the record independently and WHTG picked up on it. That's what kind of gave us a push to start playing down in the area.

We really started down the Shore at the Brighton Bar. And then we got involved with a couple promotional showcases that put four bands on the bill at the Stone Pony. We played a couple of times at the Pony that way.

The local music scene of the 80s kind of gets forgotten in Shore history. Everything focuses so much on Bruce Springsteen.
Certainly, but it was kind of an anti-Bruce Springsteen / Asbury Park sound too. It was kind of like alternative rock before there was such a term. That's the way I looked at it.

Did you guys feel like there was something going on in those days?
Oh, definitely. It was a great time that we had there. There was a great scene. There was a great bunch of bands. Really the credit should go to whoever did the booking there, which I guess was Tony Ackerino or people in his family. I think WHTG had a lot to do with it too.

Are there any Dervishes shows that really stand out for you?
My fondest and most rebellious memory was when we played at the Pony in March sometime in the late 80s. For some reason, we were asked to headline on St. Patrick's Day along with three other bands. I have a crazy friend named Frank who still lives in the area. In a dark corner with a bandanna around his head and a denim vest, he might have you thinking that he looked a little bit like Bruce Springsteen. Nothing like a close resemblance. So, we planned this little hoax while the band learned a quick medley of "Born In The USA" into "Born To Run".

There was about 300 people tops in the club. About a third full. We had planned it with a guy in the audience to have him come up and whisper something in my ear and that would start the process.

Mid-set the guy comes up and whispers something in my ear. I'm like, "Ladies and gentleman, we have an extremely special guest!' People at the Pony automatically think it's going to be Springsteen so they rush the stage. The band goes into "Born In The USA" and we bring out Frank who's very drunk. He just goes into some Iggy Pop rant over the top of the song. Meanwhile, the band shifts gears and goes into the "Born To Run" riff and by now I'm looking at the audience and I'm seeing all these nasty faces. All of a sudden, the bouncers are on stage dragging him off. I played it totally straight. I was like, "Wait a minute... you're not Bruce Springsteen!" I don't know if they knew right then, but they never had us back. We didn't get back into the Pony until it changed hands.

One time we played the Fastlane and opened for Hawkwind. They were a British acid-rock band that spawned Lemmy from Motorhead. Lemmy was the bass player in Hawkwind. They're kind of like a little known but fairly famous international band and they did a kind of special biker acid rock, which I didn't know back then. It was complete with psychedelic movies and Spinal Tap like lyrics. It's silly but cool.

We opened for them around the time we had released a movie called *Thin Mints*. It was a really sick John Waters styled movie and the star was this overweight great actor named Fred Hallow dressed like a drag queen. We decided to bring Fred up and have him sing this really corny song from the movie. The audience was restless as it was because they were really a bunch of bikers, real tough guys, and they started getting nasty. And when Fred came out and started singing this kind of sappy song that was the end of it. They started booing and stuff like that. I came out, it was a packed house, and I said, "I distinctly think I heard people booing Fred Harlow." They're like, "Yeah, get the fuck off the stage. We want Hawkwind." Then we launched into Queen's "I'm In Love with My Car" and it shut them up.

How does it feel to have a song, like your version of "The Grinch" that you always know will be played and you pretty much know when it's going to be played?
Yeah, it's amazing. The thing gets played every year all across the country. I have people calling me to say they heard "The Grinch" in Hawaii or in Philadelphia or in Giants Stadium. I just wish we wrote the fucking thing.

The way royalties work you don't get any radio royalties. We've never really made any money on "The Grinch." The thing got released several times on our label and on some better indy labels, but the money never came through.

Was it a little disappointing that they didn't use your version for the Jim Carrey movie?
That was disappointing because we got our version to the right people. They just passed on it. Jim Carrey really wanted to do it. At least I know that it got to the right people, but they passed on it. That was disappointing because they really could have used it in that.

For a lot of years, you guys had the label of probably being "the next" to break from New Jersey. How difficult was it to be playing with that kind of pressure?
Well, I mean, that never really bothered me. I'll tell you what happened. We just didn't get the right kind of breaks. I'll never forget we played - this is a funny rock and roll stupid story. There was this big shot at like Warner Brothers and we had got his interest somehow. We did a showcase at the Pony. It was like a weeknight, but we had a pretty good turnout.

You know how things go with bands, you're playing in places where labels can come out and see you, you're hoping the timing is right and the band is on. Well, about a month before this was happening, we had just met these girls that claimed they were designers. They wanted to design a look for us, which I kind of bucked from the beginning, but then I said what could hurt? I've always considered myself a good dresser, but I don't know about the rest of the guys. Anyway, these girls had come up with these designs and they wanted to try them out. I said there's no way I'm gonna try something out the night of a showcase unless I truly fall in love with it.

They were supposed to have these things ready for weeks and weeks and weeks, but sure enough the showcase happens and that's when they have them ready. We were actually in a hotel room that night when they broke out the clothes. They had me wearing a burlap robe. It reminded me of that *Lord of The Rings* crap that people are wearing or something from *Star Wars*. It was kind of an old-fashioned Robin Hood type of wear. It was like no! And we got into an argument with these girls and everybody started fighting among themselves. I really think that put a damper on our show. Anyway, they passed on us after that showcase.

I wasn't as good as I could have been. My guts tell me that. The audience was there with us but I don't know. That was just one example of a record company executive coming to see us because we were kind of quirky, you know? We had talent as a whole but there wasn't any singular talent that stood out in the band other than our songs. Who knows? It takes a lot of different things to make it happen.

We actually had kind of a resurgence years later in the early 90s. We got signed to a publishing deal with Herb Albert's company. So, I guess to answer your question about being the next big thing we kept trying to do short goals and keep things going for as long as we could, which kept us amused and enthusiastic. So, we never really got down on being the next thing. We never really took that seriously until it was all over. There was a number of bands that did get deals at that time and you don't hear anything from them anymore. Once you get your record deal that's when it really starts.

How did the evolution of Everlounge come about?

First of all, there was always that element of tongue-in-cheek cabaret in the Dervishes. There was a couple of songs that had goofy, comedic and blues - different genres of music within songs. But it was just something that evolved naturally with age. We had kind of run our course as far as we had a publishing deal but we never got signed to a major. We were running out of opportunities with the Dervishes.

Yet, I wanted to keep singing and there was a whole lot of covers that I wanted to do. I felt like ok, I'm not going to really go as far as I wanted to with this original band and the rock and roll dream is dying, but I can still do ok as a second rate singer in a cover band or lounge thing.

We've played all over the place with Everlounge. We've played some really nice clubs in New York, fancy parties, weddings. It's been fun. It's totally different. I think it was just really a survival mechanism. If we had just continued to try playing one-set gigs with the Whirling Dervishes and attract new audiences it just wasn't going to happen.

Is it a lot more fun now that you're not out there shooting for deals?
Totally, and I actually do really enjoy it. I think I enjoy performing now more than I did with the Dervishes. There was more pressure with the Dervishes and the material was rough on my voice. It was all different things. It was louder. It was harder to hear one's self.

Do you guys get an entirely different crowd now?
Well, we're so old now. It's like with bands there are generations of fans and friends. It's usually like a five-year cycle (or even shorter) where people will come out for what seems like forever and then the fans will drop off the face of the earth and a new group will come in and then they'll fall off the face of the earth. Because what happens to most ordinary folks is they do their going out and drinking and dating stuff and then they settle down and don't want to do it anymore. I guess, I just never got tired of going out. But a lot of people do.

When the Whirling Dervishes get together on stage now, how does that differ from Everlounge? All different songs?
Yeah, there's very little cross over in the songs. I think there's like one or two. Both bands do "The Grinch" and a handful of Dervish originals. For the most part, it's that kind of dark, hard alternative rock with the Whirling Dervishes and light pop sounds for Everlounge.

What would you like people to remember about the Whirling Dervishes?
Just those great nights that we had live. That's the main thing. For people that liked our records and bought our records I think that's brilliant and thank you. But really the scene was the Brighton, the Pony, the Fastlane and the Parrot. My wife looks back on those days as such a great time. I was dating her then and we got married in 1989. We all loved it and it left a mark on all of us.

37 Well of Souls

They wanted me to be that intense singer person 24-hours a day and I couldn't do it. I couldn't be that everyday. When I was on stage it was no problem, but I couldn't live in that world all of the time. It was just too intense.

--TOM KANACH

Tom Kanach, the founder of Well of Souls, is pictured here.
Photo © Debra L. Rothenberg/rothenbergphoto.com

W ell of Souls was a band on the verge of success for many years. They won the *East Coast Rocker* "Unsigned Band Contest" in 1989, had a radio hit with the song "No More Rain" and spent countless nights in New York City showcasing in front of music industry people, but never managed to get signed to a record deal.

The band was formed by Tom Kanach, a talented songwriter and electrifying live performer. Joined later on by John Pfeiffer, the two paired up to take Well of Souls as far as it would go before continuing on as the band Grimace and then Lustre. I spoke to Tom Kanach via phone about this great punk rock band and to find out what he's been up to lately.

When did Well of Souls first get together?
Well, I was in a band called Mischief until 1987 and then Well of Souls started in '87 or '88. There were a couple of different lineups but the first lineup, the "No More Rain" period, was a bunch of younger guys that were just 19 or 20 who I recruited to play with me. They played my songs my way, but after a while I wanted to play with guys that were a little bit better musically. As a result I had to give up that authoritarian control. So the "Whisper" time period was more of a band.

How would you describe Well of Souls?
I thought that we were like a bunch of punk guys trying to play pop music. My big influence was the Beatles. I really liked that and that was what I was trying to write like. But I wanted to play it a little more aggressively... like aggressive pop. That's what I listened to and to me I wanted to play fast, edgy Beatles songs. During the "Killing Frost" time period, I was trying to create the masterpiece. That was almost put together like a concept album.

I'm proud of all of it. I know this sounds arrogant, but I consider myself a great undiscovered songwriter. I mean, people hear the stuff that I do now and say "Wow, this is great! Why aren't you signed?"

How close did Well of Souls get to a deal?
We went to New York, had a manager and had real photographers take pictures of us. We used to showcase at places like CBs, we played at the Limelight, we played in Philly and Hoboken a lot. At one point in time, right as the Parrot started to end and the lineup in Well of Souls changed, we were playing in New York, Philadelphia and then playing around here in between shows to build up a fan base. We won the *East Coast Rocker* "Unsigned Band Contest", I think it was in 1989, at the Stone Pony. Then we played at the Cat Club in New York City in front of all industry people.

I remember one point of time when I was in a building in New York City with a woman who was the lawyer for Elvis Presley's estate. We were there with a guy that was pseudo managing us at the time and a couple of other people. I could see Central Park all laid out behind her as she said, "You're gonna have to make a decision which guys in the band you're gonna get rid of because this guy's this way and this guy's that way." And she was basically telling me to get rid of my friends. I remember thinking to myself that I probably don't have that killer instinct to go to the next level. And yet music is who I am. I write music, I write songs, I spent a year recording an album called *Undertoe* and it was all me done at home.

We had a production deal with Jack Ponti who is a Toms River producer. We did a bunch of stuff with him and Dennis Birk. There was a falling out with those guys and we went through some legal hassles to get out of our production deal with them. That legal stuff killed us.

Do you ever plan on releasing your new stuff? Maybe as an independent record?

I've thought about it. People have asked me about it. There's a publishing company in New York that's been trying to get me to do something with this stuff. I would like to, but at the same time, I'm very happy with my life. I'm married with four children all under the age of four. At night, I come up here and put my ideas down. It's a part of me. It probably will always be a definition of who I am. I'm a musician and a songwriter, but while I liked the rock star stuff on stage there was a lot of other parts I didn't like. It got to the point for me in the Parrot days where girls would be willing to sleep with me just based on what I was doing on stage. They wanted me to be that intense singer person 24-hours a day and I couldn't do it. I couldn't be that everyday. When I was on stage it was no problem, but I couldn't live in that world all of the time. It was just too intense.

Where did Well of Souls play?

Around that time period we played the Brighton Bar in Long Branch, J.P. Trolley Stop in Red Bank, which was booking original bands for a while back then, the Fastlane, the Green Parrot, the Pony, the Court Tavern in New Brunswick. We played a lot of colleges like Kean College and universities in upstate New York. The band had a regular college thing that we would string together. We'd leave on a Thursday and come back on a Sunday and just try to play as much as possible, try to get our CDs in the local stores and get some college airplay.

Right around the time that the Parrot went down we were doing really well in terms of draw. We opened up for people like Julian Cope, Live, Big Country... a lot of those types of bands that were headliners for smaller clubs on their national tours.

We played Christmas break at the Stone Pony one night and opened for Live. I remember being on the stage, the Pony was packed and the fire marshall came and closed the door. No one else could go in. We were the band playing directly before Live. Here I am on stage and girls were screaming and grabbing my legs and they were singing my lyrics back to me. It was cool. I loved it! I think the Green Parrot and WHTG and all of the talent in the area sort of all bubbled up to the top at the same time.

What do you remember about the Green Parrot?
I remember there was a lot of shenanigans and wackiness going on. I had a great time as a single guy around 25-26. I was the singer in a band. I had long hair... It definitely helped me to appreciate being married by getting all of that out of my system!

One of the things I really liked about that time period and what I thought was important was how everybody went out to see everybody else. It was more of a scene. There was a number of good bands who went out and saw the other bands and got along relatively well. That really helped it. As a band, we played a little bit different. We weren't as polished or as commercial as some of the bands, but on stage I'd do the big dramatic things like pouring water on my hair, dropping my guitar and jumping around. I had a lot of psychopathic girls fall in love with me from that.

What was the worst thing about that period of time for you?
It was draining... I had a lot of girlfriends at the time and all at once. It was sort of difficult not to lose yourself in that world because it's not real. I would work as a waiter when I needed to, but the rest of the time I would just goof off and live with girls or off of band money. I did whatever I could get away with. It was a really great, free lifestyle and I loved it, but I was very frustrated by the fact that I thought we were really great and we couldn't take that next step. I was actually told from somebody at a record company once that "you're from New Jersey, so we're not interested."

It was frustrating because I think for a long time we hated the Bon Jovi's and the Springsteens of the world simply because people had a pre-conceived notion of what a New Jersey band was and that was it. I always thought it was really cool that you could go to the Brighton Bar on a week night and see three completely different bands that were all fundamentally very good bands.

The other thing was that I had been in clubs since I was 16 and I got tired of it. I was never a big drinker and I saw friends go through problems and die from drinking or drugs. It didn't lend itself to a lot of stability.

When did you first start out playing?
The first place I ever played was in Asbury Park in '81-82 at a place called Garp's back when I was in Mischief. It was a go-go bar and we played in between dancer sets. It was funny because the girls would try to dance to our music and they kept coming over to complain that we were playing too fast and tiring them out. They were all skanky, biker go-go dancers. The place had fights every night. There were knife fights and all these Harley Davidson's parked outside. It was a very dark and seedy place. It was located around the corner from the Fastlane. I think it became a Mexican restaurant.

Joe DeLorenzo (later of the Blases) was in the band as well. We started when we were 16. I was in that band for seven years before Well of Souls. So, by the time that band ended I instantly had a ton of material which the other band wasn't playing. That's where songs like "No More Rain" and others came from.

Well of Souls eventually changed their name to Grimace.
Grimace was the same lineup as Well of Souls. The President of Virgin Records sent us a fax saying he really loved our stuff and that my songwriting reminded him of Elvis Costello meets Kurt Cobain. He wanted to sit down and have a private showcase with us in New York City. Then our manager got into trouble and we were there through him because he set it up, and that was it. It went away and we changed our name to Grimace to disassociate ourselves.

How long did Grimace play?
We played for about a year and a half. We had another legal deal that we were in and it got to be really prohibitive in terms that the producer wanted to change what we were doing. He was trying to make it as commercial as possible. We were artists and we didn't want to do that. So, that ended and then the drummer left and the bass player left. I wound up taking some time off.

We sort of petered out in '95. I continued writing the whole time and I played with the guitarist John Pfeiffer in a band called Lustre. We did a CD that we basically gave out to our friends. There was a song called "Isn't She Pretty" which was a finalist for the TV show "Ed" for their first season-ending show.

They were looking for a specific song and we wound up in the top three. We got all the way to the end and they picked a different song. They said, "Your song's really good, but we went with this song because it's a known artist."

Did you ever have a song publishing deal?
I've had pseudo publishing deals with guys who didn't have any money to give me, never with a really big company. But we're dealing with somebody in New York now that has a real company.

We're actually getting ready to put the band back together and start playing sometime this summer. It's all new material that we've been recording in my home studio.

What are your plans with getting the band back together?
Just to play a few shows. I've been writing all along, I have a ton of new material. I write about 50-60 songs a year and I always have. I'll throw them into my home studio on the computer and meet with John Pfeiffer and we pick the ones we like and play them.

What will the band be called?
I don't know. There's a band in Chicago called Well of Souls. It's an industrial metal band and they have a website and some other stuff. So, we're not really sure. I used to own the name for a long time. We were incorporated and a whole bunch of stuff. We tried to be businesslike back then, I guess.

How would you like people to remember Well of Souls?
If somebody remembered them I think it would be good. I think we were a really good band. I thought at the time that we were a little ahead of ourselves in terms of what happened afterwards. People were saying after Nirvana came out that our old stuff sounded like Nirvana, although I don't necessarily agree. It was just a fun period of time and I don't know if it will ever happen again around here. It seemed liked everything happened - the radio station and the club - at the right time.

38 The Bongos

The Bongos were a force of nature and performing at the Shore was a perfect combination of that energy sort of exploding. I think that the Shore area was our favorite place to play.

--RICHARD BARONE

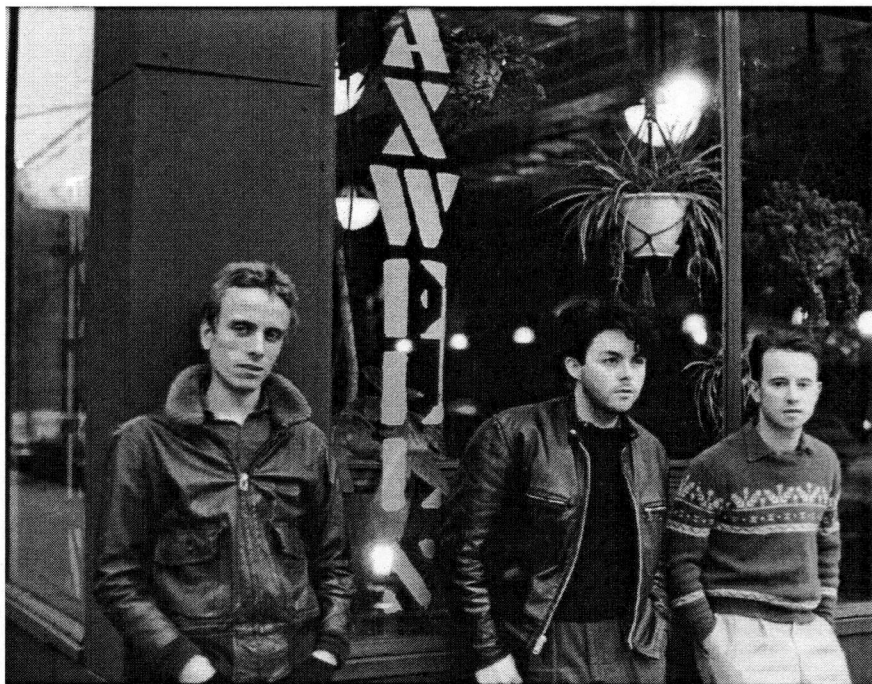

The Bongos, circa 1981, in front of Maxwell's. Left to right: Bassist Rob Norris, Richard Barone, and drummer Frank Giannini. Photo © Phil Marino

T he Bongos were one of the pioneers of early alternative music. A favorite of college radio fans, their music was an eclectic blend of pop and punk that stood just outside the mainstream. The band was originally a trio which included Richard Barone, Rob Norris and Frank Giannini with James Mastro joining the band a few years later. The Bongos released three albums that have reached near cult-like status.

Although the band's home base was clearly Hoboken, they were also an instrumental part of the Green Parrot scene along the Jersey Shore. They were introduced to the area by WHTG, the local alternative radio station that played them often. The band's mix of Beatlesque pop and punk energy with tribal rhythms was clearly ahead of its time.

The Bongos played many great shows along the Shore and Richard Barone performed many solo shows here as well. In fact, Barone was the very last artist to play at the legendary Green Parrot club. I talked to Richard via phone about the Bongos and that last night of the Green Parrot, which sadly ended an era at the Shore.

When did the Bongos first get together?
I guess it was in 1980 and the Bongos continued to perform for most of the eighties. But I started doing more acoustic music around 1987. It was just acoustic guitar with cello, vibes and percussion, a different kind of set up. That was the group I was working with at the end of the Green Parrot period.

You were part of a legendary night on the Jersey Shore, the night the Green Parrot closed. Was it a Richard Barone solo show or the Bongos that played that last night of the Parrot?
It was definitely me because the last Bongos shows were around 1987-88. I started performing as a solo artist while the Bongos were still performing. It was a schizophrenic period for me.

What do you remember about the Green Parrot club?
There was a lot of cool things about it. For one thing, it was one of my favorite places to play, both with the Bongos and as a solo artist, because the way the stage was set up was sort of really low. Usually we'd play at places where the stage was very high so you're separated from the audience. At the Green Parrot the audience was literally right in your face, which created an intimacy that doesn't always happen at a club. There was a sort of convergence of the audience and the band there because the place would be really packed and the people were pretty much on the stage. It was exciting. I loved the way it was set up there. You could really communicate with the audience.

It was so sudden when it was done. I loved that place. It went quickly, but it was great. Lots of great people played there. If I recall, the group that I had at that time had a timpani and was quite a big, almost orchestral, pop group. It was just great to do it where the audience was practically on stage with us. It was a very cool and unusual atmosphere because of that. There was a great sort of rowdiness that I liked, especially in combination with my more acoustic music. Having the wild atmosphere of the Green Parrot contrasted with the kind of music we were doing in a way.

Did you have any idea that your solo show was going to be the last night of the Green Parrot?
No, I think they told us after we finished our set. As I recall, they told us when we came off stage that it was going to be the last night of the club. Of course we celebrated all night. I mean, we really made it the last night there. I think we stayed there... well, the sun was definitely coming up. We just hung out in the club as long as possible too because we loved it!

Were you living around Hoboken then or in the city?
At that time I might have been already living in Manhattan, but certainly part of the time I was living in Hoboken. Where I live is almost an extension of Hoboken, in some ways, but across the river. I can actually see Hoboken from where I live. So, I'm very connected to it still.

The Bongos were certainly a large part of the Hoboken scene, did the band feel like a part of the Green Parrot scene as well?
Yes we did, very much. The Bongos were always connected to the Jersey Shore scene. We felt very connected to that area because of the radio station. I think that's what really started it. We got really connected with the station, which we loved, and ended up playing there a lot. I mean, we played there almost as much as we played in Hoboken.

Where did you play in Hoboken? Maxwell's?
When we started out there was a small place that we would occasionally play, but Maxwell's was the place. Maxwell's was where the Bongos would rehearse. When I first moved to Hoboken with the other guys in the Bongos, Maxwell's had recently opened as a bar/tavern/restaurant but it didn't have live music yet. So, we convinced the owner to let us rehearse in the back room. Somehow we started inviting friends to the rehearsals and it sort of became a scene from that.

So the Bongos kind of convinced Maxwell's to offer live music?
Yeah. For years the sound system was simply our rehearsal PA that we used to use when we practiced. They kept that, I think, for most of the eighties. But that's really how that started. It was a place where we practiced and eventually we started doing shows there and it was really the beginning of something great.

Wasn't there a Bongos video that was shot at Maxwells?
Actually, "The Bulrushes" video, which is obscure but very cool, was shot in the basement of Maxwells. I think that video, which I love, was ahead of its time. It was produced by a guy from Hoboken named Phil Marino. He directed it as well. The back cover of *Drums Along The Hudson* was also shot in the basement of Maxwells. Maxwell's was definitely our home base. There's no way around it.

What are your thoughts on the radio station WHTG?
It was an incredibly good radio station. I just remember it playing everything I loved. It was a great station to listen to, I only wish I could have picked it up more here away from the Shore area because it was so good. We couldn't really pick it up at home, but as soon as we were in the Shore vicinity we'd listen to it. One great song after another. They had great taste in what they played.

It was fun to do the live things there. We would often perform live on the air. Like if we were performing at the Green Parrot or in that area we would do a live segment in the afternoon, maybe an acoustic set or something like that. It was very cramped, a very crowded little station. The control room would become very crowded suddenly when we went in there because I'd bring my cellist and quite a few musicians.

Did you play any other places along the Shore?
The Bongos did over 300 shows a year so you'll have to excuse me if I'm a little vague on where we played. Those shows were over seven or eight years. We toured so much and we did play a lot at the Shore. It was always a big event when we did.

We did a live recording once... I think it was at the Tradewinds. It's never been released. RCA brought the mobile trucks there. I recently redis- covered the master tapes for that. It's one of the wildest shows. It espe- cially captures the feeling of the Shore crowd. It was so wild. You just feel the audience's energy on that recording. I'm looking into seeing if we can release it. It was recorded in 1985 on Memorial Day weekend, which made it even wilder than it would have been on a normal weekend.

Was there a particular Bongos show that stands out for you?
All of them. They just got wilder and wilder. The Bongos were a force of nature and performing at the Shore was a perfect combination of that energy sort of exploding. I think that the Shore area was our favorite place to play.

Do you still play any shows with the other guys from the band?
Sure. The Bongos have done the occasional benefit here and there for the right purpose or cause or for a special event, but they've been rare appearances. One was a performance at DJ Vin Scelsa's 50th birthday.

Have you played any shows at the Shore recently?
I haven't lately. I've been working on a new album with Tony Visconti producing and it's interesting to me because he is the producer who produced the T-Rex records that the Bongos loved and also the David Bowie records that I've always loved.

For the last year, I've been working on an album with Tony producing and while I'm recording I haven't been doing too many shows out of the New York City area. I'm just more in a recording mode than performing mode. I am doing a series of shows at Joe's Pub at the Public Theater in New York, but I haven't played at the Shore too much lately. I did do a performance at an event called WHTG's "Cultural Heritage Festival" in 2000. John Easdale played at that as well. I went up and did a solo show just with my acoustic guitar. That was my last visit to the Shore. I'd love to go back soon and when my album is ready I will be back there. It's just been one of those things where I'm enjoying the process so much. Working with Tony... it's been a nice experience to work on this album.

What would you say was your favorite Bongos album?
For me, it's hard to say. I think my favorite was the first. Maybe just because it's the first one. *Drums Along The Hudson*, that project, that whole album was so do-it-yourself and it was at a time when that was not the usual thing to do. We had so much control over that one and did it ourselves. I think it's my favorite because of that. That came out on an independent label (PVC Records) here in the states and then we went to RCA after that.

I would say my favorite Bongos album is *Drums Along The Hudson*, even though production-wise I love *Numbers With Wings* and that's the record that gets played the most. The tracks from that record have had the most exposure. They're used on many compilations of songs from that period. Plus there's the video that VH1 Classics still plays in rotation.

How pleased were you with how your records have come out?
I'm very pleased with them. My favorite is *Clouds Over Eden*. The new one, of course, is where my heart is now. *Primal Dream* would have been the tour that the last Green Parrot show was from. That material was just so great to do live. In a way, I had a larger group with sort of combined rock elements and the acoustic stuff. That was especially cool.

How did the live record *Between Heaven & Cello* come about?
After *Clouds Over Eden* was released in Europe, I did a major tour over there, with a fairly big band. But, when the CD came out here in the states a few months later, I decided to tour the states with just the cellist. It was such a stark and intense sound - guitar and cello. But, it turned out to be one of my favorite tours. I felt so free to improvise, change arrangements on the spot, and generally work without a net or a script.

We started to record all the shows on a portable DAT machine. I collected those recordings and put together *Between Heaven & Cello* which was released in Europe in the mid-90s. Two of the tracks on that album were recorded at the Shore: "Before You Were Born" was recorded at the Fastlane, and "Barbarella" was recorded at the Stone Pony.

Do you still get a kick from seeing longtime fans of the Bongos?
Yeah, they come to the shows and it's great! Sometimes it's in unexpected places. People seem to know the Bongos in a lot of different places that I travel to, which is nice. We had a sound that kind of got around in a good way.

It really was an rather eclectic sound.
Yeah, that's because the guys in the group had such different tastes. Rob Norris, the bass player, was so into stuff like Ornette Coleman, Captain Beefheart and Sun-Ra. The drummer, Frank Giannini, was really into ABBA or very melodic pop. I guess my interest, at the time, was I really loved the Velvet Underground and the Beatles and wanted to combine those opposite ends of pop music.

What are your shows like now? Do you do mostly new material?
Well, each show is different, and I'm doing an interesting mix. For the show I'm doing at Joe's Pub, half of the show is my own songs and half is songs by artists that don't normally get covered. I've found some songs that I love but that don't get played. My half is mostly music from the new album and one song from each of the solo albums and maybe one Bongos song. I don't dwell too much on the past though.

39 The Fastlane

It was just me and these other guys in this dark, dingy club listening to the band. I was like yeah, they're good, but I went back to the Pony and hung out the rest of the night with my friends. About six months later I was like, "Holy shit, I saw U2!"

--RICH ROBINSON
FORMER PROGRAM DIRECTOR AT WHTG

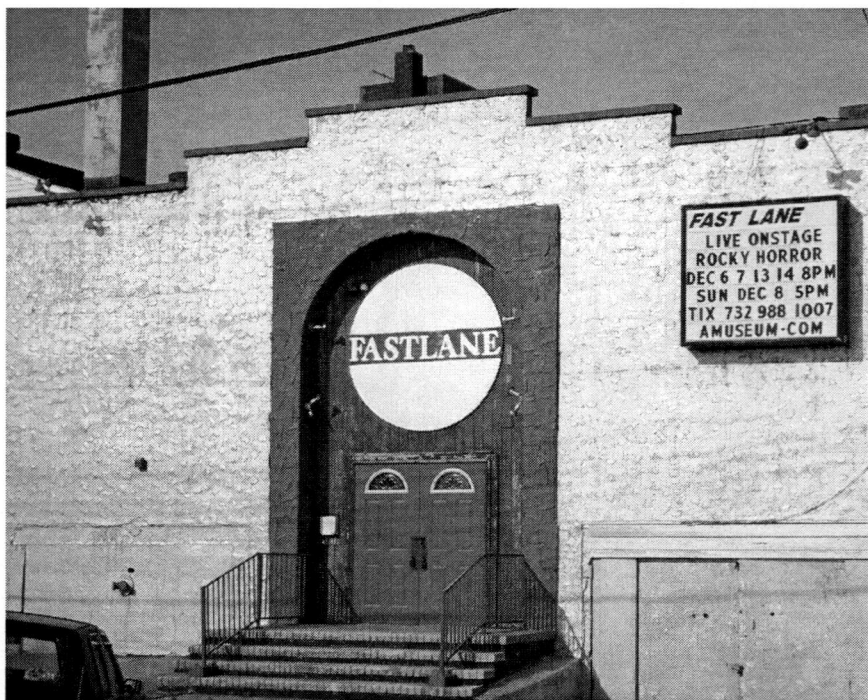

FAST LANE
LIVE ONSTAGE
ROCKY HORROR
DEC 6 7 13 14 8PM
SUN DEC 8 5PM
TIX 732 988 1007
AMUSEUM-COM

Bands like U2 and the Police played here during their first world tours and a young Jon Bon Jovi gained a following at this club.   Photo © Gary Wien

Around the world the Fastlane is noted in rock and roll history for being one of the clubs where a young Jon Bon Jovi got his start. Bon Jovi played here long before becoming famous with bands like Atlantic City Expressway, the Rest and the Wild Ones. The Fastlane was always home to several of the traditional Asbury Park musicians like Billy Chinnock and Lance Larson, but its true claim to fame lies in being the premier venue for alternative music in the area.

Bands like U2, the Police and the Psychedelic Furs all played here during tours in the early 80s. In later years, alternative favorites like Dramarama, the Connells and Concrete Blonde would pack the house. While the Stone Pony down the street was catering to those that loved the "Asbury Sound", the Fastlane offered something different. The club was a good size with a big stage and surrounded by bars. There was carpeted bleachers for years until the current owners renovated the place in the late 90s. It looked a bit like one of those classic New York dives that always had the best music in the area even when the place was empty.

"I was actually at the U2 show," said Rich Robinson, former Program Director at WHTG. "I was supposed to hook up with my friends to go hang out at the Pony, but no one was there yet. So, I went over to the Fastlane to see what was happening there. I walked in and it looked like a sausage factory. There were about 18 guys hanging out and this band on stage that was just kicking ass and taking names. They sounded really good but I was bored out of my brain. I sat there watching them for about 3-4 songs. It was just me and these other guys in this dark, dingy club listening to the band. I was like yeah, they're good, but I went back to the Pony and hung out the rest of the night with my friends. About six months later, I was like, 'Holy shit, I saw U2!'"

The biggest problem with the Fastlane was the club's history of closing then reopening, then closing again. It was never open long enough to truly gain the legendary status that the Stone Pony achieved. But for a few years, the Fastlane was the bar in Asbury.

In the early 90s, the Stone Pony was pretty much running on fumes. The bar was starting to show its age and many of the more popular acts of the day chose to play at the Fastlane instead. Mike Sauter, former DJ for WHTG, recalls that period of time. "In the early 90s, the Fastlane was the place to see alt-rock shows," said Sauter. "It was, as stated in hundreds of commercials I produced at WHTG for the club, 'the house that rocks the Jersey Shore.' I absolutely loved the set-up of the place. There was something very cool and college dorm-esque about the carpeted bleacher-style audience seating along the west wall."

The Fastlane was home to plenty of great shows during the 90s. Dramarama would play back-to-back nights at the club and the place would be wall to wall with screaming, moshing fans. Matthew Sweet, Fishbone, Henry Rollins and King Missile were some of those that stood out. Mr. Reality (currently Highway 9), a local band that gained a big following along the Jersey Shore was practically born there. The band's lead singer, Peter Scherer, used to work at the club. One day you saw him at the front door letting you into the Fastlane and the next he was on stage singing incredible covers of Don Henley songs and unbelievable originals. They played acoustic music and, for some reason, seeing a band play acoustically and sing songs with such wonderful harmonies in a club like the Fastlane was really special. Fans felt as though they were truly part of something. It was that kind of club. The bartenders knew your name, they knew what you wanted to drink and you'd go there often.

Mike Sauter recalls one of his most memorable shows at the club. "British pop-rocker John Wesley Harding was headlining a show at the Fastlane following the release of his 1991 album *The Name Above the Title*, and it happened to be the same night as Little Steven was playing the Stone Pony a few blocks away (this was an era when the Pony seemed on life support, they never seemed to book many decent bands. I seem to recall there was some sort of dispute within the club's management brain trust that ended in the opening of a competing club called the Rock Horse elsewhere in Asbury). The opening bands for the Harding show (The Judybats from Tennessee and an Atlanta group called Uncle Green, as I recall) completed their sets, and the stage crew set up the equipment for the headliner. The room was pretty packed. In those pre-America Online, pre-Playstation, not-quite-yet-Draconian-drunk-driving-laws days, people went out to live shows a lot more than now. Hell, people would even drive from New Brunswick to Asbury to see a show (and vice versa) which has become all but unheard of.

"The thick crowd at the Fastlane was heavy with anticipation at the imminent arrival onstage of the evening's top bill. But John Wesley Harding was nowhere to be seen. The between-set music pumped through the Fastlane house PA continued, as audience members began to get impatient. Maybe something happened to Harding? Perhaps he was backstage doing unspeakable rockstarish things. I was standing in the middle of the crowd, towards stage-left, and people around me were inches away from getting ugly, when suddenly the house lights went out and Harding appeared on stage, to loud cheers borne of pent-up impatient tension from the crowd. I didn't notice at the time, but the back of Harding's right hand was smudged with a sort of small dark stain.

"Later, I found out what the holdup was. Harding, a big Springsteen fan, had heard the inevitable rumors before his own show that Bruce was going to make a surprise appearance at the Little Steven show over at the Stone Pony. So Harding skipped out on his own show and snuck over to the Pony to see what was up. He paid the cover at 'the house that Bruce built' and waited around until he absolutely had to get back to play for his own audience at the Fastlane. I thought this illustrated a very important point about context. In one building, John Wesley Harding was the star of the show with cheering throngs offering an abundance of adulation. A couple of blocks away, though, he's just another schmuck with a stamp on the back of his hand, craning his neck to see if Bruce had appeared. Bruce never showed, by the way.

"The next morning when I recounted this story on my morning show, someone called me to tell me that he heard that Harding, Little Steven, and Bruce had all gone into a studio and recorded some music. That's when I first began calling Bruce the 'Asbury Park Bigfoot.' Like the mythical sasquatch, Bruce sightings were plentiful and plenty apocryphal. And the Springsteen rumor mill was capable of believing and spreading any tall tale, regardless of how much it strained credulity."

The Fastlane was once run by Mark Grubman, a man described by those close to him as a direct disciple of Bob Fischer, the guy that once ran the Sunshine In. Both were far from easy to deal with, but both had the knack for bringing great bands to Asbury Park. The Fastlane has always seemed to get the short end of the stick when people talk about Asbury Park's music history. When the plan for redeveloping Asbury Park was announced, there wasn't a big rallying cry to save the Fastlane from the wrecking ball. While fans of Bruce Springsteen and Southside Johnny rallied around the Stone Pony as if it was the Alamo, the Fastlane fans were barely noticed.

It will be a crime for Asbury Park to get rid of the Fastlane. Not simply because of its great music history, but because the current owners have spent many years and much money renovating it and the Baronet located next door. Their buildings are located in the part of town which needs redevelopment the most. People don't just drive by the Fastlane, they have to know something is going on before they head down that way. Asbury Park is lucky to have business owners that care so much about the city, and they should be able to reap the rewards should Asbury come back to life. In recent months, they have put on shows and run movies at the Baronet Theatre with after-parties held at the Fastlane. There's talk about bringing back live music to the Fastlane as well, but that shouldn't be a surprise. The club's bound to have a few more lives in it.

40 T-Birds Cafe & the Saint

> Scott, bless his heart, is one of those guys that has done everything he can to keep original music fresh and cool and just support the scene. We need more people like that.
>
> --GORDON BROWN
> HIGHWAY 9

The late Jeff Buckley performs at T-Birds Cafe, which was located on Main Street in Asbury Park. Photo © Debra L. Rothenberg/rothenbergphoto.com

E very good music scene needs that one person who goes out of their way to support up-and-coming bands, in Asbury Park that person is Scott Stamper. In the eighties, he was responsible for booking the bands at T-Birds Cafe, an intimate venue located on Main Street. After that club closed, he opened up the Saint and continued to provide new talent with a great place to play.

T-Birds Cafe was a very unique place in town. It had a look and feel all to its own. The club was dark with black lights so anyone wearing white clothing would literally glow in the dark. The walls were decorated with things like pinball machines cut in half and other weird things. It was small, but very eclectic and the shows were usually incredible and very memorable.

"I remember that when we would play there we'd usually end up doing pretty long, raucous shows there because it just seemed like that kind of place," said Bruce Tunkel, who played with the band Red House. "You'd maybe drink a little more than usual and just have a lot of fun there. I have great memories of playing T-Birds."

One thing that virtually every musician that ever played T-Birds remembers is the pole. In front of the stage there was this pole that the musicians often had to work around. "It was like dancing with an inanimate object," said Greg Di Gesu. "If you were set up near the front of the stage you would inevitably have to do some maneuvering around in order to see and be seen. But then again, with the bar about 5 feet or so across from the stage, there was never a question of not feeling intimate with the audience."

Mimi Cross laughs as she recalls the pole. For her, there were other obstacles to overcome as well. "The bar was so close to where you were playing and there was always some guy leaning against the bar with that music industry stance of arms folded and kind of glaring at you. So, you'd have to do this little psyche thing on yourself. He must think I'm cute... He thinks I'm cute that's why he's glaring."

Mr. Reality, a band which now performs as Highway 9, played their very first shows at T-Birds. "It was great," said Gordon Brown of Highway 9. "It was small and very dark in there. It was very cool. You could just walk in and do your own thing. I went with the Bon Jovi guys one night and we saw Jeff Buckley. To watch Jeff Buckley at that club and sit there and be like this guy's unreal and know that you have a room in town where you can have that kind of experience was great."

Artists like Peter Himmelman took advantage of the unique vibe at the club. He once decided to take everyone outside and simply grabbed his guitar and started playing as the crowd and him walked up the block.

T-Birds was a place designed for spontaneous jams and, for a while, there was even a night set aside just for that purpose. James Deely recalls one jam in particular. "Me and Bruce Tunkel and my bass player, Paul Ford, went down to T-Birds one night to rock with Vini Lopez at his jam night," said Deely. "We had played some covers like 'Here Comes A Regular' and 'Like a Rolling Stone' when Bruce goes, 'Ask Vini if we can play 'Incident on 57th Street." I was a little nervous but I said, 'Hey Vini, let's do 'Incident on 57th Street." He thought for a second, then said, 'Yeah, let's do it!' So guitar man Al cuts into the intro/lead and we start playing. All during the song I kept hearing this gorgeous vocal. I kept looking around trying to see who the hell was singing this great high part. Then I look over at Vini and he's back there singing his ass off! Just like the record!"

"It was just one of those places where you would stay all night listening to other people," added Mimi Cross. "And people actually listened, that's the thing. I would go and play, but I would also stay for the other bands and really listen... Everyone listened."

"I only really got to play there about four or five times before it closed down and then it was the Saint," said Danny White who was starting out in Shore clubs when T-Birds was on its last legs. "I remember the first time I played the Saint, I was like, 'This place is huge!' Because when you go from T-Birds and then you go in there... Scott pretty much said we're closing and we're gonna open down here and I'll call you when we do. He did and I played there a lot. It's like you move on."

The scene did kind of move on when the Saint opened further up the street. For years, T-Birds was left abandoned with just its sign and a message saying "reopening soon." The club never did reopen, but the arrival of the Saint made it easier to take. Dozens of national acts have played the Saint throughout the last decade. Some of the acts to grace its stage include Ben Folds Five, Chris Whitley, Creed, D-Generation, Everlast, Fun Lovin' Criminals, Incubus, Jewel, Jill Sobule, Superdrag, The The, and Matt Keating.

Clubs like the Saint are the life blood of new music. They can be found throughout the country, but rarely last as long as the Saint has. The club is entering its 10th year - a great feat for an establishment based on presenting acts largely unknown. Mike Sauter, a former disc jockey at WHTG and currently at WBJB, says that clubs like the Saint are "absolutely critical to a vibrant music scene and to live music in general. Clubs that take a chance on new bands even if they run the risk of selling few tickets are the live equivalent of the old 'HTG' - nurturing new talent even at the expense of the bottom line."

One of the most unique things about the Saint has been the addition of its Asbury Cafe shows. During these shows the crowd is asked to refrain from talking to create the effect of a listening room. Shows at the Asbury Cafe are also smoke-free, something unique for a rock club. There are chairs lined up as in a listening-room setup. The overall atmosphere is perfect for lyrically-driven performers.

New York singer-songwriter, Matt Keating, played an Asbury Cafe show early in 2003. "I was doing an on-air performance/interview with Jeff Raspe from 'The Night' (WBJB) radio station and he mentioned the club," explained Keating. "I was getting airplay there and wanted to do a show in the region.

"The last time I played at the Saint with my band it was a little overkill. Doing what I do in front of smaller audiences is much easier in a 'listening room' type of experience It's more intimate and helps you connect better with the audience. They had a great sound system, really nice people and I really enjoyed it."

"The thing is everybody is silent," added Mimi Cross. "It was the Saint, but if anything it reminded me of T-Birds because the people were really listening."

Rich Robinson, the former Program Director at WHTG, believes that clubs like the Saint clearly benefit from local commercial radio station support. Unfortunately, the only station in the area that really tries to promote the local music scene is the public radio station WBJB 90.5 The Night. Robinson recalls the period of time in 1996 when he returned to WHTG and got Everlast to stop by the station. "I really liked that song 'What It's Like' and I was friends with one of the guys on the label so I asked them to come by and do an interview before the show," said Robinson. "He came in and we hit it off really well. So what was supposed to be a 10-minute interview ending up being an hour and a half interview and his record hadn't even come out yet. That night when he played at the Saint there was a line outside the door and you couldn't get in. And when he broke into that song everyone went wild. We had debuted it on the air less than two hours before. I was like wow, the station still has it."

"Scott, bless his heart, is one of those guys that has done everything he can to keep original music fresh and cool and just support the scene," added Brown. "We need more people like that."

41 Soul Engines

But we're older now so I don't know if we can recapture the same thing again, like what we had before - ten years ago, twelve years ago. Do you catch the magic twice? Who knows? Is what we're doing still contemporary?

--MARK NUZZI

The members of Soul Engines. Pictured from left to right: Mark Nuzzi and David Kuchler (bottom) and Gino Scelza and Steve Scarpa (top).

S oul Engines was one of the most popular bands along the Jersey Shore in the early 90s. Built around the brilliant songwriting of Mark Nuzzi, the band had a largely acoustic rock sound that picked up a loyal following of music fans in Shore towns like Asbury Park and Long Branch.

The band's first independent record, *Ghosts On A Landscape*, was released in 1991 and sold nearly 10,000 copies. Soul Engines found themselves opening shows for artists like John Eddie, Glen Burtnick, the Bodeans and the Spin Doctors, while local critics frequently picked them as the band to watch from the area.

After putting out *Learning To Live*, the band landed a record deal with One World Records, a New Jersey based independent label. In late 1993, the band headed back to the studio, but the record label closed its doors before the new album was released leaving the band without a record or a record deal. Soul Engines never did get that momentum back and even disbanded for a few years. They ultimately got back together in 1997 and have released three additional records, including the long awaited *Endless Carnival* and their most recent, *Closer Still*.

Recently, Soul Engines has been doubling as a cover band under the name Mama Luke while trying to book shows for their originals. I caught up with Mark Nuzzi one night to find out whatever happened to this great Jersey Shore band.

Soul Engines was a very popular band along the Jersey Shore in the early 90s. What did playing in Asbury Park mean to you?
It was definitely special because I'm a big fan of Asbury music like Bruce Springsteen and Southside Johnny and some of the other people who passed but never made it to the same heights like Glen Burtnick and John Eddie. So, it was a big deal. But the scene was basically dead in the early 90s and thank God T-Birds opened up. It was a place to play. A small venue, very intimate, people were right on top of you. We had a great time doing that. For a certain extent, there was still a mystique about Asbury Park and Bruce Springsteen. But, at that time, he was personally living in California so he was nowhere to be found. But it still meant a lot.

Being largely from North Jersey. Was it strange to be grouped with the up-and-coming bands along the Shore?
It was a good thing. The name of the band makes reference to a Bruce Springsteen song. People always thought we were a cover band, like a Springsteen cover band. So, we were automatically lumped into that. And, no, I didn't mind at all. We're nobody's...

Soul Engines kind of disappeared for several years and resurfaced with the cover band Mama Luke. How did that band come about?
We needed to play covers so we wanted to come up with a name that was silly so we weren't playing under the name Soul Engines. Because when someone like yourself comes to see us play our own music we really can't in this atmosphere. So now we have this other identity where we just be a cover band and make money.

I don't have fun doing this. I have much more fun doing our own music. This is not fun. These people aren't here because of us. We're here tonight and there's a lot of people having a good time, but it has nothing to do with us. It could be six other musicians up there and it wouldn't matter. They're here because they're just hanging out and they hear songs that they like.

The band was kind of stuck in legal limbo after the record label fell apart. Are the legal issues completely over now?
Yeah, that's over with now. But we're older now so I don't know if we can recapture the same thing again, like what we had before... ten years ago, twelve years ago. Do you catch the magic twice? Who knows? Is what we're doing still contemporary?

Well maybe it's the right time. Highway 9 had lightning strike twice and they were playing the clubs around the same time you were.
That was the expression I was looking for "lightning striking twice". Maybe, yeah maybe. They were definitely around the same time. Well, hopefully good music is good music no matter when it is; fifty years ago, a hundred years ago or ten years ago.

What is the worst thing about being in a cover band? Is it that the crowd isn't coming to see you or the fact that you can't do your originals?
That they're not coming to see you. You can do your originals. They don't even really care about the cover music that you're playing. And there's nothing wrong with that. They come in here to hear music they know and have a good time.

I hate using the term originals because nothing is original, but when you play your own music even if three people come that's three people there to see you and hear the songs that you wrote. You could have 500 people listening and going crazy over "American Girl" or "Me & Julio Down By The Schoolyard", it's better to have three people who like something you write.

I saw that Soul Engines has a page on MP3.com now. Is the band actively marketing the new records?

No, not really. That was just a simple thing. Everyone is kind of into it right now because who knows what's going to happen with the music. We'd love for something to happen with the music. We'd love for something to happen as far as with publishing. We're not really seriously considering something happening as far as us being signed as artists because we're fat old guys.

Is the story about "You hardly even know this guy" really true?

Yeah, we were in this place, which kind of goes through the whole line of questions about cover bands. We were totally bored and once in a while when there's no one there we kind of make stuff up on the spot. And when there's no one there we do it a lot. And that night, I was totally bored and we asked the audience for a key to play in and then somebody said E-flat. Then we asked this girl who was sitting in front, I think I asked her, "What's the name of your boyfriend there?" She said, "That's not my boyfriend, I don't even know this guy." It was like a first date.

So, then we made a song up. Not the whole song, just "you hardly even know this guy, you hardly even know this guy at all." That came right at that point and then we just sat down and finished it and crafted it. Yeah, that was just made up on the spot. A lot of stuff we do just happens that way. So, Dave and I sat down and finished it. Hey, you know what? If it becomes a hit song somewhere in Hamburg or wherever that'd be great.

Do you ever see yourself pursuing some kind of a record deal?

Yeah, if we got something like in Europe where there's a little interest in us from a company in Germany right now. If we had interest there and we got signed to a European contract we would definitely pursue something that would physically enable us to put out our own music. And that would be great. But if somebody like Faith Hill came along and needed a song that would be great too.

Is playing covers needed for a band to survive?

No, you don't need it, you don't have to play cover music. We do it now because we're in a situation where we're older and we have families we have to deal with. But we didn't do it before. I had never played in a cover band before until the other thing fell apart. But, it sucks, it really sucks. I'd rather play my own music to one person. We're here tonight and there's a lot of people having a good time. But it has nothing to do with us. It could be six other musicians up there. It wouldn't matter.

42 Mr. Reality, Samhill & Highway 9

Samhill was a really cool name, but it didn't necessarily identify with our roots specifically. And so coming across the name Highway 9, we immediately felt like we were representing where we came from and our roots, our New Jersey roots. It was a great feeling to finally tie in.

--PETER SCHERER

A look at Highway 9, the second go around for members of Mr. Reality.

A
t the end of the eighties a new band took over the Jersey Shore scene. Known as Mr. Reality, the band featured the songwriting of Gordon Brown and the vocals of Peter Scherer. Together, along with Rob Tanico, they formed an acoustic trio playing sets unlike anything else. Everything seemed to move fast for the band. One day Peter was opening the door for people at the Fastlane, the next day the crowd at the Fastlane was there to see him. Mr. Reality soon was signed to a deal and released a debut record. A tour of the country followed and then just as quickly as it had started the band was finished.

After several years, the band members reunited under the name Samhill. Fans from the past spread the word to other Mr. Reality fans that the guys were back while Samhill started attracting its own fans. Record companies once again came calling and the band had another deal. They were forced to change their name after discovering another band was called Samhill. But it didn't take them long to come up with Highway 9, a name that proudly lets the world know their roots.

I caught up with Peter and Gordon after they finished playing a show at the Stone Pony on the day *The Rising* was released.

Talking with Gordon Brown

guitarist/songwriter for Mr. Reality, Samhill and Highway 9

Tell me about the early days for you and the band.
The early days for us. They weren't that long ago. We had the Pony, the Fastlane, there was a club called Murphy's Law in Long Branch. All these places we just sneaked into and did everything we could to be able to jump on stage and get a gig. It was awesome, you know. When all of the clubs were open it was kind of like the golden age for us. And that was far after what people would consider to be the peak time of Asbury.

The scene was pretty much dead back then.
Yeah, it's pretty amazing because in the late 80s and early 90s things were really calm here and with good reason. There's a lot of things that happened here that not necessarily drove people away but I think made them feel like it wasn't as safe as it used to be. And maybe it wasn't as glamourous as it used to be.

When did you guys first get together?
A little over ten years ago. We were probably about 15-16 years old when we started sneaking in and forming these bonds. And we've been very lucky, luckier than most. A lot of times we have seen bands and friends of ours not be able to keep it together and not be able to keep that bond.

There's a lot of bands that we have seen in this area that have been great through the years, too many to name actually. Many of our friends are tremendous musicians and decided that it may not have been for them to pursue the band thing because it's extremely difficult. And, for us, this record out on Epic, this is our second record deal. We've gone through the hard times and we've gone through good times. And, again, the most important thing is a band sticking together through the thick, the thin, through the record deals, through no record deals - whatever it takes. Sticking together and continuing to pursue that dream and really feel like you have something special... That comes off somehow.

The fans have stuck with you as well.
It's weird because we had no clue. I mean, we didn't sell a million records with Mr. Reality, but we sold some records. And as we were getting back out there, these people are showing up and they're like, "I can't believe we found you guys. We had no clue it was the same band."

You guys were lucky that the Internet was around.
Absolutely.

When word got out that you guys were Mr. Reality...
There's a handful of people out there that have found that as something that was hopefully special to them.

How cool is that to have people remember the band so well?
It's the best. It's the best.

And Highway 9 is basically doing the same thing that Mr. Reality did.
It's the exact same thing it's just electric now and that's what's so great. When we decided to add the other members we wanted to continue to have the vocal blend and everything that we've grown up with musically still be everything that matters to us. We could have hip-hop beats and all kinds of crazy stuff, but we'd still sound like us because Peter has an unmistakable voice. I think the consistent thing through most of the material is the harmonies.

Has Highway 9 ever played any of the old songs from the Mr. Reality record?

We have, actually. We have when we know people are coming out. We've played "Mr. Reality," we've played "Jess." A couple of things. Those were the two we're like throwing around.

That was a great album...

Thank you. Thank you very much. There's a lot of great records from here. That means a lot.

I like the Highway 9 one as well. It's a great driving record.

That was one of our goals. Listen to this one.

First time I listened to it, some songs stood out. I put it on in the car.

Right, it's a whole other thing.

Now back then, you guys did a lot of tracks that weren't on the album and were always writing stuff. Do you do that on this tour?

Absolutely, there's always songs. And the thing is that right now, when your record first comes out and you're doing everything you can to push it, the writing thing and bringing songs into the band becomes part of the back burner. Because you're really focused on getting your set together and making the band sound great. Once you're kind of on track with that and you feel good about that then you start bringing the new stuff. So it'll be a while for any of the new stuff.

We haven't done new songs that aren't on this record since we've been touring and we probably won't for a while because there's no need to. People are just getting into it and it's just the very beginning of everything.

Who are some of the people that you've played with so far on this new tour?

We toured with Rusted Root, Big Head Todd and the Monsters, Monte Montgomery, a guitar player from Austin. We played with Jeffrey Gaines on a bunch of shows and a lot of little people here and then. We've just been able to see different crowds. And it's been amazing for us to go out and play the bigger stages and really get people into the harmonies and see what we're about. It's the greatest feeling in the world.

Do you ever worry... well, this is a good opportunity right now, hopefully you guys are above this-

We're not above anything!

Ok, you have a Springsteen festival going on and a band called Highway 9. There's about thirty thousand people here spending the night, do you ever worry that they might think you were a Springsteen cover band?
You know, if they did and they came out it's all good. We picked the name of the band and, I swear to God, it had nothing to do with the "Born to Run" song.

I think it's a great name for a Monmouth County band.
That's exactly it. It was one of the roads we grew up upon and it was that or Highway 35 and we thought Highway 9 sounded better.

And you put the other in a song.
Exactly, so there's references everywhere.

Where did you grow up by the way?
In Hazlet. We are so lucky to come from a musical community that we were able to grow up in and watch guys that did this and were successful at it and were inspiring to millions of people. I tell you, if we weren't lucky enough to grow up in this area and we grew up in an area where there wasn't that kind of community it probably wouldn't have meant as much and we probably wouldn't have worked so hard to make it on our own.

When we travel now we see that and, man, I tell you we are so lucky. Nashville, L.A., New York, Cleveland - wherever there's a music scene. We're so proud to have what we have here because there's a lot of music lovers here and there's a lot of great records that came from this area and great songs and things that just fill your heart with joy.

What does the Stone Pony mean to you?
The world. We grew up in this room. Call us a house band or whatever you want to, but we love this place. It's everything that we've been about. We would never have had a living anywhere. I mean, the Saint is amazing and it's a great club. The Fastlane was another club that when we were little we used to sneak in all the time. But this has been our home.

How does it feel to be part of its history?
You know what? I don't even know if we're part of the history. We're just trying to be what we are and continue a tradition that's been a big part of our lives and we hold that very close to our hearts. And we wear it on our sleeve, wherever we go, and it's very important.

What is it like for you when guys Bruce and Bon Jovi show up?
It's awesome because these are records that we've grown up with and those are the guys that have inspired us to do this and let us know that it can be done.

The times that we've jammed with Bruce on stage or the times we've played with Jon (Bon Jovi) or any of those guys, it's an exciting feeling. You see them hanging out and you have a drink with them and it's like, this is great! You know that it's real. They came before you and they made it happen because they could and were good enough and could put the blood, sweat and tears to it. That is extremely inspiring and we live on that.

What is it about Asbury that makes it a great place to see a show?
The people. The people and the love that they have for the community. It's like when you're sitting next to someone that you know from somewhere and when you're sitting next to someone that you know has had the same experiences you do in the neighborhood, same food and going to see the movies. You share that moment of music with them and whether you know them or not it's an energy that happens and this is one of the best places in the world for that.

What would you guys think if four years from now you're going strong and so is Asbury?
It would be the greatest thing in the world. Even if we're not going strong and Asbury is it would still be great. I mean, if we're going strong and Asbury's not I'll take that too. However, we want the best for this community. Again, wherever we go everybody knows where we're from. And we make it a point, we've made it a point on our records.

So many bands don't really have a scene like Asbury Park.
You have to talk about where you come from. It gives people a sense of why they are listening to you and who you are. My favorite records in the world, that's what bands have done for me. I believe that when people get into a record and they bite into it they say, "Man, how do I get to know them better? How can I fall in love with this music even more?"

Whether people like what you do or not they see that. And that has always been our goal since we started and since we were hanging out as our little gang and trying to get into these places.

Talking with Peter Scherer

lead singer for Mr. Reality,
Samhill and Highway 9

What did it feel like when you finally changed the name from Samhill to Highway 9? That first show was a benefit for 9/11 at the Stone Pony, right?

Yeah, our first show was here and, actually, Jon Bon Jovi introduced us as Highway 9 for the first time. I think it was sometime in maybe October or November, not long after September 11th.

When we decided on changing - when we were notified that we had to change the name - we immediately started to think of things because we knew it would be difficult for us all to come across with something that we could all connect with. And, as soon as we put the idea out of naming the band after a road that we were all familiar with and I made the suggestion of Highway 9, I think there was a sense of completion, maybe in a way that we hadn't had before.

Samhill was a really cool name, but it didn't necessarily identify with our roots specifically. And so coming across the name Highway 9, we immediately felt like we were representing where we came from and our roots, our New Jersey roots. It was a great feeling to finally tie in.

The name Highway 9 will certainly bring in the Bruce connotation, especially for a band from the Jersey Shore. Did you feel any pressure to avoid the comparisons?

Personally I didn't, I never feel pressure or feel like we're put off because of Bruce Springsteen. I always feel like we are. One of the reasons why our band has been able to evolve as it has, along with our sound, is because of the music of the Jersey Shore and places like the Stone Pony and the Fastlane. Obviously those artists frequented these places and made it their home and they allowed us to do the same.

Highway 9 to me is the road that my mother drove me in our car to go buy my first record. I grew up in Marlboro. I grew up in a town off Highway 9, just two towns over from Springsteen. So, to me, we have the same backyard.

How did you guys get associated with Long Branch?
We all moved there. Actually, we all moved there a bunch of years back.

I noticed that the band still has the same mailing address. Was there always the thought that you would eventually get back together?
Yeah, I think the break that we took in between Samhill and Mr. Reality was a break that we needed. We were kids when we got together. I think that we all needed to experience some life and take some time to journey on our own so that we could bring back more of ourselves to making music. And, because I don't think our lives... our lives aren't about music. Our lives are full about other things and we bring those things, those experiences in our lives, to the music that we play.

What have you learned since the first time?
(long pause...) You know, it's amazing, most things don't change. Most things stay pretty much exactly the same, but I feel like we have become more focused on the things that we want to sing about. We realize that you have certain opportunities in a certain amount of time on the stage and a certain amount of time with an audience to listen to an album. So you want to be as focused as you can to represent those things that you feel most driven by and passionate about with that opportunity.
I think that we've gotten better with that. And picking subjects to sing about, the sound of the music that we want to help us evoke that feeling.

Speaking of the sound of the music it seems to really have a good roots rock feeling and you've got a couple of songs that could be great country hits.
Yeah, well Gordon just came back from Nashville. We recorded the album in Nashville and it's interesting, we had toured before in Tennessee and in more of the country landscapes of America and it has always moved us. And even growing up here, we grew up among farms and horses and cows.

And you were big Eagles fans too.
Big Eagles fans. And there's always been a home, down home feeling to what we're about. And I think it's really come out even more and more. I also think that by listening to our scene - Springsteen made us unafraid to explore those feelings that we had - those sounds, those ideas. We became less afraid because we saw how they embraced them in their own way. So why couldn't we embrace it in our own way? We felt good about it. It's true to who we are and so we felt comfortable.

You guys grew up in the atmosphere. In fact, didn't you used to work at the Fastlane?
Yeah, I worked there from the time that it reopened. It had been open before. I remember that one of the first staff meetings they flat out said, "We're not here to make stars, we're here to promote local bands." I wasn't singing at the time so I kept quiet and did my job and I loved working around bands and working in Asbury. So, that was definitely a place for me to be here in town.

What sort of led you towards the stage?
I guess an artist... an artist takes time to do other things, whether they read or they go off on their journey to explore things that might influence them, things that they might need to find out about themselves and about the world we live in. And I think that all artists go back to their art. If you're an artist you go back to your art. So I think it was inevitable. Just like you asked, "Why did we keep the mailing address," I guess Brian, our manager, felt it was an inevitable thing that time would find us back together. He's been very instrumental in keeping us focused on the priorities and the goals.

What do you remember about those days at the Fastlane?
They were really good times. There were no rules. We basically would have ideas about what we wanted to do and then we would do them. If we didn't want to play on the stage we would set up on the floor on a couple of stools, and everybody would sit around us. And we tried all different kinds of things, whatever we felt musically or vibe-wise. Whatever we wanted to do we had a place that embraced that, embraced us to do it and it was right here in Asbury Park. We were able to become part of this history.

The legacy...
Yeah, and that's an exciting thing. It means everything to us.

What was the biggest problem with Mr. Reality? Was it that you all were just too young? Was it label merging?
Well, we were really happy with what we did musically. It was very overwhelming to go into the studio at such a young age and be presented with all these different options and not have experience to fall back on to make those decisions. We're proud of the record that we made. I think the industry was really going through a lot of changes and it's hard to become a priority at these big, corporate companies.

This being the second time to get through the door, we've been lucky to get a record made again.

And you also realize how unlikely and special it is to do it twice. Especially when you see all the bands that you playing with struggling to get a deal...
Absolutely, and because we've been playing together for so long we appreciate everything that we're doing. There isn't a moment that goes by that we don't appreciate us playing together, our friendships, the places we play, the people we meet or our relationship with the label. We certainly don't take it for granted. I think, sometimes the people at the labels might because they have so much talent that they work with all of the time. But we are very strong and we realize that persistence is really what it's about. You have to keep at it, just keep at it.

How was it after the end of Mr. Reality? You guys were the hottest band to see at the Shore at the time. What was it like in the years after the band disbanded?
It was difficult. It was difficult in the sense that, I think, life is all full of change. And those changes can be very painful, but they bring tremendous rewards if you're willing to see them through. I think none of us were afraid to make a change at that point. We all knew that there was something, other things that we needed to fulfill ourselves with, not necessarily musical, but other life experiences that became more important than the band itself at that point. And some people will say it's unfortunate because there were a couple of years, three or four years, that went by when we didn't work musically together. But I think if we hadn't taken that time for ourselves, we would not have come back together as strong as we have.

Were you guys in other bands or did you just take time off?
I personally took time off. I didn't sing, I didn't perform or sing for a couple of years, about two years or so. And Gordon and Rob... Rob jumped into a band called the Outcry and was filling in, and Gordon was writing and recording and working on his songwriting. So those guys kept active and playing, but I don't think they pursued putting together another band. And then I showed up again after a few years ready to really get back into it.

Refreshed?
Yeah.

What was it like the first show you guys played together again?
It was fantastic! Our first show as Samhill was here at the closing night of the Stone Pony before it closed for a period of time. It was a whole weekend and that was our first show. That was really exciting. I think the stage was on the other side. They had moved the stage to the side.

What does coming back to the Stone Pony mean to you now?
It means that we, in a lot of ways, have come full circle from our roots, from where we started as an acoustic band and now, here we are, at the Pony years later as an electric rock and roll band. I think it shows how we embraced the roots music that came from here and how we've shown that because of these clubs and these rooms that it's enabled us to continue to explore musically our ideas and our songs and end up here.

On August 10th, with a new record on Epic Records and a new beginning. August 10th is really - it's going to be very special for us, for Domenic, for the Stone Pony. I think we feel like we are of the regular house bands at the Pony. There's no doubt about that.

You grew up in Marlboro. Did you ever go to Asbury as a kid?
Yeah. My parents divorced when I was 14 and my mother moved to Long Branch. I stayed with my father about 6 months more and I moved with my mother to Long Branch. The first weekend that I was here I had heard that there was a WNEW concert on the beach. So I said to my mother, "Can you drop me off?" All of a sudden my backyard was Asbury Park.

It was the Smithereens and the Hooters. And they were set up right on the boardwalk, right out here. And my mom dropped me off and when she picked me up at the end of the day I said, "Mom, one day I'm gonna play one of these shows."

They would broadcast the shows live on Memorial Day and that was a special thing. Last night, coming here for the record release party I was saying to myself. Twenty years from now we're going to look at July 30th, 2002 as the day Bruce released *The Rising* and we played the Stone Pony and had a new record out as well. Those are memories.

What's it like to be considered "the next" again?
I like to look at us as instead of the next, just that we are. Because we are. It's about today, it's about yesterday, and it's about tomorrow. And just the fact that we are a band that is from Asbury Park, from clubs like the Stone Pony and the Fastlane, we have, we are, and we will always play these rooms. It's our home. We will always have a home on stage at the Stone Pony.

What's it like when your friends jump on stage?
It's the best. When I look around and I'm with my buddies and, over the last few years, being embraced by artists like Springsteen and Bon Jovi and performing with them. It's like I said, this record and this time is a time where we realize things have come full circle and there's a sense of completion that we are.

You're one of the lucky bands where I've never been at one of your shows and heard people scream for Bruce.
Isn't that amazing?

It seems like there's a little bit of a boundary, which is nice.
I think it may be a generation thing, maybe. Maybe when people see the artists of Bruce's generation they feel more like they're thinking more about him. But we're a new generation of musicians and there's a twenty plus year difference in age.

It's cool that you get the benefit of jamming with him but you still have a crowd that's coming to see you.
Yeah, it really rocks. That's right. And what a better crowd than on events like this and other events that we've participated in that are revolving around a Springsteen event. I couldn't think of a better audience to want to play for, that really cares about music. There's a sensibility of songs and music and the community and all the things that matter to us are there in the audience. So they're always good shows for us.

What is it about Asbury and music? Is there something special?
I think there's something beyond, you know. Our community of Monmouth County is really a heart and soulful community. And all of us coming together to embrace music and songs and lyrics and each other in a venue like this is everything. It's everything musical and everything about community that can happen. But beyond that, the geography of Asbury Park with the lakes, the ocean, the architecture, the streets and the sky, there's something very special here that happens with a synergy of all of those things that isn't duplicated anywhere in the world.

We can travel from coast to coast, city to city, and you will never duplicate this town. And, so, we have a tremendous sense of pride.

43 The Outcry and Blowup

There's more than one music scene. There's the popular music scene that everybody knows because it's out there and it's popular. Then there's the music scene of people who are in this way of life. People make a decision to be in it or not to be in it.

--JON LEIDERSDORFF

The Outcry was one of the Jersey Shore's hottest bands during the 1990s. Photo © Debra L. Rothenberg/rothenbergphoto.com

The Outcry started playing the clubs in the early 90s at a time when the Asbury Park scene was in trouble. But the band certainly made the most of their opportunities. They had regular gigs at the Fastlane and the Stone Pony as well as clubs in Long Branch and musicians like Bruce Springsteen and Brian Setzer jammed with them.

Fans came to see them wherever they played. They were named the "Best Unsigned Band" by readers of *East Coast Rocker*. In 1995, the Outcry independently released their first record called *Wentworth*. They released a follow up three years later called *This Side Of Anywhere* which received great reviews and was picked up by the major label Eureka Records and contained the hit "On and On."

Jon Leidersdorff, the band's drummer, had begun writing his own material and wanted a larger place in the band's set. Ultimately, this led to the end of Outcry and to the creation of Blowup, which features the songwriting and lead singing of Leidersdorff. The band has released several records independently and is attracting major label interest and significant radio airplay as well.

I caught up with Jon Leidersdorff for a phone interview to talk about his new band Blowup and his memories of the Outcry.

When did the Outcry get started?
Well, the singer and I were playing together when we were 12 in various different bands. The bass player came when we were 14, the original bass player. We went through different bass players along the way. Rob, the bass player for Mr. Reality and now Highway 9, was with us for a bunch of years. We had another bass player, Jerry Stanick, who was popping around here.

The Outcry really got going when the scene around the Shore was pretty much dying.
It was dying. It was very much dead but we were doing really well because we were playing a lot and we had steady nights. We played at the Stone Pony and started off when I was 17 or 18 playing every Wednesday night with Bobby Bandiera. We played all the time. That's all we did. We did every Wednesday at the Pony with him and then when he stopped playing we took the night over. The Pony shut down and we went to the Fastlane and played the Fastlane every week.

Then the new Pony opened up with Steve Nasar and we went back and did every Thursday at the Pony. We were also doing every Sunday at Cheers in Long Branch. So we had two steady nights. We did really well. We also played Cafe Bar and Tradewinds on the weekends.

Outcry had a huge fanbase. Was your mailing list in the thousands?
At least... Probably more than that. We would play the Pony and have 700 people some nights there.

The band took some shots at unsigned band contests in New York and Philly.
Yeah, we did all kinds. We won the first one for the Discmakers competition and ended up 2nd overall on the east coast. We had an independent record deal through a major label too. We ended up signing a deal with a label called Eureka which was a Polygram subsidiary. Eureka bought our 2nd CD which was called *This Side of Anywhere*.

We put two independents out by ourself and other things that were small like cassette only before CDs became popular. We put out a couple of cassettes. One was a live DAT recording and another was a 4-songer. We actually put a record out in 1989 called *Legend*. That was when I was 18 years old. There were two other guys playing with us then, a keyboard player and a guitar player.

What do you remember about those early shows along the Shore?
I remember going to see Bobby Bandiera play and just thinking that he was amazing. I remember we had a night where we played at Cheers in Long Branch and Bruce Springsteen played with us. He came up and we did an entire set with him on the fly which was really neat. I mean, I was young and he was amazing.

I grew up in Freehold Boro and went to the same high schools that Bruce went to. We used to go to his shows at Giants Stadium and I covered his songs when I was 14. It was an original band but we played covers too.

Are there any other Outcry shows that really stand out for you?
There's a lot of them. Brian Setzer came and played with us one night which was great. We were playing at the Cafe Bar in Long Branch and we were just about to close. Brian Setzer was in town to play one of those WNEW things on the beach. He heard about the band and came over. They locked up the doors and we played a full set with him. It was neat. Outcry used to open up shows for the band Verve Pipe before they had their deal. We got put on before them at Michigan State University for a college show there once.

There were so many shows. There was a show that we opened up for the Spin Doctors at Lehigh University and they didn't make it. The Spin Doctors were late and we wound up playing for 3 1/2 hours.

Who would you say were some of the influences of Outcry?
I think different guys were influenced by different artists. I know my singer was a huge U2 and INXS fan. My guitar player was a huge Pat Methany fan. The bass player was... I don't even know what the hell he was listening to! He was studying bass so much back then. But everyone was influenced by different music. We would just get together and play every day.

How difficult was it for the band when you were kind of on the verge of breaking for a couple of years but never quite made it over that hurdle to take it to the next level?
It was very difficult. We felt that we were mismanaged. Some crucial mistakes were made. We probably could have had a lot more success if we had some better decisions made.

Did you feel that the local radio stations like WHTG or WRAT helped support the band?
WHTG didn't support our band much at all. They played one of our songs for a while but WRAT was very supportive. As soon as they opened we approached them and they played our independent release before Eureka picked it up. And they played it a lot. They were a radio station that really supported us. It was a great thing. We would be touring around the country and call them up in the morning and they'd put us on the air. We'd tell them about all of the crazy things that were going on. We charted at rock radio in the trade publications. I think we went as high as #31 for "On and On."

What ultimately led the band to call it quits? Was it a group decision?
Well, I don't think that we ever made a conscious decision to call it quits. I had started writing on my own and singing on my own and the guys in Outcry didn't want me to sing for the band. So, I started doing my own band and I think me taking my energy out of one and putting it into the other affected the whole equation.

Did you always want to be the singer?
No, what happened is that I just wanted to always do it and if you're not the singer and you're not the writer then you're at the mercy of other people. I think I needed to be self-reliant. I needed to always be creative. And I couldn't. And I would get frustrated having to have other guys.

How difficult is it for a band around here to make it doing originals?
Umm... I think the area does not lend itself to support original music but there's so many people in the area still trying to do it. There's some real talent in this area. There's no great college music scene which I think is one detriment. There's no indie radio station. There's not a hub. There's no independent record labels except for Indian down at Gig Records. There should be an Asbury Park Records. Think about the independent record stores... there's not many here.

Blowup already has four CDs out. You're quite a prolific writer, do you try to write every day?
It depends where I am at in my life. There were times where I was trying to write every day and times where I'm not. But I do try to stay creative every day.

What are your plans for the new CD? Are you shopping it around to record companies?
We're interested in more opportunities, definitely. It's going well, there's a lot of interest. There's a bunch of radio stations playing the new record.

Do you think the scene will be different without the Tradewinds?
Well, I don't know. I think what's going to change it is the fact that Asbury's changing and the perception of Asbury is changing. Harry's Roadhouse is doing so well that people are coming to Asbury Park. So, when people start coming to Asbury the Pony can get some of that business. They really need that energy.

The perception of the Pony is that it's an old man's club. There's not a lot of young people that are going to go there. I think it's just in a transitional phase. It could change again with a couple of good artists coming out of this area and with the clubs refocusing on creating an identity. A new identity... an evolved identity. It's a possibility.

What would you like people to remember about the Outcry?
Just that there were a lot of great songs. That there was a band that was writing their own stuff and not compromising, working hard and playing so much - creating a scene. And there was a scene. You'd go to see us Sunday night at Cheers and it would be packed. You could see us on a Wednesday night at a big club like the Fastlane or a Thursday night at the Pony and there would be a good crowd there as well. There was a great scene and a lot of people were part of that and remember that.

The most important thing was it was a way of life. It was a great way of life for us to be creating music and doing it full time. There's more than one music scene. There's the popular music scene that everybody knows because it's out there and it's popular. Then there's the music scene of people who are in this way of life. People make a decision to be in it or not to be in it. I'm one of those people that made the decision to stay. It's not about the money for us.

So you're ready to stick it out? There's no timeline in mind.
There's no timeline. This is what I do. It doesn't mean that I'm going to die if I don't get the success from the entire world. I feel successful now when a person like yourself says to me that you like the music and you're enjoying it. I mean, I enjoy making it. The process for me is very fulfilling. It's been a vehicle to help me evolve.

I started off being in a band and by being in Outcry I learned how to arrange and cover. I'm a session drummer too. I make money as a session drummer playing on a lot of records on major labels right now. From being with Outcry, I learned how to play the drums. I took lessons and from the band itself we started playing with other people and listened to music together. The band members changed and I evolved and became a good enough drummer that I could make a living as a studio drummer now. That was a great process and as I evolved musically I grew in every other way. My whole psyche changed. It's really given me a lot to make the transition from being a drummer to a songwriter and a singer and a frontman. I've learned a lot again.

When you evolve you may have enjoyed a period of your life but you don't ever want to be lesser you want to keep growing. Were there mistakes made? Yes. Could we have had more success? Yes, but I'm very happy to be where I am now and I wouldn't be where I am now if I didn't go through with this story and this process. I'm very happy. I have a tremendous band. The guys are great players and they're great guys. And the guys in Outcry are still great friends.

Is there anything that you miss from your days in the Outcry?
I miss that I was playing so often and that I could play so much but I think that's going to happen to me again. Like when I went on tour with Blowup and we played 12 shows in 2 weeks in the UK. That was just a great moment for me. I'd love to have a record and be able to tour the country and the world 300 nights a year!

44 The Pony's Crazy Ride

The Pony is not just a place, it's more of an atmosphere, attitude or whatever you want to call it. Because it's not only the place it is but it's the people that go there, who play there and the people who work there that make it what it is.

--LEE MROWICKI
STONE PONY DJ

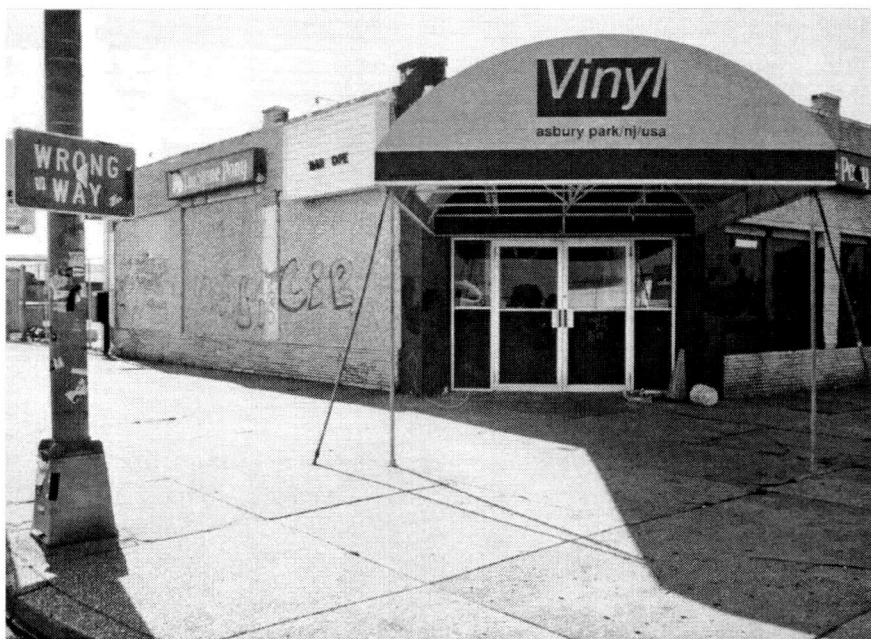

In September 1998, the Stone Pony closed and Vinyl took over. The new dance-oriented club didn't last very long. Photo © CJ Photography

The Stone Pony has always had a strange run during its history. From its early days as a disco bar to the heights of the Asbury music scene when the club would be packed night after night with lines around the block, the bar had seen it all. As the town itself moved further into ruin, the Pony remained the one constant you could count on.

"I guess people didn't realize what was going on around them," said Lee Mrowicki, the Pony's long-time disc jockey. "There was change and it wasn't change for the good it was change for the worst. The other day as I was standing outside I was trying to point out to somebody where the roller coaster was. Back in 1976 there was the Tilt-A-Whirl and the whole boardwalk was full of rides. By the mid-80s, the roller coaster was gone and so was the Tilt-A-Whirl, but the miniature golf place and the batting cages were still there. In the late 80s, that's when it was really nothing.

"The two owners were pretty astute at booking concerts, so we just continued. It was kind of weird because we were in that realm where we were in the redevelopment mode and we knew a lot of big changes were coming but nobody knew everything was going to go into a bankruptcy. We were just waiting for things to happen."

What ultimately happened was truly unexpected. The Stone Pony closed its doors when a series of drunk driving-related lawsuits forced the club into bankruptcy. Music fans from around the country were shocked while local fans went on about their business. Asbury Park just wasn't the place to go in that period of time. And if the locals did go to a show in Asbury they most likely headed over to the Fastlane which was booking the hipper, more exciting bands.

Mrowicki remembers the last day was a benefit show for Susan Hector, the wife of guitarist Billy Hector. "The next day when I had to go over to the club to change the answering machine tape, which I did every Monday, I found there was a padlock on the door," said Mrowicki. "And that was it. I called the owners and said, 'Hey, there's a padlock on the door. What's going on here?' And later the sign said closed to bankruptcy, all questions to be referred to the trustee.

"The weird thing about the bankruptcy was that originally that place had been thriving. The two owners really made a huge financial mistake in declaring bankruptcy. It wasn't that the place wasn't making money, it was just the opposite."

Several of the club's employees tried to reopen the club themselves. They hired an attorney in an attempt to get the bankruptcy settled. According to Mrowicki, the employees had been hooked up with Joe Piscopo and some real estate investors who arranged to get a mortgage for them to buy back the Pony.

"The bankruptcy court, instead of taking our mortgage took the cash that the guy from Long Branch had," said Mrowicki. "But he had been around before that. In fact, he had been introduced to me and we had long discussions about how to resurrect the place and stuff. There he was against me in federal court."

The guy from Long Branch was Steven Nasar, a man that had never run a club before. He bought the Stone Pony with the thought that the name alone with bring the crowds back. It officially reopened in October 1992, one year after it had closed. The first band to play was Carter, the Unstoppable Sex Machine. This was the first sign that things would be different this time around. Interior changes within the club itself was the second.

Nasar changed the club so much that he alienated regular customers and musicians alike. The place just didn't have the same vibe anymore. The Stone Pony had been living off of its history for years and Nasar appeared anxious to erase such memories. After several years of trying, along with some well-publicized problems with hardcore and punk shows, Nasar finally gave up on rock and roll. He decided to abandon the Stone Pony name and create Vinyl, a dance lounge aimed at attracting a Manhattan-like crowd.

The new club opened in September 1998, but the Stone Pony had one final moment to itself. It was billed as the "Stone Pony's Last Ride," three days of music celebrating the three decades in which the club was open. Such acts as Cold, Blast and Steel (ironically, the first rock and roll band to perform at the Stone Pony), the George Theiss Band, Paul Whistler and the Wheels, Cats on a Smooth Surface, Mike Dalton and the Push, Buzzed Meg, the Outcry, Samhill, Bobby Bandiera Band, Gutwrench, Union Spirit, Mudbox, Strange Environment and the Lord Gunner Group all performed.

"For the last party Eileen had called me because she was organizing the 'funeral,'" said Mrowicki, who had never been to the club under Nasar's ownership. "And I said to her, 'You're going to actually raise money for this guy to close the place?' I didn't see a reason to pay for a funeral. And I wouldn't raise money for him anyway."

There are very few clubs with such name recognition or history as the Stone Pony. In fact, many clubs are lucky to see their 10th anniversary much less find themselves still open after 20 years. Still, it was a very sad period of time for the Jersey Shore and music fans from all over the world came to say goodbye to the club that Bruce Springsteen and Southside Johnny made famous. But the club that they loved was hardly recognizable.

The dance area in front of the stage was covered with new flooring. The stage itself had been moved from its original location to the opposite wall and replaced with a smaller stage. Each of the three bars were moved to new areas as well. The dingy, dark look of rock and roll was replaced by carpeting, lounge furniture and peach colored walls.

"I remember walking into the club and thinking what a God-awful job the decorators had done!" said Maggie Powell, a European music journalist. "Dado rails and peach colored walls at the Pony? And why was the stage relocated? The decor felt wrong somehow and it didn't feel like the same Pony I was lucky enough to visit during my trip in 1995. But when the music started I very quickly forgot about the color of the walls!"

It was a strange weekend. Bands that hadn't played the Pony for years gave the final goodbyes to the club, fans that had never been to Asbury Park before came to see what they had been missing and for three more days Asbury rocked and rolled all throughout the night.

"Honestly, I personally felt very lucky and honored to be one of the bands that was asked to play that show," said Mike Dalton. "Playing the Pony was my dream when I was cutting my teeth on the Shore circuit so playing there was special enough. And then to be asked to be part of that night made me feel like a permanent part of the Pony legacy. It's a very special thing to me.

"The intensity of the crowd was very high and we fed off of it. We felt we had a really energetic and special performance. The vibe was good, but I really wish we were on the good old stage with the Pony on the wall behind me," added Dalton. "I'm not gonna lie, I didn't like it. I didn't feel like I was in the Stone Pony. It was kind of sad, but there was also the feeling that it wasn't really gonna be over. Personally, I always thought it would come back as the Pony again and it did!"

While some fans were hoping for Bruce Springsteen or Bon Jovi to make an appearance, Southside Johnny surprised the crowd by joining his buddy, Bobby Bandiera, for three songs. The odds of a Springsteen sighting were pretty slim since he hadn't made a guest appearance at the Pony since 1995. In recent years, Bruce could be more likely be found guesting with bands in clubs like the Metro in Long Branch or Tradewinds in Sea Bright. After all, it was clear that this was no longer the same club he fell in love with.

Even without an appearance from Bruce, the final weekend was ultra special for everyone involved. Each band played their sets at a slightly higher than usual level. The Pony was packed and it seemed to have that sort of energy, that sense of history in the making that always made the club more than just a bar.

"You could feel that it was electric," recalled Hal Selzer, a longtime veteran of the Jersey Shore scene who played that night as a member of the Bobby Bandiera Band. "Having everybody there and seeing all of the musicians that you knew from the whole scene was pretty cool. People were jamming with different people. Playing on stage was really fun. I remember we had the horns and Southside and everything.

"It was just as much fun being backstage because all the musicians were there. Since everybody's always gigging or touring you don't get to hang out much with your fellow musicians and friends. That night was a great excuse to get together."

Having made its mark in rock history, the stained-glass pony behind the main bar was given to the Rock and Roll Hall of Fame in Cleveland, Ohio. Robert Santelli, the Director of Education for the Hall of Fame accepted the gift. Santelli was raised along the Jersey Shore and was a regular at the Pony during the 70s when much of the club's history took place.

"I don't remember giving it a lot of thought until that night," said Selzer. "I remember hearing Bob Santelli say, 'I'm taking this to the Rock and Roll Hall of Fame' and it made me really think."

The sense of history was even more apparent for the people from around the world that came for the last weekend. "Like so many other people who live so far away from the Shore, most of what I've learned about the Shore's music history I've learned from other people," said Maggie Powell, who came all the way from Germany for the final weekend. "So, it was an incredibly special night for me to be there and see some of the artists I'd only ever read about actually perform on the Pony's famous stage."

After that weekend, Vinyl took over but it didn't stay around very long. Within a few months the former home of the Stone Pony was nothing more than a boarded up, abandoned building. Just another piece of rock and roll history discarded as the Upstage, the Student Prince and the Sunshine In had been discarded many years before. The difference this time around was found in a man named Domenic Santana.

In 2000, Domenic Santana and a partner purchased the Stone Pony with a plan to bring the club back to its former glory. Santana was a successful restaurant owner with a background in producing and holding special events. If anyone could return the Stone Pony to its rightful place in music history it was him.

The new owners spent over $500,000 to purchase and renovate the club. They not only restored it to the way it looked before but made several improvements as well. A new sound system was installed which dramatically improved the sight lines within the club. Instead of huge speakers beside the stage (obscuring the vision of anyone behind them) the speakers are now hanging from the ceiling. In addition, the club finally recognized just how important its history was to music fans. A giant collection of photographs from previous shows throughout the years was put on display along with several photographs of Asbury Park in its glory days. In effect, the Pony itself has become somewhat of a museum.

Ironically, one of the most famous images in Jersey Shore rock and roll history - the "Greetings From Asbury Park" postcard, which was featured on Bruce Springsteen's first record - actually came out wrong. Hal Selzer remembers being at the Pony the week before it opened when they discovered the mistake.

"I was talking to Domenic," said Selzer. "We look over at the wall where they've got that famous "Greetings from Asbury Park" sign. Domenic looks at it and says to the guy that just put it up, 'It says Welcome to Asbury Park, you've got it wrong! That has to change... you need to fix it!' And the guy was like, 'It's done, we can't do anything about it. It's too late.'"

The sign never did get changed and it's funny because people are literally so used to seeing the "Greetings" postcard that they don't even notice the error. Nevertheless, the Stone Pony was back in business.

"We are going to wake this city up," said Santana. "We are going to be the thunder before the storm!"

One of the most important things the Stone Pony did was bring back many of the staff members that had worked there for so many years. Tracy could be found serving drinks again, Lee was back as the disc jockey on Saturday nights - it was almost as if nothing had ever changed.

Lee Mrowicki recalls how Domenic lured him back to the club. "He had approached me actually when Eileen had been managing over at the Fastlane. They reopened that first. So I had gone there for a press conference to pay my respects to them and say hello to a few musicians and stuff. Outside Ben Buckwald said, 'The new owner of the club is upstairs and he wants to talk to you.' So I went up and this guy had been calling me a few times to try and get me to meet with him. And at that point in time, I had been pretty much semi-retired put it that way. And I didn't even know that there might be a possibility for it to come back.

"We kind of talked for a long time and the first thing he did was wave the keys in front of my face and said 'these are yours if you want them,'" recalled Mrowicki. "So I said, 'Well, let's talk.' And we talked about the possibilities of working together, what his visions of bringing back the place to the way it used to be. And he said, 'I'm not here to re-invent the wheel. You guys already did that. You did a good job of keeping it alive while the place was still running.'"

Mrowicki believes the club renovation was pretty true to its original form. "Things have to change a little bit, but everything was adapted for the better," he said. "The sound system is tremendous compared to what we used to have. In fact, we used to have to rent sound systems. Back then, I had a separate system apart from the major concert system, which was kind of really just thrown together. And everything is more professional now."

Santana and his family moved to Asbury Park, proving his commitment and love for the city. Since arriving, it's rarely been easy for him but he's not a guy that takes fighting lying down. As the Stone Pony started making headlines again, Asbury Park found itself once again involved in a redevelopment plan. The city was able to finally wrestle control of the oceanfront of the failed bankruptcy of a previous developer. Only one thing stood in its way - the Stone Pony.

The redevelopers had a plan to create condominiums along Asbury's beachfront and create a new Victorian city. Their plan called for the Stone Pony to move to the former location of the Casino. Many people were in favor of doing this, but thousands more were against it. As word got out over the Internet that the Stone Pony was going to be moved Springsteen fans banded together and an organization called "Save the Stone Pony" was created.

"Save the Pony" rallies were held to let people know about the problem. It culminated on a frigid January day when over 100 fans, undaunted by an oncoming snowstorm, showed their support for the club by waking up early to protest the city's redevelopment meeting. The fans marched from the Stone Pony to the Berkeley Carteret Hotel where the meeting took place. They gathered in front of the hotel and chanted things like "hell no, we won't go," "condos schmondos" and "1-2-3-4 no more condos on the Shore!" In the end, the voices of the people were heard. For now, at least, the club has been saved.

"You always have people that are vocal and it's a good thing that they expressed their interest and affection for the place," added Mrowicki. "We appreciate that tremendously. And it's been like that for years and years because there are people that we call regulars, people that you see on a regular basis at the club. Those people become vocal if their home is being destroyed. The Pony is not just a place, it's more of an atmosphere, attitude or whatever you want to call it. Because it's not only the place it is, but it's the people that go there, who play there and the people who work there that make it what it is. It's just such a strange combination of things that make it what it is. That's something you couldn't duplicate if you had to."

Mike Dalton & the Push play during the "Pony's Last Ride." Photos © Rob Fuzesi

Memories of the Stone Pony from a fan. Photo © CJ Photography

45 Joe D'Urso

It's funny because when you're overseas, a lot of the fans think like on Thursday night everybody has dinner together, which would be great... we should start that. We'll all go to Bruce's house for dinner.

--JOE D'URSO

Joe D'Urso shown on the Stone Pony Outdoor Stage during *The Rising* release party on July 30, 2002. Photo © Gary Wien

J oe D'Urso is one of the adopted sons of the Jersey Shore, mainly due to playing here often and because his music evokes comparisons to people like Bruce Springsteen. Born and raised in New York, Joe is a fine singer-songwriter who has released a bunch of records through his own independent record label.

Joe started in the music business by working at Premier Talent Agency where he typed contracts and collected deposit money for some of the biggest names in the world. A few years later, after leaving the world premiere of U2's *Rattle & Hum* film, he began focusing on a music career.

His early shows were at CBGBs in New York City and T-Birds Cafe in Asbury Park. He has been touring and recording new records ever since. Since he releases his records independently, Joe knows that he's got to earn new fans one at a time through hard work and great live performances. So far it's worked well in Europe where Joe has built a tremendous following for himself. And, in 2002, his band became the official house band of Harley Davidson's 100 year anniversary tour taking him all across the country.

I met up with Joe D'Urso at the office of his record label. He brought me to his rehearsal area and sat holding a guitar. Like any great musician, he just doesn't seem comfortable without one.

Before there was Stone Caravan, the band was known as "Three Chords and the Truth."
Yeah, I got it from U2's *Rattle & Hum*. "All I have is this red guitar, three chords and the truth." Bono did that. I was at the premiere of that movie in New York with U2. I went down into the subway with my roommate who played drums, and I didn't play guitar yet, I just looked at him as we're waiting for a train. We had just come out of this movie, U2 was there. It was this amazing premiere. I just said, 'You know, we've gotta start a band.' And he looked at me and goes, 'Hey, I know how to play drums. You've got to learn how to play guitar.' I went home and that winter I learned how to play.

My first guitar was an acoustic knock off. It's actually on the cover of the *Mirrors, Shoestrings* record. And there's a photo of it inside *Rock and Roll Station*. It doesn't even play anymore. It's kind of broken, but I have all my backstage passes I've ever gotten on that guitar.

Our first show was November 17th, 1989 in Long Island, City of Queens in the vacant apartment building we took over. We were living upstairs. We took over the downstairs and then December 4th it was either T-Birds or CBGBs and December 18th, either my second or third show, was at T-Birds in Asbury Park.

Before you started playing music, you were on the other side of the business working at Premier Talent Agency. What were you doing over there?

I got out of school in 1986, moved to Manhattan and started working in the music business. I got a job at Premier Talent Agency typing contracts and collecting their deposit money, as we called it. Any contract in the music business they collect 50% of the deposit up front. So I got a chance to work with a lot of really small bands, mid-level bands like the Ramones and Smithereens, Suzanne Vega. I got to work on some great artists, the Leonard Cohens, the Marianne Faithfuls. And I got to work on some big tours.

Back then, I caught the end cusp of the way agencies used to be run and the way that record companies used to think. There used to be a department called artist development. Artist development doesn't exist anymore. It's one of those reasons I started SCR Records because I became my own artist development. I'm confident now that I work hard and I make what I consider are records that I'm proud of. I like to listen and look backwards and occasionally see where I came from, but that was the development to get to here. Nowadays, you don't have development. You have a record and if you flop you're gone.

That experience must have helped you to wear all the hats later on, right? You saw the business the way most musicians never see it.

Yeah, and early on I was always embarrassed when I used to go down to Greenwich Village. I didn't start Caravan really until late 1989. I finally picked up the guitar in 1987 or 1988, somewhere around there. So when I went down to Greenwich Village, probably around 1988, I would go down there and meet with other songwriters but I would never let anybody know where I worked or what I was learning. I was very embarrassed because I thought that to be a great artist you should know nothing about the music business and you should only know about art. And there's a part of me that, maybe still believes that a little bit and has held me back at times of trying to be a better businessman. I should probably care a little bit more than I do, but I care enough to keep the ball rolling.

To this day when I walk out on stage, I'm very much the person I always dreamed I could be or wanted to be. I'm really just getting lost in the song and getting lost in the performance. And when I'm in the office I do what I need to do. Fortunately, I can just walk in here and jam for a half hour. It's one of the ways I can keep going when I get a little tired or frustrated over there. Then it becomes like, "Ok, put it down, make some phone calls." It keeps it really honest.

I noticed you are definitely hitting Europe a lot with guys like Southside Johnny and Nils Lofgren.
My co-manager is Bob Benjamin and Bob's tied into the Jersey Shore scene. I guess we have done a bunch of shows over the years. I started supporting Southside on and off when I was first starting out in 1992. I was doing some band dates with him and that was on and off, but on these European shows he didn't want bands he only wanted solo. So I've been doing a lot of solo stuff during the last 5 or 6 years.

Nils is a real nice man. That was supposed to be an evening with Nils. He was doing 30 theatre dates in the UK and he gave me 9 of them. And that was supposed to be just him playing because he plays quite a long show. So it was nice of him to give up 30 minutes of his stage time. It helps that I've been around the block a couple more times than say five or seven years ago where as people kind of know me a little bit.

And your following in Europe helps...
Yeah, it sells a few tickets. Certainly my following in Europe has helped. In the UK it really jumped up because of these Southside and Nils tours. In fact, they came out with a fanzine, a full-color, 40 page fanzine of me. Last month they mailed it to me, it's not bad... "Let The Story Be Told."

Do you read the reviews? Do you pay attention to that kind of stuff?
Some. Yeah, I read things. I've been fortunate in that I've only read one bad review of me since I started from day one. I've been really lucky.

Was that from a college paper?
That was from a college paper in Yale.

I was wondering if you had seen that one.
The funny thing is that on Google or something it's one of the ones that comes up right away. One of my co-managers, Gord Hunter, just extended an invitation to that reviewer to see me play with Huey Lewis in Connecticut later this month. It's funny because I said to Gord, "Listen there are people out there who don't like Elvis or the Beatles."

This guy really dug in. A friend of mine, we were on the phone together when I found it. I was like you've got to go to this page. We read the thing out loud to each other on the phone and we just cracked up. The next review the guy did was a violin concerto that got five stars, so I'm pretty sure this guy's a classical music fan. I've gotten some almost embarrassing good reviews as an independent artist and that's great, but that's the one. I don't mind reading them though.

What's the hardest thing about being an artist on your own label?
The hard thing for me is that if a kid in Iowa or Minneapolis trips upon my music and doesn't have access to the Internet he's not going to find my records. That's where the Sony's and the Warner Brother's come in.

I don't think it's a bad thing to hold yourself up against the great artists. The odds are slim to almost none, but hopefully if you make that your goal somewhere along the line you'll become pretty good as an artist. My goal has always been to get somewhere along the line.

Radio stations have been a tough thing. I mean, to actually get them out to radio stations in this Clear Channel/SFX world is almost cost prohibitive as an independent label. As a small independent label, I'd rather take that money and tour on it as well as live on it.

Right now, there's a part of me that likes how everything's grown. It's taken a little while, but nothing in my career at this point is bought and I can't say that for every major label or even large independent label.

How difficult is it for you being a much bigger name abroad?
It's a double edged sword. It feels good that anyone likes the music anywhere. The fact is that for years I went to a day job. I've worked very hard and now I can just really work on music. As an independent it's not easy. Sometimes when I see major label artists or people who have success complaining, it really irks me because I know what I need to get by as an artist on the financial level.

That guy who's sitting in Chestershire UK or Bern, Switzerland who's hitting my website and putting together an order for 3 CDs and 2 t-shirts is a really important person to me. Because that allows me to continue to write songs and I don't take that lightly as an artist. That's why after every show I spend a good amount of time out at the table signing cds and talking to people. Without those people I do not exist as an artist.

There's also a little part of me that's absolutely amazed that anybody buys my records. I started off a little late in this game. I was 23-24 picking up the guitar. I had this absolutely foolish belief that I could do this when no one else believed I could. Maybe one or two other people right around me said keep doing it and occasionally you'd meet someone who'd come up to your show and you'd know you got through to one. I've always believed if you could get through to one person you can get through to ten, which leads to 100, 1,000, 10,000. So, now it's down to the point where I get through to thousands of people. Will it ever get to hundreds of thousands or millions? I don't think so, but maybe. I think if a lot of people are going to know about me it's going to be from a song that just really takes off from a movie soundtrack.

I grew up on the Grateful Dead and the Dead was a big influence on me. Here's a band that never got played on MTV, VH1 or radio. And seeing what Phish has done, and Widespread Panic and Government Mule, all these bands that have been able to be quite large without that exposure. So there is a way.

I was wondering about your relation to the Grateful Dead with your bootleg series.

The only artist I've seen more than Bruce, Tom Petty and Bob Dylan is the Grateful Dead. I've probably seen about 60 Grateful Dead shows, but I don't own any CDs or cassettes. To me, they were always the live experience. It was the party that went on and the sub-culture that existed and still to the day exists around them. It always amazed me.

The thing I get from the Dead the most is I don't ever walk on the stage with a set list. The Dead never played with a set list. I usually know what I'm going to close with and, most of the times, what I may open with but I yell out the songs in-between. I just like that looseness.

I've always wanted to meld my East Coastness with the Grateful Dead. I've been working on it for ten years now. It's tough because at face value people who like the Dead don't like Jersey Shore music and people who like Jersey Shore music don't like the Dead's music. But the common element between the two of them is Bob Dylan. Bruce is by far the most popular Jersey Shore artist and the Grateful Dead is by far the most popular hippie artist and the biggest influence on both of them is Bob Dylan. So, there is something under that umbrella of both and I've been trying for years to merge those.

I did some recording with guys who were really into Phish in the mid-90s. And I kind of wish I would have experimented at the time. I wonder if I would have went down that path if that would have really brought me closer to the marriage I was looking for.

You've been very involved with benefits. What drives you with that?

The first song I ever sang on stage was "Taxi" by Harry Chapin. I tend not to believe too much in weird coincidences, but around 1997 I was asked to play the Beacon Theatre on the Springsteen tribute show called, "One Step Up… Two Steps Back," which was benefiting World Hunger Year. Bruce has certainly been an influence on me, his humanity and how he's been with charities. So, here I am being pulled into to a show by an artist who's influenced me on that level and the reason we're donating this music is because of this artist that I first sang on stage when I was fifteen years old and dreamed of this thing. It was weird.

So then I got to meet some of the World Hunger people and I really liked them. There's a part of Harry Chapin that I see sometimes as I'm out there on the road. I feel like I've met his spirit a few times. The thing I liked about the guy was that he actually believed he could stop world hunger. Now whether he could or not is not the point, the fact that you believe you can is the point. I like fools with a lot of good positive energy. It's very easy to be cynical. It's very easy to say no, to say that can't be done. It's a lot harder to say why not or even yes.

I'm not on a big label. I don't sell tons of records so I can honestly say not enough people care about me anyway. I'm a pretty honest guy. But at the same time, if a few people trip upon these CDs and like them they might turn around and get the other records. For one, it's never been about the money. I didn't get into music for money. I didn't get into music for girls. Those weren't the reasons I got into this.

I dated here and there, but I was just really blinders and focus. I really probably got about eight years of playing my first few years. I still don't play lead guitar. I'm still just a pure rhythm guitar player. I'm more interested in writing songs and trying to convey whatever it is that's making me tick. I was writing all these lyrics and I always kind of thought there had to be a reason why. Maybe there is no reason why, but for me that was the motivation.

Along the way, I'd like to see my music get out there and certainly earn a good living. I just had my first child, so now I want to make money to take care of my wife and my family and that comes into play. I've always loved the charitable aspect of music. How can I go about trying to do it all at once? Some people say you can't. They say it hurt Harry Chapin's career trying to do that. One thing I like about the music business, and maybe life in general, is there are no rules. As long as you can get to the next day and keep a roof above your head, keep everyone fed, and pay the bills there's always the opportunity for something to happen. Maybe that's why I get involved with these organizations. At my core I'm definitely a dreamer and certainly an optimistic fool.

You're sort of an adopted son of the Jersey Shore. What is it about the music of the Jersey Shore?

It pulls you in. It's almost like when people see movies and move to Hollywood to be in the movie. There is something about playing down at the Jersey Shore. I can't wait for the day when Asbury's a healthy environment again, but there is something. It almost seems like the Jersey Shore and the "Asbury Park sound" is more popular other places on the earth than it is in America and along the East Coast, which is a shame.

I remember this one quote with Bruce and Little Steven talking about "play every show like it's your last show." Now it may be, career-wise or health wise, who knows? But if it is going to be then you can look back at your last show and say, yeah.

I remember when early on, there would be five people in the crowd. Even now there's nights now as an independent band when we'll go out there and some crowds are definitely bigger than others. And we'll have people come up to us and say, "Wow, I wish there could have been more people but you played as if there was 5,000 people here tonight." To me, that's the best compliment I'm gonna get on the night. Don't waste anybody's money, don't waste anybody's time, just go out there and try to do it. I think it's probably because I used to go see concerts a lot from working in the business and when I was a kid going to see a lot of shows spending my hard earned money and just seeing some artist that didn't do it. Either they didn't have the ability to do it or they just didn't care, they were just going for the paycheck. Well, I don't get paid enough to worry about the paycheck.

How do you feel about being part of the Asbury Park scene?
Absolutely honored and love it. It's a double edged sword to belong to a music scene or to be part of. Now in the mid-90s, I started doing a lot of shows in Milwaukee, Chicago, the Midwest. I wanted to be more associated with the Replacements and the Bodeans, because of the shadow of the Jersey Shore. Bruce's shadow was quite large and I'd seen other people be overshadowed by it and get very upset by it. So, I wanted to be an Americana band from the East Coast. And I believe we've been able to pull that off. As the years have gone by I've probably grown more accepted of my Jerseyness.

I live in Rockland County in New York but the end of my street is New Jersey so I have the best of both worlds. If I want to be from New York, I'm from New York. If I want to be from Jersey, I'm from Jersey. I get letters from people saying "musicians such as yourself, Southside Johnny, Bon Jovi, Bruce Springsteen." And that means a lot to me.

I've seen reviews in Norway where people have said "Bob Seger, Joe D'Urso and John Fogerty." When I see that, it's like maybe I did pull off this whole Americana/Jersey thing.

I always wanted to put out a record called, *New York, New York* only because of Frank but it's a tough thing, it's almost the same double-edged sword as the Bruce. Being part of a music scene where you pretty much know that you're never going to eclipse the top musician from that scene is interesting shoes to stand in.

I think anybody coming out of Memphis after Elvis felt that way and anybody coming out of Liverpool after the Beatles felt that way as well. So those are the rules you've got to play with. It's either going to rip you down or you make it into something more positive. The way I've been able to make it more positive is because some fans of Bruce's music and Jersey Shore music have discovered my music. Then it becomes up to me. Do I stand in this one corner and be considered a derivative artist? Or can I take that and then turn it into who I am as a person? And that's what I've tried to do.

Now when you come out with a new record and you're working on something and everybody only wants to talk about Bruce's next record coming out it's a bit of a thing, but that's the world you live in. You either live with it or you don't. Yes it's a big shadow, but it's also a shadow I don't mind standing in because I admire the person. As a kid he was something of a musical hero. As I've grown into a man, he's more of a hero on a humanity level. I like the fact that when we see each other there's a hello. I was able to hop on stage with the E Street Band to sing "Santa Claus is Coming to Town." I kind of like that. I'm not sure if I ever want to be friends. I think it's nice to meet your heroes, but it's probably good to keep a little distance because you might find things you don't like. Kind of go about your business and do what you need to do...

But remain colleagues?
Yeah, if anybody would ever have told me when I was fifteen years old that I'd walk backstage at the Pony and Bruce Springsteen would turn around and go, "Hey Joey, what's going on?" I'd say they were nuts! And that's cool, I love that. The only way I could equate it is when Bruce was a younger artist and Elvis or Dylan acknowledging him. That's a real cool thing, but my biggest challenge is how do I turn that corner and become that other thing? I'm hoping that it's gonna be with the mixture of that Jersey Shore and my hippieness. Not that I'm a hippie, but it's the background with all the Grateful Dead stuff and being much more free and alternative to the music business.

People always say to me, "The music business is in such a sad state right now. How does that affect you?" I say, "It doesn't." I don't exist in the music business, I exist in an independent world that we've created. I'm just trying to keep moving up, but whether the music business sells 40 billion records next year or one billion doesn't affect what I do day to day.

It's funny because when you're overseas, a lot of the fans think like on Thursday night everybody has dinner together, which would be great... we should start that. We'll all go to Bruce's house for dinner.

Asbury Park is like a mythical place to many music fans around the world. When you see fans after the show that know you are sort of grouped with them, how do they view the area?

I think they look at it as the – the word mecca has religious attributes, but I'll use it anyway - the mecca of where this style of music that affects them so much comes from. If Bruce was the first artist that they tripped on and then they found out about Southside and then they found out about Bon Jovi later and then they found out about Joe Gruschecky and then they found out about John Eddie and then myself. How? Where? Why is it? How could this one area shoot off so much different music under the rock and roll umbrella.

I mean, Bruce covers a bunch of it. Johnny tends to be more R&B and horns. John Eddie has a little bit more of that Mott the Hoople / Stones kind of thing going on. We tend to be a little more Americana, a little bit harder. Gruschecky tends to be a little more stomp. Everything has its different angle within that thing. Probably one of the things that Bruce does, only because he's had a bigger career and a longer career, is that his style may have encompassed all of that.

It's a mythological thing, I think more so than any other. I'm really proud to be part of this Asbury scene. Seattle had a scene and there was some really good bands from there, but it's almost kind of quickly gone by the wayside or moved around. Liverpool had a scene but that kind of dispersed as did all of the different scenes that have happened around the world. Even though it happened twenty years ago, a lot of those artists from the Asbury scene are still playing. Now if Domenic Santana didn't reopen the Stone Pony it would have went more by the wayside.

Domenic's a character on to himself, without a doubt. But the fact is that it's a hard thing because none of these artists are going to allow themselves to be branded as a commodity like Asbury Park, USA. We did a tour once over in the UK with myself, John Eddie and Joe Gruschecky. The promoters there promoted it as "Greetings from Asbury Park, the Sounds of Asbury Park" to help the ticket sales. The funny thing is none of us are from Asbury, but we're all associated.

I don't care if you have the finances of Bruce Springsteen or the hard working sense of a Southside Johnny. They do things for the right reasons. That's one of the reasons why I like being associated with them on many levels. I've certainly learned a lot and some people say I'm trying to emulate what these people are doing. Well, these people played some of the best music I ever heard as a kid and as human beings they do the right thing, so show me where the negative side is.

46 <u>Mimi Cross</u>

When people write about my music, they compare me to every woman with a guitar from Ani DiFranco to Joan Osbourne to Joni Mitchell and I could go on and on. Now, some of those people have influenced me and maybe I do sound a little like some of them, but some of them I don't.

--MIMI CROSS

The haunting look of Mimi Cross. Photo © Danny Sanchez

Mimi Cross is not just another pretty face, she's also one of the most talented singer-songwriters on the Jersey Shore. Born in Canada, she now lives along the Shore and is a veteran of the local music scene. Mimi has graced stages from local clubs like T-Birds Cafe, the Saint and the Stone Pony to Maxwell's and the Liquid Lounge in Hoboken. She's played in clubs from New York to Boston, Philadelphia on down to Washington, DC and has opened for such artists as Sting, Bonnie Raitt, Lauryn Hill, Jeffrey Gaines, Jill Sobule and Chris Whitley.

She released her first record, *Monkey Trap*, independently two years ago and is currently working on her follow up record. As an independent artist, Mimi's songs have been heard on local radio stations and college stations across the country. She has had songs placed in independent films including the documentary, *Greetings From My Home Town,* which was directed by Takaharu Macky Makiura. And she's a two-time Asbury Music Award winner, which shows her standing in the area.

I had the chance to visit with Mimi to discuss her career and find out why she believes that men rule the world.

Your bio says you're Canadian. Where exactly are you from? How did you start out playing in Asbury Park?

Who are you? *(laughs)* That's just sort of to make me sound a little more interesting... that foreign thing. I lived in Toronto when I was a little kid. But I really grew up about an hour from here in Millburn, New Jersey. I went to school out west in Arizona and did grad school at NYU.

I started playing in Asbury Park because I was living on Long Beach Island and I didn't want to drive to New York. There was really no places except for the Tide that played original music in LBI. At the time I was in the reggae band, No Discipline. I was doing backup vocals and percussion. That was a hard working band man, we played six nights a week. Mostly it was reggae covers, but they had original stuff too. And they've been together forever. I ran into one of the guys at this gig I did at Rutgers last fall and I was just amazed that they were still doing it. I was like, "When are you going to retire to the islands or something?" I remember the coolest gig that I did with them was playing at the Stone Pony with Peter Tosh's son.

No Discipline was the first gig I ever had, I think. After that I started writing with bunches of people and also writing on my own. Then I hooked up with Will Herceck and we put together this band called Pictures and Stories, which was good. We played places like T-Birds and the Bitter End. And then I had my own band. I remember I started doing these gigs where I'd have Pictures and Stories do the first half of a gig and then I'd do the other half.

Was it difficult to be a female performer around here? There haven't been that many throughout the years.

Scott Stamper used to bring in people for us like Kristin Hall and May Moore at T-Birds and later Jill Sobule and Laurie Sargent at the Saint. These were all shows that I was on. Well, think back now when did it really start? I remember hearing Suzanne Vega for the first time and going, "Oh yeah, that's it," because you had all these women trying to be men. I was never really into the rocking women like Janis Joplin, I think she's great but I never really loved what she did. Suzanne Vega came along and she had that alternative kind of edge while all the other women I would hear had more of a folky thing or a Joni Mitchell jazz thing. So, finally there was a woman doing something alternative. Say you start with her, how long did it take to get to Alanis Morissette? There was like this little push, push, push and then Alanis just broke it open.

Now it's fair game, but it's still not really fair. I mean, just turn on the radio any given day with any given station except for maybe a college station. Turn on the radio and count how many guys you hear in a row.

Why do you think that is?

Because men rule the world! *(laughs)* Men are still in charge, it's really true. I also think that - and this has happened to me countless times over the years - when people write about my music, they compare me to every woman with a guitar from Ani DiFranco to Joan Osbourne to Joni Mitchell and I could go on and on. Now, some of those people have influenced me and maybe I do sound a little like some of them, but some of them I don't. As my Sister said, "Basically any chick with a guitar."

It's almost like that we're categorized where they really are all these different genres of music and there are clearly men in all of these genres. I think there are clearly women in all of these genres as well, but for some reason when people see a female with a guitar they only see it one way. It's definitely starting to shift, it really is, and the same thing's happening in sports. It's just a timing thing, I think. I think there's a lot of chicks playing, a lot of women playing gigs. I'm allowed to say chicks because I'm a chick.

And I'm allowed to quote it because you said it!

I better watch myself! *(laughs)* There's just more guys out there playing, although I think women are coming more into their own and being more assertive. I also think, in general, the women that you do hear on the radio are better than a lot of the men you hear. For some reason, there aren't a lot of mediocre women on the radio and that's a good thing.

Look at all of the boy bands, look at all the bands that sound like either Pearl Jam or the Counting Crows, why do we have that? Why don't we have just one Pearl Jam and one Counting Crows? You only have one Suzanne Vega. You don't have ten women on the radio that sound like Suzanne Vega.

Well, who would you say has influenced you?
Wow, I mean, there's so many people... I love great songwriting. So, Joni Mitchell, Neil Young, Bruce Springsteen, bands like the Smithereens - I love that poppy, hooky kind of stuff. I love the Beatles. In fact, on my new CD I have a cover of a George Harrison song. There's so much great music out there. My CD collection is incredibly eclectic. Another big influence is Rosanne Cash. She's sort of a mentor, I take writing workshops from her. Chris Whitley has got to be my favorite artist and he's influenced me a lot, but there's a million people.

Tell me about your record *Monkey Trap*.
I released it about four years ago, it's old now so I'm working on a new one. I have it about halfway done. I'm taking a long time because I really have no money. But I love being in the studio because I love collaborating with other people. I wrote all of the songs on *Monkey Trap*. I used to have a songwriting partner in Will Herceck when we played in Pictures and Stories, but basically I haven't been writing with anyone in a long time. So, when I go in the studio I love getting the collaboration from other musicians. There's nothing better than working with great musicians. They'll come up with a bass line or a guitar part or a really hip drum groove and that, to me, is just the greatest thing.

Do you have a steady band now or just play solo?
I don't have a band now, I'm just solo. I had a band about a year and a half ago and we just went by my name. It was good, it worked. In fact, it was really working until it sort of imploded. Being in a band is like being in a four way relationship, it can be intense.

What do you hope to do with the new CD? Will you release it independently or shop it around?
What am I doing? That's a good question. The thing is that I'm really a writer so I'm always like I'll worry about that stuff later and just sit down and write another song. Unfortunately, I've always done that. But what I'm trying to do now is just be really open and reach out. I feel like I've opened myself up recently and a couple of things have happened.

I just wrote two songs for an independent film. A friend of mine who has a film and video company ended up passing my music to the director. We ended up chatting and I met one of the writers who gave me the script. So, I wrote a couple songs and that, to me, was a complete blast! You have some interesting parameters and you get to meet some new people that have a lot of energy. I liked the script so that got me excited. And a guy I know just did a documentary and one of my songs is in that. I love movies, so I would love to do more stuff like that.

How often do you write songs?
A lot. I go through phases. It's like if I have a gig I usually practice, if I'm practicing I'm picking up the guitar and if I'm picking up the guitar then I'm going to write. One of the main reasons I do shows is to inspire my writing. And, what are you going to do with the songs after they're done? I make demos on my computer, but you can really isolate yourself with that stuff - let me add another harmony part here or throw in some Tibetan bells...

But you've got to do it, you've got to play. It's always surprising to me that I ended up being a front person at all. I mean, I love to sing and I love to write, but I don't love performing. It's just part of the process. You have to do it. Some people are lucky, they love it and they're great on stage. They have that thing about them. To me, it's part of the process. It's nice to get that feedback. It's important because when you finish a song and there's that moment where you're entrenched with the audience and you know... you don't even have to look at them, you just know that they got it. We all want to be recognized by our culture and we all want to know that we're not the only ones that feel this way. It's like when you're reading a book and you see something you relate to, you just love that feeling when you discover something that you can connect with. It's all about connecting. So, you've got to share your work.

I know I'm not 20 years old. I'm not going to be the next Madonna or Britney Spears and I never wanted to be, but I do wonder now about what I am doing with a record. I think I'll just keep doing what I'm doing; playing out some, recording and trying to do movies and television. And I love festivals and playing outside, that's another thing. I'm always thinking I should get off of my butt and do a summer festival tour or something.

I'm definitely looking for something different now. I think it's like when you're in your thirties you begin to wonder if it's gonna happen? Has it happened already? Is it going to be something different? Will it be something different than you thought, maybe a different opportunity? Like I would love to write for other people.

The best compliment I ever got was when Peter Scherer started play-ing solo again and he played a song of mine called, "Invisible Things." That was the greatest to hear someone like him sing one of my songs.

A friend of mine said that when you get in your thirties a lot of people just give up. They stop what they're doing, but there's still a place for us. People still love our music, and we should keep doing it because all those people that stop leave a void. And that void can't be filled by 20-year olds because they're doing something different. I've seen friends of mine drop right through the cracks. They get their records recorded and then either get dropped or fail to have their records promoted. I've seen it happen, so maybe it's a blessing that I never got some kind of a major deal.

What are the shows like for you now in the city?
Well, I just played Friday and it was a really different kind of show for me. I played with some songwriters that I know, so it was really fun. I played a lot of new stuff and had a lot of laughs. I haven't been playing too much. It seems like down here I've just done a bunch of benefits. I'm really in this weird place where I'm like I don't have a new band and I don't have a new CD, so why should I play?

I go through different phases in my career where it's like I'm only going to play here and here because I know certain music industry people will come. And I went through the playing for money phase where it was like I took any gig I could and I made a lot of money doing that. I played some weird shows and some really good ones. It's funny because when you go out of town you realize how tough New York really is.

Back when you started out playing in Asbury Park, did the town's history mean anything to you?
Oh yeah, absolutely. I'm a real sentimental person and I want things to mean something and Asbury Park definitely meant something. I knew that Bruce Springsteen had played at T-Birds and I knew about that whole Stone Pony thing. In the beginning when I would go to T-Birds I would only go at night. I would just play and then leave. Then one day I had to meet someone in the afternoon and I couldn't believe it when I drove into that town. I fell in love with the abandoned boardwalk and the buildings with their architecture. I loved it. I used to go for walks on the boardwalk and swim there. The town's definitely got a vibe.

I think Bruce Springsteen is the reason a lot of us are in this area. People like us that are serious about our writing, we listen to his songs and we really look at those lyrics. We've been influenced by him and we appreciate what he's done. And that's kind of what drew us to the area.

47 Danny White

No gig is a meaningless gig. If that's what it comes down to. If they start becoming meaningless gigs then don't play them. It's that simple. I mean, just tonight I'm sitting there playing and I'm like I'm pretty lucky to be standing here playing my songs and people are coming to hear them.

--DANNY WHITE

Danny White performs at the Saint in Asbury Park. Photo © Gary Wien

D anny White is proof that the Jersey Shore is still producing great singer-songwriters. The Matawan-based artist writes songs filled with stories of people you feel as if you know. His words capture their hopes and dreams like a modern street poet. He has often been compared to Bruce Springsteen, a comparison not likely to go away anytime soon.

White started out playing in clubs like the Brighton Bar in Long Branch and T-Birds Cafe in Asbury Park. As his audience grew he moved up to where he became a regular for the Stone Pony crowd. He has released a pair of critically acclaimed independent records and has received good reviews in publications like *Billboard Magazine*, the *Aquarian*, *New York Times* and the *Asbury Park Press*.

Like many Jersey Shore musicians, he has been very involved in giving his time to benefit causes. White has been part of such things as the Light of Day concerts, Musicians On Call and Jersey Jams, Jersey Cares Organization.

I caught up with Danny White in Point Pleasant where he was playing a free show in a summer pavilion. At the time he was just about to head back to the studio to work on his upcoming record due out in 2003.

When you first began playing clubs you started at the Brighton Bar in Long Branch, right?
The very first place I ever went out to with an acoustic guitar and just walked into and played was T-Birds in Asbury. And then, like right after that, I found the Brighton down there on Sundays and it used to be packed every Sunday night. There used to be open mikes. I guess they called it songwriters in the round or songwriters. Anyway, it was an acoustic night on Sunday nights and that was the first time I ever really went out consistently and played acoustic - just solo guitar. I guess it was probably right after high school.

Was it a paying gig?
No, these were just open mikes. The cool thing about both of them was that they eventually turned into that. We'd go down a couple of times, keep playing. If they liked you they'd ask you back. That was Jacko over at the Brighton. He was really great with that.

I remember the first time I went out and played. I played on a Sunday, I played three songs and I didn't get off the stage and he was like, "Hey, you gotta come back to this place. You've got to come back and play a show with a couple other songs." That was really the first place. Jacko was a good guy.

When did you start moving to places like the Pony?
Pretty much when the Pony reopened. The last time we played the Saint it was sold out, luckily you graduate.

When the Pony reopened it seemed like they tried to get the old-timers as well as the new guys to play there.
Yeah, it was good that they actually gave younger bands a chance instead of just going with the guys who had played there for years. They called you up and said, "Come on over." That was cool.

That was around the time that you were put in the category as another guy from the Shore... The next in line.
Yeah, yeah...

How do you feel about being thought of as the next in line?
Well, you know, I'm ready to take my turn.

Is that right?
The sooner the better, Gary.

Did you have many bands in high school?
Pretty much in high school I had one band, the same band and like anything else the same guys. It was called a couple different things. The longest incarnation was Parkway South.

So you had the Jersey thing from the beginning.
That was my drummer, he came up with it. We couldn't think of anything better. He was from Manasquan so whenever he drove home from Matawan he always saw the signs for Parkway South. It was actually not that bad looking back at it. Better than anything I could come up with.

Did you have any gigs?
Yeah, we did a lot of friends' parties in high school. We used to play the Deck House in Asbury Park. It was two stories and you play on the second story with the window. It's something else now. They just redid it recently. That was one of our good gigs in high school.

Were you writing songs then?
Yeah, we always did originals. That's why our covers suck now. Never had a cover band. Well, everybody does Bob Dylan, but it was always originals - better or worse.

What would you prefer to be known as: a songwriter, a performer or what? What are you most proud of?

That's a good question. If you don't have the songs... If you don't have good songs you can't - there's nothing to go out and play. And if you don't have good songs they ain't going to want you back and no one's gonna buy your CD. So, I guess, the songwriting aspect of it. Because you're just sitting there with a guitar and there's nothing and hopefully a short time thereafter there's a whole new song, you know. But it's two totally different things completely. That one has nothing to do with the other.

Who were some of the songwriters you liked while growing up?

I'm a big Tom Petty fan, Tom Petty & the Heartbreakers - always great, solid songwriting. Always his songs to me made you feel like you kind of heard them but you didn't. They're always comfortable and like your buddies. Dylan is great. U2 is a great, great band, I'm a big U2 fan. Great songs, great sound.

With newer guys there's a guy out there by the name Joseph Arthur. I don't know if you've ever heard of him but he deserves to be heard a lot more than he is. He's on Virgin Records. Two great records that he put out. So I listen to him and that kind of stuff. I like to hear a good song too. That kind of stuff.

Now something like you did today, "Small Tattoos," is that something for the future? Is that this album? How quickly after you write it does it get to the studio?

I actually wrote that one a month ago or something. If it's good, let's record it right away. But a lot of times you come up with something after you have already done recording and you put it aside or you show the band. If it sounds good then you play it while you're doing shows promoting that other CD. I think you throw it in once and awhile just to keep up on it. But this one, really we played so much after the last CD *Beautifully Preserved Wrecks*. We played so much after that - like all over the places: Boston, North Carolina, South Carolina, DC, New York, New Jersey, Philadelphia - all over. So we're playing so much that I didn't do a lot of writing actually. There was just too much other stuff to do.

It just comes around naturally where you're like hey it's time for some new songs. Like that one that you mentioned there, "Small Tattoos," that's like a month old. We did it on a TV show in a different version just me and Jim acoustic on News12. And, you know, we did it like that so that's one I would assume will be recorded. It's getting a good reaction. **Will this**

upcoming record be an independent release? Do you have plans for it yet?

A full CD just really takes too much time. Ten or twelve songs is a big undertaking to record. It takes a few months and I've got the best band that I think I've had ever so I want to play as much with them as I can. We've had some opportunities with record labels. We need better recordings.

Have you ever thought of putting the best tracks from the records you've released on one CD and then take it to record companies?

Yeah, well what we probably should have done the last time around instead of doing this whole CD, we should have taken three or four songs and had it done by a big time producer and went from there, had somebody big producing it and getting it in people's hands. But, then again, I mean with that we got a nice feature in *Billboard*. So maybe not. Because you need those other things. It all works into one.

When you had the write up in *Billboard Magazine* did that lead to a bunch of calls?

It opened up a lot of doors in other ways. Opened a lot of doors to the producers that we're talking with now. Everything leads to something else. It's not like that anymore where you go out and play and so and so from Columbia Records just happens to be there and it's like alright you're in. It's a lot of independent work.

How hard is it to get these indies sold?

Just as hard as it is to get a record deal. It's all the same. We do good selling them on the Internet. Like on our own website and Amazon.com. There's a lot of others, we mainly stick with Amazon because people know if you buy your CD that they're going to get it. And they're good in that they only take what you sell. There's no up front fee. That really helps an independent artist. And everybody's heard of Amazon. They're legitimate. That's the most important thing. You don't want someone buying your CD and then never getting it.

Tell me about the Millennium Rock and Roll Music Showcase that you guys played last year. How did that turn out for you?

Oh God, how do you know about that? Man, you do your homework! I don't remember that one. It was in Harrisburg, Pennsylvania. It was one of those indie-band showcases like CMJ or NEMA, any of those. You go to have record company people, newspaper people, journalists, and stuff.

It's in a hotel and you go and rub elbows with them. You see what they can do for you and then you play a club in the area. It's like the Boston, South by Southwest - all of them it's all the same. That's what they do. When we did the Boston one, we played a club in Cambridge. When we did this one I think we played right in Harrisburg. I couldn't remember the place at all, but it was cool. The one up in Boston was the first one we did. That's a bigger one.

You've been fortunate to land opening spots at the Garden State Arts Center in recent years. Is that the biggest place you've played?
Yeah, definitely. I think we've played with Journey, Foreigner, Chicago. I think those were the bands. It was cool, you know.

Definitely right in your backyard, huh? You could walk to the gig.
Yeah, it's easy to get to. Not a lot of gas money there...

What's your favorite place to play around the Jersey Shore?
Well, I have to say... Seriously, I don't have to say it, but the Stone Pony really is my favorite place to play. The sound guys there John and John, they do excellent work. The J & J Boys... Seriously, they do a great job and there's something about playing right in your area. Right at home and stuff. And Domenic did an incredible job putting money into it.

That place was a disaster. I didn't play there but I was there. It was a disaster. He did a great job bringing it back. It sounds great. I think it's a great place to see a show. It's a great place to come out and see a show. It's clean, good sight lines for the most part, the sound is great.

Domenic's a good guy. They're all good people there. Tracey, of course, behind the bar. It's not the Stone Pony without Tracey. She's the "Princess of the Pony." That's what I call her. But they're all cool people, you know.

The Bottom Line's a great place in the city. Alan Tepper's a great guy. Real professional. And, again, great history at that place. But they're just pros. He's a real professional. You know whatever he says is gonna happen. Same thing at the Stone Pony. Another one of my favorite places is the 9:30 Club in DC. Same deal.

Very professional again, and you don't get that a lot. It's just how some of the places are. It's the same thing like you were saying this band really means business. They've really got their act together and when they're playing on stage it looks like they're doing what they want to do. And you've got other bands who don't have their stuff together. It's the same thing with clubs and owners. Some of them don't care.

Where did you go when you first started going to see the bands?
You know, the thing was that I was always so concerned with playing and having my own band that I really never went out to check bands out. Because if I wasn't playing I was practicing. So early on, I didn't see a lot of bands, like bands that were doing the same thing I was doing. Or even today. I really don't... the only time I see another band is when I'm playing with them. If we're not playing around here than we're playing someplace else. Or we're practicing or we're recording.

Well, is this everything? Is there a day job?
This is everything right now.

So you're trying to squeeze whatever you've got?
Yeah, if you're going to do it you've got to do it. And that's that. But, you know, like Matt Witte for example. He was reading about us. It was funny the first time we played together because obviously I'd heard about him a lot and he said the same thing. He's like, "Man I read about you all the time. I see your name everyplace. You'll play on a Friday night, I'll play on a Saturday. I'll play on a Friday you'll play on Saturday. I'm in the paper one week you're in the paper the next week." But we didn't talk too much till a couple months ago. Now we've played three or four shows together. So that's what happens.

Now, you're from an area that obviously has a lot of commuters to New York and you wrote a song after September 11th.
Right. "Freedom Come to All."

What was it like being in that area during the weeks after the attack took place?
Yeah, you know what? It's funny because I told this story before. I was down - we were out in Cleveland and I went to the Rock and Roll Hall of Fame there. I would say almost exactly a year before it happened. Almost exactly because it was September that we were out there and it was that week of September too.

We went to the Rock and Roll Hall of Fame, watching the induction things and it was Bob Marley's turn. Off in the distance, I noticed something spray painted on a wall behind the museum. It was a soccer ball with the words "freedom come to all." And I was like that's pretty cool. Jotted it down, stuck it in my pocket. So, I always had that title. I had it written in my notebook or whatever. I was like maybe that will be useful one day. I thought it was kind of cool in a way.

And, in case you ever started doing reggae...

Right, I figured I'd be in! And that happened on September 11th and I'd had that title and chord changes for it. I guess that was why I had that title.

Where were you when the attack took place?

Sleeping! I'm a musician, Gary! I was in Matawan, sleeping. My girlfriend called me up and was like, "A plane just hit the World Trade Center." I'm thinking like some guy had a heart attack and rammed into it. That's awful. And then she said another just hit it too and I was like alright I gotta get up, turn the TV on. That was it for the next day and a half. Sat in front of the TV. What's gonna happen now? Don't know.

I wrote that song that night and two weeks later we played at the Bottom Line. That was a very, very strange night that was because usually that place is sold out. You can't get into it. You do two shows there and the first show was like 1/2 to 3/4 full and the next show was not even half full. The later it got the less people you saw walking around. Still out there in the air, you know. Going into the tunnel it was like the only time I never waited to get into the tunnel. There was nobody in the city. It was very eery. Nobody walking around on the streets. The smell still lingered in the air. That was an intense show. Definitely different.

Did you play "Freedom Come To All" there?

That was the first time I played it.

What was the crowd's reaction?

It was pretty intense, man. They were listening to every word. Hung on every word. Got a great reaction after it. I think it was a tough question. Should I play the song? Shouldn't I play the song? Do I just go out there and just play a rock show? Hit them with all upbeat songs to get their minds off it? But when you're there I was just like I gotta play it. And the band didn't even know it at the time. So I was like let's play it. We played it and I think it went well. I think they appreciated it. Everybody knew what happened, you gotta do it. It's there.

You've been very involved with benefit causes. That's one thing lots of Shore musicians seem to have in common.

It's us New Jersey guys, Gary, who are very giving people. You know, I don't really know what it is. I've played around enough to know and to talk to other people and it's not like that in other places. It's just not, you know. I mean, Boston's a big town, but I don't see it as much anywhere but here man. I really don't. I'm not saying that.

It definitely has to do with Bruce. Definitely think that it's something he installed in all of the musicians around here, like musicians who do it full time. I think that definitely comes right from him. I don't think there's any question about it.

What was it like doing a show like the Light of Day benefit concert?
Great! And again, it's a great cause so why not take the time to do it? And there you go. He shows up and that's a great thing for guys like me and the other guys. Whether you're fans or not. There's living proof right there that he grew up in the same kind of town that you did and he did it. You know what I mean? It's a great inspiration. And he's done it with class. There's not a lot of guys that have hung around as long as him.

What was it like the first time Bruce jumped on stage with you?
Very cool. It was great! More important than that he was just a genuine nice guy. He could have been like yeah, nice meeting you see you later. But he wasn't. You just sit there and talk to him like a normal guy. And that's it. He doesn't have to get up and do anything but he does.

I think when you see a guy that has gone to the highest level - yeah, he's got a lot of money and, which is the exact reason he doesn't have to get off his couch to do anything, but he does. You see that and I think that's been installed. That can definitely be traced right back to him.

Is it weird playing gigs like today or some fair in Freehold and thinking that Bruce played these gigs. Are they meaningless gigs?
No gig is a meaningless gig. If that's what it comes down to... if they start becoming meaningless gigs then don't play them. It's that simple. I mean, just tonight I'm sitting there playing and I'm like I'm pretty lucky to be standing here playing my songs and people are coming to hear them. And you're out by the beach and fireworks are going off. It's like alright! What it does it give you that little bit of hope when you're out there in the middle of nowhere and you're playing to two people in some little town in Virginia or something and you're like, "What the hell am I doing at here? I could be home watching a Yankees game or whatever."

Do the Springsteen comparisons ever get to you? You're a singer-songwriter from the same area as him.
That's a dangerous thing, you know. Because his fans are so fanatical that to a certain degree it's good because maybe they'll come and check you out and maybe you'll get some new fans. But if you're too closely linked it's never worked for anybody.

But it's something you deal with.
Well, you know, we're from the same area. Playing roughly the same kind of music. I mean, I don't necessary think that my songs are like his or the band sounds exactly like his. You're definitely going to get compared to them, especially somebody like me. And, hey, as long as they're not - I guess I've been kind of lucky because they're not saying he's a Springsteen ripoff and that's important.

Did you ever consider doing anything else or was it music from early on?
From early on this is definitely what I wanted to do. I'm really... I'm obviously not doing it for the money, man, because, you know, I don't have any. There isn't a lot to be made at this level. You're either way up there and you're making a lot or you're down at the bottom. There's no middle ground really. I'm sure I could. It's a lot more - I'm not going to say easy to be a lawyer, but you know what you've got to do. You go to school you do good, you go to college you do good, you go to law school you do good and more than likely you're going to have a job as lawyer. This... who knows? You've got to make your own breaks.

I think the only one who blatantly got that was John Cafferty and the Beaver Brown Band. I think John Cafferty's career never made it because he was called a Springsteen ripoff.
No comment. *(laughs)* I don't know. At least they're not saying that and it's a lot better to me being compared in some ways to Bruce Springsteen than Poison, you know what I mean?

48 Bob Burger

It's a different feeling when you're playing somebody else's tunes as opposed to playing your own tunes. In some respects when you're playing someone else's songs it's almost like you're sort of listening.

--BOB BURGER

Bob Burger takes his turn at lead vocals in a performance by the Bobby Bandiera Band at the Stone Pony. Photo © Gary Wien

Bob Burger is a member of the Bobby Bandiera Band and a longtime songwriting partner of such Jersey Shore artists as Glen Burtnick, Bobby Bandiera and Joey Vadala.   In 2002, Bob headed to the studio to record a bunch of original songs for a CD called *Cymbals At Dawn*. Backing him in the studio is Rob Tanico from Highway 9 and PK Lavengood from John Eddie's band.

If it wasn't for a successful career outside of music, Bob Burger just might be a household name by now. As a talented singer, songwriter and live performer Bob fits in perfectly with the Asbury Park music scene.

For several years, Bob Burger and Bobby Bandiera have played as a duo at the Celtic Cottage in Long Branch each week. I caught up with him one night in the summer at one of these weekly shows to talk about his role in the local scene.

You're originally from Pennsylvania, right?

Yeah, Erie, Pennsylvania. I came here in the late eighties, around 1987. I had been here a year or two, and then I got started working with Bobby (Bandiera) and Glen (Burtnick). I auditioned for Bobby many years ago as his bass player and I played with him for a couple of years. Then I kind of dropped out of the scene for a while, came back, and started playing guitar with him playing rhythm. That was kind of a new thing for me because I hadn't played guitar very much so I kind of needed a lot of help. He encouraged me and kept me going. He's been great.

Glen I met when I had a little original band and we were playing around the corner at the Brighton Bar and Glen came down to hear us. He liked the music and the songs and asked me if I wanted to write with him. "Spinning My Wheels" was really the first song we wrote together. And I was thrilled with the opportunity.   He'd had a record out and I was thinking I had a chance to get a song on a record.

Have you had a lot of bands at the Shore?

Not really, you know, I had the original band for a while then I started playing with Bobby and I've really been playing with Bobby ever since.

How long has it been?

Oh probably fifteen years, but it's kind of been an on and off thing. I play with him now - well, I do this gig with him every week, but when we play with the electric band it's only like every four or five gigs that I'm there. It's either filling in on dates or, more often, it's playing rhythm guitar when he's got a gig that hires more people. If there's five people I'll play, if there's four I'm not playing. It's kind of like that.

But it's funny that people say to me, "Who are you? Where'd you come from? I never saw you with Bobby before." I've only been playing with Bobby for years and years and years.

Does the Bobby Bandiera Band play any of your songs?
No, the only thing we play is - I wrote "C'mon Caroline" with Bobby. So that's the only one I'm really a writer in. But really, when I'm playing with Bobby, it's Bobby's band. We're doing his thing and I love Bobby so much. I've learned so much from him.

You've been playing weekly gigs with Bobby for a while now. Is it different when it's you two as a duo as opposed to the band?
It's different, but it's different and it's not different. I still try to pull out whatever I've got inside me and push it across. And that's regardless of what the form is and regardless of whether it's playing or writing or whatever it is. The only difference between this and playing in the band is that it's not as loud and there's no drums. But it's just performing. I love it.

You've written many songs with Glen. What's that like for you?
Wonderful.   I mean Glen is another guy that's been such a great encouragement to me and such a good supporter of me. He's turned me on to a lot of different gigs, different situations. I've written on all of his records - written for the Styx records. Writing with him is great because we work together so well. We have kind of an unique writing approach in that we don't always write a song together at the same time. It's sort of like he'll come down to the house and say here's some ideas that I have. Then we'll sit and bullshit for about two hours just to kind of get in tune to what the feeling of where we're going right now is all about, and then I'll go take the song and finish it or half finish it.

I had forgotten that you co-wrote "Spinning My Wheels" with Glen. I still remember the great review in *Billboard Magazine*.
It didn't translate into sales though.

As a songwriter, does it feel different playing someone else's songs?
It is a different feeling when you're playing somebody else's tunes as opposed to playing your own tunes. In some respects when you're playing someone else's songs it's almost like you're sort of listening. It's like when you ride around in the car you don't listen to your own music. I don't think anybody does. You listen to other people's music because you like the way it sounds and you're being entertained by it.

Sometimes, to certain degree, when I'm playing covers I'm being entertained by the songs as a listener even as I'm playing it. But when you're playing your own stuff you're not really entertained by it.

And you try to make the other songs your own...
Well I do. I try, more of by just trying to be yourself. I don't really think about trying to make it my own as much as trying to be what I am and who I am and letting the song come out the way it comes out in that context. I really like playing other people's songs, but I like playing my own songs too just there's not as much of a venue for it.

What keeps you coming out to tiny bars like this each week?
Only one thing - I love it. Only one thing, that it's the most fun thing that there is to do. It's the thing where most people say about a job: would you do it if they didn't pay you? The answer is yes, because it's so great.

You didn't grow up around here but you're a part of the music scene. Does Asbury Park and the Stone Pony mean anything to you?
Sure it does, because I've been here long enough. I like to think of myself as part of the scene. I wasn't here in the real heyday of it, but the Pony's a great place to play just in its own right. You don't really have to be associated with the long standing legend behind it. It's like with Bruce Springsteen and the involvement. I wasn't there when that was happening, but I've been lucky enough to actually play with Bruce Springsteen at the Stone Pony in April of this year. We played two benefit shows, the Bobby Band. It was for teachers or something, it was great though. We played two nights and it was just... what a musical experience. That was thrill enough for me. So I guess I'm part of that.

What do you think about Asbury as far as a music scene?
It's awesome! I mean, it's got its own feeling. I guess we take it for granted around here. Everybody there - you can just cut it with a knife. It's a very positive feeling. When you go there and you play or you watch somebody else play, you can feel that everybody's got a kind of together-cohesive feeling about what it is.

That's so hard to come by. It's so important to have an identity like that. That's what it has and that's why it's lasted so long, and that's why it will last a long, long time to come.

49 Jody Joseph and the Average Joes

The hardest thing I do is get on that stage and do originals. And as much as I said, you're really tempted because, of course, people are going to respond to something they know. But then, who am I? I might just as well be a cover band. It's the hardest road to take.

--JODY JOSEPH

Jody Joseph shown performing at her adopted home - the Stone Pony. Photo © Gary Wien

J ody Joseph and the Average Joes remind you of what Jersey Shore music is all about. Each show contains the mixture of good blues, R&B, and rock and roll featuring the wonderful vocals and songwriting of Jody Joseph.

Jody is a veteran of the music industry who's been burned in the past, almost gave it all up but decided to keep fighting on and finally has a band that she can believe in. After being together for just a few months, the band found themselves in the finals of the Stone Pony "House Band Search", released the CD *Ain't Done Yet*, opened up for several national acts and have become a regular on the Jersey Shore club circuit.

I caught up with Jody Joseph and her band after they opened for Marah at the Stone Pony one night.

For a band that's has been together long, you've had some very good things happen quickly. You made the finals of the Stone Pony "House Band Search", you're up for an Asbury Music Award, and you've put out an album. What's been the highlight so far?
All of them. I think that the best and biggest highlight is that for the first time in my musical career I was able to get together with a group of guys that had the same hopes, same vision and did it for the love of music. They totally look at me with utmost respect. They're so good to me and it's something that enables us to be able to have what we have. It's really a family.

When I put them together, I said I'm not looking for a band I'm looking for a family. I'm looking for people that have the same exact ideas that I do. Not to go out there and say I want to be signed because I've done that. This is the first time in my life, after all the chasing of record companies, that I finally said I'm just gonna go out and play. Because that's what I want to do - I just want to play. And I think, because of the honesty of it and the genuineness, if there's such a word, that that's why it took it to the next level because nobody was so tense and so we've got to make it.

Is it different this time around? You've been on the industry side of it. Is it almost about just getting to back to the music this time?
Oh, absolutely. There's a lot of business involved because there has to be. We sell tickets and that's hard. The CDs... you've got to be on top of stuff as far as all the little administrative stuff, but basically it's a passion we all share. It's like I look at Tony (Amato) standing right next to me - that is the highest compliment that he already has done something and he's very talented and he has stepped on board for some of these bigger gigs for us. To me, that's a veteran musician/artist that has done that.

So, are you basically just recording because you want to record or are you looking for another record deal?

Well the next one that we're gonna be releasing is actually from the Stone Pony House Band Contest. We took it off the board. I don't think that you step away and when you step away from something for a moment and just allow things to evolve it will. I think we're going to shoot for more of an independent label than anything. I'm certainly not going to turn down an Atlantic Records.

I'm involving more with my music now with Dave Mack, who's our musical director. We're doing more of a bluesier slant. It's pushed more to the side that I'm about. It's evolving. The new songs are just so much truer - not that I say any of them on the last record that I don't feel good about. They're my babies.

Who are the people that you'd say are your major influences? The first time I saw you up there I did think of Janis Joplin.

Oh, wow! What a compliment. I would say I admired her life. I respected her for what she tried to do, but she also was very weathered at the time. She went against a lot of that. She went against all the record company crap. I think she's one. I take a little bit of the soul of a Stevie Nicks, only because I can see she's a poet. And then I think that it's a combination of everything else that's ever influenced me. Joni Mitchell, Melissa Etheridge, Etta James have all influenced me. I don't really think there's any one person I can hang it on, but I can tell you that you take and it just absorbs into you.

I notice that the artists you mention are all females. As a female performer, do you look more towards a female role model or is it just the music itself?

It's the music. I stand on that stage, Gary, and I look around - we're just beginning - and I say to myself how did I ever wind up back here again? By the grace of God or something or a lot of prayers, I don't know. But it is evolved because it's meant to at this time. I don't know how I would be ten years ago.

What is it about performing live that keeps bringing you back as opposed to just writing songs for other people?

Well, I would never have a problem with other people singing my songs. They're my children and they always will be. It doesn't matter who sings them. They're pieces of my life... pages. I've bled on them literally. That's pretty gross.

It's a good quote though...

Yeah. But I have no problem with someone else seeing that same side or saying wow that hits me. I would never turn that down. I'm not funny about that, but performing is just the biggest high that you can possibly have and the biggest low. Because you can be on stage and you can - I mean, we play some gigs like cover/original and we play to eleven people. We have learned over the last seven months how to internalize ourself, the band looks to each other and laugh it off. And so we've gotten a lot stronger. We're able to face eleven people where no one claps and so when we get up and we have this show at the Stone Pony with all this energy!

We've already done the crap gigs and we'll have many more to follow, but it's a high. It's an emotional high! It's not power, but it's just like you feel for a moment that they get it. They all get it. They're all there in your heart.

How often do you write songs?

As often as I can. I start out with titles and that's like the seed. I don't write it yet. It kind of stays with me for a while and I'll just keep it there and things just keep going and moving ahead and then all of a sudden when somebody in my studio starts playing something it's like there comes the title, there comes the melody, there comes the lyrics. When I come up with the title I know the song's written already. I know that sounds weird, but they are. In my head, it's already written. So a lot of times when you're hurting, unfortunately, I pick up a pen and write in journals. As often as I can.

How great is it to play a club like the Stone Pony where you can do your originals as opposed to doing a gig where they expect 70-80% cover music?

Basically I declined some management offers because they wanted no original songs. We book our own shows because I stick in about 40% of original stuff now. We're noted, people come out to hear these songs that they can't hear on the radio or whatever. But when you - I think the hardest thing is when you're up there sometimes and you're doing your originals you're basically naked. And some of the people in this room tonight never heard of me or my songs. It's like winning them over one at a time. You make your mark but you've got to be true to it. It's so hard sometimes you just want to break out and do a Janis tune. It's like, ok I'll do that. Adrian, my assistant stays very busy and a lot of people approached her tonight, "Who are they?"

Is it different when you're playing in a club that encourages originals?
Oh, I stay true to it. You have to. The hardest thing I do is get on that stage and do originals. And you're really tempted because, of course, people are going to respond to something they know. But then, who am I? I might just as well be a cover band. It's the hardest road to take.

It's like what about my original stuff? I'm not being true to it. So, I took the harder road. I've dropped out of a lot of my duo gigs - which are my money gigs - to take the band into these rooms and play. I'll take the band in and I'll say, "Alright, I'll take the cut. I don't care." You're getting out there. When you start thinking it's about the money then you better get the heck out of that.

You'd rather play a gig with the guts to do that than have people clapping along for a Beatles tune or Stones tune.
It is guts. I've done that for years. You sound great! You sing great! Oh my God, why aren't you out there? What with other people's songs? Ok. And the funny part about it is that I'm not looking to get signed because I'm not, I don't really care. I don't give a rat's ass. Don't book me. If I can't do this and I can't go to New York and do what's true to me...

For the first time in my life I stood up for my music. All the other times I've always bailed out or people bailed on me. More people bailed on me first. And then you sit there and you write a great song like "Insecurities." Well, I won't say it's great. Because that's what its about. I wanted to give up. I'm like who am I kidding? Two years ago, I was gonna give it up. I was gonna give it all up. It killed me.

How did you get through it?
I started writing again. Then I had an idea about nine months ago and that's when I started asking around and formed it. I've never been happier with my music in all the years I've been on stage or stuck in a little corner in a bar that they call a stage. Sometimes they just move two tables out of the way and that's your stage. I've never been happier.

Where did the name Average Joes come from?
We were rehearsing at Red Bank Rehearsal. This was before we became my own house band in my house. We're standing in the parking lot, it was freezing and everybody was going back and forth, back and forth with what do we call this band? What do we call it? And I said, "Guys would you really take offense if I said Average Joes? Because that's what you are to me you're my average Joes. You've all got day jobs, and I'm not trying to be twenty years old on stage."

It's almost like Dave wrote in the bio that I have. It gives me a disclaimer when I walk in the door. And that's the perfect way of putting it. It's like nobody's gonna expect anything crazy.

Your band made it all the way to the finals of the Stone Pony "House Band Search". Did you ever imagine that your band would be able to make it so far this fast?
Well, Dave was sitting next to me. I think I got up and walked right across the front of the stage. I kept walking until you caught me and took a picture. It was incredible! You're up against these baby bands. And here you are.

Did you really think that people wouldn't pick you because you guys were older?
No, actually - yes and no. We all thought about that. I guess amongst us, what we had decided was that you know what? We're going to go in and we're gonna do what we do best and that's it. If it sticks to the wall great, if it doesn't well we had a good time. And we all, we were just proud to be picked as one of the sixteen. I didn't think we were going to get down to the last five.

So, no, it was just everybody kept saying the same thing over and over. Joe, you just got to go in and do what you do. That's all we have. We're not young. We're not this, we're not that. We've got great songs, I believe. Good songs.

Tony Amato chimes in --- Great songs.

Great songs, thank you. I can't say that because I wrote them. I have some really great talent up there and when I'm on stage I own the stage. I live it, I wear it, I breathe it - it's mine. And that's all you can do. Am I gonna have a bunch of guys get on stage and dance around me? Take my shirt off - yeah, that will work! It's not about gimmick anymore. It's just not about gimmick. It's about the music.

It's like bringing it back. Asbury wants to do that, the Stone Pony wants to do that. They're stating it's about the music. Well, so be it then. And allow me the opportunity to let it be about the music.

50 Last Perfect Thing

This is like crucial decision making time. Like get a job, start your life or pursue your music and hope for the best. And as far as we're concerned we're gonna stick with it and ride it out as long as we possibly can.

--JOE PARASOLE

Last Perfect Thing shown rehearsing at the infamous Hot Dog House in Asbury Park. Photo © Gary Wien

L ast Perfect Thing is a band based in Asbury Park that has a sound based more in punk music than it does with traditional Asbury sounding bands. They've been around since 1998 and are a regular at clubs like the Stone Pony and the Saint.

In 2002, the band traveled to California for a few showcase gigs in front of record executives. It's easy to see why the band is getting noticed. They have an explosive live show with good lyrics and a good sound. The Asbury Music Awards named them Top Rock Band. This was the fourth Asbury Music Award for the band. And they capped off a great year with the release of their latest CD, *Without Justice* on WEMAKE Records with a record release party at the Stone Pony.

Last Perfect Thing really believes in their music. Although the band members are still relatively young, they've been honing their skills along the Jersey Shore for several years and are ready to take their act national. Judging by their popularity along the Shore, It's only a matter of time before they do.

I caught up with the band during one of their rehearsals at the Hot Dog House in Asbury Park. The interview contains comments from three of the four band members: Greg Wilkens, Joe Parasole and Justin.

You've been together since 1998. Your shows consists largely of original music. Does the band have one song writer or does everyone get involved?
Joe: It's a total democracy. It's gotta be. If it's split, it doesn't happen. Everyone votes on something. Everyone puts in something. Lyrics, music, rhythms, everything. It's either gonna be all unanimous or its not happening. So, I mean, we throw away a lot of stuff that way, but we also get exactly what we want that way.

How difficult do you think it is for a band to break on to the scene playing originals?
Joe: Well, it takes a lot of time. Some of the greatest bands don't get signed for years and years and years.
Justin: Or don't ever at all.
Joe: Or don't ever at all. And it takes commitment. Especially since we're all grown up, we're all at the age, well he's 21, the rest of us are gonna be 23. This is like crucial decision making time. Like get a job, start your life or pursue your music and hope for the best. And as far as we're concerned we're gonna stick with it and ride it out as long as we possibly can.
So the key is finding a bunch of guys who are all motivated and com-

mitted?

Joe: It's a hectic life living on the road. You've got to want it. Our bass player didn't want to do it.

Justin: Not knowing where you are, what day, what time... Constantly driving.

Joe: It's crazy. It's a crazy life, but if you really want it and you've got something solid going you've got to stick with it. It's all about perseverance. The band, Finger Eleven, I don't know if you've ever heard of them - nine years it took for them to get their first record deal.

Greg: I got to drive with the drummer from Dave Matthews once. I worked up at the Meadowlands and I was the production assistant and I got to drive him to the dentist. And the fact that he was just the most down-to-earth talk about anything kind of guy made me feel real comfortable talking to him and it made me feel real comfortable giving him our CD. And when I gave him the CD he said, "Wow, you guys will make it just because you're handing me a product that you've worked on." And that was refreshing to hear from someone who's hit stardom. He's a legend in my opinion. So it's good to get encouraging words from people. You can take it and use it to your advantage and it makes you work harder.

Well, it looks like you've got a good group of guys willing to make it work. What was the hardest thing about the early days?

Joe: We'd do anything to get a buck. Even just the exposure alone and trying to make money is the hardest thing to do with an original band. I mean, you could play in a cover band and make lots of money but something doesn't sit right when we're playing someone else's songs. Especially with a lot of bad music being on the radio right now. That's my personal opinion.

Justin: I'm not about it. I hate cover songs.

Is it tough bumping into a cover band? Does it bug you knowing that anyone can do that but you're trying to do something original?

Greg: I won't even lie, I'm not impressed by it. I think it's a complete joke and I don't understand that scene really.

Joe: Yeah, people in bars want to hear stuff they know, but that's more of a job for a lot of those musicians. It just pays the bills.

So it's a job versus art...

Joe: Yeah. What a lot of people do who try to get signed with their original music their whole lives - when it gets to that point they start a cover band and make some money.

Greg: I think Fuel was a cover band.

Joe: Godsmack was an Alice in Chains cover band.

Greg: It can open doors for you. At the same time, it can hurt you because you'll be playing all these other people's songs and you'll be doing so well and then they'll try to write originals.

Joe: And they try to write and it's just like where do we go from here?

Are you guys really trying to make a conscious effort to define a sound?

Joe: Yeah, basically just trying to write the best songs you can and if they're pretty good songs people are gonna listen to them and want to hear them. That's the bottom line. People are gonna buy your records. It's just you have to make yourself out there and available and playing and pushing yourself.

The band recently came back from California, were you out there doing play shows or just doing a little showcasing?

Greg: Showcases and we played with Sum 41. We played like a big expo, a dirt bike expo. So we got in front of some good crowds and, it's like Joe was saying, we're basically trying to not play so much around here because that can hurt you.

Joe: We did about six or seven of them. A couple majors, definitely good exposure, good experience, good environment. We were out there give or take 2 1/2 months total and it was good times. I love it out in California. The weather's unbelievable. The people are pretty cool. And it was definitely a pretty good experience. We met some good contacts that we'll be using with this next release.

What were the shows like?

Joe: We played one bar that was roughly ten people. They weren't too receptive at first, but as the set went on they kind of warmed to us. Sum 41 shows were off the hook. We played in Pomona at a place called the Glass House, which is a large venue. So it was cool. We went to "Price is Right."

When people think of Asbury Park they usually think of Springsteen, does that ever come up with you guys when you tell people where you're from?

Greg: No, if we go somewhere and we say we're from Asbury they're like, 'Oh, home of the boss, Stone Pony. Do you guys play there?'

Joe: No one makes any judgements.

What do you guys think about the Stone Pony?

Justin: It's worldwide. Tourists come to take pictures of it.

Joe: The place, in general, has been all totally redone and totally different. But it just rocks because it shows how it progressed. It's pretty cool.

Greg: And how it can't go away. It can't die. It's like no matter what has happened - the Pony would close down, but then it'd be back open and a little different. So I think its very persevering.

Last Perfect Thing has been in the studio finishing up another record. Wasn't it supposed to be out several months ago?

Justin: We had to take a couple of weeks off when Joe got hurt.

Joe: Yeah, I got my face busted. I got two plates and eight screws in my face. So that was a little set back.

Greg: We were trying to be peace makers at a party and these kids were trying to crash the party.

Joe: Things got out of hand, that's the way things go. That was a little bump for us.

How long did that set you back?

Joe: A solid three and a half weeks. I couldn't play. My face looked like a "Cabbage Patch Kid".

How's the studio thing been working other than the initial delays? How has it been compared to your other records?

Joe: We're a lot more together than we were for our last record at that point in time.

Greg: We were getting our CDs the day of the CD release show for our last album. And the first thing we did, a 4-song EP, they couldn't get them to us and they had to give us CD-R copies for the CD release. It's like we have this running order of last minute. So we're trying to avoid that this time.

You picked the Stone Pony for your CD release party. Any particular reason you chose to do it there?

Joe: It's the only place to have it. It's a great spot. It sounds great and looks great.

Greg: Good energy. We also play good there.

Joe: Solid-sized club. You can hear it. It's very important to hear good on stage and at the Pony we all hear everything that's going on. At least I do anyway. I'm the drummer and that's usually rough.

What do you think of the local music scene right now?

Joe: There's probably about fifteen solid bands in the Asbury Park area that play here in places like the Saint and the Pony and it's looking better than it has since roughly 1995. That's when things kind of quieted down. Now it's kind of picking up again.
Greg: Especially with the revitalization of Asbury.

You actually see that with what you're doing?
Greg: Yeah, I see it.
Joe: It's all down our street.
Greg: We're kind of right in the middle of it. And a lot of bands are getting more attention too so it's kind of like the timing is for everything.

How important is it when local bands get signed? Does that kind of help everybody?
Greg: I think so. It kind of puts us on the map.
Joe: It brings a lot of attention to New Jersey. Right now there's a lot of hot bands coming out of Jersey like Thursday. But its bringing the focus here and a long time ago the music focus was here too.
Greg: Asbury's always has kinda been the mecca. Obviously we know who put it on the map, but I think now, more than ever, it's gonna thrive. And if anyone's gonna look anywhere in Jersey it's gonna be here.
Joe: Especially with music. The Warped Tour started in 1995 with like 4,000 kids. Now they can barely hold it. There's 20-30,000 kids. And this place has been a band rehearsal place since I don't know.

What do you guys think? Is there enough clubs to get gigs or are you having a hard time?
Joe: We could use another solid one, but we've been playing the scene, we've been together for over four years now. We've been working it for a while so personally we're tending to start touring a little bit, get a little bit outside farther. Trying to find the Saint in Kentucky, you know. Just trying to progress.

Now is this record a lot different than what you've done before? Did you meet anyone on the west coast that's part of it?
Joe: Yeah, a management company out there took some interest and put us up, recorded us out there. He had a pretty solid engineer in the studio, but for the most part - he did very well by us it's just they didn't bite this time around. You've just got to be persistent and come out with something better. Our record now is nothing like the stuff we've put out.
  It's a different vibe. It's a lot more rock. Justin adds a whole new twist

to things.   He has a five string bass, just got low end. It's a lot more rocking. More rock than pop. The last album was kind of poppy.

Some of the reviews were calling it power pop.
Joe: Yeah, exactly. We're not a power pop band.   We're a rock band.

Do you want to be known more as a rock band or a punk band?
Joe: Yeah, you know, kids put so many different labels on things... I just call us a rock band. People will say oh, you're an emo band, you're a power band. Let them put their labels as they wish. What do you think?
Justin: Uh, leave it up to the scenesters to screw everything. That's all I can say about that.

Labels suck, but that's what draws the crowd so you don't have those ten people at a gig.
Joe: True. If you label us a rock band it's gonna bring a couple more... Different crowds.

So the plan is to start spreading out the touring?
Greg: Yeah, tour, tour, tour. We got a van, gonna get a trailer and hit the road. So that's the plan of attack.

Justin, you're the newest member of the band. Were you from here originally?
Justin: Yeah, most of my life. Until I was 15. I moved down to Northern Virginia. Right outside DC.

Were you in bands there?
Justin: Just Fair Weather. They just put out a new record. Very good stuff. We were out of Fairfax. There wasn't much there. We played more like up in Baltimore. We did a full US tour last summer.
Joe: I played drums with him, that's how we hooked up. I mean, we grew up together but we never played together until I filled in with his band.

What about you guys? Have you been in a bunch of bands?
Greg: Yeah, ever since because if it's all you want to do, it's all you're gonna do.
Joe: I've been in bands since I was 12. My second band was with Justin's older brother.

Is this the longest you've been in one band?

Greg: Yeah.

Joe: This is by far the longest. Besides this was like maybe two years.

Well, it must be nice that you're getting some notice notice around here as well. It's not the Grammies, but what was the Asbury Awards like?

Greg: Yeah, that's actually our fourth Asbury Award. They've got to come up with a venue for it. They should do it at the Paramount.

Justin: The Asbury Music Awards in Sea Bright. It doesn't make sense.

How does it feel to get that kind of notice in your home turf?

Greg: It's cool. This year we won top rock band.

Joe: It's pretty cool. When we were in the Press we had like a full-page layout in the Whatever section at one point! It was kind of cool because I know that all my teachers saw that and they're like oh great, he's not wasting his life doing nothing else. But school's not for us. Not for me anyway. He's got some kind of degree.

Greg: Brookdale Associates Degree... and he was collegiate.

Justin: I dropped out to come up here.

Joe: He dropped it for music. Like I said, it's commitment. If you're gonna start an original band and try to make a dent.

Greg: You have to have dedicated people and everyone has to be on the same mind track because that's the problem. There's lots of musicians, but then again there's everyday life. We've had this room and kind of made it a point to be here and to practice. We're together everyday. This is like our clubhouse. It's just kind of like we started it with one goal in mind and luckily we've been able to follow through on that so far.

Anything you want people to know about you?

Greg: We're just trying to say that music is a creation.

Joe: There's no bad side to it.

Greg: Definitely. It's like the eighth wonder of the world. It evokes emotion.

Joe: It's the yin and yang of everything.

Greg: It's like the last perfect thing. That's what it is. That's what our name is.

Joe: We're not the last perfect thing... music is.

51 Maybe Pete

I've had people tell us that we sound like everything from Bruce Springsteen to Elvis Costello to the New York Dolls, which I think is great. It's like, "Alright they get it." Because that's what I kind of what them to hear.

--FRANKIE MCGRATH

Frankie McGrath (left) and Marc Gambino (right) of Maybe Pete are shown playing at the Saint. Photo © Gary Wien

Maybe Pete is the latest in a long list of great Jersey rock and roll bands to find a home along the Shore. The band is based out of North Jersey, but has been playing clubs like the Saint and the Stone Pony on a regular basis. Maybe Pete was formed at the end of 2000 and includes the husband-wife team of Frankie and Kelly McGrath on guitar, Marc Gambino on bass and Sal DiMaria on drums.

The band's name comes from a line in the film *Almost Famous* where the character Jeff Bebe says, "No one can explain rock and roll, except for maybe Pete Townshend." Their music shows a variety of influences from the Replacements to Bruce Springsteen to the Rolling Stones and the New York Dolls. They may not be able to explain rock and roll, but they sure understand it.

I was able to talk with Frankie McGrath and Marc Gambino after a show at the Saint in Asbury Park to talk about this band on the rise.

Where are some of the places Maybe Pete has played so far?
Frankie: We've been together for about two years. We recorded our disc about a little over a year ago, sometime around Christmas 2001. We've played shows in Asbury at the Saint and the Stone Pony, in Hoboken at Maxwells and Love Sexy and played gigs in the city at places like Kenny's Castaways. We try to keep that whole New York to Asbury thing going and hit everything in between.

And you're in the process of recording again.
Frankie: Yeah, we started on some new tracks and hope to have something out as soon as possible. We'll probably shop it around. I mean, we've got nothing to lose. You hear some horror stories about people that shop stuff around and stuff...

So, you're a little wary of labels right now?
Frankie: I'm a little iffy right now. I mean, I've heard some good things. I've heard that the industry might be changing as far as nurturing artists and that kind of thing. The bottom line is that it's supposed to be fun. If anything else came from it that would obviously be more than welcome. At the same time, I don't want to set myself up for a letdown. But you only live once, so why not go for it right?

You guys have a very sharp, sound live. Have you had many bands in your career?
Marc: I've been in three bands. I was in one band for about 9 1/2 years. We even made it to like #3 on the import charts in the UK before things fell apart.

Frankie: I've been in four or five bands now. It's a pretty wide range of stuff. Everything from punk to some blues and straight ahead rock. There's a lot of different influences. This is where my heart is at and I hope that everything I listen to is represented and comes across in what we do. I've had people tell us that we sound like everything from Bruce Springsteen to Elvis Costello to the New York Dolls, which I think is great. It's like, "Alright they get it." Because that's what I kind of what them to hear.

Here's another name to add to that list... to me, you guys sound very much like a band that was around here a decade ago - James Deely & the Valiants.
Frankie: That's really cool that you say that because one of the bands I still play in is Bruce Tunkel's band. And, I guess Bruce and James Deely used to play together at the Green Parrot way back when. Bruce tells me all the time, after a couple of beers, he's like, "I wish you would have known Deely... You and Deely would have been best buddies."

What do you do with the comparisons to Springsteen? They've come and they'll probably keep coming.
Frankie: They have come. I mean, there's a part of me that welcomes it. I'm not going to deny that he's one of my biggest influences. But, at the same time, there's a lot of influences and you don't want to be pigeon-holed into one thing. I guess it happens. It's bound to happen in Jersey.

Do you ever try playing away from Asbury to get away from it?
Frankie: Not really, I want to spread it out. You hope to make something happen up and down the East Coast. We just played in Philly for the first time a couple of weeks ago, I'd like to hit Boston eventually. Again, I'm not going to deny that I'm a die-hard Springsteen fan, but I'm also a die-hard Stones fan and a die-hard fan of a lot of bands.

Have there been any shows that really stand out with this band?
Marc: We played Kenny's Castaways in Manhattan. They're in a weird period where they have a cover band come in and take over the stage from 12:30 a.m. on and that's kind of like the headliner, but there's three or four original bands on before that. It's really about whoever draws the most or makes a connection with the crowd. We played there a few days before September 11th and it was just a magical night. There were hardly any of our own people there, but we just made the connection with everybody who was there. But that wasn't the night...

It was about a month after September 11th that we came back again. It was packed. People were out and it was just such a good thing to see people out at a club again having a good time. Frankie was winging CDs up to the people in the balconies and stuff. He said something to the effect that "it was nice to see people out again and having a good time after everything that had happened."

Frankie: For me, it's probably when we played the Saint in January. We opened for Jason Ringenberg from Jason & the Scorchers. We got to open for him and back him up on three songs. It was like we did our set and then we closed out his set. It seemed to go over really well. I thought we played a great set, his set was great and then when he pulled us back up it just felt like one of those magical nights that should happen in Asbury Park. Everything just clicked and everybody seemed to dig it. Jason was a great guy and I was very proud of my band because we stepped up and rocked with someone else. That was a departure for us because we're just so used to playing our own tunes. And I thought we nailed it! It made me feel really good.

What would you say Asbury Park music means to you?
Frankie: Wow... what does Asbury Park music mean to me? One of my biggest influences in the world was Little Steven. As much as I'm a die-hard Bruce fan, a lot of people will argue that Little Steven is the one that created the "Asbury Park Sound" and I kind of swear by that myself. Steven's one of those guys who I kind of model our band after as far as doing the straight ahead rock or the punk rock, the political rock, dance music or R&B. He's a great producer, songwriter... the whole works. If that's the "Asbury Park Sound" than it's like sacred territory, you know.

How would you describe the band's music?
Marc: Punk with an edge and catchy.

Frankie: Nice... Yeah, pop, punk, folk, Jersey, downtown New York City all wrapped into one... I hope. On our good nights we're doing it well.

What are you hoping to do with this band?
Marc: I just want to make a connection man. That's what it's all about to me. If I'm going out and playing and I'm looking out into the crowd I just want to see that there's some kind of interaction going on. That somebody's going home and thinking about us, maybe talking about us and having a good time when they see us. That's the only thing that matters.

52 Matt Witte & the New Blood Revival

I don't know if it's marketable. We're definitely not what you hear on the radio right now.   As far as being marketable, I think anything's marketable.

--MATT WITTE

Matt Witte and the New Blood Revival are shown performing on the Stone Pony's outdoor stage during *The Rising* release party. Photo © Gary Wien

Matt Witte just might be one of the most exciting artists to come out of the Jersey Shore in decades. He's known as a brilliant songwriter and tremendous live performer but what really sets him apart from others is the type of music that he plays. Matt infuses bluegrass and country influences with folk, punk and rock and roll. The result is a sound not heard around the Shore for some time.

The New Blood Revival is Matt's band. They've been building a following throughout the New Jersey/New York area from New Brunswick to the Jersey Shore; from Hoboken to New York City. They have played such well-known clubs as the Stone Pony, Maxwell's and the Bitter End.

Last year the band dominated the Asbury Music Awards winning five different awards: Top Roots Band, Top Live Performance, Listeners Choice Award and Top Record Release. In addition, Matt took home Top Male Vocalist honors.

With seven independent records already released we knew it was only a matter of time before Matt signed with a major label. Sure enough, he signed with Atlantic Records in March, 2003. I caught up with Matt during a solo show in New Brunswick to learn more about this rising star.

When did the New Blood Revival get together?
About two and a half years ago. I started playing New Brunswick acoustically about four years ago and then I met all these guys through other bands and bands breaking up. That's how we all got together. It was all based in acoustic singer-songwriter stuff, but then I met these guys and changed it.

I lived in Hawaii before I came here. There really wasn't a lot of bands to play in there. When I came here I started playing at the Harvest Moon on Monday nights. Nobody really came or anything but I started getting a small following. I wasn't really used to playing before a crowd. Then the rest of the guys started playing with me. They all came from different bands and I think that helped a lot because all of sudden there was a crowd in front of us.

Your music has been called everything from "funky, contagious folk" to "sexually-charged storytelling." How would you describe your music?
It's not really folk right now. I have a bunch of different stuff going on. I have a bluegrass thing which is called Possom. Then I'm playing with the Pumps, which is more acoustic material than what we're doing with the band and the horn section. And then there's the New Blood Revival, which is our big band.

The New Blood Revival is mostly electric now. It's a little bit louder, a lot louder than the other stuff. And so, I don't know if it's sexual. I mean, some of the older stuff definitely is. It's all stories. Sometimes sexuality is kind of a metaphor in a sense and then sometimes it's just blatant. It's whatever it says. It's a little bit of everything.

I listen mostly to really old stuff from the 20s and 30s. That's what inspires a lot of this stuff but we do everything now from swing to just about anything.

Are you actually hearing the music like on 78s or are you reading the sheet music?
All the stuff that's on 78s are on CDs now. I don't read music at all. So, it's just CDs and records. I have a lot of vinyl. The band can go anywhere. Everybody listens to everything, so there's no specific style.

How did you first become interested in that type of music?
I probably started listening when I was 18 or 19. I didn't grow up on it. I just always liked that style of guitar playing and I would hang out with people who knew more about it than I did. Even the people that I'm playing with now in Possom, they're a generation ahead of me so I learn a lot from them. I guess it started about ten years ago, that's how I got into all that stuff.

What do you like best about the music of that period?
It's really natural sounding. I like the arrangements, the chord structure, the way the song moves. And I like the country/blues progressions a lot too. It's just very real to me. I'm not from that time period. I'm not trying to replicate it or anything like that, I just like the way it sounds and I like to play that style.

I love the different styles of singing, nobody sounds the same. Everybody's got a very different sound to something that they're doing, which is relatively similar but varies from one county to the next. It's just a cool kind of music that's all. The only reason I like it is for the fact that it sounds really good and real.

You've got so many different styles of music right now. Are you ever afraid a record label will want you to go in one particular direction? Is what you're trying to do marketable?
I don't know if it's marketable. We're definitely not what you hear on the radio right now. As far as being marketable, I think anything's marketable. I think that if you go back the right way anything can be marketable.

We're not really like what's going on right now but hopefully we'll be able to acquire a pretty decent audience if we start touring on a regular basis and get some support.

Have you tried big-time touring yet?
Not really. It's mostly like small trips that work out. Well, financially they're disasters but they work out musically I guess. We want to take it national. We'll play anywhere... open for people. I honestly don't know what we're gonna do but the next step is definitely getting on the road. From there I don't know. I'm not sure where it's gonna take us.

The nice thing about us is that even though you might not be able to find something specific to define as a category we can play a lot of different venues or open up for a lot of different people. We're neither here nor there, you know. So, that's nice I guess. I mean, we could even open for a country band... old country not the new country.

Country music gets a bad rap... At least, I think it does. I'm a big Hank Williams fan. I like Pierce, Buck Owens, Jimmy Rodgers, Ernest Tubb. That stuff is killer. New country I like Hank Williams III. He does that punk rock thing and old country. He's very anti-Nashville. He's cool. I'm not into that new country stuff.

Do you ever think it might be easier for the band to get noticed if you moved to a more country atmosphere like Nashville?
No, because in Nashville they really know what they're doing! Here in New Jersey I can fake it alright. That's why we're not a bunch of strummers on stage. As far as what we're doing with the country stuff there's a lot of fast finger-picking, Danny's chicken pick, he's a flat picker... really, really good. And I'm a finger picker. So, if we went down there that's how we would be. But it wouldn't even happen, we wouldn't move there now, Nashville is more new country right now. I don't think we would fit in with what they're doing.

I read a review online where you were called a "lyrical genius."
I don't think it's like that. No, it's not like that.

Are you a writer who plays or a musician that writes?
I try to do both. It's pretty much even. I love playing the guitar too. I play a lot of guitar except when I'm with the New Blood Revival where I don't play as much guitar because we've got Danny Wacker. But I'd like to be good at both. There's a long way to go, there's a lot I have to learn and a lot of people I can learn from.

Everyday, it's like you're never completely happy with your playing and your writing. When I listen to it, I hear where I've gone from this point to that point. It's writing stories. I always think that somebody will eventually catch on like all he's doing is writing stories and stuff. Some of it is from conversations I've had, nothing is so thought out. A lot of it is written fast and furiously. It's all got a flow to it. It can't sit too long otherwise it will just die. Everything that I do I try to keep it going relatively fast and finish it. I commit myself to finish it.

Tell me about some of the records you've got out.
We've got 7 CDs but two of them we haven't really been able to print so I'm just giving out the discs. Those are the most recent and those are my favorites. They're really cool. We recorded everything in a couple of days so it's got a really nice live feel. It's my favorite stuff to date. Some of it's electric and some is acoustic. It's more mellow than the other stuff.

Was there anything behind the band's name?
Well it's like a blood transfusion, I guess you could look at it like that. It's nothing too deep or anything. I heard there are some rock stars that pollute themselves to the point where they have to get a complete blood transfusion. There's like a place in Sweden or something that does it. What they do is they take the old blood out and pump new blood in. They can't do it in the United States, it's illegal or whatever. But they go and they take all the blood out and get basically new blood and that's how they continue to live the lifestyle that they've had.

I've heard stories like that. I don't know if it's true but it's funny anyway. So that's what we're doing. Nothing is coming from me just sitting there and saying, "Oh, I'm gonna write a different style of music." It's just all old stuff that we're trying to revive not for any reason other than we love the way it sounds and we don't want it to die. But it's not dying, it's doing really well right now, I think. We're relatively young and we're playing old music. It's pretty simple. The blood transfusion thing I think is cool.

You have a following along the Shore and New Brunswick. Is it kind of a mutual scene?
Yeah, it definitely is because everybody gets along. We do events and everybody comes from north and south. It's always a good time. They seem to all get along with each other. Our crowd is our crowd. If it's light it's still a mix. I mean, when we play New Brunswick we probably don't get anybody from the Shore, but when we play the Shore we get people from New Brunswick and the Shore.

How do you see the New Brunswick scene right now?
I don't think New Brunswick is very accommodating right now to a lot of the bands that made it a good town. When I first came here there was a lot of good bands playing places from the Melody to the Budapest. All of the places had really good bands all of the time. And now, some of them are still open but the Melody's gone, the Roxy has been gone for a while. You have all these great hardcore bands, punk rock bands and others that are running out of places for them to play. And that was always the best music that came out of New Brunswick.

What do you think of the music scene all over Jersey right now?
There's a lot of talented people. I've met some of the most talented people I've ever met in New Jersey. People that I've played with, people that I don't play with anymore - just all around. So I think it's a really good place for music. I think it's just a matter of finding it. A lot of people that are really good aren't playing out.

How hard is it for bands to get noticed by the clubs?
Reputation. Build a following and then open for somebody else and prove you can bring people in. And sometimes it's hit or miss. We want to bring people in all the time, but we can't always do it. The Stone Pony has been really good to us. They appreciate music and they've been really, really good to us. It's one of our favorite places to play. It's got a lot of history. I used to come here when I was younger, before it looked this nice, but it still had a good vibe then.

Do you think there's too many bars looking for cover bands?
I think a lot of it is due to the fact that the bars have to be accommodating to the people down from up north, from New York or whatever, that want to see cover bands. And there's nothing wrong with any of that. It's just that's what thrives. I mean, we couldn't make it playing D'Jais. Nobody would come to see us. We couldn't play Bar Anticipation, I don't think anybody would come honestly. And there's nothing wrong with those places.

New Jersey is notorious for cover bands. A lot of cool things come out of here, I think New Jersey gets a bad rap.

53 DeSol

What it sounds like to me is that it speaks culture. It's actually more of a message than a sound because you walk away with a lot of different visions. Lots of different images like Latin America, indigenous people and family.

--ALBIE MONTERROSA

DeSol performs at Harry's Roadhouse, one of the newest clubs in Asbury Park, located a stone's throw from the old Upstage. Photo © Gary Wien

T he faces along the Jersey Shore have been changing as more and more ethnicities settle down here. In recent years, Spanish food markets and restaurants have opened and conversations can regularly be heard in languages other than English. So it should come as no surprise that one of the most interesting bands to hit the area in some time contains a strong Latin American influence.

DeSol plays a blend of rock and roll with Latin beats and Spanish lyrics weaved alongside those sung in English. Their weekly gig at Harry's Roadhouse (a stone's throw away from the old Upstage) bring people of all color and races together on the dance floor in a scene that is very reminiscent of the mid-70s when Southside Johnny & the Asbury Jukes used to play across town.

DeSol is led by Albie Monterrosa, the band's lead singer and songwriter. The band put out a record, largely comprised of demos, which led to a major label record deal. I had the chance to talk with Albie Monterrosa via phone to discuss the band that just might represent the "New Asbury Sound" better than anyone.

DeSol really reminds me of an updated version of Southside Johnny & the Asbury Jukes. With the increasing Latino population around the area, you're like the new face of Asbury.
Wow! That's nice. I was hoping you'd say Springsteen and the E Street Band, but I could settle for Southside! *(laughing)* I'm joking, of course.

People have told me that back in the 70s when Southside played the Pony each week, the place was packed with everybody dancing and when I first saw DeSol at Harry's Roadhouse it was just like that.
Wow, that's cool man because a lot of what we pull from, especially me from the pop world, is the old school, the movement that happened in those days. It was a movement that is not seen and hasn't been seen in a while. Maybe the last movement was the Nirvana thing or the rap thing in the 80s. But as far as a rock thing, there really hasn't been a movement like that. We pull from that and it's nice that you relate us to that. It's like circles, everything happens again and again.

What do you think of the new clubs in Asbury Park like Harry's Roadhouse?
I love it man! I think it brings new blood. I'm not putting the Pony down, I like the Stone Pony, but I wasn't attached to the Pony. I came from Queens and I didn't know much about the place. You guys like die for the Pony around here and I'm cool with that. I support it, but I think it's good to have new blood as well.

When you hear DeSol's music you hear a lot of different sounds. How would you describe what the band sounds like?

Oh my God, what DeSol sounds like? That's a good question. What it sounds like to me is that it speaks culture. It's actually more of a message than a sound because you walk away with a lot of different visions. Lots of different images like Latin America, indigenous people and family. Latinos have such big families. I went to my Grandmother's 90th birthday and it was just a get together of probably 120 members of my family. Everybody's a cousin. People walk away with that warm feeling like when you walk into a Latino's house. That's what you get.

But as far as the sound, these rhythms are old man. They're old, they're from Africa. They come from Africa literally and move to the Caribbean. That's why they call it Afro-Cuban. When you play these rhythms they open up the doorways to the ancient people, the ancestors. I think that's involved in everybody's spirit. It's innate in everyone. I guess we have a key for that when we play the rhythms. That's why everybody's up there celebrating, dancing and getting involved with it.

Was this the first time that you really tried bringing Latin elements to rock and roll?

Absolutely. I was born in Queens, New York and spent 20 years there. I moved here eight years ago and started doing the rock and roll thing around and it didn't work. I actually took a hiatus because I was trying to figure out what was next for me. I wanted to make a career out of my music. So, I went out to St. John's, Virgin Islands with a few friends and found a Latina there, a Puerto Rican girl named Wanda. I spent two months with her just jamming. She showed me a lot of the rhythms.

A lot of the rhythms I had grown up with but had never seen anybody really play, or at least never in the rock way. With her, I was jamming to stuff I had. There's one song "Spin Around" that we still play that I wrote a few years back and I was like, "Wow, these Latin rhythms, these Salsa rhythms will fit, I just have to tweak a rhythm here maybe a vocal there." So, when I came back home I said, "I've really got to find something because this is what I'm gonna do."

There's a big crossover possibility. My parents are from El Salvador. Mother always asked me to sing in Spanish. When I came back I told Ma that this was my next step. I said, "If it doesn't work this way, I guess I'll hang it up and try something else." So, I got the guys together and it all equaled DeSol. It's the first time I tried and it's been a year and a half, almost two years that we've been doing this and we're about to sign a nice little record deal for us and spread this worldwide hopefully.

When the band first began, was it difficult to get gigs or did people understand what you were doing right away?
They accepted it right away. You know what? The people accept it but the record people don't. We've had everybody and their mother come out and it's funny because you hear the same old cliches. "You're not Spanish enough, you're not American enough, we don't know where to put you; you're a niche band, you're in a gray area." All of that bullshit.

I know it's gonna blow up huge in every market. The people accept it and it shows at the gigs. People of all walks of life, all different religions, ethnicities, ages. There's 45-year olds to 22-year olds. That's what makes me believe that it can blow up. The people accepted it right away. The labels didn't accept it because they're business people not artists, I guess. They want to know what worked in the past and Santana's probably the only thing they can relate us to.

You weave English and Spanish lyrics into your songs. How do you decide which way to write a particular line?
I think that as a writer if I'm stuck on a lyric maybe I try to put a Spanish lyric in there. That's a good question. I don't really know how I do it. It just flies out where I feel naturally. I like to put a Spanglish spin on every song like maybe a Spanish line or Spanish chant or something. But, at the same time, I don't want to totally saturate it with the Spanish language. I was born in this country. My first language was Spanish, but then growing up and going to school English becomes your first language after that. I guess I write where it feels right. I always in my head say I want to definitely put a Spanish line in there.

It seems like we're seeing a change along the Shore with Spanish restaurants and shops. It's like you guys are hitting at the right time.
I think so man. I think so in the whole world. It's society. And it's kind of funny because I think the white or Anglo audience actually responds more than the Latino audience sometimes. The Latino audience is used to it and it's kicked a little new, a little different than they're used to. A lot of Latinos stick with their Salsa, straight-up folk Mexican music and DeSol comes out and we spin it a little different. They're into it, but not as much as the white audience for some reason. I think it's fresh for the white audience. Well, let me say the American audience, because what we're used to hearing on the radio is just so boring now. It's just the same shit. They definitely get into it. It's still a little new for them. This band is a grass roots band, it really is. I see it growing, flourishing. And I want to spread it to everyone.

54 JPAT

I wouldn't necessarily call Secret Sound a jam band, but sometimes I do when I can't search for anything else. A lot of times I'll say, "We get down." It's like what do you guys do? "Oh, we get down. We play a little funk, a little jazz, a little blues... but not in that order."

--JPAT

James P. Dalton Jr. (JPAT) waits in the wings for his chance to get on stage with Nicole Atkins at the Stone Pony. Photo © Gary Wien

J ames P. Dalton Jr., or JPAT as he's known, is one of the most interesting musicians along the Jersey Shore. An extremely talented singer-songwriter, he plays guitar, mandolin and harmonica and brings back the spirit of the Upstage Club to Asbury Park. Since there no longer is a place like Upstage where young musicians can go and jam, he's created his own version of that club. One night you might see him adding mandolin to the songs of Nicole Atkins, the next night he might be playing harp with Matt Witte. He's known throughout the musical community and he's jammed with just about everybody.

Outside of his solo career his focus is with the band Secret Sound and his shows with Josh Zandman. Secret Sound is a popular "jam band" around the Shore. They've had house gigs at the Saint and have played the Stone Pony plenty of times. Josh Zandman is a singer-songwriter who has peaked the interest of several record labels.

I caught up with JPAT on the boardwalk in Belmar where we talked about the Asbury music scene from an insider's perspective. And you don't get more inside the scene than JPAT.

Back in the old days the musicians would jam at the Upstage Club. You're kind of keeping that spirit alive by jamming all over the place.
I have a lot of friends that play music around here and there's a lot of guys I go and jam with. That's the great thing about Asbury Park right now, there's tons of people playing and since I live around here I know everybody. Basically, it's if it wasn't like somebody saying, "Dude I heard you play harmonica, do you want to come play?" I would say to them, "When are you gonna let me sit in with you guys and fool around a bit?" I just try to play with everybody because that's what really makes me happy.

How did you get involved with the mandolin?
Actually, I'm a bad guitar player. So, basically what happened was that I was dating this girl a few years ago and somebody at the house she was staying at left a mandolin there after a party. I picked it up and started fooling around with it and said, "I can make this work!" So I asked the girl if I could I borrow it? She said, "Yeah, just bring it back."

So, I went out and got a book, tuned it and just started playing. I actually took it out later that week to play a gig with it. I really didn't know how to play it, but I made something happen.

So there's hope for bad guitarists?
Yes, there is hope.

Is it almost like playing with a 12-string guitar? I mean, is it hard to make it sound bad?

No, it can sound bad. It really can. The thing about the mandolin is you don't need to play a lot of it. The novelty of the instrument, a lot of times, is that is just has to be there. You only need to strum a little bit and it sounds nice. So, I put subtle touches on things and that's what I do with the harmonica as well. When I play with all these different people I know that I can't try to be a giant foundation to a song, I've got to add touches or add a little color. Mandolin is the perfect instrument for that because you don't need to be too loud or too big, you just have to sound nice a bit. Just a couple of notes here and there to break the chords up.

So, that's how I got into playing mandolin. I would bring it anywhere and play with anybody that would have me. And that's what I do with the harmonica, I ask everybody can I play? I mean, I'm a singer and that's what I do but years ago I was really self-conscious about being good enough to be just a singer. The music that I listened to was bands like the Allman Brothers, Phish and Pink Floyd, which has everyone in the band playing an instrument. So, I thought I had better get myself an instrument as well.

I can't remember the last time I saw a mandolin on the Shore.

Yeah, there's not many. I'm one of the only games in town.

What do you think of the Asbury Park music scene right now? It seems like we've got some action around here again...

I think it's fantastic! A lot of people will argue with me, but I don't think they want to admit that things are going our way. There's a lot of bands signing major deals. It's crazy right now. All of the old school is getting looked at and, at the same time, you've got guys like Matt Witte, Borealis, who's a completely untraditional Asbury Park sound and Sprout. Sprout's not a band that you would think would come from Asbury Park or would be a Stone Pony house band, but they are, and that's what excites me.

There are bands coming out of here now and just a lot of really good players. New Jersey's been a hotbed for years that no one's ever noticed because everyone seems to go to New York. It's like everyone forgets they lived and grew up here, even though they made it big in New York.

I just see it as a great time. People can argue that bands signing deals is not what makes a good scene, but when you go to the Asbury Music Awards there's a ton of bands in the audience and they're just applauding like crazy for each other. Everybody knows everybody and that's what matters. That's what excites me.

Do you think there are enough clubs around here?
I think there's plenty. The one thing people need to do is support the venues that are there, places like Crossroads and the Saint specifically. The Saint's a fabulous venue. The Stone Pony is a great venue. There's enough clubs that people don't need to try building many more. But, hey if they want to build more that's fine too...

Are there enough places where you're confident you can play a show built around original music?
I think there are. There's a ton of places in the Jersey Shore area that already cater to the bands that are bringing covers in, but there aren't many in Asbury Park. The covers aren't really brewing there. I mean, no one's really doing Jimmy Buffet in Asbury Park.

What's your favorite place to play around here?
I like the Stone Pony. It's a big room, big stage, lots of space, the sound system's good and the stage is comfortable. I also like playing the Saint. I can really hear myself well there, but the stage is tight. I've got five guys in Secret Sound along with me and one of them plays a lot of keyboards, which takes a lot of room.

When you're playing originals around here you've got to showcase if you're on a bill where it's not just you all night. Opening bands at the Pony get about 45 minutes to be really good. You can't drop the ball on any song, you've got to play your strongest material everytime you're there. It can be stressful but I really dig the Pony having played there so much, and having worked there for a little while, it's kinda like hanging out with friends.

Every place has something special about it. The Saint brings in a lot of the newer names that were nobodies in 1995 but are big today. It's one of those little rooms that are all over the country. Rooms where if you sell all your tickets and 20 people show it makes for a full house. At the Pony if you've got 20 people in the room you're not getting hired again!

The Saint gives everybody the idea that they could own a bar someday. It's like, 'This place isn't much bigger than my living room.'
Well, that's the great thing about it. We were spending so much time trying to sell tickets and drag 100 people to a show every month. I'm glad we did those shows because we learned a lot and we opened up for a ton of big names, but we'd go in and there's this stress of did we bring enough people? Have all of our people shown up yet? Did every song sound good during the 45 minutes we were allocated? At the Saint, we can just relax, play a set and jam.

What do you think of the title "jam band?" Would you call Secret Sound a jam band?
There's about a zillion styles of music involving improvisation. Jam band basically means any combination of the styles where improvisation is the most important thing. I wouldn't necessarily call Secret Sound a jam band, but sometimes I do when I can't search for anything else. A lot of times I'll say, "We get down." It's like what do you guys do? "Oh, we get down. We play a little funk, a little jazz, a little blues... not in that order." I think the safe thing about being a jam band is that we can really do anything. We can play whatever we want.

So jam band is like a way to categorize the uncategorizable?
Exactly! The only thing a jam band does is improvise. Sometimes we improvise a little and sometimes we improvise a lot. So the term jam band is really the safest way to describe us. I don't think it's a bad term. A lot of people use it nastily and sometimes it comes out derogatory because there's a lot of stereotypical bands that try to sound like they're a jam band. We like funk and jazz and blues and other things that involve improvisation, so we just sort of fell right in to that kind of market.

That improvisation sounds similar to the music that was around at the Upstage. How would you describe the jam band scene now?
Well, it's just starting to come along. The one guy that has been spearheading that is Kyle Brendle. He was the guy that really said, "Look Stone Pony you need to do this." It was like, "We're going to do this night and that night and these are going to be our regular nights."

I think it's being accepted because it's good music. It's not just Solar Circus, which was the only band for a long time. It's gotten to the point where people are seeing beyond the "oh, that's a Grateful Dead cover band." There's actually bands that fall into the jam band world that hate the Grateful Dead and hate Phish and hate anything to do with any of the bands that the people that listened to them did. There are even some bands playing electronic music like techno and drum 'n bass and sounding like DJs.

Is there a danger for you to be guesting with so many artists?
I'm seeking a life in music. Well, I live a life of music, but I want to seek a living as well. I want something to move forward in a position where that will be my job. Sometimes when I'm playing with a zillion bands the mentality is that I'm having a really good time playing but there's also the mentality of well this guy might take off and so might that guy.

Playing with anybody on any stage from a business standpoint is good for business. It's always good to be out there playing with other people. It's also good for my reputation so to speak. Any guy that's playing music not just for fun, which is what I'm doing, has to keep all that stuff in mind. I'm an idealist, but I also have to be a businessman. I have to be considerate of finances as well. I can't run around and sit in with everybody all of the time. I need paying gigs too.

Sounds like you just really love music...

Music today is brilliant... it's wonderful. I can't bear listening to people when they say, "The music scene sucks, it's not as cool as it was in the sixties. Where's our Jimi Hendrix? Our Janis?" I believe they're all around us. With the way the world is now I can listen to any kind of music I want to at any given time. Great music is everywhere and you don't even have to look that hard to find it.

I don't drink so I can't just get drunk and go to a show and be impressed. I'm a really critical bastard! I stand absolutely still when I see a band. I'll stand about four feet away from the stage with people dancing all around me and I'll just stare. The drummer from Brown once told me, "Man, when you were watching us I didn't know whether we did something really bad or we did something really good." That's the way I am. I'll stand and watch and I won't move. I'll watch what everybody's doing. I'll listen to every part of the song... I care.

One of the great things about Asbury now is that a lot of the emphasis has been put on the local history. People are really looking at what happened within the past such as the Bruce days and stuff. And more than ever people around here are finding it easier to do that. With things like the Internet you can look into the past and also kind of look towards the future and see how things are going to sound. I dig into everything. I dig into old jazz tunes, old blues guys, folk music. I take the old and the future comes out later for me. Bands are building up now from listening to all that stuff and pointing it to a new direction. I've been loosely calling it the "New Asbury Sound" because it just means it's coming out of here. It doesn't sound like anything that came from here before.

55 Why Asbury Park?

It's hard to believe that there are people that come from around the world to take their picture in front of the Pony. But people are hungry for the old Asbury Park and there's not much of it left.

--KATE MELLINA
ASBURY PARK COUNCILWOMAN

Max Weinberg is shown with 100 European music fans in front of Convention Hall. Photo © Debra L. Rothenberg/rothenbergphoto.com

E ver since Bruce Springsteen released *Born To Run* and became a household name, music fans have traveled to Asbury Park to learn more about the town. They came to see the Palace, the boardwalk and the rides and to hear Madam Marie tell their future. They came to have a drink at the Stone Pony and see shows at Convention Hall. They came to imagine they were cruising down the circuit on a Saturday night. And, even after the rides disappeared and Madam Marie left town, the fans kept coming.

People in New Jersey sometimes have a difficult time understanding how a decrepit, abandoned beach town could have such meaning for others. While locals pass signs for Asbury Park and Freehold every day, fans from around the world actually take pictures of such signs. They plan vacations to the Jersey Shore just to see the images from their favorite songs come alive.

"It's hard to believe that there are people that come from around the world to take their picture in front of the Pony," said Kate Mellina, Asbury Park Councilwoman. "But people are hungry for the old Asbury Park and there's not much of it left. The day they said the Palace would be torn down, I sat across the street and cried because I always thought it was such a goofy, kitschy place."

During the brief period of time in which the Asbury Park Rock 'N Roll Museum was open, thousands of visitors from around the globe came to learn more about their favorite artists. It's a shame that the museum never made it to the Internet age. The museum could easily have double or tripled the amount of visitors each year with the added exposure.

Mellina herself has first hand experience of seeing the Asbury Park music phenomenon. Before becoming a Councilwoman she owned Cleopatra Steps Out, an art gallery in downtown Asbury. As luck would have it, the gallery was across from where the Upstage once stood. On several occasions, she saw buses of tourists from Europe stop and start walking around in awe. Many would enter her shop hoping to buy souvenirs, anything that said Bruce Springsteen or Asbury Park.

Bruce Springsteen and Southside Johnny are so closely related to Asbury Park that it's only natural to see fans throughout the city. It's rare to see an artist and a place so intertwined. Yet, neither Asbury Park nor Monmouth County nor New Jersey has ever tried reaching out to music tourists. But that may change sometime soon. On April 26, 2002, a group of music fans from Europe held a meeting at the Asbury Park Library to show how Asbury Park and the surrounding area could benefit from music tourism. Speakers included Maggie Powell, Bob Stewart, Numa Saisselin, Kate Mellina, Jane McGreery, Colleen Sheehy and Simon Osbourne.

"I got involved in the music tourism project mainly because I believe strongly that Monmouth County should be doing more to promote its unique wealth of musical heritage," said Maggie Powell, a noted rock and roll journalist from Germany. "The event was well attended by people from local and state level offices, local businesses and other key areas that would benefit from a successful music tourist industry. It was also featured on News 12 who came out with us on a whistle stop tour of some of the area's most famous places and landmarks.

"To a degree, I felt like some of what I said at the conference was 'stating the obvious,' but nevertheless, I believed I had something constructive to say and I was very glad to have had an opportunity to do so in front of such an appreciative and influential audience. And I figured if people did realize that tourists were coming for music reasons there wouldn't be any need for a meeting!"

Simon Osbourne is a property manager for the National Trust in Liverpool and is responsible for the former homes of Sir Paul McCartney and the late John Lennon. He pointed out how Liverpool had neglected the impact fans of the Beatles had on tourism in the area for a long time. But, in recent years, the city has found ways to use it to boost the amount of revenue brought in by tourism. The city now holds numerous special events and tours designed for the music fan. He believes that Asbury Park could do the same. Although, he stressed the importance of not making the same mistake that Liverpool when it destroyed the Cavern Club. Asbury Park needs to keep places like the Stone Pony and the Palace intact.

The meeting received coverage in newspapers throughout the world. That, coupled with the Today Show broadcasting Bruce Springsteen's kickoff to *The Rising* tour, showed how vital the link between Asbury Park and music really is. For many music fans, that link is as strong as ever.

"I arrived in Asbury Park on a rainy Sunday in April," said Caz from the UK. "I walked down the boardwalk with tears in my eyes... I just couldn't believe I was finally here. It was like being in a dream. It was a very emotional moment."

Giacorno Squintani, is a music fan from Europe and the creator of *Let The Story Be Told*, a fanzine about Joe D'Urso. He recalls his seeing Asbury Park for the first time in 1999. "The first words that came to my mind were welcome to Beirut," he said. "We were walking around the town, about 200 of us, and a kid shouted across the street to us, 'Why do you come here? There's nothing to see.' Not your average tourist catch phrase but what was even more stunning was that the same thing happened when I returned for the second time in 2000.

"Now I don't know if it's just coincidence, but on my last two visits that has not happened. I have been getting a more positive vibe on these trips. Although, admittedly, visually there is still little to be shown for the changes in the way the city is run. I understand it's on the up and I want to believe that's the case. It's a town that needs to strike the right balance between making the most of its musical past, which, in terms of tourism assets, is certainly its greatest. Looking to the future, you really wonder sometimes how much help that town needs before it can get itself on its feet again. But, rationally or romantically, you rarely wonder whether or not it'll make it in the end. You just feel that it will."

Gail from Jacksonville Florida was prepared to see the worst. "We'd heard the horror stories... it looks like bombed out Beirut, the 'bad' people running amuck. Yes, it was rundown but not what people had described. Heartbreakingly beautiful... the boardwalk, the Casino, Convention Hall - all of it. We wandered the boardwalk and spoke with people, a few tourists and some locals. Stayed at the Berkeley, went to the Stone Pony, took hundreds of pictures. The entire 13-hour trip home was spent trying to figure out how to get back for another vacation."

Long ago, Asbury Park was a wonderful place to visit. With its beautiful beach, thriving downtown shopping area, boardwalk attractions and amusement park rides, it was the 'Jewel of the Jersey Shore.' As years went by, the town lost its status as a premier ocean resort and music was the one thing holding the town together. The music scene found here during the 70s was every bit as strong, every bit as vital as any music scene in the world.

"The Stone Pony... it's one of a short list of genuinely famous physical locations that people can actually visit," said Mike Sauter, long-time disc jockey at the Jersey Shore currently working for 90.5 FM in Lincroft. "It would make it onto a list that also includes the Abbey Road crosswalk, Jim Morrison's Paris grave, Max Yasgur's farm, and Strawberry Fields next to the Dakota in NYC.

"That's why Asbury Park's government is today veering off into complete lunacy when they talk about getting rid of or moving the Stone Pony. You just don't do that to a place with a world-wide reputation, even if you don't care about that reputation in the abstract, it's still a potential cash cow as an engine of tourism."

Asbury, once again, is on the verge of a great music scene. Matt Witte reminds me of a talented young Springsteen with so many ways to go musically. DeSol is like the second coming of the Asbury Jukes, a home-grown band that just makes you want to get out there and dance. And JPAT is like the spirit of the Upstage himself. Asbury music is truly back!

Official Websites

To learn more about the artists featured in this book, visit these websites.

Sonny Kenn:	sonnykennband.com
Bill Chinnock:	artistgroup.com/billchinnock
Bruce Springsteen:	brucespringsteen.net
David Sancious:	davidsancious.com
The Stone Pony:	stoneponyonline.com
Southside Johnny & the Jukes:	southsidejohnny.org
Lance Larson:	lancelarsonmusic.com
Billy Hector:	billyhector.com
Glen Burtnick:	glenburtnik.com
Ray Andersen:	mrray.com
Bobby Bandiera:	bobbandiera.com
Bon Jovi:	bonjovi.com
John Eddie:	johneddie.com
The Smithereens:	thesmithereens.com
Secret Lovers (Alice Leon):	thealiceproject.com
Joey & the Works (Joey Vadala):	joevadala.com
Dramarama (John Easdale):	johneasdale.com
Red House (Bruce Tunkel):	brucetunkel.com
James Deely:	jamesd.com
Everlounge:	everlounge.com
The Bongos (Richard Barone):	richardbarone.com
The Fastlane:	asburybaronet-fastlane.com
The Saint:	thesaintnj.com
Soul Engines:	soulengines.com
Highway 9:	highwaynine.com
Blowup:	blowup.org
Joe D'Urso:	jdcaravan.com
Mimi Cross:	adoptaband.com/mimicross
Danny White:	dannywhitemusic.com
Jody Joseph & Average Joes:	jodyjoseph.net
Last Perfect Thing:	lastperfectthing.com
Maybe Pete:	maybepete.com
Matt Witte & New Blood Revival:	newbloodrevival.com
DeSol:	desolmusic.com
JPAT:	jpat.info
and for all things Asbury Park:	asburypark.net

About the Author

Gary Wien is a lifelong fan of the Asbury Park music scene. Born in nearby Red Bank, he spent many weekends in Asbury Park while growing up. He would hang out at the old Palace Amusements building, walk the boardwalk and sneak into the clubs whenever possible.

Wien graduated from Lynchburg College in Virginia with a B.A. in English in 1992. Since then he has been a freelance author, playwright and website designer. He has been printed in such publications as *New Jersey Webguide Magazine*, *Discover Guides of New Jersey* and *Princeton Magazine*. Mr. Wien currently lives in Belmar, NJ with his beautiful wife, Dr. Sherry Wien.

For more information on the bands featured in this book, please go to the book's official website at: www.asburymusic.com

ISBN 141200314-8